Contemporary Challenges to International Business

THE ACADEMY OF INTERNATIONAL BUSINESS

Published in Association with the UK Chapter of the Academy of International Business

Contemporary Challenges to International Business

Edited by

Kevin Ibeh
Professor of Marketing and International Business, the University of Strathclyde, UK

and

Sheena Davies
Senior Lecturer in Strategic Management, the University of Portsmouth, UK

First published 2009 by
PALGRAVE MACMILLAN

Palgrave Macmillan in the UK is an imprint of Macmillan Publishers Limited,
registered in England, company number 785998, of Houndmills, Basingstoke,
Hampshire RG21 6XS.

Palgrave Macmillan in the US is a division of St Martin's Press LLC,
175 Fifth Avenue, New York, NY 10010.

Palgrave Macmillan is the global academic imprint of the above companies
and has companies and representatives throughout the world.

Palgrave® and Macmillan® are registered trademarks in the United States,
the United Kingdom, Europe and other countries.

ISBN-13: 978–0–230–21845–1 hardback
ISBN-10: 0–230–21845–8 hardback

This book is printed on paper suitable for recycling and made from fully
managed and sustained forest sources. Logging, pulping and manufacturing
processes are expected to conform to the environmental regulations of the
country of origin.

A catalogue record for this book is available from the British Library.

A catalog record for this book is available from the Library of Congress.

10 9 8 7 6 5 4 3 2 1
18 17 16 15 14 13 12 11 10 09

Printed and bound in Great Britain by
CPI Antony Rowe, Chippenham and Eastbourne

Contents

Illustrations

Tables

Figures

Acronyms

ACQ	Acquiring Organization
ACEA	Association des Constructeurs Européen d'Automobiles
ARD	Annual Respondents' Database
B2B	Business to Business
BBC	British Broadcasting Corporation
BI	Born International
BG	Born Global
BP	Business Performance
BS	Business System
CAA	Civil Aviation Authority
CEE	Central Eastern European
CEO	Chief Executive Officer
CMO	Chief Marketing Officer
CoO	Country of Origin
COO	Chief Operating Officer
CO_2	Carbon Dioxide
CPA	Corporate Political Activities
DTI	Department of Trade and Industry
EBITDA	Earnings before Interest, Tax, Depreciation and Amortization
EC	European Commission
ECAM	European Common Aviation Market
EJV	Equity Joint Venture
ELV	End of Life Vehicles
ER	Employment Relations
EU	European Union
FTV	Film and Television Services
FDI	Foreign Direct Investment
FIE	Foreign Invested Enterprises
GDI	Gender Development Indicator
GDP	Gross Domestic Product
GTD	Global Terrorism Database
HDI	Human Development Indicator
HIS	High Involvement Systems
HPWS	High Performance Work Systems
HQ	Headquarters
HR	Human Resources
HRM	Human Resource Management
IB	International Business
ICT	Information Communication Technology
IHRM	International Human Resource Management

IJV	International Joint Venture
ILO	International Labour Office
IM	International Management
IMF	International Monetary Fund
INV	International New Venture
IPO	Initial Public Offering
IR	Industrial Relations
ISCO	International Standard Classification of Occupations
IT	Information Technology
JAMA	Japanese Automobile Manufacturers' Association
JV	Joint Venture
KAMA	Korean Automobile Manufacturers' Association
KBV	Knowledge Based View
KSA	Kingdom of Saudi Arabia
LCC	Low-Cost Carriers (Airlines)
LE	Larger Enterprises
LTO	Long Term Orientation
M&A	Mergers and Acquisitions
MDG	Millennium Development Goals
ME	Middle East
MENA	Middle East and North Africa
MEP	Member of European Parliament
MIPT	Memorial Institute for the Prevention of Terrorism
mMNE	Micromultinational
MNC	Multinational Company (is also known as Multinational Corporation)
MNE	Multinational Enterprise
NACE	Nomenclature générale des activités Économiques dans les Communautés européennes
NGO	Non Governmental Organization
NIE	Newly Industrialized Countries
NOK	Norwegian Kroner
NTBF	New Technology-based Firms
OC	Organizational Commitment
OCQ	Organizational Commitment Questionnaire
OECD	Organization for Economic Cooperation and Development
OEM	Original Equipment Manufacturer
OID	Organizational Identification
OSAC	Overseas Security Advisory Council
PAC	Political Action Committee
PDA	Personal Digital Assistant
PRC	People's Republic of China
R&D	Research and Development
RBT	Resource Based Theory
RBV	Resource Based View

RDE	Remote Detonated Explosives
RMB	Renminbi (Chinese currency – Yuan)
SCA	Sustainable Competitive Advantage
SI	System of Innovation
SINTEF	*Skandinavias største uavhengige forskningsorganisasjon* (the largest independent research organization in Scandinavia)
SME	Small/Medium Enterprise
SOA	State Owned Airlines
SOE	State Owned Enterprise
TARG	Target Organization
TKB	Terrorism Knowledge Base
UAE	United Arab Emirates
UCDP	Uppsala Conflict Data Programme
UNCTAD	United Nations Conference on Trade and Development
UNDO	United Nations Development Organization
UNDP	United Nations Development Program
UNIFEM	United Nations Development Fund for Women
UM	Uppsala School
US	United States
VA	Value Added
VAA	Value Added Activities
WAP	Wireless Access Protocol
WERS	Workplace Employment Survey
WTO	World Trade Organization
YD	Yamoussoukro Declaration
WOS	Wholly Owned Subsidiary

Acknowledgements

Many thanks to the Portsmouth Business School of the University of Portsmouth for hosting the 35th Annual Conference of the Academy of International Business, United Kingdom and Ireland (UKI) Chapter. Thanks in particular to Professor Colin Wheeler for organizing the Conference, the staff of the Business School, especially Valerie Anderson, Chris Fill, Rosie Booker, Grace Cheng and Paul Krycler, for co-ordinating operations and compiling the proceedings, and Ray French for his assistance at the initial stage of the editing process.

Foreword

The 35th Annual Conference of the UK and Ireland Chapter of the Academy of International Business was held on 28/29 March 2008 at the University of Portsmouth, hosted by Portsmouth Business School. This book contains a selection of papers presented at the conference on four major contemporary research areas that are focused on the theme of the conference – 'Challenges to International Business'. The book is the 16th volume in the Palgrave AIB UK and Ireland International Business series.

The importance of the conference theme was powerfully illustrated by the keynote address by Michael Stephenson from the Climate Change Programme at IBM UK. Michael's address entitled 'The response of international business to climate change' was followed by a discussion led by a panel composed of Peter Buckley (Centre for International Business, University of Leeds), Stephen Young (Centre for Internationalization and Enterprise Research, University of Glasgow) and Niina Nummela (Turku School of Economics). One of the fruits of this discussion was a decision to have responses of international business research to climate change as a standing item at future AIB UK and Ireland chapter conferences. This development reflects the developing role of the AIB UK and Ireland chapter as a promoter of new developments in international business research. As a result of this decision we expect that future books in this series, and special issues of journals, will have contributions based on papers presented at our conferences on climate change and international business.

The 35th Annual Conference attracted 110 delegates with some 72 competitive papers accepted for presentation at the conference. In addition there were 25 submissions to the Doctoral Colloquium reflecting the continuing commitment of the Chapter to encouraging the development of new researchers in international business. This work together with the output reflected in this book confirms the commitment of the Chapter to promote and develop international business research in the UK and Ireland. The Chapter is developing its work by continuing to organize the Annual Conference and by helping with the development of research agendas and resources to enhance the quantity and quality of international business research. Please visit our website to explore the work of the Chapter and to find out how to become involved with the work of the Chapter – www.aib-uki.org.

FRANK MCDONALD
Chair, Academy of International Business,
UK and Ireland Chapter

Contributors

Matthew Allen is Lecturer in Organization Studies at Manchester Business School, The University of Manchester. His research focuses on multinational corporations and national business systems, and the links between employee relations and firm performance. His work has been published in journals such as *Socio Economic Review* and the *Journal of Public Policy*.

Joseph Amankwah-Amoah is a PhD candidate at Swansea University, UK. His research interests include globalization, global strategy, institutional change and the airline industry in Africa.

Arild Aspelund, PhD, is currently Associate Professor of Marketing at the Norwegian University of Science and Technology. Dr Aspelund's primary research interests are internationalization of firms in general and International New Ventures in particular. He also does research on international economic development and on global value chain management.

Magne Sivert Berg graduated from Norwegian University of Science and Technology in 2005 with a Master's degree in Industrial Economics and Technology Management. He subsequently joined *Elkem*, a daughter company of the multinational *Orkla Corporation*, as a corporate trainee. He was shortly thereafter assigned to the start-up company *Elkem Solar* where he is now financial manager.

Oliver Borchert is a PhD candidate at the University of Strathclyde. His research interests include small firm internationalization, international entrepreneurship, international market entry strategies and international marketing channels.

Trevor Buck is Professor of International Business at Loughborough University Business School, UK, specializing in transition economies (especially China) and international corporate governance, particularly executive pay. In the past seven years, he has received large grants from the ESRC, the British Academy and the Leverhulme Trust and has published five papers in the *Journal of International Business Studies* in this period.

Yi-Ying Chang, PhD, is Lecturer in Management, Dundee Business School, University of Abertay Dundee, UK. Her research interests are in IHRM, knowledge transfer, absorptive capacity and multinationals from newly industrialized and transition economies.

Gary Cook is Senior Lecturer in Applied Economics and Director of Undergraduate Programmes at the University of Liverpool Management School. His research focuses on clustering, entrepreneurship and internationalization with particular interest in the media and financial services industries.

Brian Cooper, PhD, La Trobe University, is Research Fellow in the Department of Management, Monash University, Australia. Brian is also a lecturer in management research methods. He has extensive experience publishing survey and qualitative research. His research interests include stress and coping, employee well-being and multivariate modelling.

Ou Dai is a PhD student in International Business at Loughborough University Business School, UK. He received his MSc degree in Entrepreneurship from Bristol University. He has had ten years working experience on project management and commercial and engineering management in construction industries in different countries.

Sheena Davies is Senior Lecturer in strategic management at Portsmouth Business School. She also teaches international strategy. Her research interest is in the role of emotion in managing knowledge in organizations.

Yaw A. Debrah is Professor of Human Resources and International Management at Swansea University (University of Wales). Yaw has held academic positions at Brunel University, UK, Cardiff University (University of Wales) and Nanyang Technological University, Singapore. In addition he has worked in Africa, Canada and USA. He has edited five books and his publications have appeared in journals such as *Human Relations, Journal of Applied Psychology, Organizational Behaviour, International Journal of Human Resource Management, Asia-Pacific Journal of Management, Asia Pacific Journal of Human Resources, Asia-Pacific Business Review, Australian Journal of Management and Thunderbird International Business Review.*

Despoina Filiou is Senior Lecturer in Strategic Management at Manchester Metropolitan University Business School, Centre for International Business Innovation. Her research is in the area of co-operation and innovation in the biotechnology sector.

Mika Gabrielsson, D.Sc. (Econ.), is Professor of International Business at the Helsinki School of Economics, Finland. His teaching covers areas such as international and global marketing, and his research interests relate to rapid globalization of firms. He has published over 110 articles in refereed international journals or conference proceedings. These include for instance *Journal of International Marketing, International Business Review* and *Thunderbird International Business Review.* Before joining the academic world he held several senior positions in purchasing and marketing, for instance, at Fujitsu.

Peter Gabrielsson, D.Sc. (Econ.), is Professor of International Marketing at the University of Vaasa and Adjunct Professor of International Business, Helsinki School of Economics, Finland. His teaching covers areas such as international and global marketing and his research interests include the globalization process of firms, born globals, globalizing internationals and global marketing strategies. He has published in journals such as *International Business Review, International Marketing Review* and *Industrial Marketing Management.* He has long experience in senior management positions at Nokia and other global ICT firms.

Sougand Golesorkhi is Senior Lecturer in International Business at Manchester Metropolitan University Business School, Centre for International Business and Innovation. Her research is in the area of agency problems and monitoring costs in inter-firm collaboration.

Jussi Hätönen is finalizing his doctoral thesis on management of outsourcing processes in high technology firms at the Turku School of Economics, Finland. Currently he works as a management consultant at Capgemini, specializing and assisting firms in a variety of issues regarding their technological transformation. He has published his research in various academic conferences, books and journals, including *Journal of International Management* and *Journal of Business and Industrial Marketing*. His research interests focus on partner and outsourcing management, particularly in the context of small- and medium-sized technology firms.

Andreas Hoecht, PhD, is Principal Lecturer in Strategy and International Business at Portsmouth Business School. His main research interest is in trust and control within organizations and in inter-organizational relationships. He also has a research interest in entrepreneurship and innovation issues.

Kate Hutchings, PhD, University of Queensland, is Associate Professor and Director of the International Business Research, Monash University, Australia. She has taught in Asia and also held visiting research positions in the US, Denmark and France. She has published 3 books and 50 international refereed journal articles. Her current research interests include Chinese outward foreign investment and intercultural knowledge sharing.

Kevin Ibeh is Professor of Marketing and International Business at the Department of Marketing, University of Strathclyde, Glasgow, where he also serves as Director of Research. His recent research has focused mainly on SME internationalization and international entrepreneurship and his work has been published in peer-reviewed journals, including *Management International Review, Transnational Corporations, Industrial Marketing Management, Journal of Business Ethics, Small Business Economics, European Journal of Marketing, International Small Business Journal*, and *International Journal of Market Research*.

Irina Jormanainen is currently a PhD candidate at the Helsinki School of Economics at the Department of International Business. Her research interests cover such areas as learning from foreign direct investment (FDI) in transition economies, technological capabilities development in firms and FDI entry mode choice.

Andrew Lee is Senior Lecturer in the University of Portsmouth Business School, with a PhD in Computational Linguistics, an MBA and a degree in computing science. His current research interests include the modelling of political violence, focusing on trends and risk factors and how these influence business risk management.

Xiaohui Liu is Professor of International Business at Loughborough University Business School, UK. She received her PhD in International Economics from the University of Birmingham. Her publications have appeared in *Journal of International Business Studies, Research Policy, Entrepreneurship Theory and Practice, Journal of World Business, Management International Review, International Business Review* and *Applied Economics*.

Kamel Mellahi is Professor and Chair of International Business and Strategy Group, Sheffield Management School, Sheffield University, UK. His current work focuses on the factors that result in a loss of competitive advantage, the process of business failure and how firm-level political resources contribute to corporate success or failure in emerging economies.

Frank McDonald is Professor of International Business and Director of the Bradford Centre in International Business at the Bradford School of Management, University of Bradford. His research interests are focused on the strategic development of foreign owned subsidiaries and his work has been published in journals such as *Environment and Planning, Journal of World Business* and *Regional Studies*.

Beverly Dawn Metcalfe, PhD, Keele University, is Professor of International Management and Development at Liverpool Hope University, UK, and Research Fellow in Centre for Organizations and Development, Manchester. UK. Her research has been published inter alia in *Journal of Business Ethics, International Journal of Human Resource Management* and *Human Resource Development International*.

Niina Nummela is Professor of International Business at the Turku School of Economics, Finland. She has published in the area of international entrepreneurship, small business management and inter-firm co-operation. She has contributed to *Canadian Journal of Administrative Sciences, European Journal of Marketing, International Small Business Journal, Journal of Engineering and Technology Management, Journal of World Business and Management International Review*, among others.

Naresh R. Pandit is Professor of Management and Director of Research at Norwich Business School, University of East Anglia. His research focuses on the link between clustering and economic performance and has been funded by grants from the British Academy, the Corporation of London, the DTI, the ESRC, the European Union and the North West Development Agency.

Mélanie Elina Raukko, presently Senior Research Associate in International Business at Turku School of Economics, is finalizing her doctoral research on 'Key persons' organizational commitment in cross-border acquisitions'. She has written several conference papers on the themes of organizational commitment of acquired employees and longitudinal research in the IB field.

Mika Ruokonen, D.Sc. (Econ.), is a Senior Consultant at Deloitte. His research interests include rapid internationalization of small technology-based firms and their business networks in the internationalization process. He has published on these issues in the *European Journal of Marketing, Journal of High Technology Management Research* and *International Journal of Entrepreneurship and Innovation Management*.

Sami Saarenketo is Professor of International Marketing in the School of Business at Lappeenranta University of Technology, Finland. His primary areas of research interest are international marketing and entrepreneurship in technology-based small firms. He has published on these issues in *Journal of World Business, European Journal of Marketing, Canadian Journal of Administrative Sciences, International Journal of Production Economics and Journal of International Entrepreneurship*, among others.

Roger Sørheim is Associate Professor in Entrepreneurship at the Norwegian University of Science and Technology and Professor at Bodø Graduate School of Business. His research interests include issues related to entrepreneurial finance (informal and formal venture capital). Sørheim is one of the founders of NTNUs action based research program 'NTNU School of Entrepreneurship' (www.iot. ntnu.no/nse).

Heinz-Josef Tüselmann is Professor of International Business and Director of the Centre for International Business and Innovation at Manchester Metropolitan University Business School. His research focus is on cross-border transfer of HRM and employee relations systems within MNCs and subsidiary performance, foreign direct investment and location decisions of MNCs, and the strategic development of foreign owned subsidiaries. His work has been published in journals such as *Journal of World Business, Regional Studies, Transnational Corporations* and *European Journal of Industrial Relations*.

Sigrun M. Wagner is currently completing her doctorate at Loughborough University Business School. She holds a BA in European Studies from the University of Osnabrück (Germany) and an MSc in International Management from Loughborough University. Her research focuses on corporate political activities of multinational enterprises in the European Union, specifically in the area of environmental regulations for the automotive industry. In 2006, she spent two months as Research Fellow at the German Institute for Public Affairs in Berlin. Prior to her PhD studies, she gained work experience in Brussels in a policy consultancy.

Colin Wheeler is Professor of Marketing at Portsmouth Business School, University of Portsmouth, UK. His research interests include the internationalization of the SME and international marketing strategy. He has co-edited several books on international business and internationalization and has published in journals such as *Long Range Planning, European Journal of Marketing, International Small Business Journal, International Business Review* and the *Journal of International Entrepreneurship*.

Adrian John Wilkinson is Director of Centre for Work, Organization and Wellbeing, Professor of Employment Relations, Griffith Business School, Griffith University. His research includes many aspects of Human Resource Management and Industrial Relations. Recent research has encompassed change initiatives such as TQM, the changing nature of Employee Participation and Industrial Relations theory.

Angelika Zimmermann is Lecturer in International Business and Strategy at Loughborough University Business School, UK. Her research focuses on international human resource management, particularly with regard to China, and transnational teamwork. Her research is published in *International Studies of Management and Organization, International Journal of Cross Cultural Management* and *The International Journal of Human Resource.*

1
Perspectives on Contemporary Challenges to International Business

Kevin Ibeh and Sheena Davies

Reflecting the discontinuous, diverse and complex backdrop against which it is enacted, international business (IB) is synonymous with big challenges. Familiar challenges such as cultural and institutional differences (Hofstede, 1991; Leung, Bhagat, Buchan, Erez and Gibson, 2005; Bjorkman, Smale, Sumelius, Suutari and Lu, 2008; Peng, Wang and Jiang, 2008) are perpetually potent, but 'new' concerns are also constantly surfacing to engage the attention and interest of businesses: climate change and sustainability; international terrorism/security threats; sub-prime crisis; global credit squeeze; rising energy and food prices; threats of global recession; corruption and corporate scandals; digital piracy and intellectual property theft and so on (Goodman, 2004; Luo, 2008; Hill, 2007; Romilly, 2007). These headline issues bear varying levels of relevance to businesses operating around the world, with the extent of salience dictated by firms' geographical location, nature of industry and spread of activity. Nevertheless, international businesses tend, by their typically expansive nature, to be more exposed to these contemporary challenges than purely domestic businesses.

The preceding sentence may be interpreted as associating these challenges with consistently unidirectional – read unfavourable – consequences. This is not entirely correct, as every fresh challenge embodies, at some level, atoms of the next big breakthrough. Firms typically differ in their perceptions of external challenges, with some seeing only the problems and obstacles to passively complain about, and others sensing potential opportunities (Ibeh, 2003) that need to be investigated, understood and strategized for. More successful businesses tend to adopt the latter approach to challenges, that is, seek to understand, accommodate, neutralize and transform challenges into potential sources of competitive advantage. Indeed, international business is at its best when it is in the business of deploying strategic resources towards unearthing innovative solutions to seemingly intractable challenges.

Although the aforementioned challenges to IB are, understandably, subjects of extensive media discussion, boardroom deliberations, citizens' advocacy, interest groups' activism, and government interventions, scholarly attention by the mainstream IB field seems somewhat lacking. Relevant research is not completely absent (see, for example, Czinkota, Knight and Liesch, 2004; Suder, 2004; Liesch,

Steen, Knight and Czinkota, 2006; Rodriguez, Siegel, Hillman and Eden, 2006; Penz, 2007; Romilly, 2007; Luo, 2008), but the fluid and unpredictable nature of these challenges means that research is always struggling to catch up with new realities. In this current age of anxiety (Prasad and Ghauri, 2004; Sinkovics and Yamin, 2007), epitomized by the infamous 11 September 2001 outrage in the United States, IB researchers are particularly challenged to lead the race for knowledge on the contemporary issues that face today's international businesses. This collection, and the Conference* which spawned it, represents a clear response to this challenge.

Whilst not exhaustive, the 16 papers collected in this volume have addressed the overarching theme of this book from a number of pertinent perspectives. The chapters are laid out in four parts, which respectively focus on cross-border management and institutional challenges; SMEs and resource-related challenges; emerging market challenges and the emergent challenges of international terrorism, climate change and international fraud. Each of the sixteen chapters of the book is now briefly introduced.

Part I: Cross-Border Management and Institutional Challenges

Part I comprises four chapters that discuss from different angles, the challenges of managing employees and transferring human resources (HR) practices and strategies across the foreign subsidiaries and pertinent cultures of multinational companies (MNCs). The lead chapter, also the Conference's best paper prize winner, is authored by Zimmermann, Liu and Buck, and it focuses on the issues raised by the rising turnover of Chinese employees of foreign-owned MNCs in China. The authors drew on the HR and cross-cultural management literature to explore reasons why Chinese employees may stay with firms of one nationality rather than another. Based on a survey of 316 Western (EU/US), overseas Chinese (Hong Kong/Taiwan) and other Asian (Japanese/Korean) joint ventures operating in China, they found that firms of different nationalities face turnover challenges to different degrees, and suggested that this may be influenced by their HR practices. Tenure was highest in overseas Chinese firms, moderate in Japanese/Korean firms, and lowest in Western-owned firms. Tenure was related to the extent to which firms awarded long-term contracts and the magnitude of contributions to employees' pension funds. The authors linked these results to cultural differences (notably the long-term orientation of HR systems in certain cultures and not others) and suggested that greater appreciation of such institutional differences may lead to a better understanding of employee tenure and help to establish best practice for managing and retaining HR internationally.

The next chapter by Raukko continues with the theme of employee turnover, focusing in particular, on the challenges that MNCs often face in winning the identification and commitment of highly skilled employees of recently acquired companies. Such 'strategic resources' are often a major justification for the acquisition activity itself and their departure can affect the success of the acquisition. Based on relevant previous research and a longitudinal study of a European high-tech SME recently acquired by an Asian company, the author examined the development of organizational commitment and identification among a sample of 'inherited' employees. She found the employees' identification and commitment to be stronger towards their former organization during the early post-acquisition integration phase. Key personnel, however, tended to have significantly higher levels of identification and commitment than other personnel, probably because of their greater involvement in the integration process and contact with the new managers. The chapter highlights the need for more research into the challenge of improving organizational identification among the 'inherited' staff of acquired companies.

Chapters 4 and 5 both focus on the challenges associated with transferring HR policies across MNCs' foreign subsidiaries, including the extent to which such challenges are affected by micro-level and macro-level (home-country and host-country institutional) factors. However, while Tüselmann and colleagues' research involves home and host countries that are relatively close in cultural and institutional terms, Chang, Mellahi and Wilkinson focus on a MNC from an Asian country transferring HR policies to a subsidiary based in an economically advanced and institutionally different Western country. More precisely, Chapter 4 examines how employment policies are transferred within German-owned subsidiaries in the UK, including how this is affected by home-country factors, type of industry and level of industry internationalization. The authors used a broadly institutional approach to employment relations in MNCs, the 'four forces' framework, a series of regression models, and survey data from a representative sample of UK-based German subsidiaries and indigenous UK firms. Their results partly confirmed a country-of-origin (CoO) imprint in German MNCs in the UK, but also suggested a weakening of the traditional German model, in favour of what the authors refer to as nationally distinct hybrid employment relations patterns, the new German model. The authors claim that this new model is already apparent in many German parent firms, *albeit* in an embryonic form. The intra-German analysis revealed significant differences in employment relations patterns, not only along the degree of industry internationalization, but also in relation to characteristics such as human capital, technology and skills intensity. Based on these findings, the chapter calls for a more encompassing analysis of cross-border transfer issues, which recognizes the differential influence of industry internationalization as well as the dynamic nature of business systems and country-of-origin effect. Such an analysis, they suggested, should also consider CoO effect at the more abstract, cultural level.

Chapter 5 investigates tensions arising from Taiwanese MNCs' transfer of HR policies and practices to their UK subsidiaries, including the probable effects of CoO factors and multiple power/interest bases on the observed tensions. The focus of these authors on a developing country MNC differentiates their work from the preceding chapter and much of the literature on cross-border transfer of HR practices, which dominantly focus on MNCs from advanced economies operating in developing country markets. Analysis of interview data from 76 Taiwanese expatriates managers, British managers, and British nationals of Chinese origin in five UK-based Taiwanese MNCs suggests the extent of transfer of human resource management (HRM) practices to the subsidiary level to be strongly influenced by macro-institutional forces within home and host business systems, and the interests and perceptions of actors at the micro level of MNCs. These organizational level factors include managerial competency, previous work/international experience and functional background of expatriate and local managers. The chapter also discusses how subsidiary managers act as 'powerful agents' to promote the careers of their staff.

Part II: SMEs' Resource-Related Challenges

While the first part of this book focused on MNCs and the HR-related challenges they face in managing their cross-border activities, Part II comprises five chapters all of which discuss internationalized SMEs, highlighting the resource-related challenges they grapple with, but also offering inspiring accounts of the various ways by which they increasingly transcend the limitations of their typical resource profile.

Ibeh, Borchert and Wheeler lead off this section with their research on the activities of micromultinationals (mMNEs), a recently identified category of internationally assertive SMEs defined, not by their speed of internationalization, but, by their use of advanced entry modes across international markets. Based on a previously established taxonomy of firm resources and case study evidence from three Canadian mMNEs, the authors investigated how the focal SMEs were able to develop into significant international players despite their generally limited resource position. They found that the study firms tended to make dominant use of product and relational capabilities and rely on these to neutralize and compensate for observed gaps in physical resources and human capital. The concluding section of the chapter calls on managers of other SMEs with comparably limited resource profiles to develop appropriate coping mechanisms and compensating advantages; and on policy makers to steer well-judged support towards SMEs striving to transcend resource-imposed constraints on their global ambitions. Other highlighted contributions of the chapter include its integration and triple-strand classification of the disparate literature on FDI-using SMEs; and its adding to the limited, but increasing, empirical base on mMNEs.

The next two chapters – Chapter 7 by Gabrielsson and Gabrielsson, and Chapter 8 by Nummela, Saarenketo, Hätönen and Ruokonen – both continue on the theme of resource challenges of SME internationalization using case study evidence from fast growing software SMEs from Finland. They add real value by focusing on the largely neglected dimension of the outcomes of accelerated internationalization, including the resources and capabilities antecedent to these outcomes. Based on the view that resources and capabilities may have mixed implications for survival and growth, Gabrielsson and Gabrielsson identified four growth-survival trajectories, specifically international new venture (INV) failure, born global failure, born international survival or born global survival. They found that the nature of the outcome achieved by accelerated internationalizers may be partly explained by differences in age, resources and capabilities. Capabilities were found to be more important than resources. In particular, a combination of technology and non-technology capabilities such as customer understanding, networking and marketing capabilities seemed to be critical for success. The results also indicate that low lateral rigidity is not only crucial for the growth of born globals but also for their survival. Nummela, Saarenketo, Hätönen and Ruokonen conceptualized the outcomes of accelerated internationalization and growth in dichotomous terms, success (sustainable and profitable business in international markets) or failure (a swift exit from international markets). They identified the drivers of these outcomes and concluded that they are strongly intertwined and not clear-cut. This, according to the chapter, illustrates the complexity of the challenges that managers face in trying to put accelerated internationalizing firms on the path to international market growth and success.

Chapter 9 by Aspelund, Sorheim and Berg, and Chapter 10 by Cook and Pandit, also focus on how resource-constrained SMEs strive to overcome challenges to internationalization. While the former adopts a social capital perspective to examine how INVs use partnerships to bridge resource gaps, the latter chapter explores SMEs' use of cluster location, and the associated positive spillovers, in overcoming resource disadvantages. Aspelund and colleagues drew upon case evidence from three New Technology-based Firms (NTBFs) that achieved varying levels of international success to investigate how INVs establish partnerships and the factors that facilitate the success of such linkages. Their findings suggest that relational and cognitive social capital play different roles, with the latter playing a particularly vital role in the long-term survival and performance of international partner structures. This untangling of the concept of social capital arguably represents a key contribution of the chapter to the international business literature.

Cook and Pandit's empirical context is the UK media industry, specifically the Greater London cluster that has over the years spawned many new firms and facilitated the internationalization of many SMEs. Drawing on a combination of unique data set, an in-depth interview survey and a questionnaire survey, these authors developed relevant econometric models and a number of key conclusions. The first is that strong clusters promote international entrepreneurship, which in turn promotes cluster strength in a self-reinforcing dynamic. Internationalization is one dynamic feedback loop in cluster strength, whereby increased internationalization yields benefits to firms which spill over more widely in the cluster and lead to further internationalization. The second is that some firms are better able than others to benefit from cluster location due to superior resources and capabilities. Finally, the chapter identifies the Resource-Based View as an important theoretical framework that links cluster theory and international entrepreneurship.

Part III: Emerging Market Challenges

Part III of the book comprises four chapters, each of which provides different but important perspectives on the issues and challenges associated with managing international business within transition and developing economies.

Interestingly also, the four chapters respectively offer insights on four separate developing regions, including Central and Eastern Europe, South Asia, Africa and the Middle East.

The first of these chapters is authored by Jormanainen and it drew upon the learning in IJVs and system of innovation (SI) literature streams to develop an integrated framework for explaining how SI influences the scope of learning in IJVs. Using data on manufacturing IJVs established in Russia, the Czech Republic, Poland and Hungary in the 1998–2006 period, the author showed that the structural characteristics of SI influence the amount and quality of resources and capabilities of local firms and the nature of MNCs' subsidiaries operations. These, in turn, affect the types of IJVs established in host countries and the scope of inter-partner learning in those IJVs. This chapter contributes to the existing knowledge base by demonstrating the need to complement the dominant micro-level approach to explaining learning in IJVs with an externally aware SI approach. It also discusses how policy makers might improve the SI within their domain and, in so doing, attract more IJVs to their region and generate further learning in local firms.

In Chapter 12, Dai and Liu drew on the knowledge-based view and network perspectives to explore the relationships between knowledge, networks and firm performance in the Chinese context. Using a unique, hand-collected dataset of 353 SMEs of returning entrepreneurs and 358 local entrepreneur-owned SMEs from Zhongguancun Science Park, they found that the SMEs of returning entrepreneurs perform better than those owned by local entrepreneurs due to their technological and commercial knowledge as well as their international entrepreneurial orientation. Their results show that international networks positively affect firm performance in high-tech industries and indicate that returning entrepreneurs achieve competitive advantage by utilizing their intangible assets and international networks to exploit business opportunities in emerging economies.

Chapter 13, by Amankwah-Amaoh and Debrah, addresses the recent emergence of low-cost carriers (LCCs) in South and North Africa, including the associated challenges for the airline industry, particularly the traditional or legacy airlines operating in the region. Using an environmental drivers' framework, which incorporates aspects of the broad resource-based viewpoint (Wernerfelt, 1984; Barney, 1991) and Yip's (1992) globalization drivers, the chapter explores the internal and external actors that may explain the emergence of these African LCCs. The findings suggest the salience of several resource-related factors, including decision-maker characteristics, firms' cost management and technological capabilities as well as domestic/regional market conditions such as favourable government policies. The chapter contributes to the international business literature mainly by drawing attention to the important, but neglected, subject of the liberalization of the air transport market in Africa.

The final chapter in Part III is authored by Metcalfe, Hutchings and Cooper and it examines the challenges and barriers to the participation of Middle Eastern women in international management. This research complements previous work in the topic area, which has mainly focused on Western women and Western MNCs, and has neglected the impact of home-country national, cultural and institutional factors on women's international work opportunities. Based on their analysis of survey data from seven Islamic Middle Eastern nations, the authors found that Middle Eastern women's international work experiences were broadly similar to those of their counterparts in the West. Notable differences were, nevertheless, identified, including the tendency by the former to have greater social and network support to enable dual career status; and their lower likelihood of wanting to combine an international career with family responsibilities. An even more important distinction observed was the overwhelming importance of non-governmental organizations (NGOs) as a source of Middle Eastern women's managerial and international employment and skills development opportunities; this is unlike Western women who overwhelmingly receive international experience via MNCs. The chapter also discusses the unique social and cultural contexts under which international business is undertaken in the Middle East, highlighting, in particular, the effects of an 'equal but different' approach that governs gender relations and underpins international management policies.

Part IV: Emergent Challenges

Three chapters constitute Part IV of this book and each of these focuses on an aspect of the more contemporary challenges that face international managers in the twenty-first century, specifically international terrorism, climate change and fraudulent behaviour. In Chapter 15, Lee discusses the threat of international terrorism attacks on business targets, awareness of which has heightened since the September 11, 2001 terrorist attack in the United States, resulting in higher levels of security spending and crisis planning for businesses. He argues that the challenges that businesses face when assessing threats and mitigating risks from international terrorism attacks are unduly magnified by media reporting of terrorism incidents, which tends neither to distinguish between types of targets of attacks nor between perceived terrorism risk and actual trends based on historical data for business targets. Redressing this anomaly was the *raison d'être* for this research, which drew on the Terrorism Knowledge Base, a major 'industry' database, to answer questions, including where international terrorism attacks are more likely to occur; what types of targets are more at risk – businesses themselves or the infrastructure that supports them; and what types of tactics and weapons are used in the attacks. Analysis results showed that the perceptions of international terrorism threats by board-level business executives were significantly higher than actual trends would suggest. The chapter highlights the unfavourable cost implications of basing risk mitigation strategies on erroneous perceptions, and suggests that attacks on business targets be routinely isolated to provide a more accurate picture of the international terrorism threats facing businesses and properly guide international risk management strategies.

The penultimate chapter of the book is authored by Wagner and it investigates how multinational enterprises (MNEs) operating within the European

Union's automotive sector deploy corporate political activities (CPA) and associated resources in trying to influence the increasingly robust environmental regulations of host governments. The empirical part of Wagner's research focused particularly on the regulations pertaining to carbon dioxide (CO_2) emissions, pollutant emissions and end-of-life vehicles and it examined how MNEs of different national origins (European, North American and Japanese) deploy corporate political activities in relation to each of these environmental regulations. It also investigated the key resources and competencies that the MNEs utilize in their CPA activities. The findings are still tentative, but they indicate the critical nature of corporate political activities for corporate strategy and the paramount importance of human resources for government-business relations. The final chapter of the book is authored by Hoecht and it focuses on the rarely discussed issue of intra-community fraud among expatriate entrepreneurs. The genesis of this chapter was a 2006 study, which had originally focused on the differences in risk mitigation strategies between UK and German expatriate entrepreneurs in Spain. That study rather surprisingly revealed a significant amount of intra-community fraud, which warranted this follow up analysis. The authors, therefore, drew on a trust and network frame of analysis to explain the observed incidence of fraudulent behaviour among UK and German expatriate groups in Spain. The chapter identifies different types of expatriate entrepreneurs among the two nationality groups and suggests that groups could be more or less susceptible to intra-community fraud based on their level of use of networks and the risk minimization strategies they employ.

Conclusions

This volume has addressed the focal theme of challenges to international business from its most significant pillars. First, it reflects the reality that tensions related with MNCs' transfer of HR practices and management of employees across borders and cultures still do loom large in the FDI-MNE world. More importantly, it goes beyond mere acknowledgement of the persistence of this challenge to IB to also offer appropriately informed and insightful suggestions on how to better manage the underlying cultural and institutional factors that perpetuate the observed tensions. Second, the book tells the typically heroic story of growth-seeking SMEs that embrace the internationalization path, often with considerable success, but at other times with unfavourable outcomes. These accounts of internationalized SMEs – arguably the most exciting of actors in the IB firmament – are interesting because they highlight the difficulties these size/resource challenged firms typically face, but also embody inspiring pointers to the compensating capabilities and factors that they often leverage to their advantage. Third, the book's coverage of current issues, trends and challenges pertaining to IB in transition and developing economies seems very timely, given the rapid pace of economic progress around the world and the intensifying integration of world economies. The range of developing regions covered by the four chapters – Central Eastern Europe, South Asia, Africa and the Middle East – is remarkable; so are the additional perspectives offered on challenges that women face in international management. Finally, the book's insights on international terrorism directed at business targets, environmental regulations and MNCs' responses, and abuse of trust is invaluable, particularly in view the topical nature of these issues to the IB field and beyond.

Note

* The Academy of International Business UK and Ireland Chapter 2008 Conference was held at the Portsmouth Business School, University of Portsmouth, Portsmouth, UK, in March 2008. The theme of the Conference, chaired by Professor Colin Wheeler, was 'Challenges to International Business'.

References

Barney, J. (1991) 'Firm resources and sustained competitive advantage', *Journal of Management*, 17(1), 99–120.

Bjorkman, I., Smale, A., Sumelius, J., Suutari, V. and Lu, Y. (2008) 'Changes in institutional context and MNC operations in China: Subsidiary HRM practices in 1996 versus 2006', *International Business Review*, 17(2), 146–58.

Czinkota, M.R., Knight, G.A. and Liesch, P.W. (2004) 'Terrorism and international business: conceptual foundations', in G. G. S. Suder (ed.), *Terrorism and the International Business Environment: The Security-Business Nexus* (Cheltenham: Edward Elgar), 43–57.

Goodman, M.B. (2004) 'Meeting the Global Challenges of the Contemporary Business Environment', Royal Society for the encouragement of Arts, Manufactures and Commerce (RSA) Lecture, 1 October, New York.

Hill, C.W.L. (2007) 'Digital Piracy: Causes, consequences, and strategic responses', *Asia Pacific Journal of Management*, 24(1), 9–25.

Hofstede, G. (1991) *Cultures and Organizations: Software of the Mind* (Maidenhead: McGraw-Hill).

Ibeh, K.I.N. (2003) 'Toward a Contingency Framework of Export Entrepreneurship: Conceptualisations and Empirical Evidence', *Small Business Economics*, 15(1), 49–68.

Leung, K., Bhagat, R., Buchan, N., Erez, M. and Gibson, C. (2005) 'Culture and international business: Recent advances and their implications for future research', *Journal of International Business Studies*, 36(4), 357–78.

Liesch, P.W., Steen, J., Knight, G.A. and Czinkota, M.R. (2006) 'Problematizing the internationalization decision: Terrorism induced risk', *Management Decision*, 44(6), 809–23.

Luo, Y. (2008) 'The changing Chinese culture and business behaviour: The perspective of intertwinement between guanxi and corruption', *International Business Review*, 17(2), 188–93.

Peng, M.W., Wang, D.Y. and Jiang, Y. (2008) 'An institution-based view of international business strategy: A focus on emerging economies', *Journal of International Business Studies*, 39(5), 920–36.

Penz, E. (2007) 'Multinational companies' battle against counterfeiting', in R. Sinkovics and M. Yamin (eds), *Anxieties and Management Responses in International Business* (Basingstoke: Palgrave Macmillan).

Prasad, B.S. and Ghauri, P.N. (eds) (2004) *Global Firms and Emerging Markets in the Age of Anxiety* (New York: Praeger).

Rodriguez, P., Siegel, D.S., Hillman, A. and Eden, L. (2006) 'Introduction: Three lenses on the multinational enterprises: politics, corruption and corporate social responsibility', *Journal of International Business Studies*, 37(6), 733–46.

Romilly, P. (2007) 'Business and climate change risk: A regional time series analysis', *Journal of International Business Studies*, 38(3), 474–80.

Sinkovics, R. and Yamin, M. (2007) 'Introduction', in R. Sinkovics and M. Yamin (eds), *Anxieties and Management Responses in International Business* (Basingstoke: Palgrave Macmillan).

Suder, G.G.S. (2004) *Terrorism and the International Business Environment: The Security-Business Nexus* (Cheltenham: Edward Elgar).

Wernerfelt, B. (1984) 'A resource-based view of the firm', *Strategic Management Journal*, 5, 171–80.

Yip, G.S. (1992) *Total Global Strategy: Managing for Worldwide Competitive Advantage* (Englewood Cliffs, NJ: Prentice Hall).

Part I

Cross-Border Management and Institutional Challenges

2
The Challenge of Managing Employee Tenure in China

Angelika Zimmermann, Xiaohui Liu and Trevor Buck

Introduction

China has easily become one of the greatest arenas of cross-cultural management research. With ever rising foreign investment in China, managers and scholars have gained awareness of many cultural and institutional barriers to successful China operations. We focus on the difficulties of retaining qualified Chinese employees as a challenge that has grown so large that it can no longer be tackled by human resource (HR) professionals alone, but has become a major concern for managers at all levels. So far, this challenge has not been regarded as an international or cross-cultural issue as such, but has been investigated within firms of different nationalities. We, in contrast, argue that employee tenure is linked with firm nationality and should therefore be compared across nationalities.

Employee turnover in China has risen continuously since the nineties and has increased even more dramatically since the end of the Asian crisis in 1998. According to Hewitt Associates, annual employee turnover across industries and cities rose from an average of 8.3 per cent in 2001 to 14.7 per cent in 2007 (Sheng and Earsdon, 2007), and a Mercer study reported that the average tenure of 25- to 35-year-olds (the age group targeted by most multinational companies) fell from around four years in 2004 to around two years in 2005 (Wilson, 2006). This trend is likely to continue, as more foreign companies enter the Chinese market, existing firms expand and the shortage of talent grows.

However, the problem may not be uniform for all companies in China. A few researchers suggest that Chinese and foreign firms experience retention problems to different degrees (Wang, 2004; Sovic, 2006; Rein, 2007). Tenure may vary across different types of foreign firm (Walsh and Zhu, 2007), perhaps because of differential HR practices that promote retention, such as those identified in numerous best practice reports (Melvin, 2001; Sheng and Earsdon, 2007). Surprisingly, both tenure and HR practices have rarely been compared between firms of different nationalities in Sino-foreign JVs. Such a comparison is important, because it helps us to understand not only why Chinese employees stay with a firm or leave, but also how employee retention can be improved.

This chapter, therefore, takes the first step towards investigating whether employee tenure in China is bound up with foreign firm nationality. In particular, it asks whether different nationalities of foreign JV partners are associated with employee tenure and whether firms' HR practices are responsible for inter-firm variations in tenure. The findings from our research will contribute to a better understanding of the effectiveness of HR practices for retaining Chinese employees, as well as generate important managerial implications for HR policies in China.

The chapter is structured thus: Following a review of the literature on employee retention problems in China, including their foreign ownership dimensions and some description of HR practices relating to job retention, again with a foreign ownership element, we investigate why firms of different nationalities are likely to vary in their HR practices and employee tenure; this leads to our hypotheses. The subsequent sections then present our methods, the results and our discussion.

Firm nationality and employee tenure

Employee tenure and retention are here used synonymously, with tenure seen as the length of time that an employment post is occupied, and retention as keeping or holding employees in their posts, which implies tenure. In this section, employee retention in China is introduced, with distinctions between local and foreign-owned firms. A consideration of the employee motives for staying with a firm leads to the subsequent section on HR practices for employee retention.

Most studies on staff retention in China do not distinguish between firms of different nationality. Some include Chinese as well as foreign firms, without comparing the two (Chen and Francesco, 2000; Wilson, 2006; Sheng and Earsdon, 2007). Others examine retention in all kinds of foreign companies (Jackson and Bak, 1998). However, a few papers make an exception. Walsh and Zhu (2007) compare different foreign companies (wholly owned firms as well as Sino-foreign JVs), including European, US and Japanese. They find that turnover ranged from one per cent in a Sino-Japanese JV to 10 per cent in a Sino-German JV. Moreover, evidence from practitioners suggests that highly qualified Chinese employees leave their foreign employers for better career prospects in Chinese firms. Western firms are highly attractive employers for young management candidates, because they provide training in Western management methods and often grant higher salaries. Nevertheless, Chinese firms may be regarded as more attractive employers in the long term. An early analysis by Chow, Fung and Yue (1999) of manufacturing enterprises in Shanghai between 1989 and 1992 demonstrates higher turnover in foreign JVs as compared to Chinese state-owned enterprises (SOEs). Sovic's (2006) anecdotal evidence further suggests that many multinationals lose their Chinese employees to local companies after a couple of years of training, because employees perceive that opportunities for career development and promotion are greater in Chinese firms. The same conclusions are reached by Rein (2007), who interviewed senior executives in multinational corporations. Their view was that many multinationals run into the pitfall of 'glass ceilings' for native Chinese.

Senior ranks are commonly taken by Western or overseas Chinese expatriates. Two-tier pay systems often exist, with sometimes generous compensation packages for expatriates. In exit surveys, Chinese workers reported that the main reason they left was that they had no visible career path.

One of the most interesting enquiries is by Wang (2004). He examines the organizational commitment of Chinese employees working in SOEs compared with foreign-invested enterprises (FIEs). Wang (2004) measures different types of organizational commitment, and finds active and passive continuance commitment to be most relevant for retention. Passive continuance commitment describes an attachment due to necessity, where an individual stays with the organization due to a lack of alternatives. Active continuance commitment describes the attachment of individuals to an organization due to a feeling of individual achievement, such as awareness of an opportunity to improve oneself through promotion opportunities or on-the-job training. This attachment is seen as a reason for the employee to stay with the organization. Interestingly, participants from SOEs scored higher on passive as well as active continuance commitment than employees in FIEs. The higher passive continuance commitment in SOEs is explained by government employment restrictions, making it difficult for workers to change place of residency without losing social welfare benefits. In contrast, manual workers in FIEs are usually guest workers from other districts who do not expect residency anyway and therefore move easily from one FIE to another. The lower active continuance commitment found in FIE employees is seen as the result of an over-representation of elite employees in these firms. FIEs provide more training opportunities than SOEs. However, these are usually restricted to a small number of elite employees. In SOEs, most employees expect lifelong employment and there may be long-term developmental opportunities available (Wang, 2004). This implies that active continuance commitment would be higher for higher-level employees than manual workers in FIEs. In contrast, we argue that long-term career opportunities are limited for higher-level employees as well, given the earlier mentioned 'glass ceiling' effect. Such barriers may have a negative effect on active continuance commitment and retention of higher-skilled employees.

This difference in commitment depending on employees' skill level is investigated by Chen and Francesco (2000). They examine companies of unspecified nationality in China, and find that the higher position of Chinese employees is related to higher organizational commitment. They attribute this finding not to career opportunities, but to a cultural factor. Employees in higher positions will have stronger *guanxi*, that is, personal relationships with influential people such as the boss, which were necessary to get to this position. The *guanxi* relationship is seen to create a stabilizing effect and increase the commitment to the organization that the boss represents. In our view, stronger *guanxi* would then be another reason why higher-skilled employees have better career chances. However, even if career chances, commitment and retention are greater in higher level than in lower level employees, it is the turnover of higher-skilled employees that presents the most pressing issue.

A number of relevant conclusions can be drawn from these studies. Retention of Chinese employees may be a greater problem for FIEs than for Chinese firms. For all levels of employees, this may be due to better long-term development opportunities in Chinese firms. Higher-level employees may in addition stay with the firm due to the strong *guanxi* that brought them into this position. Retention comparisons have so far focused on Chinese firms in contrast to FIEs as a whole. Most research does not examine whether retention problems vary with the nationality of the foreign investor. Before demonstrating why such a comparison is worthwhile, we now have a closer look at the HR practices that may promote retention.

HR practices for employee retention

There are abundant suggestions regarding the HR practices that should be deployed to gain an advantage over competitors in attracting and retaining key employees (for example, Goodall and Burgers, 1998; Melvin, 2001; Speth and Doeringer, 2006). Consultancies such as Hewitt, Mercer and Watson Wyatt conduct regular surveys worldwide to capture the latest developments. Best practices are collected from firms with outstanding retention figures, and best practice employers are identified by a Hewitt study each year.

The reviewed influences on Chinese employees' continuance commitment point to the importance of certain HR practices for achieving a higher tenure of Chinese employees. Long-term career chances and social welfare are designed by human resource management (HRM) specialists. Interestingly, recent research on HRM in China converges in the view that *career prospects* have become just as relevant as *financial incentives* for retaining Chinese employees. This corresponds to the observations regarding the effect of career barriers, and it accords with Wang's (2004) explanation for higher active continuance commitment in SOEs. Personal relationships, particularly with one's boss, are also frequently mentioned. This accords with Chen and Francesco's (2000) view that *guanxi* is important for higher-level employees' intention to leave or stay with a company. Social benefits are another recommended retention tool.

To illustrate, Goodall and Burgers (1998) conducted a survey of 80 experienced Chinese managers. A greater number of respondents cited 'soft factors' as reasons to stay or leave, such as job-development opportunities and interpersonal relationships, compared to 'hard factors', including salaries. In a Watson Wyatt international survey in 2005, monetary benefits as well as career prospects and development were the most important reasons for staying or leaving, besides job stability and security (The China Business Review, 2006). Mercer Human Resource Consulting conducted a survey of 114 organizations in Greater China in 2005 (Wilson, 2006). The most highly rated methods of attracting and retaining staff were 'attractive salary and benefits package' (23 per cent of respondents), and 'opportunities for career development (19 per cent). On the basis of this study, Malila (2007) suggests that firms have to adopt a more long-term, strategic approach to HRM. They should 'build, not just buy' their workforce and sustain this grouping through training, career development and pay for performance. Upward mobility has to be ensured for talented PRC (People's Republic of China) nationals. Melvin (2001) draws on a Korn Ferry survey in 2001 and stresses that career development plans are key retention tools. The Korn Ferry research also identified relationships with one's boss as a crucial motivating factor, second behind career development and even before salary.

Many recommendations have been given regarding the other main retention tool, financial incentives. Melvin (2001) provides a useful summary, stating that salaries remain the basis of comparison between different job offers, but need to be combined with many other tangible and intangible retention techniques in order to be effective in the increasingly sophisticated Chinese job market. These can include performance-related bonuses and stock options, 'golden handcuffs', which are financial incentives for staying with the firm for a contractually speci-fied amount of time, or 'iron handcuffs', which are punitive fines for leaving the firm before the end of one's contract.

Melvin (2001) further outlines social benefits used as retention tools, which are government-mandated payments into the government-run social insurance funds. These funds include housing, pension, medical, unemployment, accident/ disability and maternity. Of these, pension funds place the largest burden on employers. Benefits are also given in terms of assistance with mortgages and hous-ing, additional accident and medical assistance, child care, extra holiday time, amongst many others. However, the effectiveness of social benefits for retaining Chinese staff has been questioned by findings from earlier research of Chinese enterprises, where the provision of social benefits was associated with the old regime and was not thought to be a beneficial element in performance manage-ment (see Goodall and Warner, 1999).

The most effective retention tools for top talent in China may have to be dif-ferentiated with regard to employees' years of service and age. Hewitt associates found in 2005 that for the age groups of 25–30 as well as 30–40, career oppor-tunities, education reimbursement and housing benefits were amongst the most important (Speth and Doeringer, 2006). The younger group additionally valued training, whilst the 30–40 year olds sought exposure to senior management. For the 40+ age group, different incentives were important, namely retirement benefits, medical benefits, long-term incentives, work/life balance and external recognition. This takes Wang's (2004) suggestions regarding the reasons for con-tinuance commitment a step further. Whilst career and development opportun-ities are likely to be more important for younger employees, older employees may be retained to a larger extent by social benefits. In the same vein, Melvin (2001) suggests that employment packages in China are more competitive if they are tailored, for example, to employees' age, gender, position and personality. As with retention figures, HR practices for retention have not directly been compared between firms of different nationality in China.

Nationality, employee tenure and HR practices

We have so far demonstrated that Chinese and foreign firms may encounter retention problems to different degrees, and outlined HR practices that may pro-mote retention. Both tenure and HR practices have rarely been compared between firms of different foreign nationality in China. We argue that such a comparison should be conducted, because different nationalities are likely to experience retention problems to different degrees. First, they may differ in their use of HR practices that help them achieve higher retention. Such HR practices are likely to be influenced by the firm's cultural, institutional and historical background. Secondly, retention problems may depend on the firm's language, and, thirdly, on their country's relationship with the People's Republic of China.

It should be noted that HR practices of foreign firms in China are usually partly adapted to the Chinese context, and therefore only partly congruent with the practices used in the foreign home country (Ngo et al., 1998; Walsh and Zhu, 2007). Moreover, in Sino-foreign JVs, the Chinese partner tends to have a significant influence on HR practices (Goodall and Warner, 1997; Walsh and Zhu, 2007). Nevertheless, the influence of the foreign partner is likely to be discernible. Bjorkman and Lu (2001) demonstrate that HRM practices in JVs were determined more by the foreign than the Chinese partner. Accordingly, Zhu and Warner (2004) find that the greater the degree of foreign ownership, the more likely it was that formal HR practices were adopted.

This suggests that HR practices in JVs vary with the nationality of the foreign parent firm. A number of studies support this view, by comparing Japanese, US American and other Western firms. Walsh and Zhu (2007) found differences between firms of Japanese, US and European (whole or partial) ownership in China. For example, US firms were more likely to have individual-based pay, larger internal wage disparities and less permanent employment contracts than Japanese firms. In Farley, Hoenig and Yang's (2004) enquiry, US firms were more likely to use merit-based employment, and Japanese firms were more likely to offer lifetime employment. In the same vein, Ngo, Turban, Lau and Lui (1998) compare companies in Hong Kong, and demonstrate greater similarities among Asian (Singaporean, Hong Kong Chinese and Japanese) firms and Western (British and US) firms, than between Western and Asian firms.

'Asian' as opposed to 'Western' HRM is also distinguished by Rowley, Benson and Warner (2004). They identify a partial convergence of HRM in China, Japan and South Korea. It is shown that HRM in each of these countries converged on parts of the Western HRM model in terms of flexible sourcing, unionism and performance-based remuneration. Nevertheless, HRM in the three countries is still distinct from HRM in the West. Generally speaking, these nationalities still seem to adhere more than Western firms to traditional, long-term HR strategies in terms of secure promotion, long-term employment and predictable promotion. Zhu, Warner and Rowley (2007) investigate HRM in the same countries and, additionally, Taiwan, Malaysia, Thailand and Vietnam. They demonstrate that all these Asian countries retain traditional, group-oriented HRM characteristics.

The question that arises is which HR practices suit the Chinese context better and are more likely to be accepted by Chinese employees? Which practices lead to better outcomes, in particular, employee retention? With regard to Western HRM, Bjorkman and Xiucheng (2002) suggest that some Western 'high-performance HRM practices' are less effective in China than in Western countries. Such limited success of Western HR practices is sometimes attributed to cultural differences. Asian firms in turn may benefit from their cultural proximity to China. In particular, Japanese, Korean, Chinese and overseas Chinese (Hong Kong and Taiwan) citizens share parts of their cultural and historical heritage. For example, Confucianism has shaped societal structures and values in these countries, and the countries score similarly on various cultural value indexes. On the Hofstede (2003) scale, they all obtain high values for long-term orientation (LTO): the degree to which a society embraces long-term devotion to forward thinking values), power distance and collectivism. Asian HR professionals may for these reasons be in a better position than their Western counterparts to understand Chinese employees' expectations, and to design HR practices accordingly.

Some researchers use cultural proximity explicitly to explain the degree of HRM effectiveness in China. For example, Jackson and Bak (1998) argue that Western reward systems do not sufficiently take into account Chinese collectivist attitudes, and certain incentives, such as housing benefits, should be used to promote loyalty and belonging. On a personal level, cultural proximity may motivate Chinese employees to build stronger guanxi with Asian than with Western colleagues and superiors, which may then be an incentive to stay with the firm (Chen and Francesco, 2003). Cultural proximity to China appears to be particularly high for overseas Chinese nationals. Ngo et al. (1998) find important differences between Japanese and Hong Kong/Singaporean Chinese companies in Hong Kong. For example, Chinese firms provided training that was more effective in increasing employee retention than that provided by Japanese firms. They conclude that researchers should distinguish between HR practices in Japanese and Hong Kong/Singaporean firms.

There are, however, some findings that contradict this cultural proximity view. Chinese employees may expect and accept Western management practices from their Western employers, and may even prefer them to Asian practices. For example, Selmer (1996) demonstrates that subordinate managers assessed the leadership behaviour of their Western expatriate bosses to be significantly closer to that of their perceived ideal boss, with American leadership behaviour being the most preferred and Japanese leader style the least preferred. Moreover, the HR practices that Asian firms apply in China may not be highly effective. For example, Taura (2005) observes that Japanese firms in China offer lower wages and less career advancement than their Western counterparts. Legewie (2002) posits that the Japanese, heavily expatriate-based system causes a 'them–we' mentality. This may create a perceived limitation for the career of Chinese employees. It is thus ambiguous whether Western or Asian firms deploy more effective HR practices in China. This makes it less certain which nationalities are likely to face greater retention difficulties.

This ambiguity regarding retention difficulties is reinforced when considering the role of language. Language difficulties for Chinese employees will be greater with some foreign firms than others. Overseas Chinese firms will be the least threatening in terms of language requirements, followed by Western organizations that use English. Japanese firms, in contrast, often maintain Japanese as the company language, which makes a career for Chinese staff in these firms very difficult (Taura, 2005). This language factor therefore supports a distinction between overseas Chinese and other Asian firms. Moreover, acquiring English language skills may be seen as an opportunity for career development. Walsh and Zhu (2007) report that employees were leaving a Sino-Japanese JV for new career development opportunities at European and American companies. These were viewed as more attractive partly because they provided 'the opportunity for employees to develop English language skills' (p. 256).

Finally, historical relationships with other countries could cause Chinese employees to feel either more or less affectively committed to employers of different nationality. It is uncertain how attractive Japanese companies are as employers, given the political and historical resentments some Chinese hold against Japan as a country. Western countries may be attractive due to the fashion of absorbing 'everything Western', whilst overseas Chinese firms may be attractive due to the common cultural grounds they share with their Chinese employees.

These cross-national comparisons illustrate that retention and HR practices may vary with the nationality of a foreign firm in China. The direction of these differences is, however, not clear-cut and is not apparent from the literature. The reviewed literature also suggests that differences in HR practices may be bound to certain nationality clusters, namely Western in contrast to Japanese and Korean, and both in comparison to overseas Chinese firms.

For our investigation, we therefore distinguished between three nationality clusters in relation to HRM and employee tenure in Sino-foreign JVs: (One) Western (EU and US), (Two) overseas Chinese (Hong Kong and Taiwanese) and (Three) other Asian (Japanese and Korean) nationality. We examined three hypotheses based on our literature review above:

> Hypothesis 1 (H1): Different nationalities of foreign partner (a. Western, b. Overseas Chinese, c. Japanese and Korean) are associated with significantly different levels of employee tenure in Sino-foreign JVs.

> Hypothesis 2 (H2): Different nationalities of foreign partner are associated with significantly different HR practices in Sino-foreign JVs.

> Hypothesis 3 (H3): The HR practices adopted by Sino-foreign JVs are significantly related to employee tenure.

Methods

Sample

We focused on employee tenure and HR practices in Sino-foreign JVs with three categories of foreign partner (a. Western, b. Overseas Chinese, c. Japanese and Korean). In these JVs, the nationality of foreign partners represents a different degree of LTO and cultural proximity. Nationality of foreign partner was the main explanatory variable together with HR practices, which were also dependent variables in the context of H2.

The paper is based empirically on a postal questionnaire survey conducted during 2006 with 316 Chinese-foreign JVs, where questions related to the period 1998–2005; 1998 was the year foreign ownership of shares in JVs was freed from State controls. We limited the sample to high-tech industries in order to control the impact of industrial affiliation on HR practices and employee tenure across the three types of foreign JVs. Three cities, Beijing, Tianjin and Qingdao, were surveyed because of their domination of the foreign JV sector in China. In particular, Japanese, Korean and Chinese JVs mainly locate in the Pan Bohai region, and these three cities accounted for 67 per cent of Korean and 40 per cent of Japanese investment in China (Wang, 1998). Selecting our sample firms from the three cities enabled us to avoid the problem of the under-representation of Sino-Korean JVs in other regions. According to lists obtained from the Beijing, Tianjin and Qingdao Industry and Commerce Bureaus, in 2006 there were 2,126 foreign JVs in Beijing, 1,075 in Tianjin and 461 in Qingdao. Each foreign JV was approached and a willingness to participate in our survey was indicated by 2,053, representing 53 per cent of the foreign JV population in these three cities.

The 2,053 JVs were then surveyed. A total of 316 useable questionnaires were obtained (a response rate of 15 per cent) with 104 JVs with US/EU partners; 103 with overseas Chinese ownership (Hong Kong and Taiwan); and 109 with other Asian co-owners (Japan and Korea). Further details of the methodology are excluded owing to space limitations, but can be obtained by contacting the lead author.

Results

Chi square (χ^2) analysis was conducted to examine relationships between categorical variables, and univariate analysis of variance (ANOVA) was used for continuous independent variables. Four sets of relationships were examined to test our three hypotheses, and the significance levels of these tests are provided in Table 2.1. We also tested the interrelationships between HR practices which were implicitly embedded in our hypotheses. These are shown in Table 2.2.

Nationality and tenure (H1)

H1 was confirmed. We found significant differences in employee tenure between the JVs with different nationalities of foreign partner ($\chi^2 = 13.89$; df = 6; Asymp. Sig. (2-sided) = .031). Figure 2.1 illustrates the differences between the different nationality clusters with regard to the means of chosen category numbers. Tenure was significantly higher in the overseas Chinese firms (Mean = 3.15) compared to Japanese and Korean firms (3.05), which in turn scored higher than Western firms (2.72). Relatedly, counts of employee tenure are provided in Figure 2.2. Again, the distribution of counts across categories was significantly different for each nationality. EU/US participants had a greater skew towards the category of 0 to 3 years of tenure, with overall 53 responses in this category compared to 37 for Japanese/Korean and 30 in overseas Chinese firms. Japanese/Korean companies had the

Table 2.1 Relationships of nationality and tenure with HR practices and control variables

	Tenure (average employee's tenure)	National origins of the JV parent firm .031* (χ^2)
The percentage of expatriates in total employees	.77 (ANOVA)	.000*** (ANOVA)
Percentage of local managers	.89 (ANOVA)	.001** (ANOVA)
Percentage of employees with a contract for over 5 years	.000*** (χ^2)	.006** (χ^2)
Average contribution of the JV to employees' pension fund (as a % of total pay)	.000*** (χ^2)	.05† (χ^2)
Pension provision is the responsibility of the company	.049* (χ^2)	.25 (χ^2)
Frequency of employee bonus payment	.058† (χ^2)	.22 (χ^2)
Largest percentage of labour force increase during the last seven years	.504 (χ^2)	.177 (χ^2)
Years of existence of company	.000*** (ANOVA)	.894 (ANOVA)

Notes: N = 316, *** p<.001, ** p<.01, * p<.05, † p<.10.

highest count in the middle category (4–5 years), whilst overseas Chinese had the greatest count in the higher category of 6–10 years, representing 33 responses compared to only 17 from the Western and 26 in the Japanese/Korean firms. The numbers for the highest tenure (>10 years) were small for all nationalities, with Japanese/Korean firms accounting for the highest.

We controlled for two potential intervening variables, age of the company and recent growth. The assumption was that higher tenure could be positively associated with older firms or those with recent employment growth. The age variable on its own was significantly related to tenure (ANOVA: df = 5; F = 24; Sig. = .000), whilst growth was not significantly related to tenure (χ^2 = 8.9; df = 6; Symp. Sig. (2-sided) = .177). We subsequently used analysis of covariance (ANCOVA) to assess the relationship between nationality and tenure after controlling for firm age and growth. The relationship was still significant (df = 2; F = 6.4; Sig. = .002; and df = 2; F = 4.3; Sig. = .014). These results are consistent with H1.

Nationality, HR practices and tenure (H2, H3)

There were mixed results regarding both H2 and H3. Both hypotheses were only partly confirmed. A highly significant difference between firms of different nationality was found regarding the amount of local and foreign staff, namely 'the percentage of expatriates in total employees' (ANOVA: df = 2; F = 9.77; Sig. = 000) and 'the percentage of local managers in total employees' (ANOVA: df = 2; F = 7.4;

Table 2.2 Relationships between HR practices

	Percentage of expatriates	Percentage of local managers	Contract for over 5 years	Contribution to pension fund	Pension responsibility	Type of bonus
Percentage of expatriates	–	.12 (ANOVA)	.18 (ANOVA)	.19 (ANOVA)	.26 (ANOVA)	.37 (ANOVA)
Percentage of local managers		–	.84 (ANOVA)	.008** (ANOVA)	.204 (ANOVA)	.05† (ANOVA)
Contract for over 5 years			–	.004** (χ^2)	.017* (χ^2)	.025* (χ^2)
Contribution to pension fund				–	.000** (χ^2)	.019* (χ^2)
Pension responsibility					–	.028* (χ^2)
Type of bonus						–

Notes: N = 316, *** $p < .001$, ** $p < .01$, * $p < .05$, † $p < .10$.
······ Interrelation.

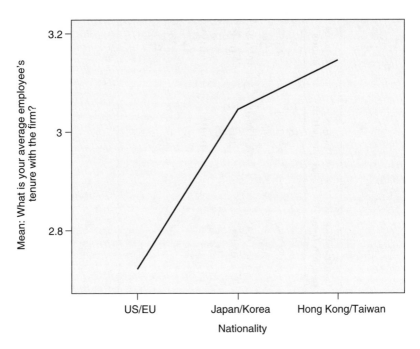

Figure 2.1   Nationality and tenure (a)

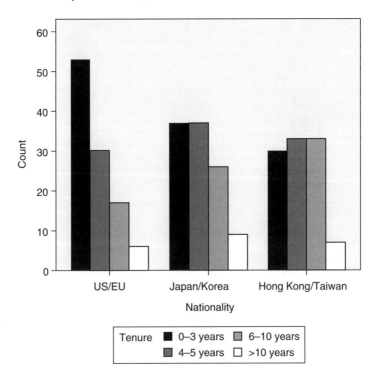

Figure 2.2   Nationality and tenure (b)

Sig. = .001). Overseas Chinese firms had the lowest percentage of foreign expatriates (Mean = 3.75), whilst Japanese/Korean firms were in the middle (6.45) and EU/US companies scored the highest (6.69). The pattern for local staff was, however, not the converse. With regard to percentages of local managers, Western firms again scored the highest (14.48) followed closely by overseas Chinese firms (13.44). Japanese/Korean firms employed the smallest percentage of local managers (10.52). Overall, Japanese/Korean firms seemed to be the least localized, given their low percentages of local managers and high number of expatriates. Overseas Chinese firms appeared to employ the least expatriates. Western firms, interestingly, scored highest both with regard to local and foreign employees. Contrary to our expectations (H2), the degree of localization, in terms of local versus foreign staff, was not significantly related to employee tenure (see Table 2.1).

We found a significant difference between nationalities regarding the percentage of employees who had signed a contract for over 5 years ($\chi^2 = 21.47$; df = 8; Asymp. Sig. (2-sided) = .006). Overall, overseas Chinese firms had the highest percentage of long-term contracts (Mean = 3.81), followed by Japanese/Korean (3.54) and then EU/US (3.26). The most striking difference was with regard to the highest percentage, that is, the category of > 30 per cent of employees who signed an over five year contract. Overseas Chinese scored highest on this category (N = 59), followed by Japanese/Korean (N = 48) and then the EU/US (N = 39). Conversely, EU/US firms scored highest on the lowest percentage of employees with long-term contracts (N = 31; compared to N = 23 for overseas Chinese and N = 19 for Japanese/Korean). Japanese/Korean firms scored highest on the middle, 6–10 per cent, category (N = 14, compared to N = 5 for Western and N = 2 for overseas Chinese). The long-term contract variable was highly significantly related to employee tenure ($\chi^2 = 214.1$; df = 9; Asymp. Sig. (2-sided) = .000), with a virtually linear relationship.

A firm's average contribution to employees' pension funds was significantly related to nationality at the border level of p = .05 ($\chi^2 = 9.47$; df = 4; Asymp. Sig. (2-sided) = .05). Western and Japanese/Korean firms had similar averages and patterns of pension contributions (Mean = 2.19 for Western and 2.21 for Japanese/Korean firms), but overseas Chinese firms had a skew towards the highest category of pension funds, and a higher average contribution (2.49). The contributions to pension funds were highly significantly related to employee tenure ($\chi^2 = 34.77$; df = 6; Asymp. Sig. (2-sided) = .000), again in a virtually linear relationship.

Attitudes towards the firm's responsibility for pension provision was not significantly related to nationality, but was significantly related to tenure (ANOVA: df = 6; F = 2.234; Sig. = .049). The pattern of relationship was again approximately linear.

The type of bonus was not significantly related to either nationality ($\chi^2 = 5.73$; df = 4; Asymp. Sig. (2-sided) = .22) or tenure, although the relationship with tenure came close to the significance level ($\chi^2 = 12.172$; df = 6; Asymp. Sig. (2-sided) = .058). However, the pattern of relationship with tenure was counter-intuitive and not linear. Short-term bonuses, that is, the collapsed categories of 'weekly' and 'monthly' bonuses, were related to the highest tenure (Mean = 2.1), yearly bonuses to the second highest tenure (1.62), and quarterly bonuses to the third highest tenure (1.86).

Interrelationships between HR practices

The clustering of HR practices is summarized in Table 2.2. It can be seen that the association between percentage of expatriates and local managers was non-significant, which corresponds to the finding that Western firms had high levels of both expatriates and local managers. In contrast, there were interrelations between all other HR variables, namely, long-term contracts, contribution to pension funds, pension responsibility and bonus types.

Discussion

As predicted in H1, the nationality of JV partners was significant in relation to average employee tenure. Tenure was the highest in overseas Chinese, moderate in Japanese/Korean and lowest in Western firms. This is consistent with the high LTO in Asian countries and low LTO in the West. Some of our results suggest that this variation in tenure may be mediated by the firms' use of particular HR practices.

Two of the six measured HR practices were significantly related to both nationality and tenure, which partly confirms H2 as well as H3. These statistically significant practices were the award of long contracts and employers' pension contributions. In contrast, four HR practices did not seem to be associated with tenure differences, because these HR practices did not relate to both tenure and nationality. Two HR practices related only to nationality (confirming H2 but not H3), one only to tenure (confirming H3 but not H2) and one to neither nationality nor tenure (refuting H2 and H3). The percentage of expatriates and the percentage of local managers varied between JVs with different nationality, but were not related to employee tenure. Conversely, the perceived responsibility to provide pension funds was related to differences in tenure, but not to nationality. The type of bonus system did not vary significantly with either nationality or tenure, although the relationship with tenure came only close to significance (Sig. = .058). We now first discuss the findings that supported our hypotheses, and then turn to the unexpected results.

The relationship of long-term contracts with nationality is in certain respects counter-intuitive. If employee tenure is a great challenge for firms in China, then firms of all nationalities should be eager to offer their employees long-term contracts. It therefore seems to be a contradiction that Western firms in our survey did not sign as many long-term contracts as Japanese/Korean did, and even fewer than overseas Chinese firms. This difference in long-term contracts may reflect the distinction between higher and lower level employees in Western and Japanese/Korean firms. It is the highly qualified employees that firms struggle to retain, and perhaps long-term contracts may be restricted to such employees in Western and Japanese/Korean firms. Offering long-term contracts to a broader group of employees may not be seen as useful for improving the retention of key employees.

However, our findings give us cause to reconsider the importance of long-term contracts for retaining employees of all levels. Long-term contracts may not be just a tool in themselves to retain employees. Instead, providing long-term contracts to a broader group of employees may be part of a company culture which signals the firm's long-term commitment to employees across all levels. Such a company culture may create more than merely contractual bonds. It may strengthen employees' psychological contracts and attachment to the firm and thereby enhance their tenure. Firms with such a culture are likely to use a set of interrelated HR practices which focus on long-term employee development and retention, that is, a long-term oriented HR system.

This speculation is supported by our finding that the HR practices that were associated with retention were also related to each other. The relationships between long-term contracts, contributions to pension funds and attitudes towards pension funds followed a clear pattern, approaching linearity. The more one of these methods was present, the more the others would be used, as well. These HR practices may therefore all be part of an integrated HR system.

The use of a long-term oriented HR system could be tied to cultural traditions. On the one hand, 'high performance work practices' (Huselid, 1995), which emphasize the importance of strategic alignment of HRM and (long-term) employee commitment, were developed in the USA. On the other hand, long-term employment contracts were more prevalent in the Asian firms of our sample. This may reflect the traditional institution of lifelong employment, which was until recently common in Japanese, Korean, as well as some overseas Chinese, companies (Zhu, Warner and Rowley, 2007). Long-term employment may be tied to these countries' strong cultural value of LTO (Hofstede, 2003). In the same vein, the emphasis on social benefits, including pension funds, may be rooted in overseas Chinese firms' strong LTO, collectivism and the Confucian value of mutual obligations between employer and employee.

However, variations in tenure are unlikely to be due to HR practices alone, given that only two of the examined HR practices were associated with both nationality and tenure. Culture may provide an additional explanation for variations in tenure between JVs of different nationality. As mentioned before, Chinese employees' relationships with their superiors seem to be important for their decision to stay with a company or leave. Due to cultural proximity, Chinese managers may be able to build stronger relations with their Chinese employees than Japanese or Western managers can. In particular, shared long-term orientation and person-orientation may lead both parties to spend more time and effort in building long-term relationships ('*guanxi*') at work. Similar cultural-meaning systems and a shared language can help to avoid misunderstandings and strongly facilitate relations between managers and employees. This issue is worth investigating in future research. International managers should understand how their cultural distance to their employees may affect employee tenure.

A number of unexpected results of this study must also be discussed. For example, we found that the percentage of expatriates and of local managers in a firm did not affect employee tenure. This is surprising, given the emphasis in previous research on the barriers to the advancement of Chinese employees. A clue to this finding may lie in the lack of a relationship between the two variables. JVs that employed more expatriates did not necessarily employ fewer local employees. This was most apparent in Chinese-Western JVs, which counted high numbers of both expatriates and local managers. Therefore, the percentage of expatriates in total employees may not always reflect a lack of career chances for Chinese employees. Conversely, the number of local managers would not depend on the degree to which higher positions are filled with foreign staff. Western companies in our sample appeared to be building a local workforce and at the same time maintaining a high level of control through the expatriates. It is then easy to understand why the percentage of expatriates in total employees was not related to the other HR practices for retention. Employing more or fewer expatriates does not appear to be counterproductive for employee tenure, unless it is associated with a lower number of local managers. It is not in itself an HR practice for retention that would form part of a long-term oriented HR system.

Correspondingly, the percentage of local managers would not in itself be a practice for retention, but only if it was associated with fewer expatriates in the firms. Nevertheless, the percentage of local managers was related to a number of HR practices for retention, namely the contributions to pension funds, and bonus types. We could speculate that firms that employ a higher percentage of local managers may be aiming to localize their operations. They may therefore tend to adopt HR practices which are common in the local, Chinese context, such as high contributions to pension funds. The relationship of local managers with bonus type, in contrast, was not linear. This may be due to factors not captured in this investigation.

There are a few other, more puzzling, findings. In line with hypothesis 2, participants who agreed that pension provision was the responsibility of the company worked in firms with higher employee tenure. Attitudes towards pension responsibility also related to actual contributions to pension fund, which differed between nationalities. Nevertheless, the views on pension responsibility did not vary with nationality. We reason that this finding may be due to factors outside the scope of the study.

It was also contrary to our expectation that bonus types had a non-linear association with tenure and with the HR variables that were related to tenure. In particular, weekly/monthly bonuses were associated with higher scores on tenure, long-term contracts, contributions to pension funds and pension responsibility than quarterly bonuses. This seems to contradict the idea of an integrated, long-term oriented HR system. However, it is possible that the time intervals covered by our bonus measures were not large enough to distinguish between different degrees of LTO. The difference between monthly and quarterly bonuses may not be sufficient for encouraging employee tenure, and may for this reason not correspond to the use of other, retention-focused HR practices.

This study was one of the first to show differences in tenure and HR practices for retention between firms of different nationality in China. The findings correspond to the research showing that Western and Asian firms use different HR practices (Farley et al., 2004; Rowley et al., 2004; Walsh and Zhu, 2007), and that there are differences in HRM between overseas Chinese and other Asian firms (Ngo et al., 1998). Our findings further implicate that some of these practices are relevant to increasing employee tenure, and may explain differences in employee tenure between JVs of different nationality. Foremost, providing long-term contracts may be an important retention tool which Western firms in China presently use less than Japanese and Korean firms, and even less than overseas Chinese firms. Contributing to employees' pension funds appears to be another effective retention method, which overseas Chinese firms apply to the greatest extent.

This can be taken as a hint for Western HR managers to learn from Japanese and Korean firms, and for Western, Japanese and Korean managers to learn from overseas Chinese firms. However, our enquiry focused only on a limited range of HR practices for retention. Insight into a wider range is needed in order to optimize a company's HR system. It is also necessary to examine HR systems in more depth, in order to understand the mechanisms by which they help achieve employee retention in China. It would be important to investigate how organizational commitment varies and affects tenure in firms of different nationality, and how it can be influenced through HR practices. In particular, the influence of cultural distance on employee commitment, including implications for cross-cultural management, should be investigated in more depth. Future research could also differentiate between employee skill levels and ages, to highlight how tenure of these different groups can be enhanced. Furthermore, one should explore other possible reasons for national differences in tenure, such as company language and relationships between local and foreign firm countries. Thus, there are numerous ways to carry this research forward, and this study provides a fruitful basis for such advances.

Note

Financial support from the Leverhulme Trust, grant number F/00 261/U, is gratefully acknowledged.

References

Bjorkman, Ingmar and Lu, Yuan (2001) 'Institutionalization and bargaining power explanations of HRM Practices in International Joint Ventures – The case of Chinese-Western joint ventures', *Organization Studies*, 22(3), 491–512.

Bjorkman, Ingmar and Xiucheng, Fan (2002) 'Human resource management and the performance of Western firms in China', *The International Journal of Human Resource Management*, 13(6), 853–64.

Chen, Zhen Xiong and Francesco, Anne Maria (2000) 'Employee demography, organizational commitment, and turnover intentions in China: Do cultural differences matter?' *Human Relations*, 53(6), 869–87.

Chen, Zhen Xiong and Francesco, Anne Maria (2003) 'The relationship between the three components of commitment and employee performance in China', *Journal of Vocational Behavior*, 62(3), 490–510.

Chow, Clement Kong, Fung, Michael Ka, and Yue, Ngo Hang (1999) 'Job turnover in China: A case study of Shanghai's manufacturing enterprises', *Industrial Relations*, 38(4), 482–503.

Farley, John U., Hoenig, Scott and Yang, John Z. (2004) 'Key factors influencing HRM practices of overseas subsidiaries in China's transition economy', *The International Journal of Human Resource Management*, 15(4/5): 688–704.

Goodall, Keith and Burgers, Willem (1998) 'Frequent fliers', *The China Business Review*, May–June, 50–52.

Goodall, Keith and Warner, Malcolm (1997) 'Human resources in Sino-foreign joint ventures', *The International Journal of Human Resource Management*, 8(5), 569–94.

Goodall, Keith and Warner, Malcolm (1999) 'Enterprise reform, labour management relations and human resource management in a multinational context', *International Studies of Management and Organisation*, 29(3), 21–36.

Hofstede, Geert (2003) *Cultures Consequences: Comparing Values, Behaviors, Institutions, and Organizations across Nations* (London: Sage Publications).

Huselid, M.A. (1995) 'The impact of human resource management practices on turnover, productivity, and corporate financial performance', *Academy of Management Journal*, 38(3), 635–72.

Jackson, Terence and Bak, Mette (1998) 'Foreign companies and Chinese workers: Employee motivation in the People's Republic of China', *Journal of Organizational Change Management*, 11(4), 282–300.

Legewie, Jochen (2002) 'Control and co-ordination of Japanese subsidiaries in China: problems of an expatriate-based management system', *The International Journal of Human Resource Management*, 13(6), 901–19.

Malila, Jill (2007) 'The great look forward: China's HR Evolution', *The China Business Review*, July–August, 16–19.

Melvin, Sheila (2001) 'Retaining Chinese employees', *The China Business Review*, November–December, 30–43.

Ngo, Hang-Yue, Turban, Daniel, Lau, Chung-Ming and Lui, Siu-Yu (1998) 'Human resource practices and firm performance of multinational corporations: Influences of country origin', *The International Journal of Human Resource Management*, 9(4), 632–52.

Rein, Shaun (2007) 'How Multinationals Err in China', *http://www.forbes.com/opinions/2007/05/24/china-glass-ceiling-oped-cx_sr_0524rein.html*. Accessed 19 November 2007.

Rowley, Chris, Benson, John, and Warner, Malcolm (2004) 'Towards an Asian model of human resource management? A comparative analysis of China, Japan and South Korea', *The International Journal of Human Resource Management*, 15(4), 917–33.

Selmer, Jan (1996) 'Expatriate or local bosses? HCN subordinates' preferences in leadership behaviour', *The International Journal of Human Resource Management*, 7(1), 165–78.

Sheng, Henry and Earsdon, Melinda (2007) 'Hewitt announces best employers in China 2007', *http://www.hewittassociates.com/Intl/AP/en-CN/AboutHewitt/Newsroom/PressReleases/2007/april-18-2007_a.aspx*. Accessed 19 November 2007.

Sovic, Nina (2006) 'Western firms find hiring, retention in China surprisingly tough', *The Wall Street Journal Online: http://online.wsj.com/article/SB115523756653432470.html*. Accessed 19 November 2007.

Speth, Matthias and Doeringer, Christian (2006) 'Key talent retention in China', *http://www.hewittassociates.com/Lib/assets/AP/en-HT/pdfs/key_talent_retention.pdf*. Accessed 19 November 2007.

Taura, Rika (2005) 'Japanese Companies' HRM strategies in China', *NRI Papers*, 86(February), 1–10.

The China Business Review (2006) 'China's Tight Talent market', *http://www.chinabusiness review.com/public/0603/ChinaData.pdf*. Accessed 19 November 2007.

Walsh, Janet and Zhu, Ying (2007) 'Local complexities and global uncertainties: a study of foreign ownership and human resource management in China', *The International Journal of Human Resource Management*, 18(2), 249–67.

Wang, YingYan (2004) 'Observations on the organizational commitment of Chinese employees: comparative studies of state-owned enterprises and foreign-invested enterprises', *The International Journal of Human Resource Management*, 15(4), 649–69.

Wang, Z. (1998) *Japanese Corporations' Investment in China* (Beijing: Chinese Economic Press).

Wilson, Brenda (2006) 'Companies in China struggling to retain staff, survey shows', *http://www.mercer.com/pressrelease/details.jhtml?idContent=1239885*. Accessed 19 November 2007.

Zhu, Ying and Warner, Malcolm (2004) 'Changing patterns of human resource management in contemporary China: WTO accession and enterprise responses', *Industrial Relations Journal*, 35(4), 311–28.

Zhu, Ying, Warner, Malcolm and Rowley, Chris (2007) 'Human resource management with "Asian" characteristics: A hybrid people-management system in East Asia', *The International Journal of Human Resource Management*, 18(5), 745–68.

3
Organizational Identification and Commitment Following a Cross-Border Acquisition

Mélanie Elina Raukko

Introduction

Cross-border mergers and acquisitions (M&As) have become common in the business world. Recent figures show that in 2006 the OECD countries witnessed the second highest level of foreign direct investment (FDI) flows and that estimates for 2007 would be close to those of 2000 – the record year for M&As (OECD, 2007). Cross-border acquisitions involve unique challenges, due to their various economic, institutional or regulatory and cultural structures (Child, Faulkner and Pitkethly, 2001). As cross-border acquisitions are challenging for managers, they provide a fruitful research arena for scholars. Many of the acquisitions made during the past decade appear to have been motivated by the need for firms to obtain critical technologies or capabilities (Ranft and Lord, 2000). Since the 1990s, acquisitions have increased dramatically in high-technology sectors (Ranft and Lord, 2002). Intangible assets such as knowledge are very important as they can even determine the success of a company, especially after mergers and acquisitions. In knowledge-intensive and innovation-driven industries, highly skilled human resources may represent one of the most valuable strategic resources in a specific company (Ranft and Lord, 2000). Nevertheless, if the primary objective of an acquisition is the acquisition of valuable knowledge, a subsequent departure of key personnel can affect the success of the acquisition (Hubbard, 1999; Ranft and Lord, 2000).

Turnover and commitment literature implies that the most important factor affecting turnover intentions is organizational commitment (Porter, Steers, Mowday and Boulian, 1974; Mobley, 1982; Allen and Meyer, 1990; Elangovan, 2001). Organizational commitment is also closely linked to organizational identification, which has been viewed as one type of organizational commitment (Mathieu and Zajac, 1990). Consequently, this research focuses on the organizational commitment and identification of a target company's employees. Moreover, this research considers the duality of identification and commitment in the context of an international merger and acquisition (Millward and Kyriakidou, 2004;

Kusstatscher and Cooper, 2005). Hence, *organizational identification and commit-ment are explored both in relation to the acquired and the acquiring company.*

The main purpose of this research is to explore the development of the post-acquisition organizational commitment and identification of the acquired employees, later also referred to as target employees. The research was conducted as a longitudinal case study in a small and medium-sized European high-tech company, which was acquired by an Asian company. The data collection started within the first 100 days (Angwin, 2004) of the closure of the deal and continued during the following year. Data was collected through both qualitative interviews and quantitative questionnaires.

This paper is divided into three main sections. First, the literature review elaborates on the concepts of organizational commitment and identification, and how mergers and acquisitions may affect commitment and identification. The second section describes the research process and the results. Finally, the main conclusions are drawn in the final section of this paper.

Organizational identification and commitment in cross-border acquisitions

Organizational commitment

The concept of commitment has been defined in various ways and studied extensively (Morrow, 1983; Cooper-Hakim and Viswesvaran, 2005). According to Morrow (1983), there are over 25 commitment-related concepts and measures, and in a more recent review Cooper-Hakim and Viswesvaran (2005) identified 24 forms of commitment. Consequently, this field of research has been fragmented and it has been marked by a lack of consensus concerning the definition of the concept or its measurement (Mowday, Porter and Steers, 1982; Morrow, 1983; Mathieu and Zajac, 1990; Meyer and Allen, 1997; Benkhoff, 1997; Hartmann and Bambacas, 2000; Cooper-Hakim and Viswesvaran, 2005). Common to all conceptualizations found in the relevant literature is the link with turnover, which demonstrates that employees who are strongly committed to an organization are those who are least likely to leave the organization (Porter et al., 1974; Mowday, Steers and Porter, 1979; Allen and Meyer, 1990).

The organizational commitment questionnaire (OCQ) developed by Porter et al. (1974) has in a sense become 'the' approach to organizational commitment as it has become the most popular measure of commitment (Mathieu and Zajac, 1990; Brown, 1996). Based on a recent literature review, it is still the most frequently used measurement tool (Cooper-Hakim and Viswesvaran, 2005). According to Porter et al. (1974) and Mowday et al. (1979), organizational commitment is defined in terms of the strength of an individual's identification with, involvement in, and desire to maintain, membership in a particular organization. Another frequently used approach to organizational commitment is the three-component conceptualization of commitment proposed by Allen and Meyer (1990). This conceptualization divides organizational commitment into affective, continuance and normative commitment (Allen and Meyer, 1990).

Committing key persons to the acquirer and the new post-integration organization can be crucial in acquisitions where the main target has been the gaining of knowledge embedded in the target company's employees. Thus, the retention of key persons can be critical regarding the success of M&As (for example, Hubbard, 1999). Furthermore, recent research suggests that organizational commitment is an important determinant of knowledge sharing (Hislop, 2003; Van den Hooff and De Ridder, 2004). Consequently, understanding how organizational commitment develops during the integration phase is important.

Recent research has been increasingly interested in the organizational commitment of the acquired employees, although research in this field is still very scarce (for example, Schraeder, 2001; Fairfield-Sonn, Ogilvie and Del Vecchio, 2002). Moreover, there is little research available on identifying changes in commitment over time or on the factors associated with these changes (Beck and Wilson, 2001). Thus, this research focuses on the organizational commitment of acquired employees during the early post-acquisition integration phase. Organizational commitment is conceptually very close to organizational identification (Riketta, 2005; Van Knippenberg and Sleebos, 2006). Thus, in order to obtain a better understanding of target employees' organizational commitment, organizational identification is explored as well. The next section defines organizational identification in more detail.

Organizational identification

Organizational identification is a more recent concept than organizational commitment (Riketta, 2005; Cole and Bruch, 2006). For decades the dominant approach to conceptualizing the strength of the psychological relationship between the individual and the organization seemed to be the organizational commitment approach (Van Knippenberg and Sleebos, 2006). However, recent research has been inspired by social identity theory, according to which, organizational identification has been viewed as a shared identity (Ashforth and Mael, 1989; Van Knippenberg and Sleebos, 2006).

Organizational identification can be described as the perception of oneness with or belongingness to an organization when an individual defines himself or herself in terms of the organization(s) in which he/she is a member (Mael and Ashforth, 1992). Consequently, the more a person identifies with an organization, the more the organization's values, norms and interests are incorporated into the self-concept (Van Knippenberg and Sleebos, 2006). Organizational identification is organization-specific, while commitment may not be; that is, a person may score high on commitment without perceiving a shared destiny with that particular organization (Mael and Ashforth, 1992). Nevertheless, it can be argued that in a cross-border acquisition both organizational identification and commitment would be organization-specific as employees identify and commit more easily to their own organization than the newly merged companies that form a new entity.

Consequently, organizational identification is closely linked to organizational commitment and it has been viewed as one type of organizational commitment (Hall, Schneider and Nygren, 1970), or at least as a close conceptual neighbour to affective organizational commitment (Mowday et al., 1979; Mathieu and Zajac, 1990; Riketta, 2005). More recent research argues that organizational identification and organizational commitment are distinct constructs (Mael and Ashforth, 1992; Van Knippenberg and Sleebos, 2006; Cole and Bruch, 2006). The core issue differentiating organizational identification from organizational commitment is that identification reflects an individual's self-definition, whereas commitment does not (Ashforth and Mael, 1989; Van Knippenberg and Sleebos, 2006). In other words, identification reflects the extent to which organizational membership is incorporated into the self-concept, whereas commitment focuses on employees' attitudes towards the organization based on their perceptions of the costs and benefits associated with the organization (Bartels, Douwes, de Jong and Pruyn, 2006).[1]

In summary, based on more recent research, this research views organizational identity and organizational commitment as distinct and separate concepts (Van Knippenberg and Sleebos, 2006). The next section describes in more detail the factors affecting the development of identification and commitment following an acquisition.

Employees' organizational commitment and identification following an acquisition

Organizational commitment and identification are very complex phenomena in the context of international acquisitions. It has been argued that the stronger the social bonding with the pre-merger organization, the more problematic is identification with the merged new organization likely to be (Bartels et al., 2006). M&As create a threat to an organization's identity and therefore also to the employees' social identification with their organization.

Previous research on how organizational identity is affected by M&As has adopted a dual perspective by distinguishing between pre- and post-merger identity (Bartels et al., 2006; van Dick, Ullrich and Tissington, 2006). The majority of studies on organizational identification have taken a post-merger perspective. Nevertheless, as previous research implies that employees identify with specific organizations (Mael and Ashforth, 1992), this chapter argues that instead of making the distinction between pre- and post-M&A identification, it is much more important to differentiate between the target and the acquiring organization. Accordingly, organizational commitment and organizational identification will, in this research, be viewed as having two dimensions: *towards the acquirer and towards the acquired/target company* (Ketchand and Strawser, 2001).

M&As per se can be expected to alter employees' identification as they essentially redraw or dissolve the boundaries of two distinct groups within the newly merged entity (van Dick et al., 2006). Moreover, as M&As threaten the distinctiveness of the pre-merger identity, it has been argued that subgroup identification may increase at the expense of identification with the post-merger entity (van Dick et al., 2006). Employees often identify with their pre-acquisition company, and it may take several years before they really feel committed to the newly merged company and develop a 'we' feeling (Kusstatscher and Cooper, 2005). It is also common for employees to feel that the new organization, despite incorporating their old organization, is no longer theirs (Rousseau, 1998; Millward and Kyriakidou, 2004). Based on the above, this paper argues that

> *During the early post-acquisition integration phase, the target employees' organizational identification and commitment is stronger towards the target organization than the acquiring organization.*

Previous research findings suggest that pre-merger identification could be a strong predictor of post-merger identification (Bartels et al., 2006). Hence, if the M&A does not involve severe feelings of threats, (that is, fear of job loss) among employees, the pre-merger and post-merger identification may have a positive relationship (Bartels et al. 2006). Moreover, it has been argued that high initial organizational identification would have a positive effect on long-term organizational commitment (Bartels et al. 2006).[2] Hence, it is likely that identification with an organization enhances support for and commitment to it (Ashforth and Mael, 1989). However, the employee has to identify with and be committed to the target company in order to adopt the new identity and commit to the new organization.

Obviously, the nature of an acquisition greatly affects how pre-merger identification and commitment evolves. In a hostile takeover, employees would be more likely to hold on to their old identities and reject the new one, while in friendly acquisitions the acquirer may be seen as an attractive organization and employees might even be eager to adopt the new identity. Hence:

> *In friendly acquisitions, the more the target company employees are able to identify with the acquiring company, the more likely it is that they will become committed to the acquirer and the new post-M&A organization.*

In summary, in contrast to previous research this study will not focus on pre- or post-M&A identification and commitment, as access is seldom obtained prior to an acquisition. Instead, this research *explores how employees' identification and commitment develops during the post-integration phase in relation to both the acquirer and the target organization.* In order to obtain a deeper understanding of the changes and developments related to commitment and identification, this research was conducted as a longitudinal case study.

Methodology

Longitudinal case study

The purpose of this research is to investigate the contemporary phenomenon of employees within a real-life context, which in this case is a cross-border acquisition (Yin, 2003). It has been argued that conducting research on organizational change and processes in a holistic and comprehensive way is often best approached by using a longitudinal research design (Pettigrew, 1990; Van de Ven, 1992). Moreover, previous studies have recommended the use of a longitudinal research design when studying both organizational identification (Bartels et al., 2006) and commitment (Beck and Wilson, 2001). Consequently, in order to obtain a deeper understanding about the phenomenon under scrutiny a longitudinal case study approach was adopted (Eisenhardt, 1989; Yin, 2003).

The case for this research was carefully selected based on several criteria. An important criterion was that the acquisition had to be relatively recent. Ideally, the researcher had to gain access to the company soon after the deal was closed. In addition, the focus of this research is on cross-border acquisitions, thus the international nature of the deal was also a pre-requisite. Finally, the researcher needed access for at least a year in order to complete the research, which meant that the company needed to be committed to the research.

The case company chosen for this research fulfils all the above mentioned criteria. It is a small to medium sized European high-tech company operating in the field of telecommunication, employing around 300 employees. It was acquired in 2006 by an Asian company, which will be referred to as Gamma. Gamma was bigger than the target company in terms of personnel, as it employed a little over 3000 employees. The nature of the deal can be defined as friendly and the acquisition can be defined as conglomerate acquisition as both companies operated in the same field (Walsh, 1988; Cartwright and Cooper, 1992), although in different areas, which meant that the technological know-how of the target company complemented the capabilities of the acquiring company. The companies shared the same goals; both companies wanted to grow and become more international. The European company needed to grow internationally and expand its customer base but its resources were limited. As competition was becoming fiercer, many companies in the high-tech sector in Europe had already transferred all or parts of their production and R&D to low-cost countries in Asia. On the other hand, the Asian company was looking for new customers, new know-how and a foothold in Europe.

The acquiring company and the target company had a rather similar company history and shared the same values to a large extent. However, the Asian and European cultures obviously brought some challenges to the integration phase, although in general both parties were very culturally sensitive from the beginning. There were concrete challenges regarding the post-acquisition integration as the European target company was geographically spread over six cities. In addition, it had grown through smaller acquisitions and in consequence the target company had two main sites; Alpha and Beta. Alpha acquired Beta in 2004 and the integration of these two organizations was still on-going at the time of the M&A. Furthermore, Alpha had smaller sites in four cities, where employees mainly worked at their customers' premises on different projects. Both Alpha and Beta had strong, distinct identities and based on the interviews the cultural differences between the organizations were substantial, even though both companies operated within the same country. Thus, the target company initially had employees with multiple organizational identities. Nevertheless, approximately six months from their acquisition by Gamma the full operational integration of Alpha and Beta was implemented and their name was changed to

Gamma Europe. In summary, the setting of the acquisition renders this case very interesting.

Data collection

The *quantitative data* was collected through two questionnaires administered within the first ten months of the acquisition. The main purpose was to measure the levels of organizational commitment and identification, as well as to analyse their relationship. The majority of the scales were borrowed from well-known and established scales in academic literature. The questionnaire was designed both in the mother tongue of the respondents and in English because there were a small number of foreign employees. Since the scales were originally in English, they were translated by professional translators. The responses were measured using the seven-point response scale ranging from one (strongly disagree) to seven (strongly agree). In addition, there was an eighth alternative, zero (I don't know), in case the respondent did not really know about the items in question (Kline, 2005). Organizational identification and commitment were measured with the same scales at both data collection times.

Organizational identification was measured using the 6-item scale developed by Mael and Ashforth (1992). This scale captures the conceptualization of organizational identification rather well and has been recommended by other researchers (Riketta, 2005). This measure is based on a narrow definition of organizational identification and has only a small degree of item overlap with the organizational commitment questionnaire (OCQ) (Mowday et al., 1979; Meyer, Becker and van Dick, 2006). The same scale was used to measure organizational identity towards the acquirer and the target company and in both cases it showed good reliability (see Table 3.1).

Organizational commitment was measured using the 15-item OCQ developed by Mowday et al. (1979). This scale has been widely used and tested (Porter et al., 1974; Mathieu and Zajac, 1990). According to Cooper-Hakim and Viswesvaran (2005), the OCQ is the most frequently used scale. The scale was made slightly shorter for measuring acquirer commitment because item 10 'I am extremely glad that I chose this organization to work for over others I was considering at the time I joined' and item 15 'Deciding to work for this organization was a definite mistake on my part' were removed, as the respondents at the target organization had not chosen or decided, as such, to work for the acquiring company when they were acquired. In both cases the scale demonstrated high reliability (see Table 3.1).

The reliability of the scales used in the questionnaire was assessed through several means. First, the items and the construct of the scales were assessed using the *Factor Analysis procedure (varimax rotation)*. Organizational commitment and identification were loaded on separate factors, which implies that these were indeed separate constructs. Secondly, the reliability of the scales was assessed through *Cronbach alpha* analysis at item-level and for the whole scale. In general, the *Cronbach alphas* were very strong, well above $\alpha > 0{,}70$ (see Table 3.1) (Hair et al., 2006).

Table 3.1 Scales and their reliability

Variable	Scale borrowed from	No items	December 2006		May 2007	
			Cronbach's alpha	N	Cronbach's alpha	N
Organizational commitment *towards target company*	Porter, Steers, Mowday & Boulian (1974)/ Mowday, Steers & Porter (1979);	15	Target α = 0,90	N = 112	Acquired α = 0,93	N = 133
towards acquiring company	(Items 10 and 15 were removed from the scale, since employees had not chosen this organization)	13	Acquiring α = 0,91	N = 72	Acquiring α = 0,92	N = 116
Organizational identification *towards target company*	Mael & Ashforth (1992)	6	Target α = 0,81	N = 131	Target α = 0,89	N = 169
towards acquiring company		6	Acquiring α = 0,88	N = 89	Acquiring α = 0,88	N = 169 N = 172

The first data collection round took place only three months after the closing of the deal in December 2006, within the first 100 days (Angwin, 2004). The second data collection round took place five months later, shortly after Alpha and Beta were integrated into one subsidiary and the target company changed its name to Gamma Europe. The questionnaire was administered electronically using software called Webropol and was sent individually via email to the entire personnel of the acquired company. The final sample for the first questionnaire was 155, which is a response rate of 56 per cent and for the second round 187, representing a response rate of 60 per cent. The panel sample was 70, of which 18 were key persons. The distribution of the respondents seemed representative of the overall organization on hierarchical and geographical terms.

In order to obtain a deeper understanding of the development of organizational identity and commitment following a cross-border acquisition, interview data was also collected. Altogether 68 interviews were conducted during 2007 in two rounds after the questionnaires. The first set of interviews was undertaken right after the first questionnaire round in early spring 2007. At that time, mainly top managers and other key persons including the Asian integration manager were interviewed (18 interviews). The second, more extensive, interview round was conducted during autumn 2007.

The interviewees for the second round were carefully selected. Based on the quantitative results, it was important for the researcher to visit all the sites of the target company Gamma Europe and also interview personnel at different organizational layers. The interviewees were selected from among those who participated in the surveys as they were considered to be interested in the research. In order to better understand how organizational identification and commitment evolves during the post-acquisition integration, the researcher identified, based on the questionnaire data, very highly and very lowly committed employees within each organizational position. However, this information was used only to identify the respondents and the anonymity of the respondents was not violated. The researcher ensured that no individuals could be identified from the results or reports. This selection method enabled the interviewing of 'extremes' regarding acquirer commitment, which resulted in richer data compared to randomly selecting the interviewees.

The majority of the interviews were conducted in the mother tongue of both the interviewer and the interviewees. Usually interviewees speak more freely in their own mother tongue (Welch et al., 2002). The interviews were tape-recorded with the consent of each interviewee. All interviews were conducted face-to-face at the organization where the interviewee works, either in a conference room or at the office of the interviewee. One interview was conducted over the telephone and recorded from the loud-speaker. The quality of the recording was equal to a face-to-face interview and the interview situation was relaxed even though the interviewee and interviewer had never met. The duration of the interviews varied from thirty minutes to one hour and twenty minutes. In addition to tape-recorded interviews, field notes were used as well (Silverman, 2000). Notes were made during the interviews merely to explain some concepts or write down the essentials of the answers in case the tape recording failed for some reason.

In summary, the mixed-method strategy, that is, combining both quantitative and qualitative data and analysis was used to improve the validity of the research, but first and foremost it was used to acquire a deeper understanding of the phenomenon under scrutiny (Hurmerinta-Peltomäki and Nummela, 2006). It has been suggested that using multiple methods in order to gain an understanding of the inputs, processes and outcomes of an organizational change (such as an acquisition) might be more useful than focusing on merely one tool (Van de Ven and Huber, 1990; Pettigrew et al., 2001). Consequently, the interview data was used to complement the quantitative data and to provide support or explanations and a deeper understanding regarding the quantitative results.

Analysis

The data was transferred from *Webropol* via *Excel to SPSS* for further analysis. In *SPSS* the data was checked and verified by analysing the descriptive statistics; specifically, the frequencies and the explorative statistics were checked for each item. The main tools of analysis were comparing means with the 'Means' function, testing statistical significance by *ANOVA* and measures of associations *(ETA), T-tests, Mann-Whitney U-tests*. In order to analyse the correlations, bi-variate correlation and *Spearman's* correlation tests were also undertaken. The researcher used mostly nonparametric tests as most of the variables were not normally distributed and the measurement scale used was a Likert-type scale, which is considered to be an ordinal scale (Kline, 2005; Hair, Black, Babin, Anderson and Tatham, 2006).

The analysis remained explorative and no causalities were analysed, mainly due to limitations of the data highlighted above: the nature of the measurement scale; the study's focus on attitudes; and the lack of normal distribution of the mean variables. The research comprised two cross-sectional data sets. The panel data, that is, respondents that participated in both questionnaire rounds, was identified by comparing the respondents for each survey. These were then recoded into 1 (panel) or 0 (not panel). Based on earlier top management research (Walsh, 1988; Krug and Hegarty, 1997), and suggestions concerning the retention of key persons in knowledge-intensive acquisitions (Ranft and Lord, 2002), key persons were identified separately, based on discussions and lists obtained from the Asian integration manager and the target company's CEO, and coded 1 (key person) or 0 (no key person). Identifying the respondents in this longitudinal research was crucial in order to enable panel analysis. However, once the coding was completed respondents were only numbers in the data and the anonymity of the respondents was assured. The longitudinal analysis was based on a comparison of the two data sets.

The interviews were analysed qualitatively. Due to the large number of interviews the recorded interviews were sent to professionals for transcription. Then the transcribed interviews were read through many times in order to identify key elements and themes. The data was coded once it had been arranged. In this research the coding was based on the theory and on the research problems, and codes also emerged from the data.

Findings and discussion

The findings lend support to the first argument by stating that during the early post-acquisition integration phase, the target employees' organizational identification and commitment would be stronger towards the target organization than the acquirer organization. No major changes in the levels of identification could be seen when comparing results only three months and ten months after the closing of the deal. There was only a slight decrease in the identification towards the target company and an equivalent increase in the identification towards the acquirer. In general, the quantitative results imply that key personnel identified more with both their organization and the acquirer; the difference between key and other personnel was significant ($p < 0.01$ and $p < 0.001$).

Based on the interview data one year after the completion of the deal, that is by autumn 2007, most interviewees identified more with the new parent organization or the new 'identity' following the name change in spring 2007. In particular, the sales people were already very 'Gammian' and the change of the target company's name was their initiative. According to these respondents, dealing with Alpha, Beta and Gamma was too confusing for the customer. However, in autumn 2007, a year after the acquisition had taken place just under 25 per cent of the interviewees stated they still identified with Alpha or Beta. Some stated that *'...well, I have tried hard to become a Gammian'* or *'...I would describe myself as a Gammian but every now and then I may still accidentally use the word Alpha when referring to my organization'.* Figure 3.1 illustrates identification towards both the European target company and the Asian acquiring company comparing the results of panel data at the two data collection times.

As the figure demonstrates, the overall levels of identification were lower towards the acquirer, which could be expected so soon after the deal (Kusstatscher and Cooper, 2005). Moreover, key persons identified more than the other personnel with both the target and acquiring organization. Based on the interviews, top and middle management and other key persons had stronger attitudes simply because they were more involved in the integration phase and were more in contact with the Asian managers or colleagues. In general, employees that are directly involved in the merger can be expected to identify more strongly with the new organization, though pre-merger identification is the strongest predictor of expected post-merger identification (Bartels et al., 2006). Accordingly, key persons who are more involved in an integration process and identify more with their organization are more likely to identify with the acquirer. In this case, they were some of the key personnel who had originally founded either Alpha or Beta or had been shareholders. Most of the key persons had been working for the organization since it was founded and were still actively engaged, for example, as top managers and/or in integration teams. Moreover, they easily identify with the acquiring company, which had a rather similar company history to the target company and in general shared the same values, identity and goals regarding the M&A. It has been argued that identification would be positively related with the expected utility of a merger (Bartels et al., 2006).

The mean scores of the key persons and other personnel responding to both questionnaires were compared to the general means for all questionnaire respondents. The trend of the panel personnel follows the trend of all the respondents

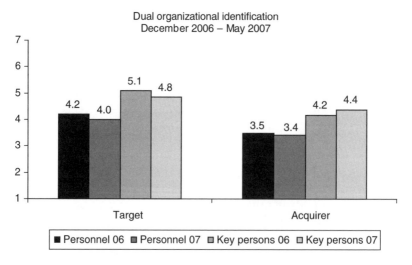

Figure 3.1   The development of organizational identification

quite well. Changes are minimal, which is understandable so soon after the acquisition. A longer time period would be needed to really identify changes. The level of identification was moderate among the personnel, and during interviews many stated that the location in which they had built their home and/or had established their families meant more than the organization as such. However, many seemed very committed to their work. It was also observed that changes in identification are more important for the key persons. Interestingly, while key persons' target identification decreases their acquirer identification increases. One reason may be that the integration of Alpha and Beta and changing the name into Gamma Europe was viewed positively and they had been pushing it forward.

The levels of organizational commitment were slightly higher than for organizational identification. In general, commitment towards the target organization was higher than commitment towards the acquiring company. However, the difference was more substantial when comparing key personnel and other personnel's commitment towards the acquiring company. According to the results, key persons in general were more committed to both the target company and the acquirer than other personnel. The difference between the groups was statistically significant (p<0,01). Figure 3.2 illustrates the changes in commitment towards both the acquirer and the target company.

The results imply that in general there was a decrease in organizational commitment levels between the first and the second data collection times (see Figure 3.2), and was more pronounced among key persons than other personnel. The differences in key persons' and other personnel's commitment attitudes results from reasons similar to those already identified above with regard to organizational identification. Several reasons may explain the drop in organizational commitment. First, based on information gathered from the interviews, the integration process turned out to be a disappointment. During the early integration phase,

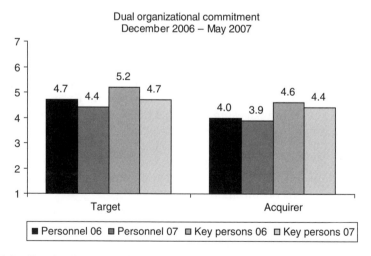

Figure 3.2 The development of commitment towards the target and the acquiring company

employees were on the whole enthusiastic about the internationalization opportunities and new challenges at work. Many were looking forward to some joint projects with the Asian parent company and larger end-to-end projects, which would render their work more challenging. Target employees had high expectations and employees became frustrated at the length of time it was taking to realize the synergies. Moreover, the cultural differences had become more evident. While the parent company had remained rather distant to the personnel, key persons were more in contact with their Asian colleagues. Based on the interviews, there were some reservations regarding the Asian way of managing and operating a European firm and how the two different organizations could be integrated.

Moreover, the level and intensity of the integration seemed to be important in the development of identification and commitment. Based on the interviews, the Asian acquirer had adopted a relatively slow approach, where the initial idea was to respect the acquired target company's culture and analyse the best practices of both companies. Consequently, the target company remained relatively independent. This approach could be referred to as the 'high road' defined by Birkinshaw (1999), that is adopting a slow approach and avoiding precipitous actions, which could scare away the staff. However, based on the interviews, the integration process could have proceeded more rapidly. The integration process took a major leap forward in spring 2007, when the target company's organization was restructured by, for example, finally merging Alpha and Beta. Consequently, the name of the European affiliate was changed and all organizations began using the name Gamma Europe. Based on the interviews, this was viewed positively. The change of the company name was expected to merge the separate Alpha and Beta identities previously coexisting in the target company into one joint, new identity.

The findings supported the argument that target identification and commitment are strong predictors of acquirer commitment. There were clear correlations between target and acquirer identification and commitment. Organizational identification correlated rather strongly with organizational commitment. Organizational identification towards the acquirer correlated strongly with commitment towards the acquiring company and identification towards the target company. The high correlation between organizational identification and commitment raises questions regarding the distinctiveness of the constructs. However, the *Factor Analysis* procedure gave support to the initial assumption that the concept of organizational identification and commitment are distinct constructs (Van Knippenberg and Sleebos, 2006; Cole and Bruch, 2006). Table 3.2 illustrates the Spearman correlation results from both the data collection times (the abbreviations OC and OID refer to organizational commitment and organizational identification, and TARG and ACQ refer to target and acquiring organization).

This result would give support to the initial idea that organizational identification is a pre-requisite or an important factor in forming organizational commitment (Ashforth and Mael, 1989). On the other hand, the results concerning key persons were contradictory. Based on the results, key persons' acquirer identification slightly increased while acquirer commitment decreased. A longer time

Table 3.2 Correlations between organizational identification and commitment towards the target and acquiring organizations

	Mean 1	SD 1	N 1	Mean 2	SD 2	N 2
OCTARG	4,81	0,94	151	4,51	0,99	180
OCACQ	4,13	1,06	151	4,01	0,97	180
OIDTARG	4,38	1,03	151	4,18	1,25	180
OIDACQ	3,66	1,17	148	3,89	1,22	179

		OCTARG	OCACQ	OIDTARG	OIDACQ
December 2006					
OCTARG	Correlation Coefficient	1			
	Sig. (2-tailed)				
	N	151			
OCACQ	Correlation Coefficient	0,815	1		
	Sig. (2-tailed)	0,000			
	N	151	151		
OIDTARG	Correlation Coefficient	0,570	0,525	1	
	Sig. (2-tailed)	0,000	0,000		
	N	151	151	151	
OIDACQ	Correlation Coefficient	0,493	0,659	0,690	1
	Sig. (2-tailed)	0,000	0,000	0,000	
	N	148	148	148	148

		OCTARG	OCACQ	ORGIDT	ORGIDAC
May 2007					
OCTARG	Correlation Coefficient	1			
	Sig. (2-tailed)				
	N	180			
OCACQ	Correlation Coefficient	0,819	1		
	Sig. (2-tailed)	0,000			
	N	179	179		
ORGIDT	Correlation Coefficient	0,631	0,641	1	
	Sig. (2-tailed)	0,000	0,000		
	N	180	179	180	
ORGIDAC	Correlation Coefficient	0,558	0,721	0,826	1
	Sig. (2-tailed)	0,000	0,000	0,000	
	N	179	179	179	179

perspective would be needed to better understand how the identification and commitment of key persons would evolve. However, the results imply that commitment to the target company is more important than identification when considering commitment to the acquiring company.

Overall, the results imply that low target identification and commitment would result in low acquirer identification and commitment. Thus, high target identification and commitment result in high acquirer identification and commitment. Consequently, the findings give support to the second argument, which states that in friendly acquisitions higher target identification would predict higher target and acquirer commitment. Figure 3.3 demonstrates the levels of target identification and commitment and acquirer identification in low, medium and high acquirer commitment groups.

In summary, it would seem that the results indicate that organizational identification and commitment are strongly related (Mathieu and Zajac, 1990; Mael and Ashforth, 1992). The differences in target and acquirer identification and commitment gave support to the importance of making a distinction between these two organizations rather than differentiating between pre- and post-M&A attitudes, as pre-merger attitudes such as target identity and commitment still prevail in some cases a year after the deal has been closed. Moreover, target identification and commitment seem to be important predictors of acquirer identification and commitment. In this case organizational identification and commitment decreased slightly between the two data collection times. A number of reasons may explain this result. For example, the slow integration may partially explain why the acquirer had remained distant from the average personnel point of view and the acquisition had not brought any changes into their daily work. In addition, key personnel's organizational identification and commitment differed significantly from other personnel. In general, key persons identified more with, and were more committed to, both the target and the acquirer organization. The reason for this was mainly due to the fact that they were more directly involved in the M&A process as a whole and had more information available and more contacts with the acquiring company.

This research has several limitations. First of all, this is a single case study conducted in an acquired high-tech company. Consequently, the results are not generalizable as such to other companies or industries. Secondly, the collected data represents the attitudes of the respondents, thus the nature of both the qualitative and quantitative data is subjective and the quantitative measures used are

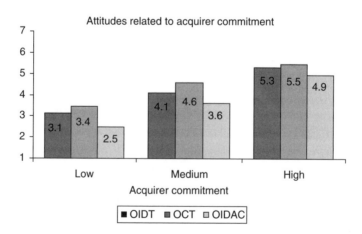

Figure 3.3   Target identification and commitment and acquirer identification in relation to low, medium and high acquirer commitment (survey May 2007 total n = 180)

ordinal. This imposes limitations on the analysis, as it did not enable the analysis of causalities, for example. Furthermore, as changes often occur over a much longer time period in M&As, a longer time frame may provide a more reliable result and a better understanding of the phenomena. Nevertheless, the validity and reliability of the present research has been ascertained by several means and the findings seem to provide meaningful answers to the questions addressed in this study.

Conclusions

Committing the target employees to the acquiring organization, especially in a knowledge-intensive industry is important for the post-acquisition integration phase and the retention of key personnel (Ranft and Lord, 2002). The results of this research demonstrated that target identification and commitment are still stronger than acquirer identification and commitment nearly a year after the acquisition (Kusstatscher and Cooper, 2005). Consequently, instead of distinguishing between pre- and post-merger identity or commitment (Bartels et al., 2006; van Dick et al., 2006), it may be more practical to distinguish between target and acquirer identification and commitment, as the pre-merger attitudes can prevail for some time during the post-acquisition integration phase. Secondly, the results imply that target identification and commitment may predict acquirer identification and commitment. More specifically, in friendly acquisitions strong target identification and commitment may lead to strong acquirer identification and commitment. Nevertheless, both identification and commitment may decrease for various reasons during the post-acquisition stage as demonstrated in this research. However, it was apparent that when acquiring SMEs the key persons tend to differ from the other personnel in respect of identification and commitment. Figure 3.4 illustrates the development of organizational identification and commitment during M&As.

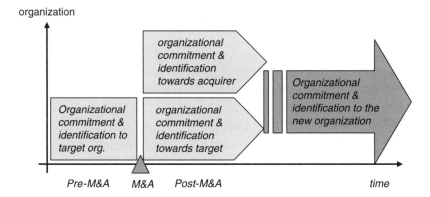

Figure 3.4   The development of organizational identification and commitment during the early post-acquisition integration phase

As the integration proceeds, the duality of organizational identification and commitment should transform into a single identification and commitment towards the new post-M&A organization, although that is dependent on the depth of the integration. A longer time perspective is needed to identify these changes. Moreover, the international aspect of M&As adds to the challenges. For example, in this research the parent company is located physically very far away in Asia and the time difference brings its own challenges in managing the post-acquisition integration. Future research could also focus on the role of psychic and physical distance related to target and acquirer identification and commitment.

In conclusion, this longitudinal study has demonstrated that organizational identification and commitment are complex phenomena when studied in the context of international acquisitions. This study contributes to research on commitment and identification by adopting a dual approach that emphasizes the organization rather than a temporal division into pre- and post-acquisition, that is, it explores both target and acquirer identification and commitment. Finally, this research has a methodological contribution, as it shows that by adopting a longitudinal approach employing several research methods, the development and change in attitudes can be understood more comprehensively.

Acknowledgements

This longitudinal research has been funded by various Foundations, namely the Jenny and Antti Wihuri foundation, KAUTE and Liikesivistysrahasto, which the author wishes to thank. The author also wishes to thank all anonymous reviewers and persons commenting on the previous drafts of this paper presented both at the Vaasa Conference on International Business 2007 and the 35th annual Conference of the Academy of International Business UKI Chapter.

Notes

1. Original source: R. van Dick, U. Wagner, J. Stellmacher and O. Christ (2004) 'The utility of a broader conceptualization of organizational identification: Which aspects really matter?' *Journal of Occupational and Organizational Psychology*, 77, 171–91.
2. Original source: J. Jetten, A. O'Brien and N. Trindall (2002) 'Changing identity: Predicting adjustment to organizational restructure as a function of subgroup and super ordinate identification', *British Journal of Social Psychology*, 41, 28197.

References

Allen, N.J. and Meyer, J.P. (1990) 'The measurement and antecedents of affective, continuance and normative commitment to the organization', *Journal of Occupational Psychology*, 63(1), 1–19.

Angwin, D. (2004) 'Speed in M&A integration: the first 100 days', *European Management Journal*, 22(4), 418–30.

Ashforth, B.E. and Mael, F. (1989) 'Social identity theory and the organization', *Academy of Management Journal*, 14(1), 20–39.

Bartels, J. Douwes, R., de Jong, M. and Pruyn, A. (2006) 'Organizational identification during a merger: Determinants of employees expected identification with the new organization', *British Journal of Management*, 17, S49–S67.

Beck, K. and Wilson, C. (2001) 'Have we studied, should we study, and can we study the development of commitment? Methodological issues and the developmental study of work-related commitment', *Human Resource Management Review*, 11(3), 257–78.

Benkhoff, B. (1997) 'Disentangling organizational commitment – The dangers of the OCQ for research and policy', *Personnel Review*, 26(1/2), 114–31.

Birkinshaw, J. (1999) 'Acquiring intellect: Managing the integration of knowledge-intensive acquisitions', *Business Horizons*, 42(3), 33–40.

Brown, R.B. (1996) 'Organizational commitment: Clarifying the concept and simplifying the existing construct typology', *Journal of Vocational Behaviour*, 49(42), 230–51.

Cartwright, S. and Cooper, C.L. (1992) *Mergers and Acquisitions, the Human Factor* (Oxford: Butterworth-Heinemann Ltd).

Child, J., Faulkner, D. and Pitkethly, R. (2001) *The Management of International Acquisitions* (New York: Oxford University Press).

Cole, M.S. and Bruch, H. (2006) 'Organizational identity strength, identification, and commitment and their relationship to turnover intention: Does organizational hierarchy matter?' *Journal of Organizational Behaviour*, 27, 585–605.

Cooper-Hakim, A. and Viswesvaran, C. (2005) 'The construct of work commitment: Testing an integrative framework', *Psychological Bulletin*, 131(2), 241–59.

Eisenhardt, K.M. (1989) 'Building theories from case study research', *Academy of Management Review*, 14(4), 532–50.

Elangovan, A.R. (2001) 'Causal ordering of stress, satisfaction and commitment, and intention to quit: a structural equation analysis', *Leadership & Organization Development Journal*, 22(4), 159–65.

Fairfield-Sonn, J.W., Ogilvie, J.R. and DelVecchio, G.A. (2002) 'Mergers, acquisitions and long-term employee attitudes', *Journal of Business & Economic Studies*, 8(2), 1–16.

Hair, J.F. Jr, Black, W.C., Babin, B.J., Anderson, R.E. and Tatham, R.L. (2006) *Multivariate Data Analysis*, 6th edn (New Jersey: Pearson Prentice Hall).

Hall, D.T., Schneider, B. and Nygren, H.T. (1970) 'Personal factors in organizational identification', *Administrative Science Quarterly*, 15(2), 176–90.

Hartmann, L.C. and Bambacas, M. (2000) 'Organizational commitment: Multi method scale analysis and test of effects', *International Journal of Organizational analysis*, 8(1), 89–108.

Hislop, D. (2003) 'Linking human resource management and knowledge management via commitment: A review and research agenda', *Employee relations*, 25(2), 182–202.

Hubbard, N. (1999) *Acquisition Strategy and Implementation* (London: MacMillan Press Ltd).

Hurmerinta-Peltomäki, L. and Nummela, N. (2006) 'Mixed methods in international business: a value added perspective', *Management International Review*, 46(4), 1–21.

Ketchand, A.A. and Strawser, J.R. (2001) 'Multiple dimensions of organizational commitment: Implications for future accounting research', *Behavioral Research in Accounting*, 13, 221–51.

Kline, T.J.B. (2005) *Psychological Testing: A Practical Approach, to Design and Evaluation* (Thousands Oaks, California: SAGE Publications, Inc).

Krug, J.A. and Hegarty, W.H. (1997) 'Post-acquisition turnover among U.S. top management teams: An analysis of the effects of foreign vs. domestic acquisitions of U.S. targets', *Strategic Management Journal*, 18(8), 667–75.

Kusstatscher, V. and Cooper, C.L. (2005) *Managing Emotions in Mergers and Acquisitions* (Cheltenham: Edward Elgar).

Mael, F. and Ashforth, B.E. (1992) 'Alumni and their alma mater: A partial test of the reformulated model of organizational identification', *Journal of Organizational Behavior*, 13(2), 103–23.

Mathieu, J.E. and Zajac, D.M. (1990) 'A review and meta-analysis of the antecedents, correlates, and consequences of organizational commitment', *Psychological Bulletin*, 108(2), 171–94.

Meyer, J.P. and Allen, N.J. (1997) *Commitment in the Workplace – Theory, Research and Application* (Thousand Oaks, CA: Sage Publications).

Meyer, J.P., Becker, T.E. and van Dick, R. (2006) 'Social identities and commitments at work: Toward an integrative model', *Journal of Organizational Behavior*, 27, 665–83.

Millward, L. and Kyriakidou, O. (2004) 'Linking pre- and post-merger identities through the concept of career', *Career Development International*, 9(1), 12–27.

Mobley, W.H. (1982) 'Some unanswered questions in turnover and withdrawal research', *Academy of Management Review*, 7(1), 111–16.

Morrow, P.C. (1983) 'Concept redundancy in organizational research: The case of work commitment', *The Academy of Management Review*, 8(3), 486–500.

Mowday, R.T., Porter, L.W. and Steers, R.M. (1982) *Employee-Organization Linkages – the Psychology of Commitment, Absenteeism, and Turnover* (New York: Academic Press).

Mowday, R.T., Steers, R.M. and Porter, L.W. (1979) 'The measurement of organizational commitment', *Journal of Vocational Behavior*, 14(2), 224–47.

OECD (2007) *International Investment Perspectives 2007: Freedom of Investment in a Changing World*. OECD Publications, http://oberon.sourceoecd.org (Retrieved 8.2.2008).

Pettigrew, A.M. (1990) 'Longitudinal field research on change: theory and practice', *Organizational Science*, 1(3), 267–92.

Pettigrew, A.M., Woodman, R.W. and Cameron, K.S. (2001) 'Studying organizational change and development: Challenges for future research', *Academy of Management Journal*, 44(4), 697–713.

Porter, L.W., Steers, R.M., Mowday, R.T. and Boulian, P.V. (1974) 'Organizational commitment, job satisfaction, and turnover among psychiatric technicians', *Journal of Applied Psychology*, 59(5), 603–09.

Ranft, A.L. and Lord, M.D. (2000) 'Acquiring new knowledge: The role of retaining human capital in acquisitions of high-tech firms', *The Journal of High Technology Management Research*, 11(2), 295–319.

Ranft, A.L. and Lord, M.D. (2002) 'Acquiring new technologies and capabilities: A grounded model of acquisition implementation', *Organization Science*, 13(4), 420–41.

Riketta, M. (2005) 'Organizational identification: A meta-analysis', *Journal of Vocational Behavior*, 66, 358–84.

Rousseau, D.M. (1998) 'Why workers still identify with organizations', *Journal of Organizational Behavior*, 19, 892–97.

Schraeder, M. (2001) 'Identifying employee resistance during the threat of a merger: An analysis of employee perceptions and commitment to an organization in a pre-merger context', *The Mid-Atlantic Journal of Business*, 37(4), 191–203.

Silverman, D. (2000) *Doing Qualitative Research – a Practical Handbook* (London: Sage Publication).

Van de Ven, A. (1992) 'Suggestions for studying strategy process: a research note', *Strategy Management Journal*, 13(Special Issue), 169–91.

Van de Ven, A.H. and Huber, G. (1990) 'Longitudinal field research methods for studying processes of organizational change', *Organization Science*, 1(3), 213–19.

Van den Hooff, B. and de Ridder, J.A. (2004) 'Knowledge sharing in the context: The influence of organizational commitment, communication climate and CMC use on knowledge sharing', *Journal of Knowledge Management*, 8(6), 117–30.

van Dick, R., Ullrich, J. and Tissington, P.A. (2006) 'Working under a black cloud: How to sustain organizational identification after a merger', *British Journal of Management*, 17, S69–S79.

Van Knippenberg, D. and Sleebos, E. (2006) 'Organizational identification versus organizational commitment: Self-definition, social exchange, and job attitudes', *Journal of Organizational Behavior*, 27, 571–84.

Walsh, J.P. (1988) 'Top management turnover following mergers and acquisitions', *Strategic Management Journal,* 9(2), 173–83.

Welch, C., Marschan-Piekkari, R., Penttinen, H. and Tahvanainen, M. (2002) 'Corporate elites as informants in qualitative international business research', *International Business Review,* 11(5), 611–28.

Yin, R.K. (2003) *Case Study Research – Design and Methods,* 3rd edn, Applied social research methods series, 5 (Thousand Oaks, CA: Sage Publications).

4
Cross-Border Transfer of Employment Relations Approaches: Country-of-Origin Effects and the Level and Type of Industry Internationalization

Heinz-Josef Tüselmann, Frank McDonald, Matthew Allen, Sougand Golesorkhi and Despoina Filiou

Introduction

The cross-border transfer of business and management practices within multinational companies (MNC) forms an important strand of research in international business. The way MNCs are shaped by their institutional environments and the impact of such forces on the cross-border diffusion of these practices have attracted increasing attention. This has led to a growing focus in the international business literature on the importance of country-of-origin effects for the management of MNCs (Mudambi and Navarra, 2002; Buckley and Carter, 2004). Furthermore, the cultural perspective (see, for instance, Hofstede, 2001) has been extensively used in the international management literature as a way of explaining why MNCs from various national origins adopt different management and business practices in the international arena (Ngo et al., 1998; Tayeb, 1998). There has also been a growing appreciation that such country-specific effects interact with globalization pressures to conform to some kind of 'best practice' template.

At the same time there is a growing recognition that pressures for international integration do not constitute a universal force, but are to considerable extent contingent upon the nature of the industry, in particular on the nature of industry internationalization (Marginson, Armstrong, Edward and Purcell, 1995; Pak and Park, 2005). This draws attention to the differential impact of industry forces on international approaches in MNCs. First, pressures for international integration are particularly pertinent in highly internationalized industries. Secondly, even in highly internationalized industries, the notion of 'best practice' is not universal across all industries, but takes an industry-specific configuration, reflecting inter alia industry-specific differentials in areas such as labour markets, human capital, knowledge and technology intensity (Dunning, 2000; Nachum and Zaher, 2005).

Thus, both the level and type of industry internationalization can be expected to influence the nature and strength of cross-border policy diffusion in MNCs.

In this context, interest has grown into the significance of the country-of-origin impact on the employment relations (ER) approaches in MNCs' international subsidiaries. An important line of inquiry focuses on the international ER approaches of MNCs with home bases in highly regulated and strongly institutionalized industrial relations (IR) contexts, such as Germany, that have subsidiaries in deregulated and weakly institutionalized Anglo-American IR settings, such as the UK. There are several reasons for this focus. First, pressures to reform the German business system (BS) in response to changes in the international economy are often seen as being particularly acute. Secondly, criticisms of traditional German ER practices and approaches are often voiced as they are viewed as unsuitable systems for workplaces abroad (Streeck, 1997). Finally, the permissive UK host-country IR context may be an attractive location for German MNCs to implement new ER patterns that would not be possible in home locations.

Central issues in this research are: to what extent, if any, do German MNCs in deregulated Anglo-American IR settings draw on the German ER model, adjust to the host-country context or adopt current 'best practice' prescriptions frequently associated with leading US MNCs (Chen et al., 2005). Therefore, the key questions are: how, and to what extent, do differential industry-specific forces (in terms of the level and type of industry internationalization) interrelate, first, with country-of-origin effects and, secondly, with pressures to adopt 'best practice' approaches to shape subsidiary ER outcomes? Although a number of recent qualitative studies have shed light on these issues, their results cannot be generalized easily. Quantitative studies into German subsidiaries in the UK (and elsewhere) are sparse and are somewhat dated. Many of the existing studies exhibit a number of limitations. (For an overview, see Harzing and Sorge, 2003; Tüselmann, McDonald and Thorpe, 2006). None of the existing quantitative studies investigating cross-border ER transfer issues has explicitly investigated the variability of the relative importance and nature of the country-of-origin effect across different subsets of industries. Despite the use of broad industry dummies in the analysis (for example, Guest and Hoque, 1996; Walsh, 2001), many previous studies focus purely on the average nationality effect. Thus, the analysis is prematurely halted.

By addressing these shortcomings, this paper aims to shed light on the relative importance, nature and variability of the country-of-origin impact on ER approaches in German subsidiaries. It is based on a representative survey of German-owned and indigenous firms in the UK. The empirical investigation follows a two-pronged approach. Firstly, a comparative analysis of German- and UK-owned firms is conducted to ascertain the average nationality effect. This enables a general picture of any differences that are associated with nationality of ownership to be set out. Secondly, an 'intra-German' analysis is performed to explore possible variations in the ER patterns of German subsidiaries along crucial industry dimensions. This is done in order to discern the possible differential impact of internationalization forces both in terms of the level and type of industry internationalization.

Key employment relations policy choices

Key ER policy choices can be analysed along two dimensions, which reflect management's relative emphasis on the collective and direct employee involvement dimension (Guest and Conway, 1999). The former involves union and non-union channels and captures the extent to which management's ER priorities are directed towards representative systems. The latter relates to the extent to which management's ER priorities are focused on the level of the individual employee. Direct involvement is facilitated through a variety of direct information-sharing, consultation and participation schemes. An emphasis on the direct ER dimension is connected with the development of HRM-style, high-involvement systems (HISs) that entail the integration of direct ER practices into a comprehensive system (Edwards and Wright, 2001). Combining the relative emphasis of these two ER dimensions results in four broad ER approaches.

Collective approaches can take two routes: the traditional collective approach, which comprises the single channel representation via collective structures (collective arrangements but no HIS), or the dual approach, which combines both collective structures and direct employee involvement in a single system (collective arrangements and HIS). The dual approach constitutes a hybrid model. Individualistic ER approaches may proceed along two avenues: the 'high road', individualized, direct-involvement approach (HIS, but no collective arrangements) or the 'low road', minimalist approach (no HIS and no collective arrangements). The former is usually associated with the mainstream unitaristic US HRM literature. It may also be viewed as an alternative to collective ER by emphasizing direct voice instead of collective voice. The minimalist variant of individualized ER involves labour-cost minimization and external, numerical labour flexibility, and is based on the absence of any meaningful employee involvement.

Employment relations in multinational companies

Within the broadly institutionalist approach to ER in MNCs, a range of influences has been identified. A useful framework for the analysis of the relative influence of the country-of-origin effect is Edwards and Ferner's (2002) 'four forces' model. In this model, subsidiary ER are influenced by a complex interplay between home- and host-country effects, dominance effects and organizational effects arising from pressures for international integration. Importantly, the model highlights that the country-of-origin effect is not a simple, universal force, but one that is variable and dynamic in nature.

The country-of-origin effect has been connected to the embeddedness of MNCs in their home-country BS, including the IR component (Whitley, 1999). The national institutional frameworks are said to shape MNC behaviour, including the way MNCs manage their international activities, such as ER issues (Ferner, 1997). The encompassing institutional infrastructure of the German IR systems, involving a high degree of regulation has traditionally imposed a relatively uniform ER template based on collective representation on companies, including

MNCs. It has been argued that such an approach facilitates co-operation in the workplace. This, in turn, helps to create competitive advantages for German firms (Hall and Soskice, 2001). Although the consensus on the benefits of the traditional ER model has weakened since the early 1990s and although ER reforms have been undertaken, there are a priori reasons to expect pronounced diffusion of home-country-influenced, collectively oriented, ER patterns to overseas subsidiaries.

The dominance effect is connected to the hierarchy of countries in the world economy (Smith and Meiskins, 1995). Those in a dominant position evolve business and management approaches that are seen as the global best practice. This is said to induce emulation in other countries. In the contemporary context, this relates to the competitive advantages associated with the business and ER models of leading MNCs that originate from the US economy, which has a strong economic record and which occupies a dominant position in the international economy. In the ER spheres, such global best practice is frequently connected with the individualistic 'high road' approach (Chen, Lawler and Bae, 2005), partly because of the supposed performance advantages attributed to it (Appelbaum, Baily, Berg and Kallenberg, 2000).

One strand of the literature suggests that the dominance effect has set in motion a shift towards Anglo-American business management and ER models, akin to those in leading US MNCs, among MNCs from non-dominant BSs such as Germany (Whittington and Mayer, 2000). In turn, this could imply attempts to pursue individualistic HIS-based 'high road' ER approaches in their international sites. However, much of the evidence points to nationally distinct pathways that incorporate US-style solutions into existing business and management models (Carr, 2005). In the ER area, there has been growing interest among German MNCs in US-style HRM innovations (Kurdelbusch, 2002). Indeed, the increasing adoption of direct-involvement practices points to an embryonic, dual approach in many German MNCs that incorporates US-style ER innovations into the existing representative structures of labour.

The extent to which home-country and dominance effects shape subsidiary ER approaches is also influenced by the nature of the IR context of the host-country BS. The permissive IR setting of the UK BS, where MNCs face relatively few institutional and regulatory barriers in the design of the ER systems in their subsidiaries, thus, provides a wide margin for the home-country and/or the dominance effect to exert an influence. The UK setting provides an attractive location for German MNCs to try out US-style ER innovations. Although this may take the form of the individualistic 'high road' approach, recent developments in ER patterns in many German MNCs suggest that this may also follow a German-specific pathway to incorporate US-style ER innovations within collective ER patterns.

Alternatively, German MNCs operating in permissive IR regimes may drop what they perceive as the constraining elements of the home-country model and pursue distinct local strategies, in particular, those based on the cost-minimizing 'low road' approach to externalize flexibility and cost pressures. Conversely, MNCs may pursue a non-strategic approach to international ER with subsidiary

ER patterns simply reflecting an adaptation to the host-country context and the adoption of local practices. In this connection, ER approaches in the UK private sector are dominated by individualistic or 'low road' ER patterns with collective ER approaches being confined to a minority of firms (WERS, 1998). However, the generally co-operative management style and ER ethos – expressed through collective or direct channels – in German parent companies may spillover to their overseas workplaces. A country-of-origin trait at this more intangible level may imply a relatively low emphasis on the 'low road' approach in German subsidiaries.

Most of the quantitative studies into ER in German subsidiaries in Anglo-American host-country contexts have found no distinctively German ER patterns, but rather an adaptation to local practices (Guest and Hoque, 1996; Child, Faulkner and Pitkethly, 2001). However, some studies highlight a somewhat more pronounced country-of-origin effect in relation to the incidence of collective ER (Cooke, 2001), as well as a distinctive German pathway to incorporate the US-style best-practice elements in the form of a dualistic ER approach (Tüselmann et al., 2006). Furthermore, several qualitative studies indicate scant use of the 'low road' approach and point to a transfer of the co-operative ethos of the German ER model (Ferner, Quintanilla and Varul, 2001; Dickmann, 2003). Although the empirical evidence remains somewhat inconclusive and although many existing empirical studies have their limitations, the following hypothesis emerges in relation to the average country-of-origin effect on the basis of the foregoing discussion.

> **H1:**   *ER approaches in UK-based subsidiaries of German MNCs exhibit a distinctive country-of-origin effect with German subsidiaries being more likely to operate with collective approaches and less likely to pursue individualistic approaches compared to indigenous UK firms.*

The degree to which MNCs are subject to competitive pressures for international integration shapes the relative strength of the effects of the home-country, the host-country and the desirability of adhering to ER models deployed in dominant MNCs on their subsidiaries. Pressures for international integration arise from the imperative for effective international operation, which in turn encourages a greater degree of co-ordination and integration of cross-border activity and the international division of labour within the MNC. This creates incentives to develop common policies and approaches across the international operations, including in the ER area. Thus, there is greater scope for the home-country or the dominance effect to exert an influence.

Competitive pressures for international integration do not constitute a universal force, but are to a considerable extent contingent upon the nature of the industry, in particular on the degree of global exposure (Dunning, 2000). MNCs operating in less internationalized industry contexts face higher pressures for local responsiveness and the adoption of local practices and lower pressures for the international integration of activities. This implies a relatively muted country-of-origin imprint in subsidiary ER. Pressures for international integration are particularly pertinent in highly internationalized industries. Here, greater cross-border integration can be achieved by using either the home-country model or the 'best practice' template. It is frequently assumed that the pressures for international integration favour the latter.

However, even in highly internationalized industries, the notion of 'best practice' has no universal meaning, but takes an industry-specific configuration, reflecting inter alia industry-specific differentials in labour markets, human capital, knowledge and technology intensity. Indeed, several studies have highlighted the differential impact of industry differences along these dimensions on international business activities (for example, Pak and Park, 2005). MNCs in more technology-, knowledge- and human capital-intensive industries are more reliant on a relatively stable and skilled workforce. In such industries, comprehensive employee voice and participation systems, investment in training and the associated longer-term employment relationships underpin competition strategies. It is frequently assumed that the terms of international competition in such highly internationalized industries exert pressures on companies to converge on the individualistic 'high road' ER patterns akin to those in leading US high-tech multinationals.

However, in situations where the IR system – in combination with other elements of the national BS – has shaped collective ER patterns that enable and support the internationally successful skills-intensive strategies (Streeck, 1992; Hall and Soskice, 2001), MNCs originating from such home-country settings and that operate in this type of industry may have an incentive to achieve greater international integration on the basis of their home-country model. In this constellation the dominance effect may interact with the home-country effect in a way that entails the incorporation of US-type innovations into the collective ER approach with a subsequent greater emphasis on a dualistic commitment to ER. Thus, even within the same type of industry the notion of industry-specific 'best practice' does not necessarily imply the 'best way' solution, but comprises nationally imbued functional equivalents.

In general, the average German MNC has traditionally been characterized as relatively decentralized with lower levels of parental control compared to the average US MNC (Child et al., 2001). However, there are reasons to expect stronger home-country and dominance ER effects in subsidiaries of German MNCs that compete in highly internationalized, skills-intensive industries. Such a strategy is, arguably, underpinned by the German IR system that enables a co-operative and collective ER approach. Many of these industries are not only export intensive, but also foreign direct investment (FDI) intensive and, hence, are mainly driven by the need to exploit ownership advantages (McDonald, Tüselmann, Hoppe and Williams, 2003). Thus, German MNCs in these industries may have an incentive to achieve international integration on the basis of their home-country model, whilst accommodating pressures arising from the dominance effect within their collective ER model, by, for instance, incorporating innovative elements of the US model, such as HISs. Such dualistic ER approaches are already apparent in an embryonic form in the home-country sites of these German MNCs.

German MNCs that compete in highly internationalized industries that are characterized by high labour, but low skills intensity can be expected to display a more pronounced preference for the 'low road' ER approach in their international operations. Investing abroad may, in these circumstances, entail a strategic desire to externalize labour-cost and numerical flexibility pressures and to pursue the 'low road' variant of the Anglo-American ER model in permissive host-country IR contexts. Alternatively, the findings of a pervasive country-of-origin imprint in German subsidiaries in the form of a transfer of the generally co-operative management style and ER ethos may imply a more muted incidence of the 'low road' approach. The incidence of this approach among German subsidiaries in less skills-intensive industries may, however, be lower compared to subsidiaries of MNCs of other nationalities that operate in this industry context.

At the time of writing, there have been no quantitative studies that have explicitly investigated the differential influence of both the level and type of industry internationalization on subsidiary ER patterns. Yet, a recent survey-based study of German subsidiaries in the UK, though employing only a unidimensional industry categorization, highlights significant variations in the ER approaches of German subsidiaries depending on their degree of industry internationalization (Tüselmann et al., 2006). On the basis of the foregoing discussion the following hypotheses emerge.

H2:   *UK-based subsidiaries of German MNCs that compete in highly internationalized skills-intensive industries are more likely to exhibit a dualistic ER approach compared to their German-owned counterparts in less internationalized industries.*

H3:   *UK-based subsidiaries of German MNCs that operate in highly internationalized less skills-intensive industries are more likely to deploy the individualistic 'low road' ER approach compared to German-owned subsidiaries in less internationalized industries.*

Data and methodology

The study is based on a representative survey of German subsidiaries in the UK and private-sector UK-owned multi-establishment firms with at least 25 employees. The data were collected using a pre-tested structured questionnaire that was sent to the managing directors of the sampled firms. The sampling frames were constructed from a range of public sources. A stratified random sampling method was used to obtain representative samples according to size and industry stratification criteria. Two representative samples of 900 establishments for each nationality were drawn. This sampling design was employed in order to ensure that the sufficiency requirements for multivariate data analysis were met (Long, 1997) for the pooled sample of UK- and German-owned establishments. The research was, therefore, designed to ensure that sufficiently high response rates from both nationality groups were obtained to avoid potential bias in the regression analyses. It, simultaneously, employs the conventional size/industry stratification criterion.

The response rates were 20.7 per cent and 33.2 per cent for UK- and German-owned establishments, respectively. The response rate for the combined samples was 27 per cent; this compares well with similar survey-based studies. Standard checks for representativeness for both nationality samples proved satisfactory and tests for non-response bias for both nationality samples suggested that the study's empirical work is not influenced by non-response bias to a significant extent. The data of both surveys were pooled for subsequent statistical analysis.

The classification of ER dimensions and approaches is based on dichotomous measures. The construction of the collective dimension was based on the incidence of trade union recognition and/or non-union representative bodies. The direct ER dimension was defined by the presence of a HIS. In the absence of a commonly agreed definition, list of practices and measurement approach, a broad working definition for HISs was adopted. Following Edwards and Wright (2001), this definition included the following practices: partly autonomous teamwork, quality circles/problem-solving groups, attitude surveys, suggestion schemes, regular meetings, team briefings, newsletters and the systematic use of the management chain. A weighted composite index was constructed using the incidence of these practices and the differential degree of employee involvement connected with them. Those subsidiaries with an above-average score on this measure were deemed to have a HIS in place; those below average did not. The suitability of this weighting scheme was verified by sensitivity analysis that used alternative scoring systems. Cronbach's alpha reliability coefficients for the collective and direct employee involvement dimension were 0.72 and 0.69, respectively. On the basis of these classifications, establishments were divided into the four broad ER approaches.

The level of the internationalization of industries was measured along the lines of the UNCTAD Transnationality Index (UNCTAD, 2006) that covers foreign and domestic sales, employment and investment. An internationalization index was calculated as the average of these three ratios for each industry at the NACE Division level. From this, the average for all industries was calculated. Industries above the index average were categorized as highly internationalized. The skills intensity of industries was ascertained by using the ILO International Standard Classification of Occupations (ISCO) and the ISCO Skill Level definition (ILO, 1997). Industries with an above-average share of highly and intermediate skilled employees were defined as skills intensive. On this basis, highly internationalized industries were further differentiated as skills or less skills intensive.

The ER approaches were treated as dependent variables. Given their dichotomous nature, the hypotheses were tested by logistic regression models. A range of control variables, drawn from the findings of relevant previous studies, were included in the regression estimates (see *Notes* under Table 4.1). In order to avoid the potential violation of the assumption of a linear relationship between continuous predicators and the logit transformation of the dependent variable, all continuous variables were transformed into categorical variables. Relevant likelihood ratio tests relating to omitted variables and data pooling raised no concerns. Checks for collinearity between the independent variables indicated no multicollinearity problems. The robustness of the logistic regression calculations was tested by altering the set of control variables and by running probit instead of logistic regressions. Unless indicated otherwise, the respective regression results concerning the explanatory variables of interest are robust.

Results and discussion

The results of the regression estimates for the pooled sample and the German sample are presented in Tables 4.1 and 4.2, respectively. The results in these tables show the extent to which the explanatory variables of interest, that is nationality of ownership in the pooled sample and industry internationalization in the German sample, are significant after allowing for the influence of the control variables. Overall, the empirical models perform well. All model χ^2s are significant at either the one or five per cent level. This demonstrates that all regressions are meaningful models. The relatively high values for the pseudo R^2s (with the possible exception of the third model in Table 4.1) are another indication for the quality of the regression models. The pseudo R^2s are, overall, good for logistic models and are, in part, higher than those in comparable studies.

Comparative analysis of German- and UK-owned firms

The results in Table 4.1 provide only partial support for **H1**. Contrary to expectations, indigenous UK firms rather than German-owned firms are significantly more likely to exhibit the traditional collective ER approach. Conversely, German subsidiaries are significantly more likely to operate with collective ER in the form of the dual approach compared to UK-owned firms. These findings indicate that

Table 4.1   Nationality-of-ownership differences in employment relations approaches

Dependent variable	Mean UK	G	Coefficient (standard error in brackets)	Model χ^2	R^2
Traditional collective approach	.19	.09	−.946 (.487)**	56.978	.302
Dual approach	.16	.33	.645 (.262)**	97.853	.366
Individualistic 'high road' approach	.28	.31	.151 (.235)	65.283	.154
Individualistic 'low road' approach	.36	.25	−.413 (.254)*	69.791	.276

Notes:
(i) Logistic regressions. R^2 is pseudo.
(ii) Number of observations: 518.
(iii) Coefficients are 1 – 0 variable: 1 is for German-owned and 0 is for UK-owned firms.
(iv) Controls: establishment size (5 categories), industry (based on NACE classification at Division level, 7 categories), region (based on Government Official Region classification, 4 categories), share of skilled labour (based on ILO classification system, 4 categories), share of part-time workers (3 categories), whether greenfield site, whether main market abroad, establishment age (5 categories).
(v) '*', '**' and '***' indicate significance at the 10%, 5% and 1% levels, respectively.

there might indeed be a German-specific pathway to incorporating US-style ER innovations. The ER patterns in UK-based German firms may, to a degree, reflect an emerging dual approach in the German workplaces. Although the dual approach is significantly associated with German subsidiaries, the magnitude of its dissemination among German subsidiaries cautions against generalizations. While this approach is more prevalent in German subsidiaries compared to UK firms, only one third of German-owned firms have developed a dual ER approach. Thus, the incorporation of the so-called 'best practice' element of the US-style individualistic 'high road' approach into collective ER patterns is a distinctive, but not a common, feature among German firms in the UK.

There is little evidence with regard to the proposed nationality difference in **H1** in relation to the individualistic ER approaches. German subsidiaries are as likely to pursue the individualistic 'high road' approach as their UK counterparts and only slightly less likely to adopt the 'low road' approach. Against the background of the collective ER orientation in the overwhelming majority of German MNCs, these preliminary findings suggest a strong host-country effect among a considerable section of German-owned UK-based subsidiaries. However, considering that the dominance effect is also connected to the diffusion of ER innovations among domestic firms, the fact that German subsidiaries are as likely as their UK-owned counterparts to develop HISs within an individualistic ER approach could also be read as the pre-eminence of the dominance effect in shaping ER patterns in a sizeable number of German subsidiaries. Although a slightly higher percentage of German subsidiaries pursue a HIS approach as part of a collective (or dual) framework, the relatively high percentage that do so as part of an individualistic ER approach could indicate dissatisfaction amongst German parent companies with their collective home-country model.

Alternatively, individualistic high road approaches in German subsidiaries may indicate a country-of-origin effect at a more abstract level. It may reflect situations where parent companies do not perceive a collective approach as providing a useful framework for international operations – even if managers still attribute positive outcomes to a collective approach in their home establishments. In such situations, the generally co-operative and consensual German management style and ER ethos may translate into direct communication rather than representative channels (Ferner et al., 2001; Dickmann, 2003). If this is so, HIS could be viewed as a German-flavoured ER style. In other words, individualistic 'high road' approaches in German subsidiaries may, in part, reflect the interaction of the dominance effect at the level of the ER approach and a country-of-origin effect at the more intangible level.

It is less likely that, compared to indigenous UK firms, German-owned subsidiaries in the UK will pursue the 'low road' ER approach. This relationship is only weakly significant. Despite this, in a quarter of German subsidiaries, employees have no meaningful voice mechanisms. This may indicate that that the co-operative ER ethos of the German model does not always translate into an Anglo-Saxon context. The use of the cost-minimizing, labour-flexibility route of the individualistic approach in a sizeable minority of UK-based German subsidiaries may in part be explained by the types of German parent company. Such parent firms may obtain or perceive few benefits from the collective home-country ER template.

The findings may also partly reflect an adoption of local practices among a certain subset of German subsidiaries in situations of significant pressures for mimetic isomorphism due, inter alia, to local responsiveness and legitimacy reasons. Moreover, regardless of the requirements of their wider business and operational environment, the incidence of this ER approach may in part merely reflect an adoption of local practices in cases where parent companies have a non-strategic approach to IR and HRM issues in their international operations and exercise little parental control. However, the analysis has so far revealed only the average nationality effect in German subsidiaries and may conceal important variations within the cross-section of German subsidiaries along crucial industry internationalization dimensions.

Intra-German analysis: industry characteristics and variations in ER approaches

The findings in Table 4.2 confirm **H2** and **H3** and therefore provide evidence that the level and type of industry internationalization have significant effects on ER approaches in German subsidiaries. With regard to **H2**, German MNCs that operate in highly internationalized skills-intensive industries are indeed more likely to draw on elements of both the German and the US model in their UK operations through the use of German-flavoured hybrid ER patterns. Compared to subsidiaries of German MNCs in less internationalized industries, they are significantly more likely to have a dual ER approach whilst being significantly less likely to pursue traditional collective approaches and 'low road' approaches.

A key observation is that the ER outcomes – as the result of the interaction of the four influences in the UK host setting and in this type of industry – are, to a considerable degree, connected with a more pertinent impact of both the country-of-origin and dominance effect. The latter is apparent in a more widespread emphasis on direct employee involvement and in the development of HISs (84 per cent) in relation to the reference group of subsidiaries in less internationalized industries (53 per cent) (see Table 4.2). The former is evidenced by a stronger preference for collective ER (62 per cent compared to 40 per cent of the reference group). However, the greater propensity to embrace the progressive HIS elements of the US model are not associated with a greater inclination to pursue these within an individualistic ER framework. A large section of German MNCs competing in highly internationalized skills-intensive industries seem to regard it as beneficial to draw on the collective orientation of the German model when operating in an Anglo-American context whilst incorporating the progressive elements of the individualistic 'high road' approach within a dualistic ER approach.

With the bulk of the large German export industries belonging to this skills-intensive category and with these firms being the main beneficiaries of the

Table 4.2 Industry internationalization characteristics and employment relations in German subsidiaries

Dependent variable	Mean			Coefficient (standard error in brackets)		Model χ^2	R^2
	LII	HISII	HILSII	HISII	HILSII		
Trade Union Approach	.18	.06	.13	−.442 (.222)**	−.136 (.352)	66.237	.314
Dual Approach	.22	.56	.10	.834 (.273)***	−.457 (.219)**	81.444	.388
Individualistic 'High Road' Approach	.35	.28	.31	−.274 (.366)	−.389 (.368)	52.676	.212
Individualistic 'Low Road' Approach	.24	.10	.46	−.586 (.214)**	1.104 (.445)***	37.892	.348

Notes:
  (i) LII = less internationalized industry, HISII = highly internationalized skills-intensive industry, HILSII = highly internationalized less skills-intensive industry.
 (ii) see Notes (i), (iv) and (v) under Table 4.1.
(iii) Number of observations: 219.
 (iv) Coefficients are for type of industry. The reference group is less internationalized industries (LII).

particular constellation of the German IR system, German MNCs in highly internationalized skills-intensive industries do indeed have an incentive to achieve greater international integration on the basis of the home-country model and to accommodate competitive pressures to adopt US-style practices within a German-specific pathway. The facts that subsidiaries in this type of industry account for over 70 per cent of the incidence of collective ER patterns and for over 80 per cent of the dual approach within the cross-section of German subsidiaries shed a different light on the findings in the preceding section. Indeed, a considerable number of UK-based subsidiaries of German MNCs that operate in highly internationalized skills-intensive industries seem to be at the forefront in developing German-flavoured hybrid ER patterns.

As postulated in **H3**, the individualistic 'low road' ER approach is a more common feature among subsidiaries of German MNCs that compete in highly internationalized, less skills-intensive industries. Compared to subsidiaries in less internationalized industries, they are highly significantly more likely to operate with such an approach. This may reflect the importance of low-cost based international strategies in this type of industry and the associated emphasis on labour-cost minimization and numerical flexibility. The findings indicate that a number of German MNCs in such sectors may associate relatively few benefits with their home-country approach and, thus, pursue a labour-flexibility cost-minimizing 'low road' ER approach in the UK. This is despite the fact that MNCs in other sectors are able to benefit from productivity-oriented skills-based strategies that are supported by the home-country framework. Such results confirm the differential impact of industry-specific characteristics on ER patterns.

At the same time, the findings in Table 4.1 also highlight that the 'low road' approach is less widespread than might have been expected. Indeed, well over half of the German subsidiaries in highly internationalized, less skills-intensive industries have either collective or comprehensive direct employee involvement and participation mechanisms in place. These results seem to confirm the insights of the case evidence mentioned above as to the working of a country-of-origin effect at the more intangible level in the form of a transfer of the co-operative management style and ER ethos of the German model.

Conclusions

This study has enhanced our understanding of cross-border transfer issues in international operations of German MNCs with particular reference to key ER policy choices. It has provided a richer picture than those conventionally obtained from quantitative studies. By including important industry characteristics not only along the dimension of the level of industry internationalization, but also in relation to human capital, technology and knowledge intensity (subsumed under the rubric of skills intensity), this study has shed new light on the interplay between home-country, host-country, dominance effects and the impact of industry-specific forces in shaping the relative strength and nature of the country-of-origin effect in German subsidiaries in the UK. The study also highlighted the importance of accounting for country-of-origin effects at the level of the transfer of the underlying principles of the home-country model and at the more intangible level of ER style, ethos and managerial mindset (Ferner et al., 2001; Dickmann, 2003). The representative nature of this study in combination with its design allow for the results to be generalized to a relatively high degree.

The comparative cross-sectional analysis of German subsidiaries with indigenous UK firms confirmed only partly the expectation of a distinct country-of-origin imprint in terms of the collective orientation of the German model. German subsidiaries are less likely to operate with collective ER patterns that have affinities to the traditional collective ER approach compared to their UK-owned counterparts and are generally as likely to operate with individualistic Anglo-American type ER approaches. However, German subsidiaries are far more likely than indigenous UK firms to use dual ER approaches that incorporate the innovative HRM-style innovations of the individualistic 'high road' ER approach within collective ER structures.

The interaction between country-of-origin and dominance effects in the UK host-country setting points to a German-specific pathway to assimilating US-style ER innovations; this can be viewed as a distinguishing Germanic feature in the comparative nationality-of-ownership analysis. This entails a nationally distinct hybrid subsidiary ER solution in the form of a selective appropriation of the progressive elements of the Anglo-American approach within a framework that reflects the collective orientation of the German approach. However, although the dual approach is associated with German ownership, the magnitude of such an approach among the cross-section of German subsidiaries illustrates that this approach is a distinctive, but not necessarily a common, ER feature among German subsidiaries. This highlights the need for a more reflective interpretation of the nationality differences.

The intra-German analysis of ER approaches revealed significant variations according to important industry characteristics, which were masked in the comparative nationality analysis because this depicted only the average German nationality effect. The intra-German analysis highlighted the mediating as well as the differential influence of the level and type of industry internationalization in shaping the relative strength and nature of the country-of-origin effect. Compared to subsidiaries of German MNCs in less internationalized and more multi-domestic industries, those operating in highly internationalized industries that also face competitive pressures for internationally integrated approaches exhibit pronounced differences in the deployment of ER approaches. These are further accentuated by the skills intensity of the industries concerned. The dual ER approach is far more pronounced in UK subsidiaries of German MNCs that compete in highly internationalized skills-intensive industries. This highlights the stronger impact of both the country-of-origin effect and the dominance effect.

German MNCs in skills-intensive industries in particular have, arguably, benefited from the specific institutional and regulatory configuration of the German IR system. This system has helped to deliver competitive advantages to German firms in these industries that have enabled them to succeed internationally. Such MNCs have an incentive to achieve greater integration of their international operations on the basis of their home-country model whilst accommodating pressures arising from dominance effects within a dualistic approach. This is more common than integration on the basis of an individualistic 'high road' approach akin to those in leading US MNCs in these industries. Indeed, with such German subsidiaries accounting for the overwhelming majority of subsidiaries with a dual approach in the total sample, a German-specific pathway to incorporating US-style ER innovations is very much a defining feature of German subsidiaries in highly internationalized, skills-intensive industries. It is not a general feature among German subsidiaries.

In contrast, the individualistic 'low road' ER variant of the Anglo-American model is associated with subsidiaries of German MNCs operating in the low skills-intensive, highly internationalized industries. Although the German IR system has generally led to a collective ER model in the parent-company home bases, the German system is less supportive of competitive advantages in these more labour-intensive industries. Though still a minority, the sizeable number of German subsidiaries that operate with a 'low road' ER approach seems to reflect the importance of low cost-based international strategies in this type of industry and the associated emphasis on labour-cost minimization and numerical flexibility. These MNCs may strategically use their subsidiaries that are based in Anglo-American host-country contexts to externalize labour-cost and flexibility pressures.

The findings of this study serve as a useful caution against the preoccupation with current 'global best practice' prescriptions and suggest that any search for 'best practice' should, at least, acknowledge that it is more appropriate to speak of 'industry best practice'. Even this needs to be understood in terms of functional equivalents, allowing for 'nationally distinct pathways of industry best practice'. The findings of this study also highlight that industry pressures in the interplay between home-country, host-country and dominance effects have a significant, but not a universal, effect. This underscores a contention of the four forces model that none of these influences is deterministic, but that their impact in shaping ER outcomes in MNCs' overseas subsidiaries operations is a matter of degree. Furthermore, the findings also underline the importance of incorporating BS dynamics and the subsequent evolving nature of the country-of-origin effect into the analytical framework. Country-of-origin effects at a more intangible level that reflect nationally embedded cultures on terms of ER style and ethos should also be taken into consideration.

Note

This paper is based on a research project on employee relations and firm performance of foreign-owned subsidiaries in the UK, funded by the Hans Böckler Foundation, Germany.

References

Appelbaum, E., Baily, T., Berg, P. and Kallenberg, A. (2000) *Manufacturing Advantage – Why High Performance Work Systems Pay Off* (Ithaca: ILR Press).

Buckley, P. and Carter, M. (2004) 'A formal analysis of knowledge combination in multinational enterprises', *Journal of International Business Studies*, 35(5), 371–74.

Carr, C. (2005) 'Are German, Japanese and Anglo-Saxon strategic decision styles still divergent in the context of globalization?' *Journal of Management Studies*, 42(6), 1155–78.

Chen, S., Lawler, J. and Bae, J. (2005) 'Convergence in human resource systems: A comparison of locally owned and MNC subsidiaries in Taiwan', *Human Resource Management*, 44(3), 237–56.

Child, J., Faulkner, D. and Pitkethly, R. (2001) *The Management of International Acquisitions* (Oxford: Oxford University Press).

Cooke, W. (2001) 'Union avoidance and foreign direct investment in the USA', *Employee Relations*, 23(6), 1–17.

Dickmann, M. (2003) 'Implementing German HRM abroad: Desired, feasible, successful?' *International Journal of Human Resource Management*, 14(2), 265–83.

Dunning, J. (2000) 'The eclectic paradigm as an envelope for economic and business theories of MNE activity', *International Business Review*, 9, 163–90.

Edwards, T. and Ferner, A. (2002) 'The renewed "American Challenge": A review of employment practices in US multinationals', *Industrial Relations Journal*, 33(2), 94–111.

Edwards, P. and Wright, M. (2001) 'High involvement work systems and performance: The strength of context-bound relationships', *International Journal of Human Resource Management*, 12(4), 568–85.

Ferner, A. (1997) 'Country of origin effects and human resource management in multinational companies', *Human Resource Management Journal*, 7(1), 19–37.

Ferner, A., Quintanilla, J. and Varul, M. (2001) 'Country-of-origin effects, host country effects and the management of HR in multinationals: German companies in Britain and Spain', *Journal of World Business*, 36(2), 107–27.

Guest, D. and Hoque, K. (1996) 'National ownership and HR practices in UK greenfield sites', *Human Resource Management Journal*, 6(4), 50–74.

Guest, D. and Conway, N. (1999) 'Peering into the Black Hole: The downside of new employ-ment relations in the UK', *British Journal of Industrial Relations*, 37(3), 367–89.

Hall, P. and Soskice, D. (eds) (2001) *Varieties of Capitalism: The Institutional Foundations of Comparative Advantage* (Oxford: Oxford University Press).

Harzing, A. and Sorge, A. (2003) 'The relative impact of country-of-origin and universal contingencies on internationalization strategies and corporate control in multinational enterprises: Worldwide and European perspectives', *Organization Studies*, 24(2), 187–221.

Hofstede, G. (2001) *Culture's Consequences: Comparing Values, Behaviours, Institutions and Institutions Across Nations* (Thousand Oaks, CA: Sage).

ILO (International Labour Organization) (1997) *Occupational Classification: Concepts, Methods, Reliability, Validity and Cross-National Comparability* (Geneva: ILO).

Kurdelbusch, A. (2002) 'Multinationals and the rise of variable pay in Germany', *European Journal of Industrial Relations*, 8(3), 325–49.

Long, J. (1997) *Regression Models for Limited Dependent Variables* (London: SAGE).

McDonald, F., Tüselmann, H.-J., Hoppe, U. and Williams, D. (2003) *Standort UK: German DFI and Employment* (London and Berlin: Anglo-German Foundation).

Marginson, P., Armstrong, P., Edward, P. and Purcell, J. (1995) 'Extending beyond borders: Multinationals companies and the international management of labour', *International Journal of Human Resource Management*, 6(3), 702–19.

Mudambi, R. and Navarra (2002) 'Institutions and international business: A theoretical overview', *International Business Review*, 11(6), 635–46.

Nachum, L. and Zaher, S. (2005) 'The persistence of distance? The impact of technology on MNE motivations for foreign investment', *Strategic Management Journal*, 26, 747–67.

Ngo, H., Turban, D., Lau, C. and Lui, S. (1998) 'Human resource practices and firm perform-ance of MNCs: Influence of country of origin', *International Journal of Human Resource Management*, 9(4), 632–52.

Pak, Y-S and Park, Y.-R. (2005) 'Characteristics of Japanese FDI in the East and the West: Understanding the strategic motives of Japanese investment', *Journal of World Business* 40(3), 254–66.

Smith, C. and Meiskins, P. (1995) 'System, society and dominance effects in cross-national organizational analysis', *Work, Employment and Society*, 9(2), 241–67.

Streeck, W. (1992) *Social Institution and Economic Performance – Studies of Industrial Relations in Advanced Capitalist Economies* (London: Sage).

Streeck, W. (1997) 'German capitalism: Does it exist? Can it survive?' in Crouch, C. and Streeck, W. (eds), *Political Economy of Modern Capitalism* (London: Sage).

Tayeb, M. (1998) 'Transfer of HRM practices across cultures: An American company in Scotland', *International Journal of Human Resource Management*, 9(2), 332–58.

Tüselmann, H., McDonald, F. and Thorpe, R. (2006) 'The emerging approach to employee relations in German overseas affiliates: A role model for international operation?' *Journal of World Business*, 48(1), 66–80.

UNCTAD (2006) *World Investment Report 2006* (New York and Geneva: United Nations).

Walsh, J. (2001) 'Human resource management in foreign-owned workplaces: Evidence from Australia', *International Journal of Human Resource Management*, 12(3), 425–44.

WERS (Workplace Employee Relations Survey) (1998) Data File MQ98SAV (Colchester: University of Essex).

Whitley, R. (1999) *Divergent Capitalisms: The Social Structuring and Change of Business Systems* (Oxford: Oxford University Press).

Whittington, R. and Mayer, M. (2000) *The European Corporation: Strategy, Structure and Social Science* (Oxford: Oxford University Press).

5

Tensions Arising from Process of Transferring HRM Practices across Borders: The Case of Taiwanese MNCs in the UK

Yi-Ying Chang, Kamel Mellahi and Adrian John Wilkinson

Introduction

Research on headquarter/subsidiary relationships and the transfer of HRM strategies and practices abroad has mainly focused on western multinational corporations (MNCs) operating in the advanced economies or developing economies (Guest and Hoque, 1996; Ferner and Quintanilla, 1998; Tayeb, 1998; Edwards and Ferner, 2004; Ferner et al., 2005). Although previous research has highlighted the need to examine these relationships in a different and dynamic way (for example, Birkinshaw and Hood (1998) envisaged the relationship as taking different forms and having different dynamics depending on the situation), little attention has been paid to the question of how MNCs' country of origin might affect the transfer of HRM practices. Possible tensions that may arise from the transfer of HRM practices by MNCs from emerging or newly industrialized economies (NIEs) operating in the advanced economies have also not been systematically investigated.

Rapid economic progress within the developing world and the spread of MNCs from the emerging economies, including Taiwan, have increased the need to pay more attention to this aspect of headquarter/subsidiary relationships. Taiwan is widely acknowledged as an emerging economy (Bae and Lawler, 2000), and Taiwanese MNCs account for an increasingly significant amount of foreign direct investment (FDI) in global markets (Yeung, 1999). A recent UNCTAD report, for example, stated that 53 of the top 100 non-financial MNCs from the developing world in 2006 originated from Taiwan and two other East Asian emerging economies (UNCTAD, 2006).

The present research examines the head office–subsidiary relationships among Taiwanese MNCs operating in the UK, including possible tensions arising from the transfer of home-country HRM practices overseas. A case study approach has been taken in this research, which reflects previous calls on international management researchers to use more qualitative methods to provide a more organic and dynamic view of the organization (Werner, 2002; Ferner et al., 2004). The present study also responds to earlier calls for more cross-national research (Werner, 2002). It emerged that the diffusion of home-country HRM practices in UK-based Taiwanese subsidiaries is influenced by the parent company's strategy; this is, however, mediated by interaction with the host-country institutional environments. Another key finding is that micro-political processes involving multiple actors at the organizational level influence how an HRM strategy or practice is actually implemented.

Analytical framework

The starting point of this framework is comparative institutionalism, which recognizes that competitiveness in the different economic systems is attuned with a broad variety of national-institutional agreements. There are systematic variations in the way different national business systems manage their economic activity through the mechanisms directing the operation of capital, labour and product markets (Whitley, 1999; Hall and Soskice, 2001). The institutional approach primarily assumes that MNCs will be influenced in their international businesses by the structures, operating models and patterns of thinking and behaviour that they have developed to respond to the national business context where they originate (Whitley, 2001). An outcome of this is that MNCs' attitudes to transferring HRM strategies and practices are likely to be influenced by the home-country HRM system. At the same time, MNCs face pressures to adapt to host-country institutional systems in which their subsidiaries operate. From an institutional perspective (Rosenzweig and Nohria, 1994; Kostova, 1999; Kostova and Roth, 2002), subsidiaries' actors can be seen as functioning between two competing institutional 'pulls' that often result in tensions: those exerted by the MNCs' headquarters (HQ) as they attempt to transfer strategies and practices to the subsidiary; and those exercised by the host institutional domain where the subsidiary operates.

The institutionalist approach has received some criticisms. For example, Gamble (2003) argues that parent and host-country effects do shape the transfer of HRM policies and practices to subsidiaries. However, as Gamble (2003) himself also indicated, HRM practices transferred from HQ could be affected where cultural distance is high, for example, between UK and China; failure by MNCs to consider HR issues as strategic in such cases could also be limiting. MNCs could still find a space to manoeuvre (Muller, 1999) in a highly constrained society such as China. As Quintanilla and Ferner (2003) suggest, every national business system contains some degree of flexibility and space, which may be used through appropriate firm-specific managerial strategies exerted by multiple managers within organizations.

Moreover, as previous research (for example, Ferner and Edwards, 1995) has argued, a power and interest perspective can complement an institutionalist approach in analysing the behaviour of MNCs (Tempel and Walgenbach, 2003; Ferner et al., 2005). First, the transfer of HRM policies and practices within MNCs is the result of power and interests held by multiple actors within subsidiaries, including the organized workforce. Moore (2006), for example, shows how expatriate managers in the London branch use their critical position on behalf of HQ as a social control mechanism to balance interests of the HQ and their own interests for career advancement.

Second, power relations interrelate with institutional pressures at the micro level of the MNC itself. Actors at different levels of MNCs may have different interests and a variety of resources with which to pursue them. In MNCs, such resources originate from the subsidiary's success and consequent credibility within the wider firm, and from its ability to exploit the local institutional context (Ferner and Colling, 2005). By acting as 'interpreters' of the possibilities and limits of the host institutional environment, particularly where they are ambiguous, subsidiary actors may 'negotiate' significant freedom of action for themselves when facing the institutional pressure from HQ and the parent-country business system. Subsidiary managers can weaken, modify or defend against disagreeable and unreasonable demands from HQ by referring to the host-country institutional arrangements or to the political power of local actors in certain conditions (Tempel, 2001; Becker-Ritterspach et al., 2002). Lastly, the tensions arising from transferring HRM policies and practices may be a consequence of the attitudes, values and ability of managers. Paik and Sohn (2004), for example, find that possible tensions and problems could be avoided in Japanese MNCs if expatriate managers have the confidence and capability to solve the problems which they face at the subsidiary level.

Also, a MNC may wish to diffuse management practices from HQ because it has successful experience with specific practices as a result of the administrative heritage of the organization (Bartlett and Ghoshal, 1989). The international experience of MNCs' actors may also be associated with the reduction of uncertainty such as risk and conflicts for the top management team (Sambharya, 1996). For instance, firms may have better performance as a result of more training of managers for international assignments (Calof and Beamish, 1994). Internationally experienced MNC managers are also likely to increase their overall value by maintaining a balance between business, functional and geographical management capabilities (Bartlett and Ghoshal, 1989).

Taiwanese HRM systems

Taiwan and the UK are both examples of 'liberal market economies' (Hall and Soskice, 2001) in which firms are related to other economic actors chiefly through arm's length contacts in markets. However, Taiwan and the UK show significant differences regarding institutional arrangements and HRM systems. Thus, a Taiwan-UK comparison provides an interesting case for propositions about the interaction between different institutional domains: what tensions arise from transferring HRM policies and practices across different national systems both at macro and micro levels?

Taiwanese companies tend to be small and medium-sized (SMEs), as is typical of privately owned Chinese enterprises (Chen, 1995). They started establishing operations in China during the 1980s due to the abandonment of martial laws in 1987 and the need to relocate their labour-intensive operations to low-cost production sites. In the twenty-first century, Taiwanese firms are typically moving from labour-intensive industries to high-technology and capital-intensive industries. Although Taiwan was not as severely affected by the 1997 Asian economic crisis as other economies in this region, it later experienced lower growth rates and a significantly higher unemployment rate partly because of global recession and competitive pressures from other neighbouring economies such as China (Chen et al., 2003). Other contributory factors might be capital flight probably arising from Taiwanese firms' shift of operations and investments and relocation of most highly skilled workers to China (Bae et al., 2003).

Taiwanese firms are largely family-owned enterprises with managerial systems influenced by Confucian culture and values (Chen, 1995; Chen et al., 2005). More than 77 per cent of the workforce is in private-sector SMEs and less than five per cent of Taiwanese workers are employed by large enterprises. Also, more than 50 per cent of the enterprises are in service sector. Management systems in SMEs and large family-owned enterprises tend to be autocratic and centralized. There is low commitment and a moderately high turnover rate among non-family members or friends in these private-sector organizations. The incidence of organized labour union is low in SMEs, but larger enterprises (LEs) and state-owned enterprises (SOEs) tend to have union organizations. Generally, the majority of indigenous Taiwanese firms have maintained harmonious and peaceful employer–employee relationships.

Taiwanese firms tend to be associated with a paternalistic entrepreneur, with a backup group of relatives and trusted close friends. The entrepreneurs exercise extensive control over the daily operation of the firm. In addition, under the influence of Confucianism, the owners of Taiwanese firms typically stress hardship and familism, which may influence the design of HRM systems. Previous research has indicated that the Taiwanese HRM system is gradually changing to a more westernized model (Yang, 1986), with greater emphasis on individual needs (for example, autonomy and self-expression) and less emphasis on collective needs (for example, order, nurture, endurance and social approval). Other researchers have, however, found that some indigenous collective values are still salient in contemporary Taiwanese society (Wu, 2004). Thus, indigenous Taiwanese firms still have participative programmes such as quality circles, goal-setting, feedback and participation in decision-making and so on.

Indigenous Taiwanese firms, particularly SMEs, often rely on informal methods of HRM (Chen, 1995). Hiring and recruiting are generally through interpersonal connections (*guanxi*). In these types of family enterprises, owners and managers emphasize individual loyalty and positive attitudes towards the firm. Evaluation is also linked with personal qualities and attitudes rather than individual performance. Training and development are also limited and viewed as costs rather than an investment in human capital. Compensation tends to be linked to seniority and is not normally linked to individual performance.

Due to changes in the institutional environments, particularly economically and politically, Taiwanese industry is moving towards high-technology product areas in which local firms can compete globally. These high-technology Taiwanese enterprises tend not to use traditional Confucian management techniques. Rather, they are increasingly adopting more strategic HRM systems (Huang, 2001) and high-performance work systems (HPWS), including increased training and pay for performance (Bae et al., 2003).

HRM systems in the UK

The UK HRM systems are typically short-term orientated, with strong focus on labour flexibility and labour cost reduction (Storey, 2001). This partly reflects the traditional reliance of large British firms on capital raised through issuing shares in the stock market and the financial institutions. In other words, the short-termist share-price approach that characterizes British firms has generated highly formalized and elaborate internal financial control systems, and given a predominant role to the finance function (Ferner and Quintanilla, 1998). HRM in British MNCs is, thus, characterized by tight control of labour costs through formal budget setting and review processes (for example, Edwards et al., 1996; Ferner and Quintanilla, 1998). While labour cost control is also a feature of Taiwanese firms, it does not have the same high profile and formalized support system of financial structures as shown in British MNCs.

British MNCs are also more likely to have worldwide systems of performance and tight financial control than Taiwanese firms. The preference of Anglo-Saxon MNCs (for example, British) for 'bureaucratic' rather than 'social' models of subsidiary control (Edström and Galbraith, 1977) is reflected in the prevalence in such companies of formal, worldwide policies (Ferner and Quintanilla, 1998), for instance, in the field of performance appraisal and remuneration of managers (Harzing, 1996). Another feature of the Anglo-Saxon model of HRM is that performance-related pay is widely used. Evidence from the 2004 Workplace Employment Survey (WERS) shows this to be the case in British firms. External sources for off-the-job training are also widely adopted by British firms, which is less common in Taiwanese firms. There is a decline in collective bargaining in workplaces in British firms as a result of changes in industrial relations laws in the 1980s and an increase in the service sector. Other contributory factors are the fall in the numbers of large manufacturing plants and manual workers and the reduced size of the public sector (Bacon, 2001).

However, there seems to be a shift in the UK institutional and political contexts towards qualified support for collective forms of employee representation, due to recent developments such as statutory union-recognition procedures and, at EU level, provisions on European works councils and information and consultation arrangements. Moreover, in a bid to improve the overall competitiveness of British industry (Bacon, 2001), management and trade unions started using 'partnership' to solve conflicts and promote co-operation in workplaces (Ackers and Payne, 1998); this is not common in Taiwanese firms.

The significant differences highlighted above in regard to the HRM systems in Taiwan and the UK suggest considerable scope for tensions between these two national business systems and, by extension, between headquarter–subsidiary relationships spanning across both countries. This study, therefore, seeks answers to the following questions: 1) what tensions are associated with transferring HRM strategies and practices by Taiwanese MNCs to their UK subsidiaries, at both macro and micro levels?; and 2) to what extent are these tensions a result of institutional distances between Taiwan and the UK HRM systems?

Methodology

Research on diffusion of best practices by MNCs tends to use large-scale surveys to explore influences of national business systems (Hamill, 1984; Bartlett and Ghoshal, 1989; Yuen and Kee, 1993). However, the survey approach may not reveal the complex processes and linkages involved during the transfer process of HRM strategies and practices (Ferner, 1997). Yin (2003) has suggested multiple case studies as an effective alternative for researching such complex phenomena and providing theoretical replications. The present study, therefore, selected five case subjects – all Taiwanese MNCs with UK subsidiaries – for systematic investigation, specifically to examine what tensions arise from the way in which Taiwanese MNCs transmit HRM policies and practices to their UK subsidiaries, and how these tensions are usually resolved in practice.

The choice of the five cases was informed by a number of criteria, including the fact that they have been in the UK for many years and have had much experience in tackling difficulties in two diverse institutional environments. The five case subjects seemed familiar with dissimilarities between expatriate and local managers in terms of communicating with local employees. They also appeared to have experience of dealing with tensions arising from the transfer of HRM strategies and practices from the home country to the UK subsidiaries.

The five companies studied in considerable depth are as follows:

- Techco, a repair and service centre for an original equipment manufacturer (OEM) of notebooks, personal digital assistants (PDA) and LCD TV assembly, based in Northern England. It has around 16,000 employees worldwide, including 150 in the UK where is has operated since 1999;
- Itco, a repair service centre for PDAs and mobile phones for UK and European customers, employing around 70 people in its UK operations, most of whom are British Chinese nationals. Its total workforce is around 5,000 globally; the UK subsidiary was established in 2004;
- Comco comprises a repair centre (for its own laptops, PDAs and ruggedized laptops) and a production centre for its Sun system. It has some 140 UK employees out of a worldwide figure of more than 20,000. Comco has operated in the UK since 1988;
- Phco, a shipping service company for UK and European customers, has more than 90 employees in the UK subsidiary, out of a global total of around 22,000, and has operated in the UK since the 1970s;

- Deco, a shipping service company with a global workforce of around 50,000, established its UK operations in 2002. This subsidiary employs in excess of 150 people and has recently taken over from Germany as the European HQ of the parent company.

For reasons of confidentiality, pseudonyms are used throughout this paper. A total of 76 semi-structured interviews (between 10 and 22 for each company) were conducted with a range of respondents in the UK subsidiaries of the five case subjects, including Taiwanese managers, British managers and British nationals of Chinese origin. Of these, 19 interviews were with expatriates in the UK; 34 were conducted in Mandarin and 42 in English. Interviews concentrated on how home-country and host-country factors influenced the transfer of HRM strategies and practices and tensions that may have arisen from so doing. Interviews were tape-recorded and fully transcribed. Some interviews were recorded using note-taking and were then transcribed within 24 hours. Additional documentary material was collected from company sources and company websites as well as magazine archives. In all cases, managers were probed in the course of in-depth interviews, averaging from one to one-and-a-half hours in length, for detailed illustrative information on the problems they identified. Moreover, the extensive engagement with the company and the relatively high number of interviews conducted allowed the researcher to triangulate the picture of problems from different managerial accounts at the subsidiary level.

Findings and discussions

Tensions between the home country and host country seemed to take different forms. These include macro-level tensions between HQ and subsidiary typically arising from the adoption of home-country practices without consultation of the subsidiary; and micro-level tensions between expatriate managers and host-country nationals stemming from differences in approach to managing people and communicating with local employees. Tensions at macro level arising from the of adoption of home-country HRM practices at subsidiary level.

Tensions were observed at macro-institutional levels in the process of transferring parent country's HRM practices, including the performance appraisal system and approach to overtime and redundancy, to the UK subsidiaries. The performance appraisal system was justifiably aimed at monitoring subsidiaries' productivity targets and maintaining quality control standards, but was diffused without prior consultation with, and involvement of, the local managers. This meant that top expatriate management were using performance evaluation criteria devised by the HQ to assess local managers and employees without prior background explanation to the local staff. This caused problems and misunderstanding between HQ and local managers and led to complaints of lack of consultation and involvement from local managers and employees. One of the local HR managers commented thus:

> ... HQ in Taiwan decides all HR practices and policies. I just follow what they approve. Performance appraisal form is a good example. All the performance appraisal form

and criteria follow HQ. But I do not think it is appropriate for British employees here ... there are too many items for managers to fill in about the day-to-day operation and productivity results. I do not [know] who can fill out all the items in the perform-ance appraisal form here.

The nature of the tensions varied within the five subsidiaries. Both Techco and Deco received robustly expressed concerns from local British managers regarding the adoption of HQ performance appraisal criteria. However, due to the strong control of the HR department at HQ and a significantly lower number of local managers in the UK subsidiaries, top expatriate management still had their way. A similar approach at Itco led to complaints from local employees and, eventually, a high turnover of local employees. At Comco, the insistence by the HR manager at the HQ to retain overall decision-making power over the subsidiary's product-ivity targets and implementation of the performance appraisal system resulted in tensions with the expatriate MD in the UK. Subsequently, Comco adopted a mix of HQ performance appraisal systems and local-country performance appraisal practices such as pay for individual performance.

The adoption of overtime practices by most of the subsidiaries (including Techco, Itco, Comco and Deco) as a means of achieving HQ-driven productivity targets caused tensions and complaints from local employees. Although this HR practice is commonly adopted in the home-country's institutional environments, difficulties seemed to have arisen because expatriate MDs just used their power to ask local managers and employees to do overtime without proper explanation.

The implementation of HQ redundancy policy also caused tensions between top expatriate management and local managers and local employees, particularly at Comco, which has experienced two redundancy programmes. This was due to the fact that HQ decided to close the non-profit production site at Comco without con-sulting subsidiary expatriate management. Moreover, top expatriate management, especially the MD did not communicate or consult local managers and employees regarding why and how to implement the redundancy programme. This caused a high level of misunderstanding and distrust between HQ and local managers and employees. The local managers felt despondent at their lack of involvement.

The other four subsidiaries reported fewer tensions regarding this issue, because they have had no need to lay off employees in the UK. However, the expatriate MDs of the four subsidiaries commented that they probably would use the same approach as Comco during redundancy. This is because expatriate managers, in particular MDs, have to accept HQ management policy, especially in employee reduction/expansion as a result of the strict cost control pressures exerted by HQ over subsidiaries. As one of the expatriate MDs remarked, *'We are here to implement HQ policy and everything is subject to HQ labour cost control.... We have to reduce num-ber of employees if HQ wants us to do so...'*

Tensions at micro level

The two main sources of tensions or conflicts observed at micro level are dif-ferences in management style and communication approach between expatri-ate and local managers. Tensions in management style tended to stem from the power imbalance and differences in interests and previous working/international/ industry experience between expatriate and local managers. These differences influence the way expatriate managers manage local employees regarding job requirements. As Gomez and Werner (2004) argued, the experience and tenure of expatriate managers will often lead them to emulate home-country practices, that is, focusing on efficiency and adopting the HQ performance appraisal criteria regarding productivity targets. The evidence on the top expatriate management of the five subsidiaries studied is that they tended to focus on statistics rather than further discussion with subordinates. This reflects their previous experience in the Taiwanese industry and demand by HQs. The following quotes from two of the expatriate management staff seem instructive:

> *Our industry aims to achieve accuracy, efficiency, and timing. Under these critical requirements for our industry, we have to select the person who can work with us well. Then he/she can follow up the correct communication and plan to do the right thing. So, I can tell you that our strategy until now is to let local people do the implementation, you see what I mean. Then we can avoid lots of delays because of communication problems (expatriate MD).*

> *... I have to say I got lots of influence from my previous manager in Taiwan. ....I think I have very strong loyalty [to] my boss in Taiwan. I have been working in the same company in Taiwan since I graduated from university ... Characteristics of Taiwanese companies especially HQs are to demand overseas subsidiaries to achieve targets and financial figures. Normally, HQ just uses statistics/figures to ask us why we cannot achieve the set targets, monthly or annually ... then expatriate management team, especially the MD, have to explain to HQ. Obviously, we are not used to explain[ing] to local manager or employees ... because we did not get explanations from HQ ... (assistant MD).*

By contrast, British managers were prepared to spend time communicating with local employees rather than simply using statistics to push employees on job performance. Also, British managers, especially HR managers, tended to use their previous working experiences, for example, experiences in Japanese MNCs in the Midlands area, to persuade top expatriate management to adopt more host-country practices, such as more off-the-job training for management and employee levels, and pay attention to career prospects issues. Local managers, especially HR managers, generally try to enhance local employees' interests in job security and career advancement by persuading expatriate MDs to invest in training. As one of the HR managers noted:

> *Taiwanese [staff] like to do on-the-job training without qualifications (Taiwanese philosophy). ....But I asked the MD: Why don't you start to think of management training courses? Most managers and employees cannot find a job if they are laid off by the company here. Most of the rest of the managers joined the company in a junior class with lower administration skills. As we found, Comco production advisors have no formal qualifications, and found that it is difficult for these people to get jobs.*

I tried very hard to persuade two MDs to have a management training course or off-the-job training course in other professional institutions for staff here. However, they are not convinced by me on the issue of training and development.

Differences in functional background of expatriate managers and local managers also caused tensions in the way staff are managed in the UK subsidiaries. The majority of expatriate managers, especially expatriate MDs, had an IT and telecommunication degree and functional background. They, therefore, tended to be familiar with functional knowledge in the IT and telecommunications area rather than have sound management knowledge, especially in the HRM area. Consequently, expatriate managers, especially expatriate MDs, tended to use an institutionalized approach, influenced by their previous managers at HQ, in managing local staff.

There was less tension stemming from management style differences between expatriate managers and local managers in Phco. This is due to the expatriate MD having worked for many years in Europe compared to other expatriate MDs in the other four subsidiaries, which made him familiar with foreign institutional and cultural environments. In other words, the international experience of the expatriate MD at Phco helped to reduce some potential conflicts arising from lack of knowledge of how to effectively manage people in the host country, and adapt to the host-country institutional environments. The expatriate MD's management style was to let local managers have more involvement in management issues.

Tensions were observed between the top expatriate managers and local managers in relation to communicating with local employees. Top expatriate management appeared unwilling to release company strategic and financial information to local managers owing to HQs' seeming distrust of local managers and fears that research and development (R&D) information might be passed on to their competitors through local managers and employees in the UK. Other observed sources of communication-related tensions include the local actors' (especially local managers) limited 'voice' in the local subsidiary's overall decisions, both at strategic and implementation levels; and lack of opportunity to discuss or provide input on HQ targets, or challenge such issues during meetings. Faced with such limited communication opportunities, local managers, especially HR managers, tended to link up with and co-opt local employees to pursue their common interests with top expatriate management.

There were fewer tensions in communication at Phco compared to the other four subsidiaries as the majority of the management team were British nationals who were more willing to communicate. Again, the expatriate MD's attitude was an important factor in lessening tension in communication, seemingly owing to his experience in dealing with western people during his previous international work in Europe.

Conclusions

The present study has explored tensions arising from the transfer of HRM policies and practices by Taiwanese MNCs in the UK, and finds that these tensions have macro- and micro-level dimensions. While the macro-level tensions can be explained by twin pressures from home-country and host-country business systems (Kostova, 1999; Kostova and Roth, 2002), the micro-level aspects can be clarified by power and interests held by different actors, as well as variations in managerial beliefs and values and previous working experiences, including international experience held by expatriates and host-country managers. In particular, the case of the five subsidiaries indicates the value of interaction of organizational actors at micro level and reveals that local actors, especially HR managers, tend to protect their own interests by gaining power through their position and familiarity with host-country institutional environments. Indeed, HR managers are a major interest group at the subsidiary level and they perform aggressively to maintain their legacy and interests, rather than merely act as 'interpreter' of host-country institutional environments. They also strive to become 'powerful agents' by using their symbolic position and gestures to promote the interests of host-country actors that may be seeking more training and career advancement opportunities. This reflects previous findings that executives work as 'political brokers' to reflect subjective concerns for career development within MNCs (March, 1962).

Furthermore, the appearance of a micro-political phenomenon within the investigated five subsidiaries supports the power relations perspective (Ferner and Edwards, 1995), in that actors observedly use power arising from their positions to impede a full transfer of home-country management practices or adoption of host-country practices. This is particularly true in the case of Comco and Phco, whose local managers tended to use more British-style practices such as a formal communication scheme and individual performance-related pay, while expatriate managers were more likely to use home-country practices such as informal communication to secure their positions. These observed tensions suggest the need for improving communication between HQ and subsidiary and within the subsidiary operations. They also indicate that the case firms are far from meeting Nohria and Ghoshal's (1997) standard that effective multinational management will 'improve inter-functional and inter-departmental, HQ-subsidiary communication' (p. 93).

The present study evidence further suggests that the more differences there are between preferred management and communication style and the reality experienced at the subsidiary level, the more tensions there will be. Whilst the study data does not suggest either management style to be superior, it does highlight that there are very different Taiwanese and British institutionalized conceptions of what a manager should be and do. This does not deny that power relations are important sources of tensions at micro level. It rather indicates that a combination of perspectives or cross-level evidence – national business systems, power components, managerial values and previous working experiences and functional background – would offer a more viable route to understanding the issues raised by the transfer of management practices across MNCs' overseas subsidiaries.

One possible shortcoming of the study is its limited empirical base. Although the findings are not generalizable, it still sheds light on tensions from cross-level evidence and shows how subsidiary actors try to actively protect their interests under the constraints from home and host-country business systems and multiple power sources operating at the subsidiary level. Further research should investigate the transfer of HRM practices by MNCs from emerging or newly industrialized economies that operate in advanced economies with strong national business systems such as Germany. This is likely to shed further light on how subsidiary actors seek to shape or influence contrasting institutional pressures and manipulate power sources to act as influential brokers within MNCs.

References

Ackers, P. and Payne, J. (1998) 'British Trade Unions and partnership: Rhetoric, reality and strategy', *International Journal of Human Resource Management*, 9(3), 529–50.

Bacon, N. (2001) 'Employee Relations', in T. Redman and A.J. Wilkinson (eds), *Contemporary Human Resource Management* (London: Pearson Education Ltd).

Bae, J. and Lawler, J. (2000) 'Organizational and HRM strategies in Korea: Impact on firm performance in an emerging economy', *Academy of Management Journal*, 43(3), 502–17.

Bae, J., Chen, S., Tai Wai David Wan, T.W.D., Lawler, J.J. and Walumbwa, F.O. (2003) 'Human resource strategy and firm performance in Pacific Rim countries', *International Journal of Human Resource Management*, 14(8), 1308–32.

Bartlett, C. and Ghoshal, S. (1989) *Managing across Borders: The Transnational Solution*, 2nd edn (London: Century).

Becker-Ritterspach, F., Lange, K. and Lohr, K. (2002) 'Control mechanisms and patterns of reorganization in MNCs', in M. Geppert, D. Matten, K. Williams (eds) *Challenges for European Management in a Global Context: Experiences from Britain and Germany* (Basingstoke: Palgrave Macmillan).

Birkinshaw, J. and Hood, N. (1998) 'Multinational subsidiary evolution: capabilities and charter change in foreign-owned companies', *Academy of Management Review*, 23(4), 773–95.

Calof, J. and Beamish, P. (1994) 'The right attitude for international success', *Business Quarterly*, 59(1), 105–10.

Chen, M. (1995) *Asian Management Systems: Chinese, Japanese, and Korean Style of Business* (London: International Thomson Press).

Chen, S., Lawler, J. and Bae, J. (2005) 'Convergence in human resource systems: A comparison of locally owned and MNC subsidiaries in Taiwan', *Human Resource Management*, 44(3), 237–56.

Dickman, M. (2003) 'Implementing German HRM abroad: Desired, feasible, successful?' *International Journal of Human Resource Management*, 14(2), 265–83.

Edström, A. and Galbraith, J.R. (1977) 'Transfer of managers as a coordination and control strategy in multinational organizations', *Administrative Science Quarterly*, 22 (June), 248–63.

Edwards, P., Ferner, A. and Sisson, K. (1996) 'The conditions for international human resource management: two case studies', *International Journal of Human Resource Management*, 7(1), 20–40.

Edwards, T. and Ferner, A. (2004) 'Multinationals, reverse diffusion and national business systems', *Management International Review*, 44(1), 49–79.

Ferner, A. (1997) 'Country of origin effect and HRM in multinational companies', *Human Resource Management Journal*, 7(1), 19–37.

Ferner, A. and Quintanilla, J. (1998) 'Multinationals, national business systems and HRM: The enduring of national identity or a process of "Anglo-Saxonization"', *International Journal of Human Resource Management*, 9(4), 710–31.

Ferner, A.P., Colling, T. and Edwards, T. (2005) 'Policies on union representation in US multinationals in the UK: Between micro-politics and macro-institutions', *British Journal of Industrial Relations*, 43(4), 703–28.

Ferner, A., Clark, I., Colling, T., Edwards, T., Holden, L. and Muller-Camen, M. (2004) 'The dynamics of central control and subsidiary autonomy in the management of human resources: Case study evidence from US MNCs in the UK', *Organization Studies*, 25(3), 363–91.

Ferner, A.P. and Colling, T. (2005) 'Institutional theory and the cross-national transfer of employment policy: The case of "workforce diversity" in US multinationals', *Journal of International Business Studies*, 36(3), 304–21.

Ferner, A. and Edwards, T. (1995) 'Power and the diffusion of organisational change within multinational enterprises', *European Journal of Industrial Relations*, 1(2), 229–57.

Gamble, J. (2003) 'Transferring human resource practices from the United Kingdom to China: The limits and potential for convergence', *International Journal of Human Resource Management*, 14(3), 369–87.

Gomez, C. and Werner, S. (2004) 'The effect of institutional and strategic forces on management style in subsidiaries of U.S. MNCs in Mexico', *Journal of Business Research*, 57(10), 1135–45.

Guest, D. and Hoque, K. (1996) 'National ownership and HR practices in UK greenfield sites', *Human Resource Management Journal*, 6(4), 50–75.

Hall, P.A. and Soskice, D. (2001) 'An introduction to varieties of capitalism' in P.A. Hall and D. Soskice (ed.) Varieties of capitalism: The institutional foundations of competitive Advantages (Oxford: Oxford University Press).

Hamill, J. (1984) 'Labour relations decision making in multinational corporations', *Industrial Relations Journal*, 15(2), 30–34.

Harzing, A-W. (1996) 'Environment, strategy, structure, control mechanisms, and human resource management in multinational management', Focused company report doctoral research project (Maastricht: University of Limburg).

Huang, T.C. (2001) 'Human Resource Management in Taiwan', in P.S. Budwar and Y.A. Debrah (eds) *Human Resource Management in Developing Countries* (London: Routledge).

Kostova, T. (1999) 'Transnational transfer of strategic organizational practices: A contextual perspective', *Academy of Management Review*, 24(2), 308–24.

Kostova, T. and Roth, K. (2002) 'Adoption of an organizational practice by subsidiaries of multinational corporations: Institutional and relational effects', *Academy of Management Journal*, 45(6), 215–33.

Muller, M. (1999) 'Human resource management under institutional constraints: The case of Germany', *British Journal of Management*, 10(3), 31–44.

Nohria, N. and Ghoshal, S. (1997) *The Differentiated Network: Organising Multinational Corporations for Value Creation* (San Francisco: Jossey-Bass).

Paik, Y. and Sohn, G.D. (2004) 'Expatriate managers and MNC's ability to control international subsidiaries: The case of Japanese MNCs', *Journal of World Business*, 39(1), 61–71.

Quintanilla, J. and Ferner, A. (2003) 'Multinationals and human resource management: Between global convergence and national identify', *International Journal of Human Resource Management*, 14(3), 732–49.

Rosenzweig, P.M. and Nohria, N. (1994) 'Influences on human resource management practices in multinational corporations', *Journal of International Business Studies*, 25(2), 229–51.

Sambharya, R.B. (1996) 'Foreign experience of top management teams and international diversification strategies of U.S. multinational corporations', *Strategic Management Journal*, 17(9), 739–46.

Storey, J. (2001) *Human Resource Management: A Critical Text*, 2nd edn (London: Thomson).

Tayeb, M. (1998) 'Transfer of HRM practices across cultures: An American company in Scotland', *International Journal of Human Resource Management*, 9(2), 332–58.

Tempel, A. (2001) *The Cross-National Transfer of Human Resource Management Practices in German and British Multinational Companies* (Múchen/Mehring: Hampp).

Tempel, A. and Walgenbach, P. (2003) 'Global standardization of organizational forms and management practices? Combining New Institutionalism and the Business-Systems Approach', Working Paper (University of Erfurt).

UNCTAD (2006) *UN World Investment Report* (Switzerland: United Nations Publications).

Werner, S. (2002) 'Recent developments in international management research: A review of 20 top management journals', *Journal of Management*, 28(3), 277–305.

Whitley, R. (1999) *Divergent Capitalism: The Social Structuring and Change of Business Systems* (Oxford: Oxford University Press).

Whitley, R. (2001) 'How and why are international firms different? The consequences of cross-border managerial coordination for firm characteristics and behaviour', in G. Morgan, P.H. Kristensen and R. Whitley (eds) *The Multinational Firm: Organizing across Institutional and National Divides* (Oxford: Oxford University Press).

Wu, P. (2004) 'HRM in Taiwan', in P.S. Budwar (eds) *Management Human Resources in Asia-Pacific* (London: Routledge).

Yang, K.S. (1986) 'Chinese personality and its change in the psychology of the Chinese people', in M.H. Bond (eds) *The Psychology of Chinese People* (Hong Kong: Oxford University Press).

Yeung, H. W. (1999) 'Regulating investment abroad? The political economy of the regionalization of Singaporean firms', *Antipode*, 31(3), 245–73.

Yin, R. (2003) *Case Study Method: Design and Methods*, 2nd edn (London: Sage).

Yuen, E. and Kee, H.T. (1993) 'Headquarters, host-culture and organizational influences on HRM policies and practices', *Management International Review*, 33(4), 361–83.

Part II
SMEs' Resource-Related Challenges

6
Micromultinationals: Transcending Resource Challenges in International Business

Kevin Ibeh, Oliver Borchert and Colin Wheeler

Introduction

Micromultinationals (mMNEs) are a recently identified category of small- and medium-sized enterprises (SMEs) that are defined not by their speed of internationalization, as is the case with the increasingly ubiquitous 'born globals', but by their use of advanced market servicing modes in controlling and managing value-adding activities (VAA) across international markets (Dimitratos, Johnson, Slow and Young, 2003; Ibeh, Johnson, Dimitratos and Slow, 2004). This recourse to advanced foreign market servicing modes sets mMNEs apart from the other types of internationally active SMEs that dominantly employ the export modes (see Borchert and Ibeh, 2006, for typical differences between mMNEs and other types of internationalized SMEs). It also suggests that they have the ambition, strategic intent and potential to develop into more substantial international players, much in the manner of the conventional MNEs. This observed high growth potential and future impact (Dimitratos et al., 2003; Ibeh et al., 2004) may account for the growing recognition of mMNEs within the academic and research communities (Allison and Browning, 2006; Mathews and Zander, 2007). Although mMNEs share several behavioural characteristics with conventional MNEs (see Table 6.1), their limited resource position, or *liability of smallness*, typically restricts them to having a smaller degree of international value-adding activities represented by physical assets, *and to managing* and *controlling* foreign operations without necessarily *owning* these (Dimitratos et al., 2003). Stated differently, mMNEs tend to transcend size-related limitations on their global ambitions by exploring and embracing feasible strategic options, including resource-augmenting collaborations and alliances (Gomes-Casseres, 1997; Lu and Beamish, 2001). Their emergence in recent years reflects a new found resolve among smaller firms to capitalize upon the opportunities presented by the modern, global marketplace to transform themselves into more substantive international players, with greater local market presence.

Table 6.1 Typical characteristics of micromultinationals and conventional multinationals

Typical characteristics of firm type	Micromultinationals	Conventional MNEs
Firm size	Small to medium	Large
Resource base	Limited but stretchable	Strong
Pattern of internationalization	Mixed	Mostly incremental
Motives for internationalization	Various	Various
Internationalization stimulus	Typically proactive	Mixed
Use of advanced entry modes	Yes	Yes
Undertaking of value-added activities in international markets	Yes	Yes

Source: Adapted from Borchert and Ibeh (2006).

A significant body of research has accumulated regarding SMEs' engagement in foreign direct investments or use of advanced foreign market entry modes. This literature, some of whose key works are summarized in Table 6.2, can be categorized into three strands. The first relates to survey evidence and summary statistics emerging from occasional studies on the internationalization of SMEs by national and supranational organizations, including the European Commission, OECD and UNCTAD. These policy-focused studies, taken together, point to a significant level of foreign direct investment activity by SMEs. More specifically, the percentage of SMEs involved in FDI (either through subsidiaries or joint ventures) averaged ten per cent in OECD countries (OECD, 1997) and five per cent in EU countries (European Commission, 2007); the latter represents an increase from three per cent reported in a previous survey of European SMEs (European Commission, 2004). The European Commission (2007) study also reported a number of European countries (including Belgium, France, Ireland, Luxembourg, Portugal and Turkey) as having ten per cent or more of their SMEs involved in FDI. Asian SMEs seem to be doing even better, as they accounted for about ten per cent of total FDI in their region, with Korean SMEs' share of FDI rising from 16 per cent in 2000 to 37.6 per cent in 2002 (OECD, 2005).

The second strand of SMEs' FDI literature pertains to academic studies that examined one or more aspects of the international market behaviour of foreign investing SMEs without clearly identifying their focal firms as mMNEs. These studies also generally lacked sufficient details to enable the reader to verify their sample firms' status as mMNEs, that is, small- and medium-sized firms that use advanced market servicing modes in controlling and managing value-adding activities across international markets (Dimitratos et al., 2003; Ibeh et al., 2004). Previous work identified within this strand include Buckley (1989), De Maeseneire and Claeys (2007), Fujita (1997, 1998), Eden, Levitas and Martinez (1997), Kohn (1997), Lu and Beamish (2001), Beamish and Lee (2003), Manolova (2003), Kuo and Li (2003), Almor and Hashai (2004), Suh, Khan and Bae (2004)

Table 6.2 Summary of key SME-FDI research

Author(s)	Sample	Foreign market servicing modes	Theme(s)	Strand of SME-FDI literature
Almor & Hashai (2004)	52 Israeli firms	FDI	Competitive advantage	Not mMNE-specific (Strand 2)
Beamish & Lee (2003)	42 Japanese, US, Western European firms	FDI	Characteristics & performance of (Korean) subsidiaries	Not mMNE-specific (Strand 2)
Buckley (1989)	n/a (conceptual)	FDI	SME FDI	Not mMNE-specific (Strand 2)
De Maeseneire & Claeys (2007)	32 Belgian firms	FDI	Financial constraints	Not mMNE-specific (Strand 2)
Dimitratos et al. (2003)	1 Greek, 2 UK, 2 US firms	Export Contractual FDI	Profiling mMNEs	mMNE-specific (Strand 3)
Dimitratos et al. (2005)	42 Greek, 78 UK, 50 US firms	Contractual/ FDI	Differences between SME types	mMNE-specific (Strand 3)
Dimitratos et al. (2007)	15 Scottish firms	Export Contractual FDI	Core competencies of mMNEs	mMNE-specific (Strand 3)
Eden et al. (1997)	n/a (conceptual)	FDI	Technology production, transfer, spillover	Not mMNE-specific (Strand 2)
European Commission (2004)	Firms from 15 EU countries, Iceland, Liechtenstein, Norway, Switzerland (number n/a)	Exporting Contractual FDI	SME internationalization	Survey evidence & summary statistics (Strand 1)
European Commission (2007)	Firms from 27 EU countries, Iceland, Norway, Turkey (number n/a)	Contractual/FDI	Foreign business partnerships (subsidiaries/JVs)	Survey evidence & summary statistics (Strand 1)

Continued

Table 6.2 Continued

Author(s)	Sample	Foreign market servicing modes	Theme(s)	Strand of SME-FDI literature
Fujita (1998)	132 firms from 14 developed countries	Contractual/ FDI	Transnational SME characteristics, activities	Not mMNE-specific (Strand 2)
Ibeh et al. (2004)	204 Scottish firms	Export Contractual Investment	Entry mode usage of mMNEs	mMNE-specific (Strand 3)
Kirby and Kaiser (2005)	12 German, 9 UK firms	FDI	JVs in China	Not mMNE-specific (Strand 2)
Kohn (1997)	214 US firms	FDI	Foreign strategies	Not mMNE-specific (Strand 2)
Kuo & Li (2003)	143 Taiwanese firms	FDI	Decision model of SMEs' FDI	Not mMNE-specific (Strand 2)
Lu and Beamish (2001)	164 Japanese firms	Export FDI	Internationalization effects on performance	Not mMNE-specific (Strand 2)
Manolova (2003)	n/a (conceptual)	FDI	Determinants of FDI by SMEs	Not mMNE-specific (Strand 2)
OECD (1997)	Firms from OECD countries, some Asian countries (number n/a)	Export Contractual Investment	SME internationalization	Survey evidence & summary statistics (Strand 1)
OECD (2005)	Firms from OECD and other countries (number n/a)	Export Contractual Investment	SME internationalization	Survey evidence & summary statistics (Strand 1)
Suh et al. (2004)	Korean firms (number n/a)	n/a	Experiential knowledge and foreign expansion	Not mMNE-specific (Strand 2)
UNCTAD (1998)	Firms from developing Asian countries (number n/a)	FDI	SME FDI	Survey evidence & summary statistics (Strand 1)

and Kirby and Kaiser (2005). Some of these researchers have apparently sought to distinguish their FDI-using SMEs from other internationalized SMEs, by applying terms such as 'small multinationals' (Eden et al., 1997; Manolova, 2003), 'mini multinationals' (Eden et al., 1997), 'small and medium sized multinationals' (Beamish and Lee, 2003; Almor and Hashai, 2004) and 'multinational SMEs' (Suh et al., 2004).

The final strand of the SME-FDI literature encompasses research that explicitly investigated firms fitting the 'micromultinationals' definition, as outlined in the preceding paragraph. Four such studies (Dimitratos et al., 2003; Ibeh et al., 2004; Dimitratos, Hood, Johnson and Slow, 2005; and Dimitratos, Johnson and Ibeh, 2007) have been identified. They provide meaningful insights on a combined total of 394 mMNEs from different countries – see Tables 6.3 and 6.4 for summary evidence on these mMNEs' demographic characteristics, international activities and key success factors. Briefly put, this aggregate evidence suggests the investigated mMNEs as having an average of 78 employees and using a variety of investment and contractual modes to effect value-adding activities in international markets. These international markets accounted for a markedly high proportion of turnover, particularly for mMNEs from small domestic markets (Dimitratos et al., 2003; Ibeh et al., 2004). Some also undertake VA activities in over ten markets, including, one, Alpha, with presence in 40 international markets and value-adding activities in 13 of these (Dimitratos et al., 2003).

Despite their slightly different orientations, the above strands of SME-FDI literature commonly recognize and highlight the challenges associated with undertaking FDI or using advanced foreign market servicing modes by typically resource-lacking SMEs (Lu and Beamish, 2001; Suh et al., 2004). This raises the question of how these SMEs manage, in a manner of speaking, to achieve so much with so little, that is, to transcend their limited resource base to become significant international players (Almor and Hashai, 2004; Kuo and Li, 2003; Kirby and Kaiser, 2005; De Maeseneire and Claeys, 2007).

Providing a well-researched answer to the foregoing question is the *raison d'être* for the present study, which aims to investigate, using recent Canadian data, how mMNEs overcome or neutralize the effects of their limited resource position whilst undertaking FDI or related advanced entry initiatives. It is believed that greater understanding of these SMEs' behaviour would benefit policy makers aiming to increase their population of potential global players (Ibeh et al., 2004).

The remainder of the chapter is organized as follows. First, relevant literature on the main resource types is discussed replete with appropriate propositions on mMNEs' typical resource gaps, coping mechanisms and compensating advantages. This is followed by a discussion of the methodology employed in generating data on the study firms. The data pertaining to these Canadian mMNEs is then presented and discussed in the context of the stated propositions. Finally, conclusions are drawn and recommendations for future research made.

Table 6.3 Profiles of previously studied micromultinationals

	Dimitratos et al. (2003) (1 Greek; 2 UK; 2 US firms)					Ibeh et al. (2004) 204 Scottish firms	Dimitratos et al. (2005) 42 Greek; 78 UK; 50 US firms	Dimitratos et al. (2007) 15 Scottish firms
	Alpha	Beta	Gamma	Delta	Nota	All Firms	All Firms	All Firms
Country	US	US	UK	UK	Greece	Scotland	Greece, UK, US	Scotland
Sector	IT	IT	Electronics	IT	Clothing	Various	Various	Various
Primary Product(s)	Telecom solutions (hardware & software)	Database marketing software & consulting	Networked video solutions	Corporate knowledge management software	Garments & underwear	Various	Various	Various
Founded	1983	1994	1994	1994	1962	Various	Various	Various
Size								
– employees	240	70	30	40	112	60 (avg)	Small firms	75 (avg)
– revenues	US$ 81m	US$ 44m	£2m	£4m	€5m	£: various	n/a	£: various
Ratio of Int'l Sales	23% (+25% indirectly)	20–25%	95%	75%	n/a	n/a	n/a	Various (2 firms derive all sales from int'l mkts)
No. of Int'l Mkts	40+	n/a	n/a	n/a	15+	n/a	n/a	n/a
Motives for undertaking Int'l VAA*	market-seeking	market-seeking	market-seeking	market-seeking	resource & market-seeking	various	n/a	n/a
Type of Int'l VAA* Undertaken	R&D production sales service	sales (?) service (?)	sales	sales	production distribution	R&D production sales service	n/a	n/a
Advanced Modes Employed	n/a	licensing etc.	n/a	n/a	WOS	contractual FDI	n/a	contractual FDI

Note: (*VAA = value-added activities).

Table 6.4 Success factors of previously studied micromultinationals

	Dimitratos et al. (2003) (1 Greek; 2 UK; 2 US firms)					Ibeh et al. (2004) 204 Scottish firms	Dimitratos et al. (2005) 42 Greek; 78 UK; 50 US firms	Dimitratos et al. (2007) 15 Scottish firms
	Alpha	Beta	Gamma	Delta	Nota	All Firms	All Firms	All Firms
Source(s) of competitive advantage	products (leading-edge tech)	products (flexible)	products (leading edge)	n/a	products (unique, innovative, high-quality)	n/a	n/a	n/a
Mkt/product strategy	key product strategy (products designed for int'l mkts)	n/a	effective mktg strategy	focus on core technology	n/a	n/a	n/a	target mkt niches; become global players
Top Mgt Characteristics	*Founders:* IB experience; respect for technology in other countries	*Founder:* clear global vision to become int'l leader in its niche; prior IB knowl & experience; open-minded re int'l issues; *Senior Mgt:* int'l experience	*Founder:* strategic vision; experience; focus on funding; entrep mindset *Senior Mgt:* competent; clear view of the mkt	*Founder:* blind ambition; strong drive to success	*Founder & Senior Mgt:* achieve objectives in domestic & int'l mkts	n/a	n/a	proactive strategists; listen to customers; visionary leadership

Continued

91

Table 6.4 Continued

| | Dimitratos et al. (2003) (1 Greek; 2 UK; 2 US firms) | | | | | Ibeh et al. (2004) 204 Scottish firms | Dimitratos et al. (2005) 42 Greek; 78 UK; 50 US firms | Dimitratos et al. (2007) 15 Scottish firms |
	Alpha	Beta	Gamma	Delta	Nota	All Firms	All Firms	All Firms
Relationships and Networks/ Networking	strong links with OEMs (which resell products abroad); effective networking with other firms	strategic alliances & partnerships with prominent computer firms reselling its software	partnerships with prominent OEM manufacturers in US, Japan, Europe	n/a	effective networking on int'l scale	n/a	n/a	effective networking
Other Success Factors	n/a	products require little adaptation to int'l mkts	quality of & support for its personnel; regards itself as a US firm	access to capital; tech & marketing staff; seen as US firm; recognition of technical & business differences between UK & US	capable personnel	n/a	n/a	n/a

Resource types, resource gaps and micromultinationals

Conventional wisdom largely views firm size as a proxy for resource position. Based on this logic, SMEs, including mMNEs, are thought to be characterized by limited resource foundations and pervasive resource gaps (De Maeseneire and Claeys, 2007). The impressive performance of some SMEs in all sorts of markets and their increasing engagement in FDI, however, suggests that these firms may be endowed with certain resources that allow for this and which compensate for deficiencies of other resources. It seems appropriate, therefore, that instead of perpetuating the view that *SMEs equals resource poverty*, more effort is made at identifying the resources empowering an increasing number of these firms to behave in some ways like conventional MNEs (see Table 6.1) despite their limited overall resource endowments.

The growing body of empirical work on the resource-based view of the firm (RBV) indicates that the abilities of resources to generate advantage vary by their type. Studies (for example, Galbreath, 2005) suggest that intangible resources, particularly capabilities, have a greater impact on firm success than tangible resources. Consequently, capabilities, which are embedded within and need to be built by organizations since they cannot be bought easily or at all (Teece, Pisano and Shuen, 1997), are increasingly regarded as one of the most likely sources of sustainable competitive advantage (SCA), a viewpoint supported by empirical tests of the RBV (Newbert, 2007). This also appears to apply to SMEs, with the few studies that have tested the RBV in relation to these firms indicating that their SCA is based on certain capabilities and that one or more of these underpin their strategies. These include innovation capabilities (ability to develop new products and processes and achieve superior technological and/or management performance); production capabilities (ability to produce and deliver products to customers, while ensuring competitive priorities such as quality, flexibility, lead time, cost and so on); market management capability (ability to market and sell its products effectively and efficiently) (Rangone, 1999); and, in the context of firm internationalization, human capabilities (the possession of general human capital, managerial and industry know-how and an ability to acquire financial capital) (Westhead, Wright and Ucbasaran, 2001).

Other empirical, resource-based studies relating to SMEs seem to confirm the importance of these capabilities to the international development of such firms (for example, Mockaitis, Kriauciunas, Makovec and Nicolescu, 2006, in relation to production capabilities). Where intangible resources in general are concerned, these appear to affect the speed of a firm's internationalization (Rialp and Rialp, 2006). On a more general level, Ahokangas (1998) found that firms have different mechanisms by which they adjust their resource base during their international development, and points out that the boundary between internal and external resources becomes blurred as firms mobilize resources residing within their organizations and those belonging to other actors in their networks. The fact that small firms leverage strategic assets residing with other firms through idiosyncratic inter-firm collaboration or other external linkages is well known due to the efforts of network researchers and other scholars (see, for example, Chetty and Wilson, 2003; Etemad and Lee, 2003).

In view of the apparent importance of capabilities as advantage-generating resources for SMEs, it would seem logical that these and other strategic resources may be partly responsible for the impressive international performance of mMNEs. To consider this further, a more nuanced assessment should be undertaken of SMEs' standing in relation to the different resource types identified in previous literature. Such an assessment can be aided by extant taxonomies of resource types. Ibeh (2005), for example, drew upon previous effort (for example, Barney, 1991; Grant, 1991; Srivastava, Shervani and Fahey, 1998; Westhead et al., 2001; Chetty and Wilson, 2003) in classifying firm resources into 'managerial resources', 'physical resources', 'organizational resources' and 'relational resources'. These categories are broadly similar to that employed in Rialp and Rialp (2006). What follows, then, is an assessment of mMNEs' position relative to these resource types.

Managerial or human capital resources. The pertinent evidence from previous mMNE and SME-FDI research can be summarized as follows: the attributes of certain founders or top management (including strong leadership, vision, ambition, determination and international experience) are associated with better international performance; a minimum employee size threshold or critical mass tends to be needed (Withey, 1980) for a firm to commence value-adding activities internationally or to become a mMNE; and larger SMEs are more likely to engage in FDI or VA activities than their smaller counterparts (Kuo and Li, 2003; Kirby and Kaiser, 2005; European Commission, 2007). Evidence from research into other internationalized SMEs suggests that the experience of the managers drives a global mindset; and that managerial experience and a global mindset are important factors in the degree of a firm's internationalization (Reuber and Fischer, 1997; Nummela, Saarenketo and Puumalainen, 2004). SMEs typically lack human resources and managers in such firms have to alternate between managerial and operational roles due to this (Andersson and Florén, 2008). Hence:

P1(a): *mMNEs and other FDI-using SMEs tend to lack requisite human capital resources.*

P1(b): *Managerial resources possessed by mMNEs and other FDI-using SMEs tend to be crucial to their international performance.*

Physical resources. Previous mMNE and FDI-SME research suggests that physical assets – finance, plant and equipment, favourable location – are a major area of resource weakness for mMNEs and other FDI-using SMEs. Although turnover data is largely lacking for the mMNEs covered in previous research, it is instructive that the available annual revenue figures ranged from the equivalent of about four million US dollars to 81 million. This indicates a relatively limited financial base, which coupled with previously noted financial limitations experienced by SMEs in undertaking FDI and related activities (Buckley, 1989; Hollenstein, 2005;

De Maeseneire and Claeys, 2007) suggests that

P2:   *Physical capital resources are among the most challenging for mMNEs and other FDI-using SMEs.*

Organizational resources. Previous mMNE research and that relating to other internationalized SMEs (for example, Knight and Cavusgil, 2004) suggests that these firms' product offerings, including such advantage-generating aspects as product uniqueness, quality and technological content, contribute to their remarkable strides in international markets. These product-related strengths appear to compensate, in part, for a number of weaknesses, including relatively inferior capabilities in marketing (Almor and Hashai, 2004), advertising and branding. Hence

P3(a):   *mMNEs and other FDI-using SMEs tend to perform strongly on product-related capabilities.*

P3(b):   *mMNEs and other FDI-using SMEs tend to compensate for gaps in human, physical and organizational resources with their product-related capabilities.*

Relational resources. Evidence from previous mMNE research identifies the quality of the relationship ties that the mMNE forges and nurtures with key customers and other firms in the context of its international activities as a major success factor. This effective networking ability appears to assist them to plug resource gaps and develop international market activities, by leveraging assets (including market knowledge and positions) from other actors. OECD (2005) reported that among FDI-using European SMEs, 32 per cent engage in alliances and networks, mostly with larger or multinational enterprises. Further SME-FDI research also found that SMEs' collaborations with local players can be an effective strategy to overcome the deficiencies they face in resources and capabilities when they expand into international markets (Gomes-Casseres, 1997; Lu and Beamish, 2001). Hence

P4:   *mMNEs and other FDI-using SMEs tend to compensate for their human capital and physical resource gaps with their relational capabilities.*

Methodology

To shed further light on the nature of the mMNE and provide data against which propositions on this organizational category can be tested, three mMNEs based in Canada were studied as cases [1]. A qualitative approach was taken since research into mMNEs is still in its infancy. Moreover, such an approach is consistent with the 'growing trend towards qualitative methods in empirical enquiries at the marketing/entrepreneurship/internationalization interfaces' (Bell, Crick and Young, 2004, p. 30). The case study strategy was adopted as it allows for an in-depth understanding of complex phenomena, and for richly detailed, holistic and meaningful insights to be obtained (Yin, 2003). The case firms have

250 or fewer employees; are independent entities; operate in diverse industries (knowledge-intensive and traditional); and use advanced (contractual or invest- ment) modes of international market entry to control and manage one or more value-added activities in at least two countries – firms whose international VA activities are limited to the marketing and sales must have exportable manufac- tured goods or separable services. Data collection for the construction and ana- lysis of the cases was undertaken during the summer of 2005 through personal interviews and the review of published data. In-depth interviews with appropri- ate persons within the case firms, typically a key decision-maker with detailed knowledge of the historical and current international market entry mode selec- tions, were conducted either face-to-face or by telephone. The interviews were semi-structured in design to allow the interviewer to explore the issues being investigated while maintaining an element of control. An interview schedule was used to direct the flow of questions.

Published data relating to the international activities of the firms studied were reviewed separately, the sources of which included the websites of the firms them- selves, business directories and research databases covering relevant Canadian and other publications. The secondary data were gathered as necessary both before and after the interviews in order to obtain relevant contextual informa- tion and to confirm the accuracy of and supplement the data obtained through the interviews. The drawing and use of data from multiple sources supported con- struct reliability in the case studies (Riege, 2003).

Data obtained from the case studies were analysed systematically and rigor- ously. The analysis, which employed methods that have been widely accepted, was both intra-case and cross-case. Every interview was recorded and transcribed. This provided 'rich' data and enhanced the validity of the study (Maxwell, 1998). The data obtained from the interviews were supplemented with those acquired from published sources, were then reviewed, and assigned categories. Key themes and patterns were looked for, with the data having been rearranged and categor- ies redefined as necessary until clear patterns emerged. Findings from the indi- vidual case studies were then synthesized and analysed collectively to determine similarities and differences between the cases (Yin, 2003).

Findings

Details of the three Canadian mMNE case firms are summarized in Table 6.5. In line with the firms examined in previous research on mMNEs (Dimitratos et al., 2003; Ibeh et al., 2004; Dimitratos et al., 2005; and Dimitratos et al., 2007), the Canadian firms are relatively small. The firms have 23, 25 and 110 employees respectively (53 employees on average) and, in two of the three cases, a similar turnover figure of approximately C$15 million; revenue data for the third case is unavailable. Regarding their age, the firms are respectively 8, 23 and 27 years old (19 years on average). The case firms, in effect, consist of two established firms and a new venture (CanMed).

Despite their small size and limited resources, the Canadian mMNEs, like the mMNEs examined in the four aforementioned studies, have an internationalization

Table 6.5 Profiles and success factors of Canadian micromultinationals

	Case 1 (CanMat)	Case 2 (CanMed)	Case 3 (CanSoft)
Sector	Construction & industrial materials	Medical supplies	IT
Primary product(s)	Coatings, roofing, resins	Diagnostic kits	Software for mapping of earth/environ
Founded	1978	1997	1982
Size			
– employees	23	25	110
– revenue	C$15 m	C$ n/a	C$15 m
Ratio of int'l sales	70%	90%	85%
No. of int'l mkts	30	65+	150+
Motives for undertaking VAA* in int'l mkts	market-seeking	market-seeking	market-seeking
No. of int'l mkts in which VAA* undertaken	3 (China, UK, US)	1 (Netherlands)	3 (India, UK, US)
Type of VAA* undertaken in int'l mkts	production (China) marketing & sales (UK, US)	production	marketing & sales (all) service (all)
Range of advanced modes employed	equity JVs (China, UK) WOS (US)	equity JV (Netherlands)	EJV (India) WOS (UK, US)
Reasons for advanced modes	better serve customers (US); leverage partner resources (China, UK); cost/resource minimization (China, UK, US); control over marketing & sales (UK, US); control over production (China); overcome tariff barriers (China); improve chances of success (China); protect assets from possible litigation (US); be seen as US firm (US).	shorter lead times to market; control production; cost/resource minimization.	more effectively undertake VAA* activities (India, UK, US); increase and better serve distributors & end users (India, UK, US); be seen as US firm (US); develop close relations with key firms & gov't agencies (India, US); cost/resource minimization (India).
Source(s) of competitive advantage	products (global reputation for quality & innovativeness)	products (cost, quality); production capabilities.	products (few alternatives)
Mkt/product strategy	continuous product innovation	develop niche markets	enhance product value for customers

Continued

Table 6.5   Continued

	Case 1 (CanMat)	Case 2 (CanMed)	Case 3 (CanSoft)
Top management characteristics	*Founders:* industry experience; open-mindedness to different cultures; long-term views and expectations.	*Founder:* immigrant to Canada; aware of int'l mkt opportunities due to work as physician in LDCs; determined for firm to become global player.	*Top Mgt:* aware of need to pursue int'l opportunities; extensive int'l experience; intent on firm leading its field.
Relationships and networks/networking	good relations with existing distributors in China and UK resulted in EJVs with them; networking significant but not crucial.	forged relationships with local firms in int'l mkts due to lack of own commercial experience; good relationship with Dutch distributor led to EJV; founder's personal/ professional networks crucial to int'l develop & success.	Indian partner's contacts and efforts instrumental in development of S Asia; networking significant but not crucial for success.
Other success factors	all int'l business managed by firm's two founders; took advantage of booming construction markets (ME, SEA, etc.) to establish firm internationally; US customers see firm as American.	only use distributors with strong market positions, selecting them against stringent criteria and only after probationary period.	restrained itself from over-investing in int'l mkts.

Note: (*VAA = value-added activities).

profile that corresponds more to firms with substantially larger size and resource endowments. The firms clearly rely on international markets since they derive between 70 per cent and 90 per cent of their sales outside their relatively small domestic market (Canada). The number of international markets in which they are active, through exporting or more involved activities, ranged from 30 to over 150. Where VA activities are concerned, the firms carry out production (in the case of two of the three case firms), marketing and sales (ditto) and after-sales service (one firm) in a number of key international markets. Of these activities, sales and production are the most common VA activities that the firms effect internationally. They also use investment modes only, specifically equity joint ventures (EJV) and wholly owned subsidiaries (WOS), and do not resort to any form of contractual mode. The ability of these small firms to project an international presence that, at first glance, seems out of sync with their limited resources is due to the nature of their resource configuration and how these mMNEs leverage their resource mix. While they are deficient in some important resources (perhaps most basically, financial assets), they overcome this deficiency with strengths in others.

Managerial or human capital resources. In view of their size, it is not surprising that the firms are managed by a small number of individuals. In the case of CanMat (with 23 employees) and CanMed (25 employees), the two co-founders and single founder respectively still look after all aspects of the businesses, including international activities. The primary reason that these firms have not followed CanSoft (with 110 employees, the largest of the firms) in delegating responsibilities to career managers is that they cannot afford to hire such personnel; where CanSoft itself is concerned, having charged a handful of managers with its development, financial constraints mean that these managers are burdened with too many responsibilities. The need for more senior managers is most evident in the cases of CanMat and CanMed, where a lone individual manages the firms' international activities, often resulting in an inability to establish closer relations with many foreign intermediaries (distributors) and a reluctance to undertake more VA activities internationally, both requiring considerable managerial time and effort., Such over-reliance may prove costly in the event that this person is unable or unwilling to continue performing this task. This realization, perhaps, informed the following comment by the co-founder of CanMat, who single-handedly developed its business outside of North America over 24 years: *'I've got to get more people into our international business.'*

The extensive nature of international activities undertaken by the case firms suggests that the responsible individuals possess certain qualities. This is indeed the case. All of the respective individuals show a clear understanding of the importance of international markets, a determination to succeed in them (those of CanMed and CanSoft are intent on their firms being global players), and a requisite long-term perspective. These individuals also have considerable international experience and industry knowledge, primarily through their previous work. Even where their prior international experience was not substantial (for example, in the case of CanMat's co-founder), an international orientation (as illustrated by a prior interest in other countries and an understanding of cultural and other differences) is evident.

The foregoing appears to support P1(a), that human capital resources are a critical challenge for mMNEs and other FDI-using SMEs, and P1(b), that managerial resources possessed by mMNEs and other FDI-using SMEs tend to be crucial to their international performance.

Physical resources. As with smaller firms in general, the case firms have limited physical assets, particularly financial ones. The bulk of these resources are dedicated to securing product development (especially for CanSoft) and/or production capabilities (both CanMat and CanMed), which provide them with competitive advantages. The substantial investments made by the case firms in relation to such capabilities manifest themselves in products that have a competitive edge. They also manifest themselves in Canadian-based manufacturing facilities akin in size to those of much larger firms (CanMat), in facilities that are relatively small but advanced and flexible (CanMed) and in sophisticated software-design facilities staffed with highly qualified personnel (CanSoft). Such allocation of their limited physical resources has tended to constrain the ability of particular case firms to, for example, establish sole venture operations internationally (CanMed) or establish such operations in additional markets (CanMat and CanSoft). P2, that *physical capital resources are among the most challenging for mMNEs and other FDI-using SMEs, therefore, appears to be supported.*

Organizational resources. As mentioned above, the case firms' channelling of their limited physical resources into product development and/or production capabilities has resulted in their being able to offer products with a competitive edge. The firms' products have an international reputation for quality and innovativeness (particularly CanMat's), low cost (CanMed) and technical sophistication (CanSoft). They also require little adaptation for international markets; for example, CanSoft's sophisticated software products are easily customized for different geographic markets, mainly by its local distributors. Furthermore, the firms' targeting of niche or underserved product markets gives them the advantage of competing against a small number of firms and having few alternatives to their products (especially CanSoft). As well as leveraging their strong product offerings and opportune market positions, the firms also draw on other organizational resources to develop their international business. These include the high international profile associated with the use of their products in major projects (for example, CanMat's products' use in the construction of Canary Wharf in London), or by government agencies (for example, NASA's use of CanSoft's).

The foregoing suggests strong support for P3(a) and P3(b), that mMNEs and other FDI-using SMEs tend to perform strongly on product-related capabilities, and use these in compensating for gaps in human capital, physical and organizational resources.

Relational resources. The case firms' international development and market presence would have been much more limited had they not been able to leverage considerable relational resources to fill key gaps, mainly in financial and managerial capital. The involvement of other firms has been at two levels. The first has been at the principal-intermediary level, whereby the case firms forged relations with export intermediaries (principally distributors) in numerous international markets to market and sell their Canadian-made products within these. Such intermediaries were, at least in the early stages of the case firms' internationalization, often located through personal and professional contacts. Building close ties with important distributors assisted the case firms in plugging gaps in their knowledge of local markets and successfully entering numerous international markets.

The second, much more intensive level of involvement with other firms came about as a result of the case firms' appreciation of the need to undertake particular VA activities in key markets, and their realization that they could not do so on their own due to a lack of particular resources, especially physical resources (financial assets and, where production is involved, plant and equipment). The firms have overcome this challenge by collaborating with a small number of their export intermediaries with which they have close relationships. Using equity joint ventures, an investment mode of market entry, the firms have been able to secure the resources they lack to effect VA activities in some international markets (production in the case of CanMat and CanMed; marketing, sales and after-sales service in India in that of CanSoft).

There is, thus, strong support for P4, that mMNEs and other FDI-using SMEs tend to compensate for their human capital and physical resource gaps with their relational capabilities.

Discussion and implications

This paper has drawn upon recent case study data from Canada to examine mMNEs' apparent success in transcending the constraining effects of their typically low resource position and undertaking FDI or related advanced entry mode initiatives. Taking the view that these firms must possess certain compensating resource advantages to explain their internationalization behaviour, the study jettisoned the rather conventional *SMEs equal resource poverty* viewpoint in favour of a more nuanced perspective of mMNEs' resource configuration, which evaluates their position relative to each of the main resource types identified in previous literature. It emerged that the resource types mostly lacked by the investigated mMNEs were financial assets and human capital, in that order, and that the firms seemed able to compensate for these observed resource gaps with their product capabilities and relational assets. The investigated mMNEs were also boosted by certain characteristics associated with their top management team, notably international orientation, long-term focus and previous relevant experience.

These findings are interesting as they represent one of the first attempts at understanding how this group of globally ambitious SMEs fare in relation to different aspects of their resource base. Indeed, the study of mMNEs' observed ability to offset their financial and human capital resource shortcomings with appropriately fine-tuned capabilities in product innovation and development, production, relationship management and so on, represents an important lesson for other SMEs with comparably limited resource profiles. Such firms could still become substantial and impactful international players, by developing appropriate coping mechanisms and compensating resource advantages.

The foregoing has potentially significant policy implications, in terms of informing thinking and guiding action on where to channel and target external support to shore up or augment the resource positions of mMNEs and other FDI-using SMEs. For example, the observed higher susceptibility of these firms to financial resource gaps suggests the need for innovative solutions aimed at facilitating their access to investment funds. To ensure compliance with appropriate multilateral competition laws (notably those of the EU, UNCTAD and WTO), such public sector support may take the form of creating enabling conditions for the emergence, within respective home economies, of a vibrant cluster of venture capital firms, banks and related financiers that are keen to partner globally ambitious SMEs in their journey toward global impact.

Bridging or mitigating the physical resource gaps confronting mMNEs and similar SMEs could also assist with the other major challenge that they appear to face: inadequate level of human capital. The argument here is that greater access to finance could enable these firms to recruit more needed staff and give them not only critical mass but the pulling power to optimize more of the opportunities, which they would normally pass up owing to lack of capable staff. Having more requisitely qualified staff could minimize the incidence of mMNEs and similarly-minded SMEs spreading themselves too thinly and losing out on potentially transformational opportunities on the global stage.

It remains to outline some of the main contributions of the present study; these include its consolidation of previous findings from mMNE research undertaken in a number of countries; its additional set of empirical data, which adds to the limited but expanding body of empirical evidence on mMNEs; and its status as the first scholarly effort, as far as the present authors are aware, to integrate the disparate SME-FDI literature. This paper has made an important start in this lattermost direction, by identifying three distinct strands within this research stream. It is hoped that future research would build on this start, to further deepen understanding of the behaviour of SMEs that seemingly pursue growth, scale and long-lasting impact in the global arena. It is also hoped that more studies within this research stream will take the mMNE perspective in advancing the knowledge-base on FDI-using SMEs.

Note

The number of cases deemed sufficient in multiple case studies varies by study. It is not determined by a formula as in the case of sampling design, but by replication logic (Yin, 2003). In the present research, it was considered appropriate not to carry out further case studies after it was determined that the (three) case studies already undertaken sufficed for the purposes for which they were carried out.

References

Ahokangas, P. (1998) *Internationalization and Resources: An Analysis of Processes in Nordic SMEs*, PhD thesis, University of Vaasa, Finland; published as Acta Wasaensia, No. 64.

Allison, M.A. and Browning, S. (2006) 'Competing in the cauldron of the global economy: tools, processes, case studies, and theories supporting economic development', *International Journal of Technology Management*, 33(2/3), 130–43.

Almor, T. and Hashai, N. (2004) 'The competitive advantage and strategic configuration of knowledge-intensive, small- and medium-sized multinationals: A modified resource-based view', *Journal of International Management*, 10(4), 479–500.

Andersson, S. and Florén, H. (2008) 'Exploring managerial behavior in small international firms', *Journal of Small Business and Enterprise Development*, 15(1), 31–50.

Barney, J.B. (1991) 'Firm resources and sustained competitive advantage', *Journal of Management*, 17(1), 99–120.

Beamish, P.W. and Lee, C. (2003) 'The characteristics and performance of affiliates of small and medium-size multinational enterprises in an emerging market', *Journal of International Entrepreneurship*, 1(1), 121–34.

Bell, J., Crick, D. and Young, S. (2004) 'Small firm internationalization and business strategy: An exploratory study of "knowledge-intensive" and "traditional" manufacturing firms in the UK', *International Small Business Journal*, 22(1), 23–56.

Borchert, O. and Ibeh, K.I.N. (2006) 'Micromultinationals and their international market entry mode selection: Further insights from Canada', in *Regional and National Drivers of Business Location and Competitiveness*, Proceedings of the 32nd Annual Conference of the European International Business Academy (EIBA), Fribourg, Switzerland, 7–9 December.

Buckley, P.J. (1989) 'Foreign direct investment by small- and medium-sized enterprises: The theoretical background', *Small Business Economics*, 1(2), 89–100.

Chetty, S. and Wilson, H.M. (2003) 'Collaborating with competitors to acquire resources', *International Business Review*, 12(1), 61–81.

De Maeseneire, W. and Claeys, T. (2007) 'SMEs, FDI and financial constraints', Vlerick Leuven Gent Management School Working Paper Series, No. 2007–25; retrieved 2 January, 2008 from http://ideas.repec.org/p/vlg/vlgwps/2007-25.html.

Dimitratos, P., Hood, N., Johnson, J. and Slow, J. (2005) 'Reframing international entrepreneurship: Insights from a three-country study', in E. J. Morgan and F. Fai (eds), *Innovation, Change and Competition in International Business*, Proceedings of the 32nd Annual Conference of the Academy of International Business (AIB) UK Chapter, Bath, England, 8–9 April (Bath: University of Bath).

Dimitratos, P., Johnson, J. and Ibeh, K.I.N. (2007) 'Core competencies of micromultinationals: Evidence from Scotland', Paper presented at the 10th McGill International Entrepreneurship Conference, University of California at Los Angeles, 27–29 September.

Dimitratos, P., Johnson, J., Slow, J. and Young, S. (2003) 'Micromultinationals: New types of firms for the global competitive landscape', *European Management Journal*, 21(2), 164–74.

Eden, L., Levitas, E. and Martinez, R.J. (1997) 'The Production, transfer and spillover of technology: Comparing large and small multinationals as technology producers', *Small Business Economics*, 9(1), 53–66.

Etemad, H. and Lee, Y. (2003) 'The knowledge network of international entrepreneurship: Theory and evidence', *Small Business Economics*, 20(1), 5–23.

European Commission (2004) *Internationalization of SMEs*, Observatory of European SMEs series (No. 4, 2003), Luxembourg: Office for Official Publications of the European Communities.

European Commission (2007) *Observatory of European SMEs – Analytical Report*, published as Flash Eurobarometer No. 196; retrieved 05 January, 2008 from http://ec.europa.eu/enterprise/enterprise_policy/analysis/observatory_en.htm.

Fujita, M. (1997) 'Small and medium-sized enterprises in foreign direct investment', in P.J. Buckley et al. (eds) *International Technology Transfer by Small and Medium-Sized Enterprises: Country Studies*, 9–70 (Basingstoke: Macmillan).

Fujita, M. (1998) *The Transnational Activities of Small and Medium-Sized Enterprises* (Boston: Kluwer Academic Publishers).

Galbreath, J. (2005) 'Which resources matter the most to firm success? An exploratory study of resource based theory', *Technovation*, 25(9), 979–987.

Gomes-Casseres, B. (1997) 'Alliance strategies of small firms', *Small Business Economics*, 9(1), 33–44.

Grant, R.M. (1991) 'The Resource-Based Theory of Competitive Advantage: Implications for Strategy Formulation', *California Management Review*, 33(3), 114–35.

Hollenstein, H. (2005) 'Determinants of international activities: Are SMEs different?' *Small Business Economics*, 24(5), 431–50.

Ibeh, K.I.N. (2005) 'Toward a greater level of international entrepreneurship among agribusiness firms: Resource levers and strategic options', *Management International Review*, 45(3, Special Issue), 59–81.

Ibeh, K.I.N., Johnson, J.E., Dimitratos, P. and Slow, J. (2004) 'Micromultinationals: Some preliminary evidence on an emergent "Star" of the International Entrepreneurship Field', *Journal of International Entrepreneurship*, 2(4), 289–303.

Kirby, D.A. and Kaiser, S. (2005) 'SME foreign direct investment: An examination of the joint venture experiences of German and U.K. small and medium sized Firms in China', *International Entrepreneurship and Management Journal*, 1(1), 83–104.

Knight, G.A. and Cavusgil, S.T. (2004) 'Innovation, organizational capabilities, and the Born-Global firm', *Journal of International Business Studies*, 35(2), 124–41.

Kohn, T.O. (1997) 'Small firms as international players', *Small Business Economics*, 9(1), 45–51.

Kuo, H.-C. and Li, Y. (2003) 'A dynamic decision model of SMEs' FDI', *Small Business Economics*, 20(3), 219–31.

Lu, J.W. and Beamish, P.W. (2001) 'The internationalization and performance of SMEs', *Strategic Management Journal*, 22(6), 565–86.

Manolova, T.S. (2003) 'Small multinationals in global competition: An industry perspective', in H. Etemad and R. Wright (eds), *Globalization and Entrepreneurship: Policy and Strategy Perspectives*, 59–81 (Cheltenham: Edward Elgar).

Mathews, J.A. and Zander, I. (2007) 'The international entrepreneurial dynamics of accelerated internationalization', *Journal of International Business Studies*, 38(3), 387–403.

Maxwell, J.A. (1998) 'Designing a qualitative study', in L. Bickman and D.J. Rog (eds), *Handbook of Applied Social Research Methods*, 69–100 (London: Sage Publications).

Mockaitis, A.I., Kriauciunas, A.P., Makovec, M. and Nicolescu, L. (2006) 'An investigation into the capabilities that influence the internationalization of Central and Eastern European SMEs', in *Regional and National Drivers of Business Location and Competitiveness*, Proceedings of the 32nd Annual Conference of the European International Business Academy (EIBA), Fribourg, Switzerland, 7–9 December.

Newbert, S.L. (2007) 'Empirical research on the resource-based view of the firm: An assessment and suggestions for future research', *Strategic Management Journal*, 28(2), 121–46.

Nummela, N., Saarenketo, S. and Puumalainen, K. (2004) 'A global mindset – A prerequisite for successful internationalization?' *Canadian Journal of Administrative Sciences*, 21(1), 51–64.

OECD (1997) *Globalization and Small and Medium Enterprises (SMEs)*, Vol. 1 (Paris: OECD).

OECD (2005) *OECD SME and Entrepreneurship Outlook 2005* (Paris: OECD).

Rangone, A. (1999) 'A resource-based approach to strategy analysis in small-medium sized enterprises', *Small Business Economics*, 12(3), 233–48.

Reuber, A.R. and Fischer, E. (1997) 'The influence of the management team's international experience on the internationalization behaviors of SMEs', *Journal of International Business Studies*, 28(4), 807–25.

Rialp, A. and Rialp, J. (2006) 'Faster and more successful exporters: An exploratory study of born global firms from the resource-based view', *Journal of Euromarketing*, 16(1/2), 71–86.

Riege, A.M. (2003) 'Validity and reliability tests in case study research: A literature review with "hands-on" applications for each research phase', *Qualitative Market Research: An International Journal*, 6(2), 75–86.

Srivastava, R.K., Shervani, T.A. and Fahey, L. (1998) 'Market-based assets and shareholder value: A framework for analysis', *Journal of Marketing*, 62(1), 2–18.

Suh, T., Khan, O.J. and Bae, M. (2004) 'Experiential knowledge of multinational SMEs and their perceived attractiveness of foreign expansion: A Korean context', in W.L. Cron and G.S. Low (eds), *AMA Winter Educators' Conference*, American Marketing Association, 15, 231–32 (Chicago, IL: The American Marketing Association).

Teece, D.J., Pisano, G. and Shuen, A. (1997) 'Dynamic capabilities and strategic management', *Strategic Management Journal*, 18(7), 509–33.

UNCTAD (1998) *Handbook on Foreign Direct Investment by Small and Medium sized Enterprises: Lessons from Asia*, Geneva: United Nations publications, Sales No. E.98.II.D.4.

Westhead, P., Wright, M. and Ucbasaran, D. (2001) 'The internationalization of new and small firms: A resource-based view', *Journal of Business Venturing*, 16(4), 333–58.

Withey, J.J. (1980) 'Differences between exporters and non-exporters: Some hypotheses concerning small manufacturing business', *American Journal of Small Business*, 4(3), 29–37.

Yin, R.K. (2003) *Case Study Research: Design and Methods*, 3rd edn (Thousand Oaks, CA: Sage Publications).

7
Survival and Failure of Born Globals: The Case of Software Firms

Mika Gabrielsson and Peter Gabrielsson

Introduction

Scholarly interest in the survival of born globals has increased quite recently (Sapienza et al., 2006; Mudambi and Zahra, 2007). This aspect is important since only those that survive can benefit their national economies. As they move toward 'adulthood', born globals face three risks: (a) they do not succeed in growing beyond their initial phase and hence become more like traditional internationalizing firms; (b) they run into financial problems and are acquired by a larger firm; or (c) they go bankrupt. Hence, the objective of this chapter is to understand (i) what born globals become after their early international growth period and (ii) the extent to which this trajectory is influenced by the age at which the foreign business began, and the resources, capabilities and lateral rigidity of the firm and its founder.

Literature review

The growth of born globals has so far been the central theme of most born global research (Rialp et al., 2005). However, only few researchers have measured or been concerned about the extent to which the born global firm grows beyond the initial export phase to become a 'grown-up' global firm. Researchers from Europe, in particular, have noted that some born international firms internationalize rapidly within Europe, but do not globalize to other continents to any great extent. Others have, nonetheless, observed 'true born globals' that achieve global growth (Madsen and Servais, 1997; Luostarinen and Gabrielsson, 2006).

As noted by Zahra (2005), we know very little about either the survival of new international ventures or what becomes of those new international ventures that are established. This is important, as we do know that new international ventures are disadvantaged with regard to two liabilities that influence their survival. First, with regard to their foreign local competitors, they suffer from the liability of foreignness (Zaheer and Mosakowski, 1997) and with regard to already established firms, they experience the liability of newness (Stinchcombe, 1965). Hence, it is not surprising that earlier research has recognized that accelerated

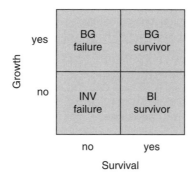

Figure 7.1   Born global trajectories

internationalization involves significant risks and, thus, requires risk management with respect to foreign revenue exposure, country risk and entry mode commitment within the portfolio of markets entered (Shrader et al., 2000). When we consider these risks against the growth options for stage-wise internationalizing versus simultaneous expansion to regions across the world, we can understand that the survival/failure rates may vary depending on which of those growth strategies are chosen.

The born globals can be seen to have four different trajectories – see Figure 7.1. The born global that survives is one that seeks to operate in regions across the world and does so successfully. The firm that settles for lesser growth is either traditional or born international, depending on whether the foreign business is initiated soon after foundation or later. The mere fact that a new venture has survived does not mean that it can be regarded as an overall success. We cannot classify a firm as a successful born global if it sets out to conquer the world, and then after an initial period of growth has to withdraw from all markets except nearby ones and its home market. It has failed when the original vision and mission are compared with the actual results. Nevertheless, if the home region has been conquered it can be regarded as a successful born international (BI). Another scenario comprises firms that are bought over by other firms. They can be considered either successful or unsuccessful born globals depending on whether selling out was the initial objective of the founders. Finally, there are the outright failures. An international new venture (INV) failure is one where the firm has not yet grown globally and has already failed in its initial internationalization efforts. In contrast, a firm that has initially succeeded in global growth, but then failed and gone into bankruptcy can be regarded as a born global failure.

Theoretical framework

The theoretical framework consists of antecedent factors, and survival and growth outcomes – see Figure 7.2. Earlier research has recognized a number of factors important for the survival and growth of born globals (for example, Mudambi and Zahra, 2007). These can be grouped into industry factors and firm factors.

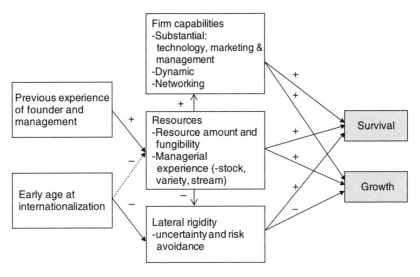

Figure 7.2 Framework for survival and growth of born globals

With regard to industry factors, industry growth (Hennart and Park, 1993), penetration by foreign firms and seller concentration in an industry (Driffield and Munday, 1997) can be expected to significantly influence a born global's survival (Mudambi and Zahra, 2007). In this study we are more interested in firm characteristics, the above industry factors have been controlled by focusing on a single industry, in this case software firms.

Firm factors that are important when survival and growth are concerned include age at initiation of foreign business (Autio et al., 2000); resources consisting of managerial experience (Reuber and Fischer, 1999; Eriksson et al., 2000); resource fungibility (that is, 'the attributes of the resources that allow or inhibit their deployment for alternative uses') (Sapienza et al., 2006, p. 916); different types of capabilities (Teece et al., 1997) and finally the lateral rigidity of decision-makers (Luostarinen, 1979). The antecedent factors are not expected to influence survival and growth to the same extent. These two key outcomes have proved to be conceptually distinct, and their empirical relationships are far from clear (see for example, Romanelli, 1989; Delmar et al., 2003; Sapienza et al., 2006). Hence, there is a need for a better understanding of their relationships.

Resources

The resource-based view originating from Penrose (1959) and Wernerfelt (1984) is useful in relation to the survival and growth of born globals. Research on resources has typically focused on the impact of resource abundance on survival and growth, the criterion of valuable resources, and the role of managerial experience. Research evidence on the impact of resource abundance on growth and survival is, however, mixed. Although most researchers usually argue that an abundance of resources is necessary for survival and growth (Hannan, 1998; Laanti et al., 2007), some assert that they can also cause problems (Autio et al., 2000). According to the resource-based approach, resources must meet four conditions. They must be useful in exploiting opportunities or neutralizing threats, they must be rare among the firm's current and potential competition, they must be imperfectly imitable, and they cannot be replaced by another resource (Barney, 1991). However, in the often volatile environment of born globals, no resource can be valuable for long unless it is constantly enhanced and deployed in the most efficient way (Hannan, 1998). Accordingly, Sapienza et al. (2006) assert that resource fungibility, the extent to which resources may be deployed for alternative uses at low cost, is more important.

In assessing the role of managerial experience in international growth and success, it is important to distinguish between stock, variety and stream (Reuber and Fischer, 1999). According to these scholars, the former refers to the experience that the founder or manager has when entering the firm and the latter to the subsequent routine or non-routine learning that takes place and which benefits the firm. In addition, it is important to consider the breath and depth of the experience, or in other words its variety.

Firm capabilities

In the born global firms, the capability to have a critical effect on performance has been noted (Knight and Cavusgil, 2004). The difference between resources and capabilities is that the latter aim at deploying and co-ordinating different resources (Verona, 1999). Barney (1991) emphasizes that a firm must have capabilities to obtain a sustained competitive advantage by implementing strategies that utilize their internal strengths in responding to environmental opportunities, while at the same time neutralizing external threats and avoiding internal weaknesses. Capabilities can be of a substantive or dynamic nature. We follow Winter (2003) and Zahra et al. (2006) in distinguishing between substantive and dynamic capabilities. Substantive capability refers to sets of abilities that enable solving a problem or achieving an outcome, whereas dynamic capabilities refer to a higher-level ability to change or reconfigure existing substantive capabilities. Based on the above, we regard as substantive capabilities: (i) technological capabilities; (ii) marketing capabilities; and (iii) management capabilities (Verona, 1999). In contrast, dynamic capabilities (see for example, Teece et al. 1997) can be seen as the firm's ability to integrate, build and reconfigure internal and external competences to address rapidly changing environments.

On top of the substantive and dynamic capabilities, a third capability type is essential for born globals: that is, networking capability. Since the born global start-up suffers from resource limitations compared with the need to reach world markets (Oviatt and McDougall, 1994), it must often network with larger established firms (Gabrielsson and Kirpalani, 2004). By interacting with international network actors and developing relationships, they can exploit and enhance their own resources and gain the benefits of those of others (Cook & Emerson, 1978; Ford et al., 1998). Hence, born globals can globalize their activities by using their activity links, resource ties and actor bonds (Håkansson and Snehota, 1995). However, this is not possible without networking capability (Mort and Weerawardena, 2006).

Lateral rigidity in decision-making

It can be expected that the survival and growth of a born global is closely related to the outcomes of its decision-making. The stage-wise internationalization model (Johanson and Vahlne, 1977; Luostarinen, 1979) builds on the behavioural theory of the firm (Cyert and March, 1963), which describes the firm's decision-making as having a number of conflicting goals, being short-term oriented, seeking simple-minded decisions and learning. A central characteristic of the company's decision-making is lateral rigidity, meaning that companies try to stick to their plans, and even when faced with an impulse or shock they make only small changes in their behaviour (Vaivio, 1963). Luostarinen (1979) argues that the internationalization of firms is especially characterized by a laterally rigid decision-making process, in which companies are rigid in a lateral direction towards new alternatives, but are elastic forwards towards known alternatives (Tan et al., 2007). In other words, the lateral rigidity enhances the probability of the survival of the firm by suggesting a risk-cautious path, but eventually decreases growth in the international market.

How then do born globals grow rapidly and also survive? Autio et al. (2000) argue that firms that are relatively young when they internationalize benefit from the learning advantages of newness, which is due to the fact that they adopt more novel approaches to internationalization. These young firms have fewer routines and simpler decision-making, and their propensity to seek opportunities and new information is also higher. However, according to Autio et al. (2000), these qualities decrease with age and the incentive and ability to pursue growth outside home markets decreases the longer the firm waits to internationalize. This behaviour is compatible with the laterally rigid decision-making described earlier for established firms if the age of the born globals is seen to moderate lateral rigidity. Innovative born global entrepreneurs may be less rigid and also possess previous experience that lowers the lateral rigidity that would otherwise prevail. Hence, the younger the firm is at first international entry, the lesser the lateral rigidity in decision-making and the higher the probability of growth. However, as illustrated in Figure 7.2, when lateral rigidity is low due to youth the odds for survival also decrease.

Propositions

Born global growth

The resource-based view (Penrose, 1959; Wernerfelt, 1984; Barney, 1991) guides us to suggest that the resources play a critical role in the growth of born globals. Since these firms often suffer from resource limitations (Oviatt and McDougall, 1994), the amount of resources (Hannan, 1998), resource fungibility (Sapienza et al., 2006) and managerial experience in terms of stock, stream (Reuber and Fischer, 1999) and variety (Eriksson et al., 2000) become central. Resources do not, however, provide growth for the born global firm if it does not possess capabilities for deploying and co-ordinating the different resources (Verona, 1999). Based on earlier research it may be asserted that long term growth can be achieved only if these capabilities are of a substantive (technology, marketing, management) and dynamic nature (Zahra et al., 2006). However, the founders and management should be experienced enough so that the firm does not suffer from lateral rigidity in decision-making (Luostarinen, 1979), which may limit the search for growth alternatives and steer the firm towards known alternatives. Also, if they internationalize early on they may benefit from the learning advantage of newness, through simpler decision-making, good information flow and novel approaches to internationalization. Hence, the following can be postulated:

Proposition 1: Born global growth is positively related to the amount of managerial experience and resources, the resource fungibility, the existence of substantive and dynamic capabilities and a low level of lateral rigidity in decision-making.

Born global survival

When a born global enters foreign markets it needs to create routines and to adapt to them (Sapienza et al., 2006); this requires substantial investment (Zott, 2003). These investments can be expected to be particularly high for born globals due to the liability of foreignness (Zaheer and Mosakowski, 1997) and the liability of newness (Stinchcombe, 1965). Hence, Sapienza et al. (2006) propose with respect to born globals that internationalization decreases survival following international market entry. Resources and capabilities play a central role. For instance, in the short term, born globals can secure their survival if their capabilities are adequate for obtaining financing such as venture capital (Gabrielsson et al., 2004) or other endowments from, for example, the founders (Hannan, 1998), although in the longer term accelerated internationalization will still involve significant risks (Shrader et al., 2000). This is particularly what the stage-wise internationalization model (Johanson and Vahlne, 1977; Luostarinen, 1979) told us. It is less risky to advance following the stages model than to jump over stages. We also assert that in the case of born globals, the more lateral rigidity (Luostarinen, 1979) there is in decision-making the higher the probability of survival. The changes in decision-making that come with aging (Autio et al., 2000) would indicate that lateral rigidity may increase as a firm ages and, thus, born globals face the greatest risk of failure in their initial internationalization efforts. Hence, we propose as follows.

Proposition 2: Born global survival is positively related to the amount of managerial experience and resources, the resource fungibility, the existence of substantive and dynamic capabilities and a high level of lateral rigidity in decision-making.

Born global survival and growth

Under what conditions do born globals have the highest probability of both rapid growth and survival? From propositions 1 and 2 it seems that this may be difficult since growth and survival call for a different type of decision-making. The existence of lateral rigidity (Luostarinen, 1979) improves the odds of survival but restricts growth, and vice versa. Based on earlier research, the capabilities of the firm play a central role, and particularly the networking capabilities (Mort and Weerawardena, 2006). Networks increase the growth rate of born globals by helping them to identify international opportunities and establish credibility (Reuber and Fischer, 2005) that often lead to strategic alliances and other co-operative strategies (Oviatt and McDougall, 2005). Furthermore, born globals can globalize their activities without making large investments and facing unnecessary risk by using their activity links, resource ties and actor bonds (see also Håkansson and Snehota, 1995). It has been suggested that SMEs build networks in a strategic manner to fill resource and knowledge gaps at various firm stages (Loane and Bell, 2006). Hence, the capability to network and exploit and enhance their own resources is crucial (Cook and Emerson, 1978; Ford et al, 1998; Gabrielsson and Kirpalani, 2004) if born globals are to gain the benefits of established players and grow successfully. Hence, we postulate the following:

Proposition 3: Born global survival and growth is positively related to high networking capabilities.

Methodology and case descriptions

This research is a multiple case study (Yin, 2003) based on in-depth interviews of five Finnish software born globals. The five case companies were chosen on the basis of recommendations by Miles and Huberman (1984), Eisenhardt (1989) and Yin (2003) for research extending existing theories by being typical representatives of the population rather than emerging through random selection. In studies working on small samples, such as case studies, the objective is to select informative and typical cases rather than to obtain a statistical representation of the total population (Ghauri et al., 1995; Stake, 2000; Saunders et al., 2003; Silverman, 2005). The purpose of the case study in this research is mainly to generalize back to theory, not to population (Yin, 2003).

The case companies selected also meet Oviatt and McDougall's (1994) definition of a born global company mentioned in the introduction section, and they all met the following criteria: the company was Finnish; it had a clear global vision from its inception; and it started its international activities early, within 3 years of establishment (Knight and Cavusgil, 1996). Finland is an especially interesting country in which to study the globalization of wireless technology born globals since it is a small and open economy and is a forerunner in internet and mobile software. The companies were selected to match the four different quadrants of Figure 7.1 as follows:

- *INV Failure firms* that achieved some international sales, *albeit* mostly with their home continent (external share <25 per cent), and then went bankrupt. The case representing this group was Wapit.

- *BG Failure firms* that achieved foreign sales both within their own continent and outside of it (external share >25 per cent), but then went bankrupt. The case selected to represent this group was Riot Entertainment.
- *Born International Survivor*, which achieved foreign sales mainly within their home continent (external share <25 per cent). The cases that represent this group were Small Planet and Cidercone.
- *Born Global Survivor*, which achieved foreign sales both within their own continent and outside it (external share >25 per cent) and are still growing well (annually over 100 per cent). The case representing this group was Sulake.

Most of the primary data for the analysis were collected from in-depth interviews of the CEOs and/or entrepreneurs/founders of the case companies. Besides the authors of this paper, the project involved several researchers who gathered the data (Rinkinen, 2000; Koskimies, 2005; Näkkäläjärvi, 2005; Hotakainen, 2007). The interviews were recorded and the database was created to help maintain the planned case study protocol and to ensure validity. The interviews were semi-structured, starting with open questions. Moreover, financial data, company presentations, product definitions and news releases were used to provide support. A short description of the cases will follow. Table 7.1 indicates key information of the case firms.

Table 7.1   Case descriptions

Case firm	Product	Establ. year	First intern. activ.	Current internat. degree	Other remarks
Wapit (INV Failure)	Internet and mobile phone software and services	1998	2000	Only limited foreign sales. Bankrupt in year 2001	120 employees (at the most).
Riot Entertainment (BG Failure)	Wireless entertainment developer and publisher (software and services)	2000	2000	90% foreign sales in first year (most of that outside Europe) Bankrupt in year 2002	120 employees (at the most), 60 on average.
Small Planet (BI Survivor)	Content management solutions for existing messaging and data infrastructures (software and service)	1998	2000	60% foreign sales. (Europe: 48%, Outside Europe: 12%) (year 2006)	15 employees (year 2006). High growth firm which downsized their operations in year 2003, but has recovered from that

Continued

Table 7.1   Continued

Case firm	Product	Establ. year	First intern. activ.	Current internat. degree	Other remarks
Cidercone (BI Survivor)	Wireless and web-based solutions for mobile workers (software and services)	2000	2003	30–50% foreign sales (mainly Europe) (year 2006)	90 employees (year 2006); 5 years growth rate 2086% (2001–2005)
Sulake (BG Survivor)	Interactive entertainment; Habbo hotel online game (software and service)	2000	2001	Out of 14 million Euros turnover in 2004 app. 90% foreign sales. (Europe: 70%; USA and Japan: 20%). Recently the global growth has intensified and it fulfils the 25% criteria set for sales external to Europe	300 employees (year 2007); 5 years growth rate 8095% (2001–2005)

Source: Compiled by the authors from the individual case descriptions (Rinkinen, 2000; Koskimies, 2005; Näkkäläjärvi, 2005; Hotakainen, 2007).

Cross case analysis

Early internationalization and experience

All of the born globals examined in this study had a technological innovation in a global niche business area (see also Madsen and Servais, 1997; Karagozoglu and Lindell, 1998). The contribution of innovative products in the successful globalization of born globals seems to be extremely important (Laanti et al., 2007). The case firms were all very young when they undertook their first international activity. Interestingly, those firms that reached global status took the least time to begin their first international sales activity: in the case of Riot Entertainment within the first year of existence and in case of Sulake during the first year after foundation. The time to start internationalization was only somewhat longer in the cases of the two born internationals, Small Planet (2 years) and Cidercone (3 years). The above-mentioned Riot Entertainment, which engaged immediately in international business, was also one of those that went bankrupt.

We also noted that the founders of the examined case firms were not particularly experienced in either international business or in establishing firms. This is consistent with some of the earlier studies (Luostarinen and Gabrielsson, 2004), which found that entrepreneurs of born global companies are young and technologically competent, but have little international business experience. Typically, the founders had work experience that had brought them technological knowledge, but usually lacked international management and marketing experience. With the exception of the founder of Riot Entertainment (who had a degree in business) and one of the founders of Cidercone (who had attended some training), none of them seemed to have had any business education. However, some of the firms had early on been able to bring in experience by involving knowledgeable investors. This was the situation in Wapit and Sulake. To conclude, contrary to some earlier research suggestions, the importance of earlier business experience on the part of the founders was not found to be an important factor in explaining the growth or success of the examined born global firms (Madsen and Servais, 1997).

Entering international or global markets was the objective of all of the examined firms right from inception or soon thereafter. Also, their international and global expansion was extremely rapid, although, the case firms mainly focused on establishment of sales offices abroad and not production facilities. This is consistent with some of the earlier findings in which born globals have favoured sales subsidiaries over production subsidiaries (Laanti et al., 2007). It seems that the most global firms – Sulake and Riot Entertainment – had effectively used marketing co-operation with global firms to their advantage (Gabrielsson and Kirpalani, 2004). Furthermore, both of the firms were dependent on online sales via the Internet (Singh and Kundu, 2002), which presumably reduced psychic distance (Yamin and Sinkovics, 2006). However, they differed in the way that Sulake effectively used Internet-based sales revenues to back up their establishment of sales offices, whereas Riot Entertainment seemed to rapidly establish offices in anticipation of sales revenues which, however, did not meet their expectations.

Resources, capabilities and lateral rigidity

The examined case firms varied to a great extent with regard to the resources they had to finance their growth. Wapit, Riot Entertainment and Sulake had based their rapid international growth heavily on venture capital funding. The failure to gather money in the second round of financing was decisive for Wapit and Riot Entertainment, whereas Sulake was able to extend its venture capital funding from domestic sources to international and even global sources. Two of the case firms, namely Small Planet and Cidercone, had proceeded differently. Small Planet decided after the initial period to change its growth model from fast growth financed by venture capital to revenue-based growth and Cidercone has from the beginning relied on extremely fast growth based on revenues. One can conclude that the results support the earlier research asserting that an important barrier for small companies wishing to globalize has been their limited financial resources (Buckley, 1989; Luostarinen and Welch, 1990). However, the results also indicate that it is no guarantee for success, and actually suggest that the survival is better guaranteed if the growth model is revenue-based, as was the case in Small Planet and Cidercone (Arenius, 2002). The study results also confirmed earlier research findings that in addition to founders and banks, government subsidies, private investors such as business angels, venture capital, initial public offerings and strategic investors such as big corporations could be important financing sources (Acs et al., 2001; Gabrielsson et al., 2004; Laanti et al., 2007).

The firm capabilities, however, seem to be the most important factor contributing to the survival and growth trajectories of born globals. Despite their high innovativeness and creativeness, the two failed firms Wapit and Riot Entertainment had severe weaknesses in their international marketing and management capabilities. They were able to create a technically fascinating product, which did not, however result in actual customer acceptance and sales revenues. Innovation capability has been found to be fundamental for achieving a competitive advantage in global markets (Madsen and Servais, 1997; Karagozoglu and Lindell, 1998), although, it seems that customer orientation and marketing capabilities are the crucial factors. Small Planet and Cidercone were highly customer-oriented and cited this as their key capability. This was also true of Sulake. It seems that all of the examined firms had good networking capabilities. This is consistent with earlier research, which has shown that networks can offer a way to surpass the resource limitations usually facing start-up companies (Baum et al., 2000). However, it seems that networking capability without customer and marketing capability is not enough, as Wapit and Riot Entertainment illustrated. This is probably why earlier research has found that marketing capabilities should seldom be externalized, and are better kept in house (Hashai and Almor, 2004).

With regards to lateral rigidity, we found that the firms were surprisingly innovative and ready to pursue new avenues and were not particularly rigid in their decision-making. However, the interviews with the entrepreneurs that had gone bankrupt, such as Wapit and Riot Entertainment, revealed that perhaps a change in their strategy toward a more revenue-driven model and temporal change in their resource base, exemplified by Small Planet, could have saved them. This finding is consistent with the assertion that resource fungibility (Sapienza et al., 2006) and low lateral rigidity in decisions (Luostarinen, 1979) may be crucial to the success of born global firms.

Examination of the propositions

Proposition 1 seems to have received strong support based on Tables 7.2 and 7.3. Indeed, the resources of the firms in terms of finance, employees and their experience were found to be important. Clearly, the firms that have rapidly globalized such as Riot Entertainment and Sulake had, at least in the early phase, a better situation resource-wise than for instance Small Planet and Cidercone. Also, the study found evidence that growth requires strong substantial capabilities not only in technology, but also in international marketing and management. This is logical, since resources (Penrose, 1959; Wernerfelt, 1984; Barney, 1991) are unlikely to provide successful growth for the born global firm without necessary capabilities (Verona, 1999). The learning advantages of newness, which result from low lateral rigidity (Luostarinen, 1979) in decision-making

Table 7.2 Founders and their experience and the early internationalization

Case firm	Founder/s and their experience	Vision	International market entries	International operation strategy
Wapit (INV Failure firms)	Founders a Finnish musician and an internet expert. The business experience was brought by a major owner of an international Finnish ICT firm, who acted as a business angel.	The company had a global vision. It had a plan to enter all lead markets with its Internet and mobile services.	It obtained a major Finnish telecom operator customer and was able to inter-nationalize within 2 years of establishment by first co-operating with Nokia and then on its own to Singapore, the Philippines, the USA and many other countries.	Headquartered in Helsinki, Finland. It had a sales office in Singapore and was planning to establish offices in Great Britain and America. The business model was based on franchising the service to telecom operators.
Riot Entertainment (BG Failure firms)	The CEO had a Master's degree in Business administration and the other founders are former entrepreneurs. Nokia Ventures joined in financing the firm during the first year of operation.	A global vision from inception. According to their mission statement, 'We don't make games, we create riots'.	The first foreign market entered within one year was Asia, then Europe (the UK, Italy, Germany and France) and the USA.	Headquartered in Helsinki, Finland. It had sales offices in Singapore, Manila, London, Paris, Berlin, Rome and Los Angeles. Marketing co-operation with global partners such as the Fox film studios. The actual service was downloadable via the Internet.
Small Planet (BI Survivor)	The founders CEO and COO did not have any prior international business experience of establishing a company. Neither did they have business degrees.	The company initially did not have a global vision, but very shortly after the inception they realized that the Finnish market was too small.	They internationalized within 2 years of foundation to the UK and Sweden. They globalized within the 4th and 5th year to Far East Asia and South America. Currently, their emphasis is on Scandinavian market, South America and the Middle-East.	Headquartered in Helsinki, Finland. Sales office in USA and present also in Russia via a subsidiary firm.

Continued

Table 7.2 Continued

Case firm	Founder/s and their experience	Vision	International market entries	International operation strategy
Cidercone (BI Survivor)	Founder and CEO did not have international business or entrepreneurial experience. He had, however, experience from working earlier in technology companies and had participated in management courses.	A vision from the beginning to internationalize their operations. There were not enough large customers in Finland in the niche segment that require work solutions for remote mobile workers.	Internationalization started within the 3rd year in France and Switzerland. Currently operates all over central Europe, especially in Scandinavia, and the UK. Global activities in the USA, South Africa and Australia.	Headquartered in Helsinki, Finland. Sales offices in Nice in France, and in Frankfurt in Germany. In markets external to Europe they operate via intermediaries.
Sulake (BG Survivor)	Founded by two persons and a Finnish Advertising agency Taivas Group. The founders previously worked in the Finnish new media company Satama as a programmer and graphic designer, respectively.	Vision to become a world class interactive entertainment company, which has a broad range of products. Earning logic based on selling virtual goods, furniture and equipment with which to decorate the game enthusiasts' virtual rooms.	Internationalization started within 1 year, globalization within 3 years. Market entries first to the UK, Switzerland, then Japan, Australia, Canada and the USA. Currently present in 31 countries on all five continents.	Habbo Hotel is a system that can only be accessed via the Internet. However, sales subsidiaries have been established worldwide to retain control and to be close to customers. The marketing is carried out by global channel partners based on revenue sharing.

Source: Compiled by the authors from the individual case descriptions (Rinkinen, 2000; Koskimies, 2005; Näkkäläjärvi, 2005; Hotakainen, 2007).

Table 7.3 Resources, capabilities and lateral rigidity

Case firm	Resources	Firm capabilities	Lateral rigidity
Wapit (INV Failure firms)	The founder and managing director of the early phase was replaced in end of 1999 with a former Chief Financial Officer and member of the Board of Directors of Nokia. Also, other experienced persons were employed. The critical resource was financing, which they first obtained from the founders and from an English investment bank. However, they were unable to get financing for the second round in 2001.	The firm was among the first in the world to offer WAP services. The R&D although innovative was too ambitious and lacked a clear focus. Also, it seems that the marketing capabilities were not adequate and hence the revenue income was too slow. The market expansion, for instance to Asia and many other countries, was too rapid and became a major cost burden. They had difficulties in finding the right customers, that is operators, and to manage the alliance partners.	The firm was not laterally rigid, but innovative and ready to experiment new things. The major problem was the excessive R&D and market expansion expenditure which was not evened out with revenues. They were rigid and did not adjust these R&D resources to match the changed conditions.
Riot Entertainment (BG Failure firms)	The management was innovative, but business-wise inexperienced. They also spent the money received in financing from Nokia Ventures Capital Fund and Softbank UK Ventures, Carlyle and others carelessly. It seems that personnel were increased too rapidly and without quality concern.	There were severe weaknesses in the substantial technology, marketing and management capabilities. The technology was delayed and not working properly. The networking skills seemed good as they were able to negotiate exclusive wireless interactive game rights to Fox film studios, and to co-brand effectively by leveraging the resources of MNCs.	The lateral rigidity was very low at the time of founding the firm. The entrepreneurs were young people, who had personally experienced the mobile lifestyle. The entrepreneurs promised the financers more than their firm was able to deliver. They were unable to adjust to changed conditions.
Small Planet (BI Survivor)	The firm has restructured themselves from the venture-capital-driven growth model to revenue-dependent growth. Only	The key substantial capabilities are related to understanding what their customers as well as end-users want from mobile services. The technology	The firm was able to change their business model from the high venture-capital-driven model to a more revenue-based

Continued

119

Table 7.3 Continued

Case firm	Resources	Firm capabilities	Lateral rigidity
	3 out of 15 employees do non-technical work. In the beginning of 2004 an American investment company made a strategic investment.	allows them to use product platforms from which they can offer slightly adapted products very efficiently. Consultants and channel members are important network partners and compensate for some of the shortcuts they have in their organization.	model. This reflects a low level of lateral rigidity.
Cidercone (BI Survivor)	The firm has been relying on organic growth and has not used venture capitalists or other investors. Out of 90 persons 20 work in R&D.	The substantial capabilities are in technology and in developing products that meet better the customer's needs than their competitors. External networks have been useful overall, but rather for receiving market information than for internationalization.	The firm has been able to stay flexible and use the available opportunities efficiently.
Sulake (BG Survivor)	Sulake has funded its growth with the initial investment by Taivas corporation and debt, followed up by both domestic and foreign (US/UK) venture capital. The firm has become profitable. The personnel have expanded extremely rapidly.	The substantial capabilities seem to lie in the innovativeness of the founders and personnel. The Habbo Hotel service concept combines an interactive communication platform with attractive pixel graphics. Also, Sulake has shown capabilities to network in their marketing with their channel partners such as Coca-cola, T-Online and MSN.	Extremely innovative firm that is far from laterally rigid in their behaviour.

Source: Compiled by the authors from the individual case descriptions (Rinkinen, 2000; Koskimies, 2005; Näkkäläjärvi, 2005; Hotakainen, 2007).

and resource fungibility (Sapienza et al., 2006) were associated with the high growth firms.

With regard to survival, it seems that proposition 2 was only partly supported. The amounts of resources were found to be important, but it seems that also with regards to survival the capabilities are much more critical. Tables 7.2 and 7.3 show that the capabilities of Small Planet, Cidercone and Sulake were stronger than in those of Wapit or Riot Entertainment. Furthermore, all of the cases internationalized at an early stage and benefited from the learning advantages of newness indicated by Autio et al. (2000). The cases deviated, however, in the sense that contrary to our expectations, they seemed more likely to survive with lower lateral rigidity, not higher (Luostarinen, 1979), and higher resource fungibility (Sapienza et al., 2006) and other dynamic capabilities (Teece et al., 1997). Wapit and Riot Entertainment were not flexible enough to change their growth model when the circumstances required such a response, and hence failed. This indicates that the flexible, creative and open-minded search for alternatives is important not only during the introductory phase of the born global, but also during the growth and mature phases.

Based on the evidence presented in Table 7.3, support was only partially found for proposition 3. Although the born global case Sulake, which had grown rapidly and also been successful, had co-operated with large MNCs in their marketing and shown relatively high networking capabilities, the same was true of Riot Entertainment, which went bankrupt. Hence, we conclude that whilst networks or networking capabilities (Cook and Emerson, 1978; Håkansson and Snehota, 1995; Ford et al., 1998) may reduce risk and increase the growth rate of born globals (Oviatt and McDougall, 2005), especially when they involve large MNCs (Gabrielsson and Kirpalani, 2004), they will not guarantee survival without customer understanding and marketing capabilities.

Conclusions

Previous born global research has focused extensively on the early phases of new international ventures (Oviatt and McDougall, 1994). This chapter deals with the question of what these firms become when they grow up by looking at their survival and failure (Sapienza et al, 2006). It presents a matrix that illustrates the four different trajectories of born globals. The research suggests that these trajectories cannot be explained by relying only on the age at internationalization (Autio et al., 2000), managerial experience and resource fungibility (Sapienza et al., 2006) and the extent of substantive and dynamic capabilities (Zahra et al., 2006). A fourth construct becomes important, the extent of lateral rigidity in the decision-making (Luostarinen, 1979) of these firms. The chapter suggests that in order to reduce globalization-related costs and the risk of failure, it is necessary for born globals to leverage the resources of network actors (Cook and Emerson, 1978; Ford et al., 1998; Gabrielsson and Kirpalani, 2004). Although network capabilities were found to be important they do not eliminate the need to develop substantial capabilities with regard to customer understanding and marketing.

The novelty of this study is its examination of the trajectories of born globals as they become adult. It, therefore, contributes to the newly emerging research stream focused on the survival of born globals (Sapienza et al., 2006; Mudambi and Zahra, 2007). In addition to depicting the trajectories of born globals, the study examines propositions regarding the relationship between the antecedents and the trajectories; this can be seen as an important contribution. Managers can also learn from the results of this study. They need to assess their resources, capabilities and nature of decision-making and select a growth strategy that will generate optimal growth, whilst also taking the risk of failure into account. Moreover, active development of network and marketing capabilities may facilitate growth and increase the odds of survival.

There are many interesting avenues for future study. Clearly, the survival and failure trajectories need to be further researched to improve understanding of the actual phases that born globals go through and the capabilities that facilitate their simultaneous survival and growth.

References

Acs, Z.J., Randall, M.K. and Yeung, B. (2001) 'Entrepreneurship, globalization, and public policy', *Journal of International Management*, 7(3), 235–51.

Arenius, P. (2002) '*Creation of Firm-level Social Capital, Its Exploitation, and the Process of Early Internationalization*'. Doctoral Dissertation, Helsinki University of Technology: Helsinki.

Autio, E. Sapienza, H.J. and Almeida, J.G. (2000) 'Effects of age at entry, knowledge intensity, and imitability on international growth', *Academy of Management Journal*, 43, 909–24.

Barney, J. (1991) 'Firm resources and sustained competitive advantage', *Journal of Management*, 17(1), 99–120.

Baum, J.A.C, Calabrese, T. and Silverman, B.S. (2000) 'Don't go alone: alliance network composition and startups' performance in Canadian biotechnology'. *Strategic Management Journal*, 21(3), 267–94.

Buckley, P.J. (1989) 'Foreign direct investment by small- and medium-sized enterprises: The theoretical background', *Small Business Economics*, 1, 89–100.

Cook, K.S. and Emerson, R.M. (1978) 'Power, Equity and Commitment in Exchange Networks', *American Sociological Review*, 3(5), 721–39.

Delmar, F., Davidsson, P. and Gartner, W.B. (2003) 'Arriving at the high-growth firm', *Journal of Business Venturing*, 18, 189–216.

Driffield, N. and Munday, M (1997) 'Industrial performance, agglomeration and foreign manufacturing investment in the UK', *Journal of International Business Studies*, 31(1), 21–37.

Eisenhardt, K. (1989) 'Building theories from case study research', *Academy of Management Review*, 14 (4), 532–50.

Eriksson, K., Johanson, J., Majkgård, A. and Sharma, D.D (2000) 'Effects of variation on knowledge accumulation in the internationalization process', *International Studies of Management and Organization*, 30(1), 26–44.

Ford, D., Gadde, L.-E., Håkansson, H., Lundgren, A., Snehota, I., Turnbull, P. and Wilson, D. (1998) *Managing Business Relationships* (New York, NY: John Wiley & Sons, Inc.).

Gabrielsson, M. and Kirpalani, V.H.M. (2004) 'Born globals: How to reach new business space rapidly', *International Business Review*, 13(5), 555–71.

Gabrielsson, M., Sasi, V. and Darling, J. (2004) 'Finance strategies of rapidly-growing Finnish SMEs: Born internationals and born globals', *European Business Review*, 5(6), 590–604.

Ghauri, P., Gronhaug, K. and Kristiansund, I. (1995) *Research Methods in Business Studies: a Practical Guide* (Hemel Hempstead: Prentice Hall).

Håkansson, H. and Snehota, I. (1995) *Developing Relationships in Business Networks* (London: Routledge).

Hannan, M. (1998) 'Rethinking age dependence in organizational mortality: Logical formalizations', *American Journal of Sociology*, 104, 126–64.

Hashai, N. and Almor, T. (2004) 'Gradually internationalizing "born global" firms: An oxymoron?' *International Business Review*, 13(4), 465–83.

Hennart, J-F. and Park, Y.R. (1993) 'Greenfield vs acquisition: the strategy of Japanese investors in the United States', *Management Science*, 39(9), 1054–70.

Hotakainen, M. (2007) *'The Resources and Core Competencies Enabling Rapid Internationalization of Knowledge-Intensive Born Globals'*, Helsinki School of Economics, Master's Thesis.

Johanson, J. and Vahlne, J.-E. (1977) 'The internationalization process of the firm – A model of knowledge development and increasing foreign market commitments', *Journal of International Business Studies*, 8(1), 23–32.

Karagozoglu, N. and Lindell, M. (1998) 'Internationalization of Small and Medium-sized Technology-based Firms: An Exploratory Study', *Journal of Small Business Management*, 36(1), 44–59.

Knight, G.A. and Cavusgil, S.T. (1996) 'The Born Global Firm: A challenge to traditional internationalization theory', in Cavusgil, S.T. (ed.), *Advances in International Marketing*, 8, 11–26 (Greenwich, CT: JAI Press).

Knight, G.A. and Cavusgil, S.T. (2004) 'Innovation, organizational capabilities, and the born-global firm', *Journal of International Business Studies*, 35, 124–41.

Koskimies, N. (2005) *'Failures of Finnish Born Global Companies'*, Helsinki School of Economics, Master's Thesis.

Laanti, R., Gabrielsson, M. and Gabrielsson, P. (2007) 'The globalization strategies of business-to-business born global firms in the wireless technology industry', *Industrial Marketing Management*, 36(8), 1104–17.

Loane, S. and Bell, J. (2006) 'Rapid internationalization among entrepreneurial firms in Australia, Canada, Ireland and New Zealand: An extension to the network approach', *International Marketing Review*, 23(5), 467–85.

Luostarinen, R. (1979) *'Internationalization of the Firm'*. Doctorate dissertation, Helsinki School of Economics, Finland.

Luostarinen, R. and Welch, L. (1990) *International Business Operations* (Kyriiri: Helsinki).

Luostarinen, R. and Gabrielsson, M. (2004) 'Finnish perspectives of international entrepreneurships', in L.P. Dana (eds) *Handbook of Research on International Entrepreneurship* (Cheltenham: Edward Elgar).

Luostarinen, R. and Gabrielsson, M. (2006) 'Globalization and marketing strategies of Born Globals in SMOPECs', *Thunderbird International Business Review*, 48(6), 773–801.

Madsen, T. and Servais, P. (1997) 'The internationalization of Born Globals-An evolutionary process', *International Business Review*, 6(6), 1–14.

Mort, G.S. and Weerewardena, J. (2006) 'Networking capability and international entrepreneurship: How networks function in Australian born global firms', *International Marketing Review*, 23(5), 549–72.

Miles, M.B. and Huberman, M.A. (1984) *Qualitative Data Analysis: A Sourcebook of New Methods* (Newbury Park: SAGE Publications Inc.).

Mudambi, R. and Zahra, S. (2007) 'The survival of international new ventures', *Journal of International Business Studies*, 38(2), 333–52.

Näkkäläjärvi, P. (2005) *'Finnish Born Globals: Financing of internationalisation'*. Helsinki School of Economics, Master's Thesis.

Oviatt, B.M. and McDougall, P.P. (1994) 'Toward a Theory of International New Ventures', *Journal of International Business Studies*, 25(1), 45–64.

Oviatt, B.M and McDougall, P.P. (2005) 'Defining international entrepreneurship and modeling the speed of internationalization', *Entrepreneurship Theory and Practice*, 29(5), 537–53.

Penrose, E. (1959) *The Theory of the Growth of the Firm* (Oxford: Oxford University Press).

Reuber, A.R. and Fischer, E. (1999) 'Understanding the consequences of founders' experience', *Journal of Small Business Management* (April), 30–45.

Reuber, A.R. and Fischer, E. (2005) 'The company you keep: How young firms in different competitive contexts signal reputation through their customers', *Entrepreneurship: Theory & Practice*, 29(1), 57–78.

Rialp, A., Rialp, J. and Knight, G.A. (2005) 'The phenomenon of early internationalizing firms: what do we know after a decade (1993–2003) of scientific inquiry?' *International Business Review*, 14(2), 147–66.

Rinkinen, L. (2000) *'Born Global: Globalisation Strategies of Small and Medium-Sized High-Quality Service Companies'*. Helsinki School of Economics, Master's Thesis.

Romanelli, E. (1989) 'Environments and strategies of organization start-up: Effects on early survival', *Administrative Science Quarterly*, 34, 369–87.

Sapienza, H.J., Autio, E., George, G. and Zahra, S. (2006) 'A capabilities perspective on the effects of early internationalization on firm survival and growth', *Academy of Management Review*, 31(4), 914–33.

Saunders, M., Lewis, P. and Thornhill, A. (2003) *Research Methods for Business Students*, 2nd edn (Harlow: Pearson Education Limited).

Shrader, R., Oviatt, B.M. and McDougall, P.P. (2000) 'How new ventures exploit trade-offs among international risk factors: Lessons for the accelerated internationalization of the 21st century', *Academy of Management Journal*, 43(6), 1227–47.

Silverman, D. (2005) *Doing Qualitative Research* (London: Sage Publications Ltd).

Singh, N. and Kundu, S. (2002) 'Explaining the growth of e-commerce corporations (eccs): An extension and application of the eclectic paradigm', *Journal of International Business Studies*, 33(4), 679–97.

Stake, R. (2000) 'Case Studies', in N. Denzin and Y. Lincoln (eds) *Handbook of Qualitative Research* (Cheltenham: Edward Elgar).

Stinchcombe, A.L. (1965) 'Social Structure and Organizations', in J. March (ed.) *Handbook of Organizations*, 142–93 (Chicago, IL: Rand McNally).

Tan, A., Brewer, P. and Liesch, P.W. (2007) 'Before the first export decision: Internationalisation readiness in the pre-export phase', *International Business Review*, 16, 294–309.

Teece, D.J., Pisano, G. and Shuen, A. (1997) 'Dynamic capabilities and strategic management', *Strategic Management Journal*, 18(7), 509–33.

Vaivio, F. (1963) 'Sivusuuntainen jäykkyys yrityksen käyttäytymispiirteenä', *The Journal of Business Economics*, 269–82.

Verona, G. (1999) 'A Resource-Based view of Product Development', *Academy of Management Review*, 24(1), 132–42.

Wernerfelt, B. (1984) 'A Resource-based View of the Firm', *Strategic Management Journal*, 5, 171–80.

Winter, S.G. (2003) 'Understanding dynamic capabilities', *Strategic Management Journal*, 24, 991–96.

Yamin, M. and Sinkovics, R.R. (2006) 'Online internationalisation, psychic distance reduction and the virtuality trap', *International Business Review*, 15(4), 339–60.

Yin, R. (2003) *Case Study Research: Design and Methods*, 3rd edn (Thousand Oaks, California: Sage Publications).

Zaheer, S. and Mosakowski, E. (1997) 'The dynamics of the liability of foreignness: A global study of survival in financial services', *Strategic Management Journal*, 18(6), 439–64.

Zahra, S.A. (2005) 'A theory of international new ventures: A decade of research', *Journal of International Business Studies*, 36, 20–28.

Zahra, S.A., Sapienza, H.J. and Davidsson, P. (2006) 'Entrepreneurship and Dynamic Capabilities: A Review, Model and Research Agenda', *Journal of Management studies,* 43(4), 917–55.

Zott, C. (2003) 'Dynamic capabilities and the emergence of intraindustry differential firm performance: Insights from a simulation study', *Strategic Management Journal,* 24, 726–43.

8
The Challenge of Accelerated International Growth: A Focus on Winners and Losers in the Finnish Software Sector

Niina Nummela, Sami Saarenketo, Jussi Hätönen and Mika Ruokonen

Introduction

Internationalization can be defined as a growth process that is tightly intertwined with the company's other activities. However, during the last decade we have witnessed clear acceleration in this process, as the time span in all areas of business development has shortened. It is not surprising, therefore, that researchers have also started to emphasize the temporal dimension of internationalization (Hurmerinta-Peltomäki, 2003; Jones and Coviello, 2005; Zucchella, Palamara and Denicolai, 2007).

Time is also the key element distinguishing earlier studies on SME internationalization from the more recent research on international entrepreneurship (Jones and Coviello, 2005). The focus in this emergent field of research at the interface of international business and entrepreneurship is on the accelerated internationalization of new ventures (Jones and Coviello, 2005; Rialp, Rialp and Knight, 2005). The international growth of these companies may follow any of several routes, and the growth patterns vary a great deal (Aspelund, Madsen and Moen, 2007). This is particularly true of knowledge-intensive firms operating in volatile high-tech markets (Jones, 1999; Crick and Spence, 2005).

Knowledge-intensive firms are interesting as study objects in that they face specific challenges in their international growth. They typically engage in work of an intellectual nature, carried out for the most part by well-educated, qualified employees (Starbuck, 1992; Alvesson, 2000). Furthermore, these companies claim to produce valuable products and/or services (Alvesson, 2000). Software firms, together with life-science and consultancy companies, for example, are often regarded as typical examples of knowledge-intensive firms.

This study describes the initial steps in the rapid international growth of Finnish software firms. It investigates such growth in terms of success and failure, and particular emphasis is placed on the challenges that they encounter during the

126

process. It should be noted that the focus of the study is predominantly on the rapidity of international growth,[1] and rapidly internationalizing firms include both international new ventures and so-called 'born-again globals'.[2]

Successful international growth – what is it?

Internationalization is rather often seen as one type of company growth. This notion can be traced to Ansoff's (1965) four primary strategies for growth, one of which is market development: in other words, a company actively seeks growth by entering new markets with its current products. The concept of growth has been somewhat neglected in the literature on SME internationalization. Early studies emphasizing the incremental nature of the phenomenon (Johanson and Vahlne, 1977; Luostarinen, 1979) included the concept of growth only implicitly, whereas later on the authors more clearly coupled internationalization with organizational growth and learning (Vahlne and Nordström, 1993).

Although the field of international business has somewhat neglected the aspect of growth of small firms, it is a relatively well-researched area in the context of entrepreneurship. Recent studies have supported the assumption that there is no single route to growth, and that there are several alternative but slightly overlapping strategies (Delmar, Davidsson and Gartner, 2003). As Yli-Renko, Autio and Tontii (2002) suggest, we assume that organic growth is the most feasible option for knowledge-intensive small firms. However, for SMEs even organic growth is not achieved in isolation, but it often requires resources and support from the company's network. We should also keep in mind the fact that organic growth is not a unidimensional concept, and knowledge-intensive firms can take various routes to international markets.

For decades, researchers in the field of entrepreneurship have been trying to understand the determinants of growth and profitability. However, the findings of empirical studies are slightly contradictory (Liao and Welsch, 2003), not least because of the use of various, often unidimensional measures of growth (Delmar et al., 2003). Empirical studies have also highlighted the fact that small firms are by no means a homogeneous, growth-oriented group – as many theoretical approaches assume – and in fact, the majority of them are neither entrepreneurial nor growth-oriented (Davidsson, 1989; Liao and Welsch, 2003; Heinonen, 2006). For these reasons it is crucial to make explicit what we mean by successful international growth.

The question of how to distinguish successful from unsuccessful international growth is intriguing. In general, the former could be defined as the achievement of desired, planned or attempted growth in international markets. In other words, the achieved international growth should be compared with the performance targets that companies presumably set for their international activities (Bernardino and Jones, 2003). However, the operationalization of success in this context is not quite straightforward.

Previous studies (Katsikeas, Leonidou and Morgan, 2000; Leonidou, Katsikeas and Samiee, 2002) have commonly measured international success in terms of indicators or proxies of the export or sales ratio and of the number of export markets. Accelerated internationalization probably requires other types of measures, however, (Moen and Servais, 2002); for example, the speed of internationalization might be an appropriate quantitative alternative (Aspelund et al., 2007). Then again, traditional growth measures such as ROI are questionable in this context (McDougall and Oviatt, 1996). Nevertheless, obtaining objective information may be difficult, and in practice researchers often have to rely on the subjective judgements of key persons. Particularly in the case of studying failures in retrospect, objective information may be scarce. Additionally, it has even been argued that subjective measures of performance and profitability may provide more meaningful information in the context of SMEs (Spanos and Lioukas, 2001).

Given the exploratory nature of this study, we thought a rather broad definition of successful international growth would be appropriate. It would allow us to include multiple growth patterns in the analysis, and to take better account of the company- and context-specific features that may have an impact on the process. Although accelerated international growth is a huge challenge for SMEs, and mere survival could be considered proof that the greatest hurdles have been overcome, in our opinion that does not yet verify that the company is successful. We rather suggest that successful international growth is something that is demonstrated not only in developing plans for internationalization but also through accumulated sales from international markets.

Earlier studies have examined the differences between successful and unsuccessful new ventures in knowledge-intensive settings too. Successful ventures appear to follow multiple patterns of strategic behaviour; that is, performance was superior when two or more strategies were used in concert (Kakati, 2003). It should also be noted that the development of new technology or products does not in itself guarantee commercial success for firms operating in high-tech industries. Instead, technological expertise needs to be balanced against business skills and capabilities. It is also suggested in the literature (Berry, 1996) that technology-based firms must go through a (sometimes radical) transformation of management philosophy. The business has to change its primarily inward orientation focused upon technical inventiveness towards an outward orientation, meaning that the management/entrepreneur increasingly devotes attention to the needs of customers and the market. This echoes the findings of McDougall and Oviatt (1996), who argue that only the INVs that are capable of strategic change would remain profitable.

Challenges in the rapid international growth of knowledge-intensive firms

We have chosen the dynamic and technology-driven software industry as our context in the empirical part of this study. It is an industry in which rapid international growth could be considered a necessity, not a strategic choice. Consequently, these companies encounter major challenges in their internationalization.

There has been increasing interest in knowledge-intensive firms in the recent literature on international business. The attention stems from the fact that their international growth patterns seem to be very different compared with those of non/less knowledge-intensive firms (Crick and Spence, 2005). For example, we know from earlier research that knowledge-intensive firms often:

- adopt an international if not a global focus from the beginning due to the rapid obsolescence of their offerings (Preece, Miles and Baetz, 1999; Bernardino and Jones, 2003);
- base their internationalization on an entrepreneurial culture, opportunistic strategies and short-term goals somewhat in conflict with what was proposed in the stages models of internationalization (Crick and Spence, 2005);
- lack a strong industry structure and a long history, but have the 'learning advantages of newness' and are thus quick to learn to adapt to changing environments: this may be more important than the (domestic) knowledge acquired earlier, which could result in overly rigid and slow decision-making and path dependency (Autio, Sapienza and Almeida, 2000);
- rely strongly upon networks (especially at the beginning) to speed the internationalization process as partner networks facilitate the acquisition of experiential knowledge about the foreign markets (Bell, 1995; Coviello and Munro, 1995, 1997; Madsen and Servais, 1997; Bernardino and Jones, 2003).

So far our knowledge of the outcomes of rapid international growth is limited (Zahra, 2005) and our understanding of how companies react to growth-related challenges is as yet insufficient. This study therefore focuses on the underlying forces that have led some knowledge-intensive software firms down a successful path to international markets, but have set others on a more disastrous course. We are particularly interested, as suggested by Aspelund et al. (2007), in how the strategic decisions made during the internationalization process influence the further development of the firm.

Strategic decisions and accelerated internationalization

Rapid internationalization is not an objective as such and most, if not all, internationalizing companies aim at sustainable and profitable international growth. Among knowledge-intensive firms rapid international growth is often considered to be the consequence of a deliberate, planned strategy. However, this is not always the case because management teams anticipate and react to internal and external factors differently (Crick and Spence, 2005). All in all, the role of the entrepreneur or management team is decisive in the strategy process (Andersson, 2000). Additionally, variation in international marketing strategies may be due to the founding process of the firm, organizational factors and environmental conditions (Aspelund et al., 2007).

The choice of country and entry mode could be considered as key strategic decisions in the firm's internationalization (Andersen, 1993, 1997) and these two decisions are strongly intertwined in SMEs (Papadopoulos, 1987). It has often been argued that knowledge-intensive firms tend to initiate their internationalization in lead markets and when these become saturated expand to other countries (Rialp et al., 2005). However, according to Crick and Jones (2000), rapidly internationalizing firms often utilize a two-phase strategy in their market selection: first, market-spreading in order to identify opportunities globally and then focusing their resources on selected, most promising markets.

On the other hand, researchers appear to agree that in order to reduce resource constraints and the risks involved, rapidly internationalizing firms choose low-commitment entry modes (Aspelund et al., 2007). This is in line with the findings of Mullins and Forlani (2005) that high-growth successful companies are very risk-averse, particularly when investing their own money. After all, later change of entry mode may be costly, risky and laborious (Pedersen, Petersen and Benito, 2002; Petersen and Welch, 2002). It may be that the use of networks in the selection of entry mode and market (Crick and Jones, 2000; Moen, Gavlen and Endresen, 2004; Crick and Spence, 2005) is an attempt to decrease the risk related to these decisions. In this respect, rapidly internationalizing firms do not seem to differ significantly from firms that internationalize at a slower pace. This is probably due to the fact that the choice of entry mode reflects the company's resources and capabilities, which need to be adjusted if it is to pursue its growth strategy (Bernardino and Jones, 2003).

No decisions are made in a vacuum: in other words, the industry context is also of importance (see, for example, Johanson and Mattsson, 1988; Boter and Holmqvist, 1996). The chosen strategy should fit the context in which the company operates (Andersson, 2004). Knowledge-intensive firms often operate in nascent industries in which there is so far no direct competition. On the other hand, these industries are also quite fast moving and volatile, which often requires speedy adaptation and decision-making (Eisenhardt and Brown, 1998; Autio et al., 2000; Crick and Spence, 2005). Therefore, in order to be successful the companies should select strategies that are flexible and support constant opportunity recognition from the environment.

Research design

This study investigates the accelerated internationalization of Finnish software companies. In order to capture the factors affecting the growth process we chose a case-study approach. As a research strategy this allows inductive, in-depth investigation of the research topic, analysis of the phenomenon in its contextual setting and more holistic coverage of the companies selected (Ghauri, 2004). In order to minimize the effects of environmental and situational factors we limited the number of cases to six Finnish software-development companies. The selection of cases is a crucial decision in the research process and should therefore be made after careful consideration and a critical evaluation of the alternatives. Random selection is neither necessary nor desirable, and theoretical sampling is recommended (Eisenhardt and Graebner, 2007). This involves choosing cases that are likely to replicate or extend the emergent theory (Eisenhardt, 1989). The theoretical qualifications of the case also have to be kept in mind, in other words how well they fit the conceptual categories and the extent of their explanatory power (Eisenhardt, 1989; Smith, 1991).

Besides being Finnish software developers, all the case companies shared the following characteristics:

- after initiation, the internationalization process proceeded rapidly;
- they could be labelled growth companies;[3]
- their internationalization took place in the early 2000s.

Because of the significance of the context in the decision-making we considered the timing of internationalization particularly important as it could have a significant impact on the company's success or failure. Additionally, as our intention was to identify drivers of success, we included companies with diverse histories.

In line with the recommendations of Huber and Power (1985) we gathered the data for the research in face-to-face interviews with the most knowledgeable informants available, in other words the key decision-makers (CEOs, directors) in the case companies. We considered these people key informants because international growth reflects company strategy, which is based on their decisions. The persons involved in the internationalization were willing to speak about their experiences, which increased the validity of the study. However, in order to preserve the anonymity of the informants, the case companies were disguised (they are given fictional names in the case descriptions, for example).

The data obtained was further analysed in several phases (Yin, 1994). First, the interview recordings were transcribed and a within-case analysis of each company was conducted (Eisenhardt, 1989). Consequently, the information from the interviews was reorganized to form descriptive narratives, which helped us to identify the key events and the background of each case. We then augmented the interview data with some additional information available from databases and company websites. The internationalization of each case company was described as a critical-event analysis in terms of its internationalization activities, strategy and market development. Finally, we included a cross-case comparison in order to reveal the similarities and differences between the companies.

The internationalization of the case companies

MobileAd

MobileAd is a small Finnish software company providing solutions to enable and ease advertising in mobile terminals. It was founded in 2000 by a group of internationally experienced employees of a mobile-handset manufacturer. The aim of the business was to provide a standardized marketing-campaign management platform for mobile telecom operators – a novel business area in which there was practically no competition at the time. When it started the internationalization process its product was still in the development phase. However, the potential for international market development seemed very favourable in general terms. On the basis of the country-level information and initial feedback received from some potential target customers, the company started developing direct sales channels simultaneously in the UK, the US and Germany, which it considered the leading markets for its solutions (Figure 8.1). At this point the management team did not consider it necessary to conduct an in-depth study of the needs of its target customers, or of their acceptance of the new innovation, since the founders believed they understood the market given their previous work experience. The foreign sales offices were staffed with personnel from the home country, and a few local sales persons were employed. The establishment of sales offices in multiple countries simultaneously was also fully supported by the venture capitalists, who actually encouraged the management team to take more risks in their activities on foreign markets.

Although the country-level market information provided a favourable view of the development of the mobile advertising business, it soon became obvious that MobileAd was far too early in the market: both the business area and the technology used were quite new to the key customers.

In 2003, it realized that its customers were not ready to adopt the new solution, and that there was no longer venture capital available to finance its operations. Consequently, MobileAd had to run down all its foreign sales offices and to operate only in the domestic market. These drastic changes in the company strategy had several consequences. For instance, the personnel had to be reduced from 55 to 10 in a short period of time. In addition, the growth in turnover had been very modest during the previous few years and was heavily negative during one fiscal year.

Surprisingly, despite the previous experience of the management team, the primary reason behind the international failure of the firm lay in their insufficient knowledge of the market readiness. For instance, only after establishing the US subsidiary did they find out that the US markets at the time were 'a mobile wasteland', as the CEO put it. Yet, driven by pressure from the investors to achieve rapid growth, MobileAd internationalized with rather limited country-level information of the target markets and clearly did not achieve the objectives set for internationalization.

eDiary

eDiary is a small Finnish software company providing electronic diaries and wireless data-collection solutions for the biopharmaceutical industry. Founded in 1999, it has developed a standardized design tool that enables the collection of data from patients within short timescales, and the flexible conduct of complex clinical trials. The company started its international operations only a year after its establishment, when it launched sales subsidiaries in the US, German and Swedish markets almost simultaneously (Figure 8.2). At the time of its establishment, the managerial attitude towards internationalization was very favourable and the home market was seen only as a test market for its

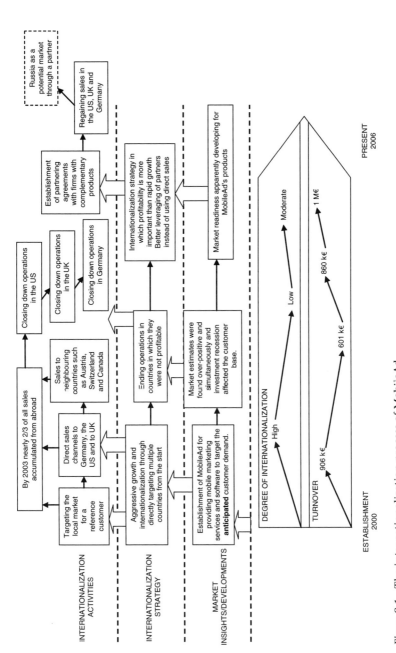

Figure 8.1 The internationalization process of MobileAd

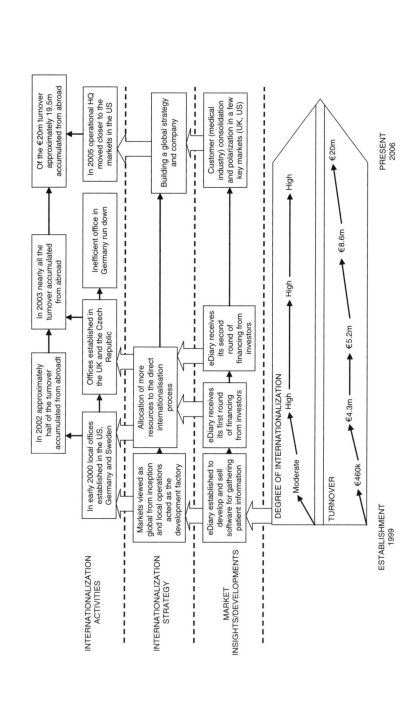

Figure 8.2 The internationalization process of eDiary

global activity. The international activities were financed with a small amount of venture capital.

Following the first rapid growth phase, the international development of eDiary was swift. The German sales office was closed down later, however, as the company realized that its key global customers were located in the US, All sales and delivery activities are co-ordinated from the UK office, while the Finnish main office focuses on product development. Since its establishment in 2000 the company has been very successful in providing software for its global customers. Its turnover in 2006 was about 20 million euros and it employed a total of 120 persons. The main sales growth in terms of annual percentage was generated from the US and UK markets.

The company clearly achieved the internationalization targets that were set. The process began only a year after its establishment, and only three years later nearly all of its revenues accumulated outside its home markets. One of the success factors behind its extremely rapid international growth could have been the fact that it received funding from investors when others did not due to the IT 'recession' that affected Finland; the latter stemmed from the consolidation of the customer base and the preponderant concentration of strategic decision-making concerning IT investments at the HQs – which were basically in the US or the UK. Although the product was still in its infancy, the company tried to get close to its customers and to monitor their needs. It later used the information obtained both in its product development and in developing its sales arguments.

4mobile

4mobile was established in 1997 and started its internationalization in 1998 (Figure 8.3). However, for a few years the process remained rather moderate and more or less sporadic, despite the delivery of a few overseas projects in the late 1990s. In 2000 it made the strategic decision to change its entire business logic from providing labour-intensive project work to becoming a solution provider using software products. This change enhanced its further internationalization.

Even with the new more scalable business logic the company did not make any internationalization plans, and considered its markets to be on the local level. However, after delivering a few solutions to local network operators the managers realized the international potential of their products. The expansion was further fuelled by the investment recession that hit the local telecom markets. The managers understood that further growth would require international growth. In fact, the CEO stated that internationalization per se was not its primary goal. The primary goal was growth, and internationalization was the only way to achieve it.

Consequently, 4mobile established sales subsidiaries abroad. This entry mode was chosen largely due to the inability to find suitable partners. The company had discussions with prospective partners, but in the end they were not interested in promoting products that were new and thereby unknown in the global arena. However, later it has gradually shifted towards partnering instead of using its own sales offices.

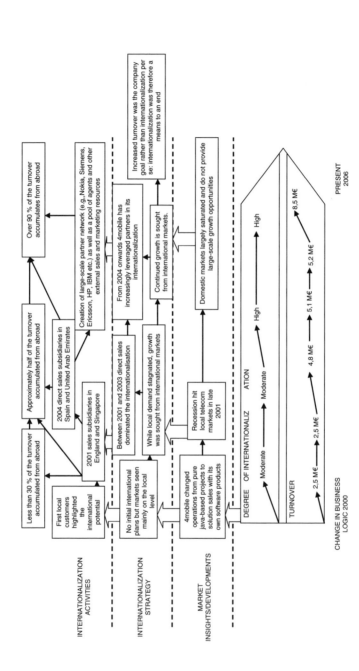

Figure 8.3 The internationalization process of 4mobile

Whether or not 4mobile achieved its internationalization goals is difficult to evaluate in terms of objectives, given the lack of explicit objectives. Internationalization was rather seen as a means to an end in achieving its targets for continued growth. In fact, between 2001 and 2006 the company grew organically in terms of turnover by approximately 28 per cent a year on average. This would not have been possible in local markets: currently over 90 per cent of all its sales revenues originate from foreign markets. Consequently, we consider the company's internationalization as successful.

mNet

mNet was founded in 1995 to provide mobile Internet solutions for B2B (business to business) markets. It started with domestic markets but when the internationalization process began in 1999 the growth was rapid (Figure 8.4). This small Finnish company used a mixed-mode entry method: it established both its own sales units and formed partnerships to sell its solutions internationally.

The internationalization challenges facing mNet were mainly related to marketing in that it had to work hard to educate its potential customers in the use of the latest technology, thus partly developing the demand themselves. On the other hand, they soon realized that their solutions were too innovative for the end-customers to adopt. Their sales- and marketing-related business partners also realized this, and gradually decreased their commitment.

Furthermore, the company was not able to develop proper mechanisms for collecting end-user information or for analysing this information systematically. Thus, the products were never properly attuned to providing significant value for the end-customers. Realizing this, their sales- and marketing-related partners were not willing to continue the relationships, and mNet had to set up sales subsidiaries.

In summary, mNet did not achieve its internationalization goals, mainly because of their aggressive internationalization strategy which allocated all of its invested capital to international expansion. When the markets collapsed, the investments stagnated, and yet it had built a considerable international organization. Soon afterwards, it was bought by its larger competitor.

mCon

mCon focused its business on tailor-made Internet and mobile-based software solutions and consulting services. It provides customer-specific software for implementing comprehensive intranet and extranet as well as e-business solutions through the use of the Internet and mobile technologies. It began its operations on domestic markets, and experienced intensive growth during its first years of operations (Figure 8.5).

In 1999 mCon realized that its international competitors were beginning to expand even more quickly, and that many European countries as well as the US markets were becoming heavily competitive. On the other hand, the domestic markets seemed to have limited growth potential. Given these challenges, the management team decided to explore market opportunities in developing

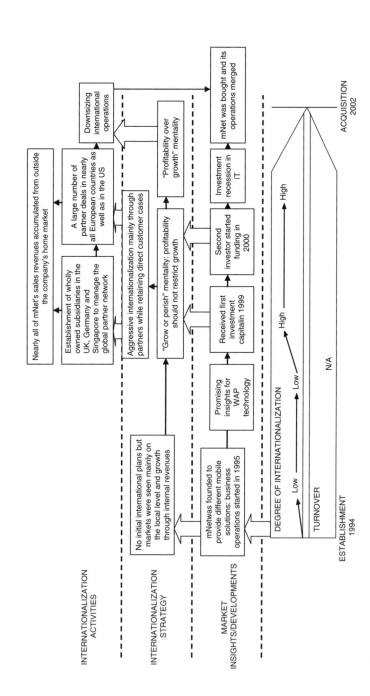

Figure 8.4 The internationalization process of mNet

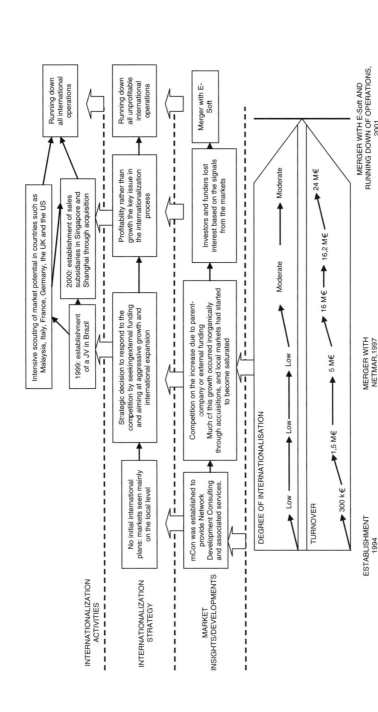

Figure 8.5 The internationalization process of mCon

countries, in which the company could grow without exposing itself to fierce competition. Having conducted desk research on a selected few countries, the company decided to enter the promising Brazilian market by forming a joint venture with a local consulting firm. This venture very soon resulted in the acquisition of a Brazilian subsidiary. At this point, an IPO (initial public offering) was held in Finland in order to raise more capital to fund the international growth. Following its initial international action in Brazil the company extensively studied a number of other countries, both on its own initiative and through external consultants. It held meetings with local customers and obtained general information about the market conditions and the competitive environment. As a consequence, in 2000 it entered the rapidly developing Internet consulting markets in Asia.

In this case the greatest challenge was to create an effective multinational service organization. The most difficult task for the company was to support the geographically distant offices. It soon became evident after the first marketing efforts that knowledge transfer was challenging and time-consuming given the extended cultural and geographical distances involved. Moreover, because of rapid growth in the domestic market the company was not able to dedicate enough technologically and culturally competent human resources to support the international service units in selling and delivering competitive technologies.

These challenges led to a situation in which the quality and the price level of the implemented projects varied considerably across countries. What was more detrimental, however, was that it did not accumulate any generic company-wide knowledge about serving customers uniformly. As a result, none of the foreign business units turned profitable and the company had to end all foreign operations by the spring of 2001. This change in strategy brought a significant decrease in turnover, and the personnel had to be almost halved during a period of only a few months. Later in 2001 the company merged with another Finnish consulting company that focused solely on domestic markets.

ServSystem

ServSystem offers design, consultation and implementation services with regard to tailor-made open-source software-based client and server systems. It was originally incorporated in 1988 (mainly for businesses other than software), but the current business model and software-product offerings were launched on the domestic market in 2001. The first tailor-made solutions were developed for customers in the telecom and pharmaceutical industries, and soon after that the acquired project experience was leveraged to other industries.

Since it began its current operations, ServSystem has been very interested in leveraging its knowledge base to foreign markets (Figure 8.6). It sold its first international implementation of a tailor-made open-source solution to Vietnam in 2002, as a result of which it established an office with sales and production functions in the target country. The motivation for the internationalization was the French-Vietnamese origin of one of the founders, which helped in operating in the Vietnamese market. Following these initial developments the company has

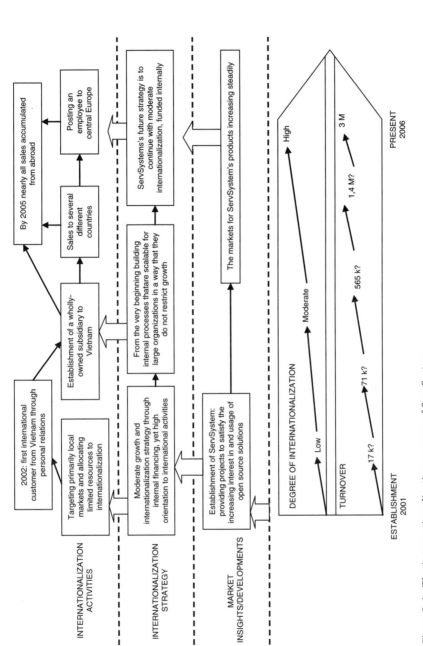

Figure 8.6 The internationalization process of ServSystem

leveraged its knowledge to various countries (including the US, the UK and Japan) by delivering projects globally – and also by approaching large multinational organizations.

ServSystem chose a highly customer-driven approach in its internationalization. From the start, the aim of the foreign operations was to establish direct contacts with the target customers and to obtain a profound understanding of their businesses. Market-level data on the target countries was collected to support the decision-making, and was swiftly validated by customers following market entry. As the market for open-source software is still developing, there have not been many competitors in the global markets, and thus the company has been able to keep abreast of the competitive environment from the very beginning of its internationalization process. Furthermore, the few competitors have co-operated in marketing actions in order to tailor the market to their quite similar solutions, and they have thus shared information about market developments.

In order to secure a standardized level of response to customer needs, the company has also developed a virtual organizational structure in which all customer projects are implemented co-operatively by more or less all of the employees working in a particular electronic network environment. Regardless of the location of the employees, these effective information-sharing activities have ensured the continuous generation of company-wide market intelligence to the benefit of all business units alike. ServSystem currently employs about 50 persons in Finland, Vietnam and Hungary. Its annual turnover has grown very rapidly during the last few years: it was more than three million euros in 2005, of which a large proportion was generated from sales abroad. Thus, we consider its international growth successful.

Cross-case analysis

Our cases offer fertile material for analysing the accelerated internationalization of software companies. The time period – from the late 1990s to the early 2000s – was challenging for all companies in the industry and the case descriptions tell different survival stories. We have focused in our cross-case analysis in identifying potential explanations for success and failure (Table 8.1).

As expected, obtaining objective information on the international growth of the case companies – particularly the unsuccessful ones – proved to be difficult. However, on the basis of the key decision-makers' subjective performance evaluation, we conclude that three of the six cases could be considered successful in that they have been able to create a long-term presence in international markets.

Interestingly, the case descriptions offer several explanations for the success or failure of the companies. The key drivers of either positive or negative development in the internationalization process seem to be related to the strategic decisions and chosen strategy in general, the ability to read the market and adapt accordingly and access to external finance. Surprisingly, all the cases – including the successful ones – included some form of de-internationalization. In terms of

Table 8.1 Cross-case analysis

	MobileAd	eDiary	4mobile	mNet	mCon	ServSystem
Objectives	not achieved	achieved	achieved	not achieved	not achieved	achieved
Drivers of success/ failure	* lacking knowledge of customer needs * lack of external finance	* adaptation to customer needs * access to venture capital	* strategic change * commitment to internationalization	* lack of information of customer needs * inability to bring about strategic change	* challenges in the management of the organization	* systematic market intelligence * flexible organization
Entry mode and market selection	sales offices in multiple countries, later partners	sales offices in multiple countries	sales offices in multiple countries, later partners	partnerships and sales offices in multiple countries	one joint venture, sales offices in multiple countries	virtual organization in multiple countries
Timing	market creation	market creation	market creation	market creation	market expansion	market expansion

success, the key question was how they handled this challenging task of changing strategy or operational mode, for example.

The cases confirmed that the role of venture capitalists is a double-edged sword – on the one hand they offer the finance required for rapid growth, and on the other hand they stress the importance of rapid international growth – the managers themselves might prefer a more risk-averse strategy. Venture capital seems to be (at least in some cases) a necessary but not a sufficient condition for rapid international growth. However, sustainable long-term growth requires the ability to make strategic changes (McDougall and Oviatt, 1996), particularly in situations involving a mismatch between the finance obtained and the resources required.

In terms of context, the decisive factor is related to the timing of market entry. Even a small, rapidly growing company can be successful with a first-mover strategy (such as our eDiary case), but it must be able to 'read' the weak signals from the market and to develop close collaboration with its customers. Additionally, companies entering markets early may need to change their operational mode. Although potential partners might not be interested in a newcomer at first, they might seize the chance to engage in a more efficient, low-commitment operation mode.

Conclusions

From the results of our study, and in line with Zucchella et al. (2007), it seems that the drivers of precocity (the early start of international activities) and subsequent rapid international growth are different. Whereas early internationalization requires the rapid identification and efficient exploitation of opportunities (McDougall, Shane and Oviatt, 1994; Autio et al., 2000), further profitable growth in international markets necessitates different types of managerial capabilities and skills. These are reflected in timely and appropriate decisions as well as in the ability to act proactively and to change the organization accordingly.

Although experience, market knowledge, language skills, a global mindset and other entrepreneurial characteristics are significant antecedents of early internationalization (see, for example, Autio et al., 2000; Nummela, Saarenketo and Puumalainen, 2004; Zhou, 2007; Zucchella et al., 2007), their importance decreases with time. It should also be kept in mind that the same factor may be both a positive and a negative driver – depending on the context. Thus, factors that often are considered to have a positive impact, such as the previous experience of managers, may have a negative effect on success. For example, in the case of MobileAd the management team assumed they knew the market because of their earlier experience in the business, when in fact the strategic choices – particularly related to the international marketing strategy – were more decisive. Additionally, serendipity – the ability to recognize 'chance' opportunities and to exploit them – may prove to be a crucial driver of success (Crick and Spence, 2005). Therefore, we suggest that these firms may pursue different growth trajectories.

Our findings from the six exploratory cases highlight the cyclical nature of accelerated internationalization in two ways. First, the internationalization processes of these companies were cyclical rather than linear, including phases of de-internationalization and re-internationalization, and success depended on the managers' ability to manage this. On the other hand, there is also a loop between the market, the company strategy and its international activities. A company that is rapidly growing in international markets should carefully follow the market changes, adapt its strategy accordingly and act immediately. In the best case, the actions which reflect the chosen strategy will have a positive effect on the market. In order to overcome the challenges of accelerated internationalization, these companies should try to be flexible and agile, thus to utilize the common strengths of SMEs and to avoid the lateral rigidity that is so typical of larger organizations.

Notes

1. Time in company internationalization has three different dimensions: precocity, rapidity and pace (Zucchella et al., 2007, see also Jones and Coviello, 2005). This study focuses on only one of them – the speed of international growth and its challenges.
2. In line with Bell et al. (2001), traditional firms are defined here as companies that follow the incremental internationalization process; international new ventures (or born globals) are international from inception; and born-again globals are well-established firms focusing on domestic markets at start-up, but which later start a rapid internationalization process.
3. Except for MobileAd, the case companies grew in terms of turnover between the years 2001 and 2005 by between 21 per cent (4mobile) and 300 per cent (ServSystem) per annum on average. MobileAd was established in 2000, and in 2001 already achieved a turnover of close to one million euros. Thus, although the company had only marginal growth between 2001 and 2005, the intensive growth prior to that clearly labels it as a growth company.

References

Alvesson, M. (2000) 'Social identity and the problem of loyalty in knowledge-intensive companies', *Journal of Management Studies*, 37(8), 1101–23.

Andersen, O. (1993) 'On the internationalization process of firms: A critical analysis', *Journal of International Business Studies*, 24(2), 33–46.

Andersen, O. (1997) 'Internationalization and market entry mode: A review of theories and conceptual frameworks', *Management International Review*, 37(2), 7–42.

Andersson, S. (2000) 'The internationalization of the firm from an entrepreneurial perspective', *International Studies of Management & Organization*, 30(1), 63–92.

Andersson, S. (2004) 'Internationalization in different industrial contexts', *Journal of Business Venturing*, 19(6), 851–75.

Ansoff, H.I. (1965) *Corporate strategy* (New York: McGraw-Hill).

Aspelund, A., Madsen, T.K. and Moen, Ø. (2007) 'A review of the foundation, international marketing strategies, and performance of international new ventures', *European Journal of Marketing*, 41(11/12), 1423–48.

Autio, E., Sapienza, H.J. and Almeida, J.G. (2000) 'Effects of age at entry, knowledge intensity, and imitability on international growth', *Academy of Management Journal*, 43(5), 909–24.

Bell, J. (1995) 'The internationalization of small computer software firms: A further challenge to stage theory', *European Journal of Marketing*, 29(8), 60–75.

Bell, J., McNaughton, R. and Young, S. (2001) ' "Born-again global" firms: An extension to the "born global" phenomenon', *Journal of International Management*, 7(3), 173–89.

Bernardino, L. and Jones, M.V. (2003) 'The role of resources/capabilities in the internationalization and performance of high-technology small firms: Mode choice and performance', in C. Wheeler, F. McDonald and I. Greaves (eds), *Internationalization: Firm strategies and management*, 187–207 (Houndmills: Palgrave Macmillan).

Berry, M.M.J. (1996) 'Technical entrepreneurship, strategic awareness and corporate transformation in small high-tech firms', *Technovation*, 16(9), 487–98.

Boter, H. and Holmqvist, C. (1996) 'Industry characteristics and internationalization processes in small firms', *Journal of Business Venturing*, 11(6), 471–87.

Coviello, N.E. and Munro, H.J. (1995) 'Growing the entrepreneurial firm: networking for international market development', *European Journal of Marketing*, 29(7), 49–61.

Coviello, N.E. and Munro, H.J. (1997) 'Network relationships and the internationalization process of small software firms', *International Business Review*, 6(4), 361–86.

Crick, D. and Jones, M. (2000) 'Small high-technology firms and international high-technology markets', *Journal of International Marketing*, 8(2), 63–85.

Crick, D. and Spence, M. (2005) 'The internationalization of "high performing" UK high tech SMEs: a study of planned and unplanned strategies', *International Business Review*, 14(2), 167–85.

Davidsson, P. (1989) 'Continued entrepreneurship and small firm growth'. Doctoral dissertation, Stockholm School of Economics, Stockholm.

Delmar, F., Davidsson, P. and Gartner, W.B. (2003) 'Arriving at the high-growth firm', *Journal of Business Venturing*, 18(2), 189–216.

Eisenhardt, K.M. (1989) 'Building theories from case study research', *Academy of Management Review*, 14(4), 532–50.

Eisenhardt, K.M. and Brown, S. (1998) 'Time pacing: Competing in markets that won't stand still', *Harvard Business Review*, 76(2), 60–69.

Eisenhardt, K.M. and Graebner, M.E. (2007) 'Theory building from cases: opportunities and challenges', *Academy of Management Journal*, 50(1), 25–32.

Ghauri, P. (2004) 'Designing and conducting case studies in international business' in R. Marschan-Piekkari and C. Welch (eds), *Handbook of Qualitative Research Methods for International Business*, 109–124 (Cheltenham: Edward Elgar).

Heinonen, J. (2006) 'Why should we study growth entrepreneurship?' in J. Heinonen (ed.), *The Nature and Elements of Growth – Finnish SMEs in Focus*, Small Business Institute, Turku School of Economics, 14–26 (Tampere: Esa Print).

Huber, G.P. and Power, D.J. (1985) 'Retrospective reports of strategic-level managers: Guidelines for increasing their accuracy', *Strategic Management Journal*, 6(2), 171–80.

Hurmerinta-Peltomäki, L. (2003) 'Time and internationalization: Theoretical challenges set by rapid internationalization', *Journal of International Entrepreneurship*, 1(2), 217–36.

Johanson, J. and Mattson, L.G. (1988) 'Internationalization in industrial systems – A network approach', in N. Hood, and J.E. Vahlne (eds), *Strategies in Global Competition*, 287–314 (London: Routledge).

Johanson, J. and Vahlne, J.E. (1977) 'The internationalization process of the firm – A model of knowledge development and increasing foreign market commitments', *Journal of International Business*, 8(1), 23–32.

Jones, M.V. (1999) 'The internationalization of small high technology firms', *Journal of International Marketing*, 7(4), 15–41.

Jones, M.V. and Coviello, N.E. (2005) 'Internationalization: Conceptualising an entrepreneurial process of behaviour in time', *Journal of International Business Studies*, 36(3), 284–303.

Kakati, M. (2003) 'Success criteria in high-tech new ventures', *Technovation*, 23(5), 447–57.

Katsikeas, C.S., Leonidou, L.C. and Morgan, N.A. (2000) 'Firm-level export performance assessment: Review, evaluation and development', *Academy of Marketing Science*, 28(4), 493–511.

Leonidou, L.C., Katsikeas, C.S. and Samiee, S. (2002) 'Marketing strategy determinants of export performance: a meta-analysis', *Journal of Business Research*, 55(1), 51–67.

Liao, J. and Welsch, H. (2003) 'Social capital and entrepreneurial growth aspiration: A comparison of technology- and non-technology-based nascent entrepreneurs', *Journal of High Technology Management Research*, 14(1), 149–70.

Luostarinen, R. (1979) 'Internationalization of the firm'. Doctoral dissertation. *Publications of the Helsinki School of Economics and Business Administration*, Helsinki.

Madsen, T.K. and Servais, P. (1997) 'The internationalization of born globals: An evolutionary process?' *International Business Review*, 6(6), 561–83.

McDougall, P.P. and Oviatt, B.M. (1996) 'New venture internationalization, strategic change and performance: A follow-up study', *Journal of Business Venturing*, 11(1), 23–40.

McDougall, P.P., Shane, S. and Oviatt, B.M. (1994) 'Explaining the formation of international new ventures: The limits of theories from international business research', *Journal of Business Venturing*, 9(6), 469–87.

Moen, Ø. and Servais, P. (2002) 'Born global or gradual global? Examining the export behavior of small and medium-sized enterprises', *Journal of International Marketing*, 10(3), 49–72.

Moen, Ø., Gavlen, M. and Endresen, I. (2004) 'Internationalization of small, computer software firms. Entry forms and market selection', *European Journal of Marketing*, 38(9/10), 1236–51.

Mullins, J.W. and Forlani, D. (2005) 'Missing the boat or sinking the boat: a study of new venture decision making', *Journal of Business Venturing*, 20(1), 47–69.

Nummela, N., Saarenketo, S. and Puumalainen, K. (2004) 'Global mindset – A prerequisite for successful internationalization?' *Canadian Journal of Administrative Sciences*, 21(1), 51–64.

Papadopoulos, N. (1987) 'Approaches to international market selection for small- and medium-sized enterprises', in P.J. Rosson and S.D. Reid (eds), *Managing export entry and expansion*, 128–158 (New York: Praeger Publishers).

Pedersen, T., Petersen, B. and Benito, G.R.G. (2002) 'Change of foreign operation method: Impetus and switching costs', *International Business Review*, 11(3), 325–45.

Petersen, B. and Welch, L.S. (2002) 'Foreign operation mode combinations and internationalization', *Journal of Business Research*, 55(2), 157–62.

Preece, S.B., Miles, G. and Baetz, M.C. (1999) 'Explaining the international intensity and global diversity of early-stage technology-based firms', *Journal of Business Venturing*, 14(3), 259–81.

Rialp, A., Rialp, J. and Knight, G.A. (2005) 'The phenomenon of early internationalizing firms: what do we know after a decade (1993–2003) of scientific inquiry?' *International Business Review*, 14(2), 147–66.

Smith, N.C. (1991) 'The case-study: a vital yet misunderstood research method for management', in N.C. Smith and P. Dainty (eds), *The Management Research Handbook*, 145–58 (London: Routledge).

Spanos, Y.E. and Lioukas, S. (2001) 'An examination into the causal logic of rent generation: Contrasting Porter's competitive strategy framework and the resource-based perspective', *Strategic Management Journal*, 22(10), 907–34.

Starbuck, W.H. (1992) 'Learning by knowledge-intensive firms', *Journal of Management Studies*, 3(4), 262–75.

Vahlne, J.-E. and Nordström, K.A. (1993) 'The internationalization process: Impact of competition and experience', *The International Trade Journal*, 7(5), 529–48.

Yin, R.K. (1994) *Case Study Research – Design and Methods*, 2nd edn (Thousand Oaks, CA: Sage Publications).

Yli-Renko, H., Autio, E. and Tontti, V. (2002) 'Social capital, knowledge, and the international growth of technology-based new firms', *International Business Review*, 11(3), 279–304.

Zahra, S.A. (2005) 'A theory of international new ventures: a decade of research', *Journal of International Business Studies*, 36(1), 20–28.

Zhou, L. (2007) 'The effects of entrepreneurial proclivity and foreign market knowledge on early internationalization', *Journal of World Business*, 42(3), 281–93.

Zucchella, A., Palamara, G. and Denicolai, S. (2007) 'The drivers of the early internationalization of the firm', *Journal of World Business*, 42(3), 268–80.

9
International New Ventures and the Development of Partnerships: A Social Capital Approach

Arild Aspelund, Roger Sørheim* and Magne Sivert Berg

Introduction

International New Ventures (INVs) are firms which from inception seek to establish themselves in the international marketplace (McDougall, Shane and Oviatt, 1994). The frequency of INV establishments has increased rapidly during the last few decades (Aspelund and Moen, 2001) and now constitutes a significant part of the economy in most developed economies (Aspelund, Madsen and Moen, 2007). Studies have found that INVs differ from traditional exporters in several ways (McDougall et al., 1994; Madsen, Rasmussen and Servais, 2000; Rialp, Rialp and Knight, 2005; Aspelund and Moen, 2005) and that they follow a different path to success than traditional exporters.

The INV phenomenon was neglected for a long time in international marketing research, but this is no longer the case (Rialp et al., 2005; Aspelund et al., 2007). The past decade has seen extensive research on INVs and many interesting aspects of INVs have been revealed. Among the most intriguing is evidence that INVs, despite their lack of financial capital, manage to get access to sufficient resources to establish a fully-fledged international expansion (Oviatt and McDougall, 1994). Access to the necessary resources is often secured through different types of partnerships, like alliances with larger partners with more resources or small partners with complementary assets (Coviello and Munro, 1997; Gabrielsson and Kirpalani, 2004). We also know that the initiation of these partner structures are often a result of structural social capital, that is, the partnerships are based on social relationships resulting from an already existing relationship between actors employed in two different firms (McDougall et al., 1994; Coviello and Munro; 1997; Yli-Renko, Autio and Tontti, 2002; Sharma and Blomstermo, 2003). However, few studies have looked in-depth into the social factors that regulate the nature of the collaboration and contribute to long-term survival and performance of the partnership. This study seeks to narrow this gap by adopting a social capital approach to investigate the role of social capital in the international expansion of INVs. The main research questions addressed are: To what extent are different dimensions of social capital necessary for and conducive to the establishment and long-term development of international partnerships? In which phases are the effects of social capital most prominent?

Theoretical background

Arguably, the most intriguing aspect of the INV phenomenon is the fact that the firms are able to successfully internationalize despite liabilities of newness, smallness and foreignness (Arenius, 2002). Their young age and small size negatively impact the amount of financial, human and intellectual capital available within the firms (McDougall et al., 1994; Oviatt and McDougall, 1994; Bell, 1995; Coviello and Munro, 1997; McAuley, 1999). Furthermore, company size and age are correlated to reputation and number of network ties, and thus it is to be expected that newly launched INVs will struggle for legitimacy in new markets (Arenius, 2002). Together, these three liabilities result in a daunting resource gap which new ventures that want to become international actors have to overcome.

The answer to this challenge seems to be that INVs acquire access to other organizations' resources and use them to carry out necessary steps in the internationalization process (McDougall et al., 1994; Gabrielsson and Kirpalani, 2004; Rialp et al., 2005; Aspelund et al., 2007). There are multiple examples of this in the INV literature. For example, Keeble, Lawson, Smith, Moore and Wilkinson (1998) found that many INVs were engaged in collaborative research arrangements across national borders and that the subsequent internationalization was a result of extensive domestic networking. Coviello and Munro (1997) investigated young international software firms and found that they were all engaged in partnerships with larger international firms, which supplied the necessary international distribution network. Oviatt and McDougall (1994) even found use of partnerships so common among INVs that they listed it as one of four necessary and sufficient elements for the existence of INVs. Hence, it seems likely that partnerships play a key role in internationalizing new firms and that social capital are important to establish and govern these alliances.

Social capital

The concept of social capital initially appeared in community studies (Nahapiet and Ghoshal, 1998), but has later been put to use in a wide variety of research fields. Social capital is roughly understood as *'the goodwill that is engendered by the fabric of social relations and that can be mobilized to facilitate action'* (Adler and Kwon, 2002, p. 17). Nahapiet and Ghoshal (1998) define social capital as the sum of the actual and potential resources embedded within, available through and derived from the network of relationships possessed by an individual or social unit. This means that social capital comprises both the network and the resources that can be accessed through it. Moreover, social capital can be possessed either by a person or a social unit, such as a firm.

The main insight of social capital is that an actor's network and his or her friendship ties can be used for other purposes, such as information gathering, or advice and that social capital thus is appropriable (Adler and Kwon, 2002).

The dimensions

There exist three different views on social capital; the bridging, the bonding and the neutral view. The bridging view focuses on the ego and how it is coupled to other actors. In this view, social capital can be used to explain the differential success of individual actors in their competitive rivalry since it is an actor's external relationships that determine what resources the actor can possibly mobilize. The second view – bonding – focuses on social capital as a collective (that is, organization, community, nation and so on) and its internal structure which may constitute a cohesiveness that facilitates the pursuit of common goals. The last of the views is neutral to the internal/external argument. The promoters of this view argue that the distinction between internal and external view is largely a matter of perspective; a relation that is external at one abstraction level can be internal at a higher one. Moreover, the internal and external views are not mutually exclusive because an actor's actions will be influenced by both the external linkages and the cohesiveness of the network fabric (Adler and Kwon, 2002). This chapter will encompass all three views through the adoptions of Nahapiet and Ghoshal's (1998) three dimensional analytical tool for social capital. This tool involves viewing social capital as consisting of three dimensions: the structural, the relational and the cognitive dimension (see Figure 9.1).

The structural dimension concerns the overall pattern of connections between actors (who reaches whom and how). Important aspects to consider are the pattern of linkages in terms of density, connectivity and hierarchy (Nahapiet and Ghoshal, 1998). Burt (1993) emphasizes the importance of this dimension in understanding the role of the entrepreneur; an entrepreneur earns his or her profit from taking advantage of a position as the only link between two or more groups. The relational dimension is closely connected to terms such as trust and trustworthiness, norms and sanctions, obligations and expectations and identity

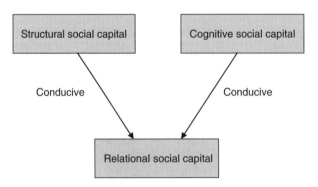

Figure 9.1   How the dimensions relate to each other

and identification. These are assets that are created in and leveraged through relationships, and their existence impacts the behaviour and motivation of the actors involved (Nahapiet and Ghoshal, 1998). Finally, the cognitive dimension refers to the aspects surrounding the existence of shared representation, interpretation and meaning among the actors. Facilitating such shared understanding is shared language, codes and narratives (Nahapiet and Ghoshal, 1998). Shared vision is according to Arenius (2002) the major manifestation of cognitive social capital, and it plays an important role as an antecedent of some of the assets belonging to the relational dimension, for example, trust and trustworthiness (Tsai and Ghoshal, 1998; Sørheim, 2003).

Studies that have directly investigated the relationship between social capital and INV internationalization are very few. Among these notable exceptions is the work of Helena Yli-Renko and her colleagues. In their 2002 study, they found that development of internal and external social capital had a positive effect on the accumulation of knowledge within the organization. This knowledge intensity is positively related to international growth. So, Yli-Renko et al. (2002) emphasize that social capital is a key resource for developing knowledge-based competitive advantage in foreign markets. This implies that social capital must be regarded as a key resource in the process of internationalization of young growth-oriented ventures. This key resource must be effectively managed and developed and not be seen as a by-product of other key activities performed by the firm.

Methodology

The purpose of this paper is to empirically investigate how INVs make use of social capital in order to develop partnerships. This is an exploratory, inductive study that uses the case study research strategy (Yin, 1989). In accordance with the purpose of the paper, we are looking at actions at the inter-organizational level, which implies that the unit of analysis will be the firm.

The case firms were selected using four criteria. First, we chose INVs defined as firms with significant international sales within six years of establishment (McDougall et al., 1994). Second, we wanted the firms to be new, technology-based firms. These first two criteria were set in order to ensure that we selected firms with international ambitions from inception and resource limitations due to newness and parallel technology development costs. Third, we selected companies that had some years of experience to be able to assess the long-term development of the partnerships. Finally, we selected cases that have had reasonable success with their international expansion, but not necessarily been successful with all their international partnerships.

Data was collected through personal participant interviews. The interviews had a semi-structured approach, which implies that the respondents were briefed about the research topic in advance, thereby focusing the interview while still allowing the respondents to elaborate on relevant issues. In order to have insightful and rewarding interviews, respondents from each case firm were selected on the basis that they had been involved in the entire internationalization process, and thus had intimate knowledge of what had happened.

Each case was analysed separately and then compared against each other in a cross-case analysis, using replication logic to discover relationships. Any contradictions were considered opportunities for refining and extending the emerging theory (Eisenhardt, 1989). The principle of maintaining a chain of evidence is to allow the reader to follow the logic path of the study, from initial research questions to the final conclusions (Yin, 1994). This paper follows this principle by providing the reader with citations directly from the research data bank and then presenting the reasoning behind the propositions and conclusions.

Case presentations

In this section we will present the case firms, their main strategy and the role of relational and cognitive social capital in international expansion.

MaXware

MaXware is based in Trondheim, Norway, and develops and sells identity management solutions. The company started in 1998 under the name MaXware International, when two employees at a large Norwegian software corporation bought the international rights of some products that the mother firm was not interested in internationalizing. In the first years of operations the firm grew organically, but steadily, and in 2005 MaXware found the time was right to bring in venture capital to finance more rapid growth. At this point MaXware already had 200 customers on four continents, 95 per cent of total sales abroad with main markets in Europe, USA, Australia and Japan. In May 2007 MaXware was acquired by a large multinational company.

MaXware's competitors are large international software vendors with access to large pools of financial and intellectual capital. Hence, MaXware adopted a differentiation strategy to avoid head-to-head competition. MaXware's strategy was to become the market's technology leader, and best on service and support. The management also emphasize the importance of being perceived as trustworthy by potential customers and partners.

In the early stages the company lacked financial resources and therefore tried to catch a few large and highly visible customers that could later be used as reference customers. This strategy also involved identifying reliable partners that could sell MaXware's products internationally. This was not easy as MaXware faced challenges related to the liabilities of newness, smallness and foreignness:

> *Often they say 'Perfect technology, but usually we buy from one of the large vendors'. Then they are worried that we are small, that we are situated in a place far away (Trondheim, Norway) which they fear may negatively impact the support we can deliver. Finally, they are worried that we will not be here tomorrow.*

MaXware in Australia

The company attended several fairs and was eventually approached by an Australian and a British actor. The Australian company was a specialized agent and wanted an exclusive distribution license for MaXware's products in Australia. MaXware saw this as an interesting opportunity, but was reluctant to give exclusivity as it could limit MaXware's choices in the future.

The Australian firm managed to sell MaXware's solutions to one large customer, but failed to bring in new customers after that. MaXware also received word from the Australian customer that they were not given sufficient service and support. This, together with the fact that the partner was failing to fulfil his financial obligations, made MaXware to open a wholly-owned subsidiary in Australia. This was done by employing an Australian person they knew from previous dealings to be technically brilliant and by sending down a person from headquarters in Norway to take control of sales and marketing.

MaXware in the UK

The British corporation that approached MaXware was not looking for a partnership, but was in need of MaXware's solution. MaXware seized this opportunity and allocated resources to assist the customer in the commissioning of the systems:

> We chose to work tightly ... and help and support him so that could prove to the rest of the corporation that it was right to choose our technology. ... We managed to establish several more points of contact within the firm, and if they now try to push us out, it will hurt them – and that was the idea.

The relationship between MaXware and the British corporation evolved over time, and UK representatives eventually proposed to become MaXware's distribution partner in the UK. By using the British corporation as a reference customer and agent, MaXware managed to attract several more customers in the UK, and eventually it became necessary to open a subsidiary. The British corporation saw the importance of having a MaXware office in the UK, and even allowed MaXware to recruit one of their employees as head of the office:

> We took a person from the customer ... and employed him at MaXware. He was to work with our products towards his old employer and other customers in the market. We recruited a customer's employee, and that may be difficult and create trouble, but in this case it happened in understanding with the customer. The corporation understood that it was sensible; they needed local support from us.

Through the partnership with the British company the UK became, and still is, MaXware's most important and most successful market.

We see that MaXware relies on partnerships to enter new markets. In addition to large partner networks MaXware has also established subsidiaries in a few of the most important markets. However, these were not established until after the company had acquired initial relations in the relevant markets. The reason for this, according to the CEO, is that MaXware does not possess sufficient resources to enter new markets on its own, and is thus dependent on partner structures to succeed.

Relational social capital

Findings suggest that MaXware is trying to build trust in partner and customer relations in order to bridge gaps caused by liabilities of foreignness and newness. We see from the MaXware case that it takes some relational social capital to establish the partnerships and MaXware had to work hard to build sufficient trustworthiness to attract the first customers and partners.

MaXware relies on the relational capital from its partners to extend its trustworthiness and access to new customers. This is particularly evident in MaXware's entry into the UK market. It seems MaXware was able to build this relationship from a mere customer relationship to a full strategic partnership by investing in relational social capital even after the relationship was established. In Australia the partnership was established with little (if any) relational social capital and eventually ended when the partners failed to build further relational social capital after the partnership was established.

Cognitive social capital

The Australian partnership is a good example. First, the Australian partner wanted exclusivity, but MaXware did not share that vision for the relationship. Secondly, MaXware believed superior customer service and support was the key to staying competitive, a view that was not shared by their Australian partner. Finally, when it became clear that the firms did not even share the interpretation of the financial terms, the lack of cognitive social capital became evident and the partnership was terminated.

In the case of the British corporation, there definitely exists a shared understanding of the relationship and the market and the relationship also evolved differently. MaXware's CEO attributes the failure of many partnerships to lack of shared understanding on the nature of the partnership:

> Since it is not strategically founded at the partner, it does not develop much.

The importance of cognitive social capital also became evident when MaXware sought to develop their presence in the UK by establishing their own subsidiary. Both MaXware and the partner believed the UK to be a very important market for MaXware's products, and both saw the need for having MaXware support capacities located nearby.

Powel

Powel is a software and hardware supplier for the energy, water supply and sewage sectors based in Trondheim. Powel was founded in 1996 as a spin-off from SINTEF, one of Europe's largest research foundations. The purpose was to take advantage of the deregulation of the Norwegian energy sector in the early 1990s and further deregulations assumed to follow in other European countries and North America. The company grew considerably during the first years and had operating revenues of 152 million NOK[1] and employed 200 people in 2005. The same year they also went public on the Oslo Stock Exchange.

Powel identified three main markets for its products and services: Scandinavia, North America and the rest of Europe. The Scandinavian markets are served through wholly-owned subsidiaries in Göteborg and Jönköping in Sweden and Oslo, Bergen, Bryne and Trondheim in Norway. The North American markets are served by offices in St. Paul (USA) and Victoria (Canada), which are results of acquisitions Powel made in 2001 and 2005. In addition Powel has entered three European markets, Denmark, Germany and the Czech Republic through a partnering strategy. This presentation will deal with activities in the latter three European markets.

After selecting which European markets to enter, Powel initiated a structural process to identify partners. First they established a desired partner profile and then got help from external parties to identify candidates that fit the profile. Important aspects of the profile were market related, such as existing customer base and potential complementarities in computer systems and services. But the CMO also stresses that the candidates had to be willing to invest significantly in the relationship:

> *And not at least that they are willing to invest in you, that they become a bit dependent on doing business on your software. Feel that they will invest, so it does not become 'okay, partners in case we are lucky and stumble into a potential customer'.*

When the candidate was identified and the agreement was signed Powel and the new partner enter into a learning phase where representatives of Powel travel abroad to educate the partner on Powel's technology, installation routines and maintenance. The process of knowledge transfer is both time-consuming and expensive. In the learning phase, Powel also tried to build relationships with the partner's employees:

> *We have to build some glowing souls at our partners ... I quickly see how glowing they are by how much we talk to them on the phone, and the number of e-mails we receive from them. How motivated are they really? ... Very important to find some ambassadors, someone who is willing to fight your cause. You must keep them motivated.*

Relational social capital

In addition to Powel's investments in training and building personal relationships they also use other strategies to build trust. Especially, they leverage their reputation as an industry specialist and actively use the global reputation of their mother company, SINTEF, in order to build trust and credibility.

To some extent we market ourselves through the foundation that we are a daughter of...they are very able at marketing us... That is a way of increasing the (market's) awareness of Powel. ... We hire in people from the foundation, and when they get here they put on their Powel hat and represent Powel.

Cognitive social capital

The footprints of cognitive social capital are very clear in the international expansion of Powel. First, the company has chosen to focus on one business sector and stay there. This facilitates the understanding between Powel and their foreign partners that also do business in the same industry. Another example is that Powel has formalized a set of corporate values that they actively use in their strategy to identify potential partners. These values are honesty, fair practices, loyalty and openness, and Powel try to ensure that potential partners share these fundamental values before entering into a formal agreement.

That is what is a bit despairing with what I am saying, because gut feeling and chemistry – how we feel they (the candidates) fit with our (corporate-) culture are 100 per cent more important than what we can get consent for in a contract... The contracts are not worth the paper they are written on if not some of the other aspects like communication and 'you like to work with me, and I with you' are in place.

In addition to seeking out these values a priori, Powel also used the training period to communicate Powel's view on how business should be performed in the industry. They firmly believe that it is important for the firms to have the same ideas and ways of doing business in order to achieve healthy and long-term relationships.

Q-free

Q-free is a Trondheim-based company that develops and sells electronic systems for collection of road tolls and systems for collection of fares in the public transportation industry. The company was started up in the mid-1980s by a group of entrepreneurs. The firm was lead by one of these entrepreneurs until 2004 when he and the rest of the management resigned after several years with large deficits. The new management initiated a major reorganization of the firm that has turned the firm around. In 2007 the revenues were close to 400 million NOK with a solid 12 per cent EBITDA.[2] During the early 1990s, the company began focusing on international markets, and now has operations in all continents except Africa. Subsidiaries have been set up in Norway, Portugal, Greece, Brazil, Malaysia, China and Australia.

The customers of Q-free are mostly public agencies or private concessionaires responsible for road networks. Due to the industry's young age, few intermediaries exist, and Q-free have therefore contacted the customers directly, sometimes using personal contacts established at trade fairs or conferences.

The co-operation with the agencies and concessionaires has sometimes been very close, and functioned more like R&D-relationships than supplier-customer relationships.

The initial corporate strategy was to become a complete supplier and often even do the installation themselves. This strategy has made it necessary to have company employees stationed in the countries where Q-free have won contracts, making it natural to establish wholly-owned subsidiaries. Thus, Q-free only used partnerships to a limited degree in the initial phases of their international expansion. However, this strategy has been problematic and as the industry has matured and more potential partners have emerged the company has altered its strategy:

> *If I try to take the whole thing I get many enemies – let me see if I cannot get a few friends instead. That is why I split it (the contract) up and say: 'That part I want for myself because it is what I am good at. However, you may have those parts.' Then I try to find someone who is clever at those parts.*

In one of its more recent engagements the company has employed its newly found strategy of partnerships. The partner contacted Q-free after discovering that it had an opportunity to find a customer for Q-free's technology. After initial conversations, representatives from the two organizations began to meet frequently to build a relationship and learn to understand each other:

> *So what did it involve? Much weight was placed on personal relations, understanding each other and building shared understanding. I know the particular culture very well, I know their community and can tell you a lot more about politics there than about Norwegian politics. I watch their TV broadcasts. So, we had common language and way of speaking from the start, shared foundation to tell jokes and that type of things. We got a very close relationship, very high degree of trust.*

Q-free has full confidence in the partner, and has not seen it necessary to formalize the co-operation with contract, and is for now satisfied with a 'gentlemen's agreement', although a formal contract will be put in place as business starts to build.

Relational social capital

Tolling systems are extremely complicated to market and sell and the Asian case shows that a partner strategy in some cases is a precondition to get contracts at all in this industry. Q-free also emphasizes the importance of personal relationships and trust:

> *Especially in the business we operate, because what we do is to deliver the heart of a revenue model, the artefact that generates the customer's income stream. He must trust the technology, he must trust the solution. If he cannot trust me, he cannot trust the solution either. Trust is the be-all and end-all.*

In order to find trustworthy partners, the CMO of Q-free emphasizes the importance of using the existing networks to identify candidates, and then spending some time learning to know each candidate:

> *How do we do it – how do we find partners? The same way: networks, meeting people, visiting them, feel the environment and the attitude, see if we get their attention. Find out if they perceive the market the way we do, and if they got the right competence. It is a process.*

Cognitive social capital

In terms of cognitive social capital the Q-free case offers similar insight as MaXware and Powell. The Q-free CMO clearly states that Q-free will not engage in a relationship with an actor with views and goals that differ substantially from Q-free. The reason for this is that they believe it will be difficult to reach agreements with such actors over time.

According to Q-free's CMO cultural distance hampers communication and makes it a challenge to understand what the other actor really thinks. To ease this problem Q-free normally sets up local subsidiaries and recruits local people as Q-free's local representatives. They are careful to assure that they understand the other party's intentions:

> *One thing is that we communicate openly and honestly, we do that. We can tell what we can do and what we cannot do. The second is that we try to understand what the other party wants, thinks and means. Show that we understand that. It [building trust] is probably as easy as maintaining a relation between what one promises and what one does.*

Hence, Q-free emphasizes that the candidates must share the company's view of the market and the goals. This can be seen in relation to the creation of a foundation for trust, but there are also matters of effectiveness and efficiency to consider; if they do not perceive the market the same way and do not have the same goals, it will be difficult to get the relationship to function over time. The findings from the Q-free case also indicate that cognitive social capital is strongly related to relational social capital, and that lack of cognitive social capital will make it difficult to achieve the level of trust needed to establish and get the partnerships to function over time.

Cross-case analysis and discussion

The case firms of this study have relied on partnerships to different degrees. On one hand, we have got MaXware who has used partnerships extensively in its internationalization process, and on the other hand, Q-free who has barely used partners at all up until recently. The Powel case can be positioned somewhat between these two firms, as the company, to a large degree, has combined foreign direct investments and use of partnerships. We believe there are several reasons for the differences in the use of partners.

The owners of MaXware are primarily its employees, who do not possess capital that can be placed at the company's disposal for making foreign direct investments. The company's access to financial capital has been very restricted, and it has been forced to choose less capital-intensive market entry modes.

Unlike MaXware, Powel has access to large amounts of financial capital through its owners who predominantly are financial institutions, and through its extensive domestic operations that supply a cash flow. This has made it possible for Powel to choose a more control-oriented entry mode through direct investments than was possible for MaXware. In addition, Powel has a business model that incorporates service, support and consulting activities that set higher demands of local presence. However, more uncertain markets have been entered through partnerships, thereby reducing the risk and the capital requirements.

Q-free is very different from the other companies in this study since it operated in Norway for some years before having its first international sales, and thus had established a significant cash flow from domestic operations that could support an ownership-oriented internationalization process. Even if Q-free wanted to pursue a partnership strategy it might not have been feasible since the industry was too young and suitable partners was hard to find.

Relational social capital

The data from the case study indicates that at least some relational social capital must be present in the relationships prior to the establishment of a partnership. This interpretation can partly be attributed to the INVs' and the partners' fear of wasting time and resources. Without presence of relational assets like trust and positive expectations, our investigation shows that companies might not find it worthwhile. Hence:

> P1:   *Relational social capital secures trust and positive expectations, and thus must be present for partner structures to be established.*

However, regardless of the time one spends to get to know each other there always exists the danger of opportunism. The Powel case offers an example: Powel invests a lot of time and money in transferring knowledge to every new distribution partner. If the partner should receive this education, and then decide that it can use the knowledge more profitably itself and subsequently end the partnership with Powel, it would be opportunism. The table can also be turned if Powel is to use the partner's network and reputation to acquire a customer base in the relevant area, and then decide to set up a wholly-owned subsidiary that takes control and seizes all profits related to service, support and new products.

The likelihood of opportunism occurring can be lowered by the use of social contracts. The loss of reputation that would come from acting opportunistically would endanger the ego's future profits since other actors would keep away from him or her. In addition to the economical aspects, there is also the personal cost for the managers at the firm that has acted opportunistically such as loss of personal reputation, self-esteem and friendships. Following this reasoning it is possible to see why relational social capital is conducive to the long-term survival and performance of partnerships. In this study all three cases consciously and systematically invested in social capital on all levels of the partner organization in order to build long-lasting and efficient collaborations. Thus, we propose:

> P2:   *Relational social capital reduces the probability of opportunism, and is thus conducive to the long-term survival and performance of partnerships.*

Cognitive social capital

The literature propose that cognitive social capital functions as an antecedent of relational social capital (Tsai and Ghoshal, 1998; Sørheim, 2003) and this gives us a starting point for understanding why cognitive social capital is important for the establishment of partnerships. If the parties possess cognitive social capital and thus are better able to understand each other, it becomes easier to live up to the other party's expectations. The Q-free case shows how the CMO is able to build trust between the company and a European partner by utilizing the shared understanding and interpretation flowing from the fact that the European partner and the CMO has the same nationality.

In addition to its role as an antecedent of relational social capital, cognitive social capital is also believed to have a positive effect directly on the effectiveness and efficiency of partnerships. Shared understanding, interpretation and vision make it easier to communicate efficiently since the parties know what, when and how to communicate information (Nahapiet and Ghoshal, 1998; Tsai and Ghoshal, 1998). The MaXware case does not, however, support the rationale that cognitive social capital is a precondition for the establishment of partnerships. Rather it is a facilitator for its establishment. However, the findings should be seen in relation to the company's degree of dependence on partnerships and their strategic freedom to choose partners. Hence:

> P3:   *Cognitive social capital is conducive to the establishment of partnerships due to its role as an antecedent of relational social capital.*

As mentioned previously, Q-free and Powel do not enter into partnerships unless the necessary level of cognitive social capital is present because they know from experience that lack of cognitive social capital will likely cause problems for relationships in the long run. MaXware also offers a great example as their Australian venture failed as a direct consequence of not sharing basic ideas of partner roles, the importance of customer service and support and ultimately financial obligations. We propose:

> P4:   *Cognitive social capital is necessary for the long-term survival and performance of partner structures due to its role as antecedent of relational social capital and positive impact on the effectiveness and efficiency of the partner structures.*

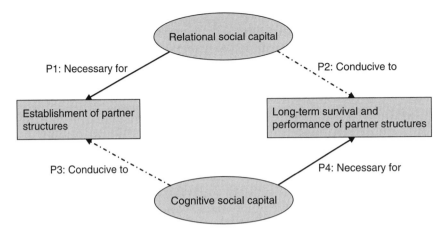

Figure 9.2 Propositions on the role of social capital in the internationalization of international new ventures

The main findings and propositions on the role of social capital in the internationalization process of INVs are summarized in Figure 9.2.

We find relational social capital to be necessary for, and cognitive social capital to be conducive to, the establishment of partner structures. We also find cognitive social capital to be necessary for, and relational social capital to be conducive to, the long-term survival and performance of partner structures.

Conclusions

In this qualitative study of three Norwegian INVs we have investigated the role of partnerships and social capital in their internationalization process. We found that all of the case companies use partnerships in their international strategy, but to a different degree and to different ends. Most of these variations can be explained by looking at the case companies' access to financial capital, market conditions and companies' strategy.

In terms of social capital we found that relational social capital motivates the actors to co-operate, reduces the probability of opportunism and thus the fear of being vulnerable. Relational social capital is necessary for the establishment of partnerships. Furthermore, the long-term development and performance of partnerships are also positively related to the level of relational social capital.

In the case of INVs we find cognitive social capital to be an antecedent of relational social capital and have a direct positive impact on both the tendency to establish and the subsequent effectiveness and efficiency of the partnership. This causes cognitive social capital to be conducive to the establishment of partner arrangements and necessary for the long-term survival and performance of partnerships.

Limitations and suggestions for further research

This study has a few limitations that demand considerations. The first question that arises is whether these cases are representative of INVs in general. Even though they match the definition of INVs as proposed by McDougall et al. (1994) and the quantitative cross-sectional study of Norwegian INVs by Aspelund and Moen (2005) we have to conclude that they might not be typical. The three case companies in this study outperform the average growth rate of INVs found in Aspelund and Moen's quantitative study (2005). A likely explanation is that these companies have had more access to financial capital that most firms. Particularly, Powel and Q-free both possessed substantial resource reserves that might not be associated with the typical INVs. This could also explain their limited use of partnerships. MaXware on the other hand is more of a typical INV in this comparison.

Another obvious weakness is that we have only talked with the INV side of relationships. This is problematic since social capital is never possessed by one actor alone, but is always tied to relationships (Nahapiet and Ghoshal, 1998; Adler and Kwon, 2002). Thus, we really only have got half the story in this study and a more balanced view of the accounts could be retrieved by investigating both parties. Moreover, our investigation gave a retrospective view of the partnerships as interviews were conducted at a time when managers would conclude whether the partnership was a success or not with certainty.

To address these limitations we believe that future research on social capital of INVs should be longitudinal and two-sided in the sense that qualitative data is collected from both/all sides of the collaboration. We will also suggest that case selection should be based on other criteria than 'success'. Finally, we conclude that the INV – social capital relationship is well suited for qualitative analysis and that more research efforts should be put into understanding the different aspects of the relationship.

Notes

* Corresponding Author
1. NOK = Norwegian Kroner. 1 Euro ~ 8 NOK
2. EBITDA = Earnings Before Interest, Tax, Depreciation and Amortization

References

Adler, P.S. and Kwon, S-W. (2002) 'Social capital: Prospects for a new concept', *Academy of Management Review*, 27(1), 17–40.

Arenius, P.M. (2002) 'Creation of Firm-Level Social Capital, Its Exploitation, and the Process of Early Internationalization', Doctoral Thesis, Helsinki University of Technology, Institute of Strategy and International Business.

Aspelund, A., Madsen, T.K. and Moen, Ø. (2007) 'International new ventures: A review of conceptualizations and findings', *European Journal of Marketing*, 41(11/12), 1423–74.

Aspelund, A. and Moen, Ø. (2001) 'A generation perspective on small firm internationalization: From traditional exporters and flexible specialists to born globals', *Advances in International Marketing*, 11, 195–223.

Aspelund, A. and Moen, Ø. (2005) 'Small international firms: – Typology, performance and implications', *Management International Review*, 45(3), 37–57.

Bell, J. (1995) 'The internationalization of small computer software firms: A further challenge to "stage" theories', *European Journal of Marketing*, 29(8), 60–75.

Burt, Roald (2000) 'The Network Entrepreneur', in Sweberg, R. (ed.), *Entrepreneurship – The Social Science View,* 281–307 (Oxford Management Readers, Oxford: Oxford University Press).

Coviello, N. and Munro, H. (1997) 'Network relationships and the internationalisation process of small software firms', *International Business Review,* 6(4), 361–86.

Eisenhardt, K.M. (1989) 'Building theories from case study research', *Academy of Management Review,* 14(4), 532–50.

Gabrielsson, M. and Kirpalani, V.H.M. (2004) 'Born globals: How to reach new business space rapidly', *International Business Review,* 13, 555–71.

Keeble, D., Lawson, C., Smith, H.L., Moore, B. and Wilkinson, F. (1998) 'Internationalisation processes, networking and local embeddedness in technology-intensive small firms', *Small Business Economics,* 11, 327–42.

Madsen, T.K., Rasmussen, E. and Servais, P. (2000) 'Differences and similarities between born globals and other types of exporters', *Advances in International Marketing,* 10, 247–65.

McAuley, A. (1999) 'Entrepreneurial instant exporters in Scottish arts and crafts sector', *Journal of International Marketing,* 7, 67–82.

McDougall, P., Phillips, Shane, S. and Oviatt, B. M. (1994) 'Explaining the formation of international new ventures: The limits of theories from international business research', *Journal of Business Venturing,* 9, 469–87.

Nahapiet, J. and Ghoshal, S. (1998) 'Social capital, intellectual capital, and the organizational advantage', *Academy of Management Review,* 23(2), 242–66.

Oviatt, B.M. and McDougall, P.P. (1994) 'Toward a theory of international new ventures', *Journal of International Business Studies,* First Quarter, 45–64.

Rialp, A., Rialp, J. and Knight, G.A. (2005) 'The phenomenon of early internationalizing firms: What do we know after a decade (1993–2003) of scientific enquiry', *International Business Review,* 14, 147–66.

Sharma, D.D. and Blomstermo, A. (2003) 'The internationalization process of Born Globals; a network view', *International Business Review,* 12, 739–53.

Sørheim, R. (2003) 'The pre-investment behaviour of business angels: A social capital approach', *Venture Capital,* 5(4), 337–64.

Tsai, W. and Ghoshal, S. (1998) 'Social capital and value creation: The role of intrafirm networks', *Academy of Management Journal,* 41(4), 464–76.

Yeoh, P.-L. (2000) 'Information acquisition activities: A study of global start-up exporting companies', *Journal of International Marketing,* 8(3), 36–60.

Yin, R.K. (1989) *Case Study Research* (Newbury Park: Sage publications).

Yin, R.K. (1994) *Case Study – Research Design and Methods* (Newbury Park: Sage publications).

Yli-Renko, H., Autio, E. and Tontti, V. (2002) 'Social capital, knowledge, and the international growth of technology-based new firms', *International Business Review,* 11, 279–304.

10
Clustering and the Internationalization of SMEs in the Media Industry*

Gary Cook and Naresh R. Pandit

Introduction

Geographical clustering is a major characteristic of industrial growth and has recently become the subject of intense interest in academic (Porter, 1990; Saxenian, 1994; Swann et al., 1998), business practitioner (Owen, 1999), and government policy (DTI White Paper, 1998) circles. Porter (1990, 2000), in common with much of the literature in economic geography, has identified two key trends which are powerfully shaping the context for corporate strategy in the twenty-first century: on the one hand the manifest rise in importance of local concentrations of economic activity and excellence; and on the other, a fast paced increase in the globalization of business. The intense interest among economic geographers, including relevance for corporate strategy (Clark et al., 2000; Scott, 2000), stands in contrast to the relatively more muted impact within the management and specifically the strategy and international business fields (Buckley and Ghauri, 2004). What makes this particularly odd are first, that the intense interest of policy makers has been stimulated by the seminal work of strategy scholar Michael Porter (1990) and secondly Porter has repeatedly emphasized the benefits of membership of strong clusters for enhanced international competitiveness.

This chapter attempts to provide some modest evidence in support of the relationship between clusters and international entrepreneurship, by incorporating the regional dimension. Regional cluster strength helps provide a basis which firms can exploit both to grow and internationalize. The positive spillovers available in clusters help SMEs overcome their liabilities of smallness and newness, which are apt to be particularly acute in hindering internationalization, by providing access to resources, capabilities and networks which can be drawn on to support survival and growth. As will be argued below, some of these positive spillovers promote growth generally, whether within domestic or international markets, whereas others bear particularly on efforts to succeed in international business.

The UK media industry provides an important case study for examining these interlinkages. First, the emergence of a cluster of entrepreneurial SMEs is of comparatively recent origin, fostered by the establishment of Channel 4 and Five as

164

broadcasters which did not have in-house production capacity. The second major change was the Broadcasting Act 1990 which inter alia brought in competitive tendering for Independent Television (ITV) network contracts and obliged the BBC and ITV companies to commission 25 per cent of most types of new programmes from external sources. A comparatively small number of the hundreds of independent firms which have sprung up over the past 25 years have not only survived but grown and internationalized relatively rapidly. Indeed, internationalization has been an important component of their growth strategies. What this paper will demonstrate is that the region in which the firm is located is one of the fundamental influences on both the prospect and the extent of internationalization, thus indicating a neglected dimension in the extant literature on international entrepreneurship.

Literature review

Clusters and competitive advantage

The majority of the literature acknowledges and builds on the classic insights of Marshall (1927) into the sources of superior performance in clusters (industrial districts in Marshall's terms): labour market pooling; the emergence of specialized input suppliers; and technological spillovers. A distinction has long been made in the literature (Hoover, 1948) between two potential sources of (urban) dynamism: urbanization economies, which refer to the benefits of size and diversity within a city; and localization economies which refer to the benefits of large scale *in a particular industry* in a particular location, essentially related to the classic Marshallian externalities.

Several authors have championed the region as the most important spatial scale over which clustering processes operate (Florida, 1995; Storper, 1997; Cooke and Morgan, 1998; Scott, 2001). Jacobs' (1972) analysis lays considerable importance on the nature of external linkages a city has, especially import and export activity – a point also emphasized by Hall (2000) – as a powerful contributor to periods of creative flourishing in cities. The importance of external connectivity for remaining at the forefront of innovation has been widely acknowledged in the literature (Boggs and Rantisi, 2003), as it provides a constant stream of fresh ideas and helps prevent insularity and homogenization. In a seminal article, Amin and Thrift (1992) argue persuasively that the emphasis on local production complexes is overdone as it does not recognize the importance of emerging global corporate networks and interconnected global city regions (Scott, 2001). Bathelt et al. (2004) suggest that multinationals provide important 'pipelines' within which tacit knowledge (among other types) can flow in a way which would be less easy between third parties at equivalent distance. Thus, the literature of economic geography sees international linkages of firms in the cluster as being essential to cluster success and dynamism.

A challenge to cluster theory is to account for why some firms appear to benefit more than others from membership of a particular cluster. In recent articles (Pinch et al., 2003; Tallman et al., 2004), an important and bold attempt has been made to meld insights from strategic management and economic geography to argue how membership of key clusters can be the foundation for sustained competitive advantage, which appeals in part to the Resource-Based View (RBV) (Wernerfelt, 1984; Barney, 1991). Whilst not denying the importance of other types of resource, these authors place particular emphasis on knowledge-based resources. They lay importance on the firm's *absorptive capacity* to assimilate and make use of new knowledge (Cohen and Levinthal, 1989). The link with spatial clusters is made by arguing that there exist cluster-level knowledge systems, which some firms are better able to exploit than others. This account of the differential ability of firms to benefit from cluster membership is in principle applicable to entrepreneurial SMEs.

Small firms have long been viewed as an integral part of dynamic industrial districts or clusters (Piore and Sabel, 1984; Scott, 1988), yet entrepreneurs have been conspicuous by their absence in much of the literature on clusters (Acs and Varga, 2005). A growing literature is examining the ways in which dynamic clusters themselves may promote entrepreneurship (Rocha and Sternberg, 2005; Scott, 2006). Scott explicitly argues that as a cluster develops, so increasing agglomeration economies will emerge as more firms are formed and in turn form denser networks which will anchor firms to a particular location. Scott also highlights that the rich social institutions in clusters may be particularly supportive of new firm formation and growth. This indicates an important dynamic interaction in which entrepreneurial firms strengthen clusters and strong clusters promote entrepreneurship.

Internationalization strategies of small firms

The literature on internationalization of SMEs has evolved with three distinct strands, each of which casts some light on the factors that may influence firms to internationalize, and more widely on the means and process by which they will do so. In brief, these are the stages model of the Uppsala School (hereafter referred to as UM) (Johanson and Vahlne, 1977, 1990), the International New Venture (INV) school (Oviatt and McDougall, 1994) and the business network approach (Johanson and Vahlne, 2003; Coviello, 2006). Each of these approaches will now be reviewed to distill the key features which they suggest will influence the prospect, mode and extent of internationalization. Some reflections will also be made on how each of these approaches might interface with insights derived from the clustering literature.

The UM is a behavioural model predicated on fundamental assumptions that risk-averse agents pursue profit under bounded rationality and imperfect information. This leads to the central proposition that firms, especially SMEs, internationalize in an incremental fashion, *albeit* that large firms may have the resources to internationalize in a non-incremental way. One aspect of this is that they typically start with *ad hoc* export orders, move on to a more structured approach through the use of overseas sales agents, then plausibly further develop by establishing their own overseas sales activities and possibly, eventually, overseas production. The second aspect of incrementalism is that firms are argued to pursue markets which are 'psychically close' first and then move on to more 'psychically distant' markets as they acquire experience (Johanson and Vahlne, 1977, 1990). From a clusters perspective, learning can take place within rich circuits of information in highly networked and dense agglomerations. With respect to international business, this will be particularly powerful in major global hubs, which have a heavy presence of domestic and overseas multinationals. It would also help if such hubs were populated by firms with much import and export experience and substantial international movements of labour, providing a pool of labour rich in tacit knowledge regarding overseas markets and the conduct of international business.

The importance of industrial networks has long been appreciated by the Uppsala School. All firms are embedded to a greater or lesser degree in networks comprising suppliers, customers and peers. To the extent that firms are embedded in networks which are international in scope, this may smooth the path of internationalization. Johanson and Vahlne (2003) argue that experiential learning continues to play a vital role in the context of internationalization within business networks. Here, the emphasis is on learning about inter-firm relationships rather than overseas markets. From a clustering perspective, such networking skills, which are important in international business, may be effectively developed in a dense cluster typified by high levels of networking and a global node in Amin and Thrift's (1992) sense will provide important connections to highly internationalized networks.

The basic Uppsala model has long been prone to the basic objection that not all firms internationalize in small steps and that the sequential model is too mechanistic. This basic thought has been effectively crystallized in the theory of international new ventures (INV) set out by Oviatt and McDougall (1994), motivated in part by evidence that firms are increasingly establishing international relationships and operation from a very early stage. Import activity is raised to a higher status in the INV literature than had traditionally been the case in the literature on internationalization, which has been unduly preoccupied with the export side of the equation (Fletcher, 2001).

One of the four key elements which constitute the necessary conditions for the emergence of international new ventures is that the firm must have unique resources as a basis for being competitive in international markets. In this regard, Oviatt and McDougall (1994) explicitly appeal to Barney's (1991) RBV. Resources are also likely to have an influence on choice of entry mode. A typical perspective is that SMEs lack both management and financial resources and that they may therefore need to leverage the resources of sales agents or other export intermediaries either domestic or overseas in order to exploit overseas opportunities without undue risk (Zacharakis, 1997), or may enter joint ventures (Lu and Beamish, 2006). The ability to exploit previous experience in international business has been one of the reasons advanced in the INV approach to explain how rapid internationalization is possible. What clusters theory contributes is the idea that such experience is more abundantly available in some locations than others both because there will be more firms, hence labour, which have international experience in stronger clusters and also because the labour markets, particularly in major global nodes, are highly international in scope.

Conclusion

Two propositions emerge from the above discussion that will be explored in the evidence to be presented below.

Proposition 1. Strong clusters promote internationalization through contributing to firm competencies through spillovers, promoting entrepreneurship and providing access to international networks.

Proposition 2. There will be a differential ability of firms to benefit from cluster membership which will manifest itself in the form of differing growth rates and differing levels of internationalization.

Methodology

The main empirical evidence for the present study is based on a series of econometric models, described more fully in the results section, aimed at identifying the principal influences on the decision to internationalize through importing or exporting and the extent of internationalization. The basic dataset on which this analysis was conducted is the UK's Annual Survey of International Trade in Film and Television Services (FTV). The survey examines sources of export and import revenues by country and as such provides a unique and detailed resource. In order to produce meaningful analysis of the pattern and extent of export and import activity, the FTV data was merged with a variety of additional databases maintained by the UK's Office for National Statistics: the Annual Respondents Database (ARD) and the Business Structure Database (further details available from the author on request). Analysis in the regression models was based on those firms with fewer than 600 employees, which was a natural break in the firm-size distribution and broadly consistent with the conventional cut-off for SMEs of 500 employees.

The interpretation of the econometric results is underpinned by evidence from two studies previously conducted by the authors investigating the principal advantages of strong clusters and the key processes which underpin them. The first was a comparative analysis of three city-regions, specifically London, Bristol and Glasgow, based on 74 interviews. The second was a questionnaire survey of firms in London conducted between January and April 2004 which resulted in 204 usable responses (further details available from the author on request). This more detailed evidence is important given the observational equivalence problem which confronts the econometric evidence taken in isolation. The superior growth of firms in stronger clusters, principally London, may be due to inherent advantages of the location, such as its position as a major transportation node connecting important markets or the existence of a large pool of human, physical or financial resources, rather than being due to processes involving the interconnection of firms, especially those requiring conscious co-operation.

Empirical evidence on small firm internationalization

Logistic models of participation in import or export activity

The first set of models estimated were logistic regressions based on a 1,0 dependent variable examining whether the firm was engaged in international activity, exporting or importing, or not. The basic model had the form:

$$L_i = \beta_1 Size_i + \beta_2 Overseas_i + \beta_3 Age_i + \beta_4 MP_i + \beta_5 OthMP_i + \beta_6 TV_i + \beta_7 Locquo_i + \beta_8 Totemp_i$$

where L_i is the log of the odds ratio $Ln(P_i/(1 - P_i))$ and P_i is the probability that the firm either exports or imports respectively. The coefficients reported for the logistic regression show the change in the log-odds ratio for a one unit change in the independent variable, therefore a coefficient less than 1 indicates an increase in the independent variable made, respectively, importing or exporting less likely.

- Size was measured by numbers of employees, measured in natural logs due to the strong positive skew. This proxies resource strength and is thus expected to be positive in both the import and export equations.
- Overseas was a 1,0 dummy variable taking the value 1 where the firm had a code indicating it was ultimately owned by an overseas corporation. This is a priori expected to have a positive sign.
- Age is the age in years of the firm since first registration, sign expected positive.
- MP is a 1,0 dummy indicating that the firm was classified to SIC 92111, motion picture production, which is expected to take a negative coefficient due to the lower propensity to engage in trade relative to the default category SIC 92120, motion picture and video distribution.
- OthMP is a 1,0 dummy variable indicating that the firm was classified to SIC 92119, other motion picture and video production. This SIC contains some post-production companies which have been relatively successful in international markets, however it also contains numerous very small companies which barely survive on intermittent production work, hence the expected sign is ambiguous.
- TV is a 1,0 dummy indicating the firm belongs to SIC 92202, television activities. Despite the recent rise in international activity in TV, the expected sign is negative as the majority of independent programme production companies are very small and serve the domestic market (often a regional market).
- Locquo is the location quotient of the region in which the firm is located. The location quotient is constructed as the ratio of total media employment in the region to that of all media employment in Britain divided by the ratio of total employment in the region to all employment in Britain. The location quotient thus represents the extent of clustering in the region. A quotient above one indicates that the region has a disproportionate share of media employment relative to its total employment. The prior expectation is that the coefficient

will be positive representing the positive effect of stronger clusters which will manifest itself, in part, in stronger export performance.

• Totemp is total employment in the region. This crudely represents the extent of urbanization economies in the region, sign expected to be positive.

The strongest influence on propensity to engage in either export or import activity is firm size (see Table 10.1), which may be given a crude interpretation as indicating the importance of resource strength. Firms with resource strength would be expected to grow larger, controlling for age and also to accumulate resources through the process of growth. Age has a negative influence, although not significant and virtually indistinguishable from zero in the export equation. This is consistent with the INV literature, which argues that it is resource strength rather than age which is the principal influence on whether or not a firm will engage in international activity. A somewhat speculative interpretation of the larger (negative) coefficient on age in the import equation may be that as firms mature, they become better able to produce internally goods and services they previously imported. Penetrating export markets is more demanding of resources and also experience and contacts accumulated over time, therefore one would not expect export activity to diminish with age in the same way. The location quotient has a positive coefficient and is highly significant in both equations implying that firms located in stronger clusters are more likely to be engaged in importing and exporting. Total regional employment has a barely positive effect and is quite far from conventional significance, indicating that it is regional strength in media employment which is the principal source of the positive influence, as far as having at least some international activity is concerned. As would be expected, being

Table 10.1   Logistic regression for probability of engaging in importing and exporting

Variable	Import model			Export model		
	Coefficient	z	Marginal effect	Coefficient	z	Marginal effect
Size	1.7201	6.27	0.05220***	1.5785	6.01	0.06645***
Age	0.9739	−1.46	−0.00254	0.9997	−0.02	−0.00004
Overseas	1.4094	1.01	0.03540	1.4057	1.21	0.05239
MP	0.3868	−1.92	−0.07453*	0.8706	−0.35	−0.01970
OthMP	0.5845	−1.34	−0.04820	1.1457	0.39	0.02011
TV	0.8121	−0.56	−0.01949	0.9553	−0.14	−0.00662
Location quotient	1.2666	2.36	0.02275**	1.2300	2.43	0.03014**
Total regional employment	1.0001	0.29	0.00001	1.0002	0.81	0.00003
N observations	597			597		
Wald χ^2	103.16***			89.87***		
Pseudo-R^2	0.22			0.17		

Notes: *** significant at 1% ** significant at 5% * significant at 10%.

a subsidiary of an overseas firm is positively associated with the likelihood of being engaged in import or export activity, although a little outside conventional significance levels. The generally negative coefficients on the industry dummies are consistent with expectation.

Import and export intensity

A set of models were run to examine the principal influences on export/import intensity. This was measured as exports/imports per employee due to the fact that only a small number (64) of firms had turnover data available (very small firms are not required to file turnover data in the UK). The Heckman (1979) two-step procedure is required as we have censored observations of export and import activity. Failing to take into account the fact that firms have made *a prior* choice to either import or export through the selection equation would lead to biased estimates in the export/import intensity equations. The export/import intensity equations were as follows, with a full and a restricted model being separately estimated. The selection equation in each case (not reported for brevity as it is highly similar to the logistic regressions reported in the previous section) was as follows:

$$Y_i = \beta_1 Size_i + \beta_2 Overseas_i + \beta_3 Age_i + \beta_4 MP_i + \beta_5 OthMP_i + \beta_6 TV_i + \beta_7 Memp_i$$

where Memp is total media employment in the sector.

Restricted model

$$Y_i = \beta_0 + \beta_1 Size_i + \beta_2 Overseas_i + \beta_3 Age_i + \beta_4 MP_i + \beta_5 OthMP_i + \beta_6 TV_i + \beta_7 Locquo_i + \beta_8 Totemp_i$$

Full model

A more extensive model was estimated in cases where additional financial information for a sub-set of firms was available, in order to capture more firm-specific effects.

$$Y_i = \beta_0 + \beta_1 Size_i + \beta_2 Overseas_i + \beta_3 Age_i + \beta_4 MP_i + \beta_5 OthMP_i + \beta_6 TV_i + \beta_7 Locquo_i + \beta_8 Totemp_i + \beta_9 Productivity_i + \beta_{10} Advertising/sales_i + \beta_{11} R\&D/sales_i + \beta_{12} Meanwage_i + \beta_{13} Investment\ intensity_i$$

- Productivity is measured as gross value-added per head. The expected sign is positive as greater productivity implies greater cost competitiveness.
- Advertising/Sales is a standard proxy for a resource strength in product differentiation. The expected sign is positive.
- R&D/Sales is a standard proxy for resource strength in innovation. The expected sign is positive.
- Mean Wage. The expected sign here is ambiguous. A high value might imply resource strength in terms of a labour force skewed towards more highly

skilled employees. Alternatively it may represent a disadvantage of relatively high costs.
• Investment intensity is measured as net capital expenditure/sales, expected sign positive.

Considering first the restricted export and import models, size and being under foreign ownership take positive signs as expected, although the coefficients are far from conventional significance. Age is positive in the export equation (see Table 10.2) but negative in the import equation. The negative sign on age in the import equation (see Table 10.3) is consistent with the logistic regressions of the probability of being engaged in exporting or importing. Again, importing may be easier for younger firms compared to exporting and younger firms may be more reliant on importing, lacking resources. There is an interesting contrast in the behaviour of the regional variables in the export and import models. The coefficient on the location quotient becomes barely distinguishable from zero. The coefficient on total employment remains positive and is close to significance in both equations, implying that as far as export and import intensity go, urbanization economies may be more important than localization economies. Sectoral dummies behave

Table 10.2   Heckman two-step model of export intensity second step results

Variable	Restricted model		Full model	
	Coefficient	z	Coefficient	z
Size	248.5235	0.45	0.5943	0.22
Age	0.4494	0.03	6.1479	0.45
Overseas	289.0943	0.59	203.1317	0.71
MP	−115.2359	−0.28	350.1079	0.95
OthMP	−1.2121	−0.00	206.3557	0.58
TV	56.8050	0.17	394.4886	1.17
Location quotient	97.8228	0.35	4.2176	0.05
Total regional employment	0.2870	1.38	0.0548	0.28
Productivity			0.8236	1.50
Advertising/Sales			1636.98	1.26
R&D/Sales			6858.712	0.21
Mean Wage			0.4275	0.12
Investment Intensity			27.3772	0.07
Rho	1.0000		0.5630	
Sigma	1559.6933		273.7773	
Lambda	1559.6933		154.1408	
N observations	597		493	
Censored obs.	464		464	
Uncensored obs.	133		29	
Wald χ^2	83.06***		58.06***	

Notes: *** significant at 1% ** significant at 5% * significant at 10%.

much as expected, the positive coefficient on TV in the export model probably reflecting the small core staff in television production companies which inflates the export intensity ratio.

The results from the full model clearly need to be treated with extreme caution as they have a very small number of uncensored observations. Nevertheless, there are a few pertinent observations. As expected, the inclusion of a greater array of firm-specific variables generally moderates the influence of the variables included in the restricted model. The impact of the regional variables, in particular total regional employment, is clearly weakened, implying that for the larger firms remaining in the restricted model, for which a greater array of financial data is available, firm resources play a greater role in supporting international activity relative to regional externalities. In both equations productivity, advertising intensity and investment intensity have the expected positive sign, with advertising intensity being significant in the import model. The negative coefficient on R&D intensity in the import equation is hard to rationalize. The negative and highly insignificant coefficient on mean wage reflects the ambiguous a priori influence of this variable. Similar results regarding the generally positive effects of these measures of resource strength were evident in a number of other

Table 10.3 Heckman two-step model of import intensity second step results

Variable	Restricted model		Full model	
	Coefficient	z	Coefficient	z
Size	47.750	0.15	1.1749	0.67
Age	−8.5736	−0.49	−1.5401	−0.31
Overseas	264.6040	1.00	137.1647	0.97
MP	−366.2376	−0.64		
OthMP	−431.0996	−1.23	328.3660	1.78*
TV	−175.8165	−0.86	517.9682	2.31**
Location quotient	27.8352	0.19	−28.4118	−0.62
Total regional employment	0.1558	1.53	0.0086	0.15
Productivity			0.5628	1.60
Advertising/sales			4206.9810	3.37***
R&D/sales			−87745.1500	−0.66
Mean wage			−1.2367	−0.61
Investment intensity			545.2009	0.29
Rho	0.8792		0.8436	
Sigma	666.8622		183.0189	
Lambda	586.2995		154.3889	
N observations	587		520	
Censored obs.	498		498	
Uncensored obs.	99		22	
Wald χ^2	96.11***		56.03***	

Notes: *** significant at 1% ** significant at 5% * significant at 10%.

regression models which are not reported. In summary, the evidence is consistent with the RBV/INV perspective that firm resource strength will be an important foundation of successful internationalization.

Geographic and psychic distance

The models estimated to explore the propensity to export to or import from more heterogeneous markets were based on the count of the number of separate markets each firm was engaged in, in either an import or an export capacity. The appropriate modelling technique was negative binomial regression as the presence of a small number of firms exporting to and importing from a very large number of markets meant that the over-dispersion test of Cameron and Trivedi (1990) rejected the restriction implicit in the Poisson model that mean and variance be equal.

In both models size is positive and significant as expected (see Table 10.4) and exerts a stronger influence than age as the INV and RBV literatures would predict. Consistent with the previous models, age has a stronger influence in the export equation. The location quotient is negative and insignificant in the export equation, yet positive and significant in the import equation. This may reflect the importance of the UK as a market for imported motion pictures and television programmes, with London, which has by far the highest location quotient, being the hub of this trade. Total employment is positive in both equations, being significant in the export equation and just outside significance in the import equation, again implying that urbanization economies may be more important than localization economies in influencing the extent of exporting and importing once the decision to engage in export or import activity has been taken. The sectoral dummies are negative, in line with expectation.

Table 10.4 Negative binomial regressions of number of export and import markets served

Variable	Import model			Export model		
	Coefficient	z	Marginal effect	Coefficient	z	Marginal effect
Size	0.3320	4.19	0.7521***	0.2790	3.57	1.2337***
Age	0.0015	0.10	0.0034	0.0222	1.38	0.0981
Overseas	−0.2414	−0.83	−0.5460	0.0632	0.18	0.2798
MP	−0.9019	−2.12	−1.5387*	−1.1606	−2.93	−3.6069***
OthMP	−1.0307	−2.82	−2.0452***	−1.1442	−3.59	−4.3908***
TV	−0.3839	−1.28	−0.8338	−0.4383	−1.29	−1.8485
Location Quotient	0.1833	2.10	0.4151**	−0.0520	−0.65	−0.2300
Total regional employment	0.0002	1.13	0.0005	0.0005	2.04	0.0024**
N observations	155			155		
Wald χ²	70.84***			113.33***		

Notes: *** significant at 1% ** significant at 5% * significant at 10%.

Discussion

The set of models examining the propensity to internationalize lead to some tentative conclusions. Taken together, they indicate that firm-specific factors are generally more important than regional clustering effects. Size and, to a lesser extent, age and foreign ownership, were shown to have an influence on both the fact of engaging in export and import activity and its extent. Where included in the export and import intensity models, an array of variables indicating firm-specific advantages such as productivity, advertising intensity and R&D intensity were influential. Moreover, the generally low fit of the models indicates omitted variables, many of which, according to the literature review, would be expected to be related to firm-specific factors on which data was simply not available in the current study. There was some evidence, however, that regional influences do matter. Localization economies as represented by the location quotient were seen to have a strong positive influence on the propensity to internationalize, but much less influence on the eventual extent of that internationalization. The basic fact that imports and exports are dominated by firms based in London, above and beyond the proportion of firms located there, also suggests cluster effects on internationalization. Urbanization effects, as represented by the scale of total regional employment, had a greater association with the magnitude of international activity at the firm level than did the location quotient. The greater importance of total regional employment may be picking up a number of effects associated with London and the South East. These general conclusions are robust for a range of dependent variables.

The results above indicate that regional effects positively influence small firm internationalization. This begs the question of what is underpinning that relationship. Recent econometric research conducted on the British broadcasting industry (Cook et al., 2001) has yielded results which show that stronger clusters have higher rates of surviving new firm start-ups and those firms also grow more quickly on average. This broad pattern is consistent with Scott's (2006) theory of how dynamic clusters evolve with increased firm formation leading to higher specialization and greater networking, supporting the further formation of new enterprises in a positive feedback loop.

The importance of social capital in supporting positive spillovers in media clusters is very manifest. The interview evidence and reading of the trade literature does reveal that substantial support, both in terms of advice and resources, can be forthcoming for entrepreneurs starting new businesses. Firms are often also able to draw on personal networks and the reputations of their founders to attract business and secure necessary supplies and services following formation. An important section of the questionnaire asked about why it was important to have close proximity to other firms in London. Collectively these factors achieved the highest ratings, with prime importance being placed on face-to-face contact, interpersonal relationships and the ability to establish trust. Three of the other top ten benefits of a London location revealed in the questionnaire survey were support from customers and suppliers in innovation and the ability to secure help from colleagues in other firms. These factors indicate the importance of networking within the London cluster. The strength of the labour pool provides another three of the top ten benefits of a London location. The broad mix of media industries concentrated in London supports the fine-grained division of labour, which is important for dynamic productivity growth and innovation.

Regarding international connectivity, as Cook and Pandit (2007) report, the impression from the questionnaire evidence is that MNEs are somewhat less reliant on the cluster than non-MNEs, yet they are also quite closely engaged and embedded within it and are drawn into the cluster by the same positive spillovers as enjoyed by other firms. One implication is that MNEs are likely to have a beneficial impact on the dynamism of the cluster. They gain strength from being in the cluster and due to their engagement in the cluster they are more likely to give rise to positive spillovers to other firms in the cluster, including non-MNEs. The dynamic strength of the cluster is likely in the future both to give rise to more overseas multinationals being attracted into the cluster and to more domestic firms taking the step of becoming multinational. MNEs also draw human and financial resources into the cluster, as well as being important hubs in international networks of production and distribution, which can all support the internationalization processes of small firms.

What of possible feedback effects from internationalization on firm and cluster strength? Internationalization strategies in post-production are essentially export based. There are a small number of notable examples of companies which have made FDI moves, three leading examples being the creation of New York subsidiaries by CFC Framestore, The Mill and thirdly, Smoke and Mirrors. International sales in film, advertising and broadcast television post-production are for high value-added work. This is above all the case for high-end special effects on Hollywood blockbuster movies (Film Council, 2003). This export-based activity is an important part of the dynamics of the London cluster, since work on these projects both develops skills and allows investment in the latest technology. It also adds to the reputation of the cluster and specific firms within it. Only a limited number of companies in London have the scale and capability to compete for high-end film work, the most significant being CFC Framestore, the Mill, MPC, Double Negative and Cinesite (non-UK). There is evidence of a 'trickle down' effect to other local companies of the techniques and technology used in the most cutting-edge work (Oxford Economic Forecasting, 2005).

FDI has not been a major feature of independent programme production. The UK is second-largest exporter of TV programmes, albeit a distant second to the USA. Many small companies in television programme production do not benefit to any great extent because they rely on sales intermediaries, which may be broadcasters or independent distributors, since they lack the resources and know-how to penetrate international markets on their own account. A small minority of firms have, however, managed to retain a greater share of the revenues from international sales by selling directly. This fact is important, as exploiting intellectual property through international sales is a rich source of cash flows as the marginal costs involved are very small, therefore any revenues earned are almost pure profit. Once a company has a stronger and diversified revenue stream it is much better placed to raise outside finance (Television Research Partnership, 2005). The vast majority of these firms are based in London.

Conclusions

This chapter has presented a few strands of evidence relating to the question of the interconnections between clusters, entrepreneurship and international expansion. Proposition 1 is supported. Those firms which have seen the greatest success in terms of international expansion have almost all been London based. This accords with Requena-Silvente's (2005) finding that geographic spillovers promote SME exports. Clusters, entrepreneurship and internationalization are mutually reinforcing. Exports and outward direct investment provide not only revenues but also develop skills by serving demanding overseas customers. The high value-added work which overseas sales typically involve also helps attract MNEs and highly skilled labour into the London media cluster at a global scale. The fact that London is a major global node in the industry is an important ingredient in its dynamism. The stronger the cluster, the stronger existing firms become. In the internationalization regressions, cluster strength in terms of media concentration was found to be positively associated with the likelihood of firms exporting and importing. It was less influential in explaining the extent of internationalization, with urbanization economies, as proxied by total regional employment, being more to the fore.

The pattern of development in both programme production and post-production supports proposition 2. In both sectors a small number of dominant, independent firms have arisen and are highly important in international sales. It is the programme production firms which have exploited their intellectual property essentially under their own steam that have enjoyed the highest success. They have also gained experience and developed networks through their involvement in international sales and co-production. Those firms forced to rely to a greater degree on third parties for distribution have not flourished to the same extent. In the internationalization regressions, firm-specific factors of size and, to a lesser extent, age and overseas ownership were seen as influences on the fact and extent of internationalization. There was also limited evidence that a broader array of firm-specific factors which indicate resource-based advantages were positively associated with import and export intensity.

This paper has some important implications for the literature. The INV literature catalysed by Oviatt and McDougall (1994) has rightly focused attention on the resource strengths and capabilities of new firms as being fundamental influences on the timing and extent of internationalization. A key contribution of this paper is to provide evidence that the ability to develop such strengths and capabilities, or to mitigate their absence by tapping into external sources, is influenced by geographic location. In short, stronger clusters support internationalization and, indeed, firm growth more generally. The theoretical and empirical treatment of the relationship between internationalization and cluster success, however, needs to be more nuanced. The current state-of-the-art in terms of understanding internationalization patterns needs to be better informed with an understanding of why some firms are better able than others to capitalize on the advantages presented within clusters.

Note

* This work contains statistical data from ONS which is Crown copyright and reproduced with the permission of the controller of HMSO and Queen's Printer for Scotland. The use of the ONS statistical data in this work does not imply the endorsement of the ONS in relation to the interpretation or analysis of the statistical data. This work uses research datasets which may not exactly reproduce National Statistics aggregates.

References

Acs, Z.J. and Varga, A. (2005) 'Entrepreneurship, agglomeration and technical change', *Small Business Economics*, XXIV, 323–34.

Amin, A. and Thrift, N. (1992) 'Neo-Marshallian nodes in global networks', *International Journal of Urban and Regional Research*, XVI, 571–87.

Barney, J.B. (1991) 'Firm resources and sustained competitive advantage', *Journal of Management*, XVII, 99–120.

Bathelt, H., Malmberg, A. and Maskell, P. (2004) 'Clusters and knowledge: Local buzz, global pipelines and the process of knowledge creation', *Progress in Human Geography*, XXVIII, 31–56.

Boggs, J.S. and Rantisi, N.M. (2003) 'The "relational turn" in economic geography', *Journal of Economic Geography*, III, 109–16.

Buckley, P.J. and Ghauri, P.N. (2004) 'Globalization, economic geography and the strategy of multinational enterprises', *Journal of International Business Studies*, XXXV, 81–98.

Cameron, A. and Trivedi, P. (1990) 'Regression-based tests for over-dispersion in the poisson model', *Journal of Econometrics*, XLVI, 347–64.

Clark, G.L., Feldman, M.P. and Gertler, M.S. (eds) (2000) *The Oxford Handbook of Economic Geography* (Oxford: Oxford University Press).

Cohen, W.M. and Levinthal, D.A. (1989) 'Innovation and learning: The two faces of R&D', *The Economic Journal*, XCIX, 569–96.

Cook, G. and Pandit, N.R. (2007) 'International linkages and entrepreneurship in media clusters: Evidence from the UK', in *Uddevalla Symposium 2006*. Research Reports 2007:01 (University West, Sweden).

Cook, G., Pandit, N.R. and Swann, G.M.P. (2001) 'The dynamics of industrial clustering in British broadcasting', *Information Economics and Policy*, XIII, 351–75.

Cooke, G. and Morgan, M. (1998) *The Associational Economy: Firms, Regions and Innovation* (Oxford: Oxford University Press).

Coviello, N. (2006) 'The network dynamics of international new ventures', *Journal of International Business Studies*, XXXVII, 713–31.

DTI White Paper (1998) *Our Competitive Future: Building the Knowledge Driven Economy* Cmnd. 4176 (London: HMSO).

Film Council (2003) *Post-Production in the U.K.* (London: DTI).

Fletcher, R. (2001) 'A holistic approach to internationalization', *International Business Review*, X, 25–49.

Florida, R. (1995) 'Toward the learning region', *Futures*, XXVII, 527–36.

Hall, P. (2000) 'Creative cities and economic development', *Urban Studies*, XXXVII, 639–49.

Heckman, J. (1979) 'Sample selection bias as a specification error', *Econometrica*, XLVII, 153–61.

Hoover, E.M. (1948) *The Location of Economic Activity* (New York: McGraw-Hill).

Jacobs, J. (1972) *The Economy of Cities* (Harmondsworth: Penguin).

Johanson, J. and Vahlne, J-E. (1977) 'The internationalization process of the firm – a model of knowledge development and increasing foreign market commitments', *Journal of International Business Studies*, VIII, 23–32.

Johanson, J. and Vahlne, J-E. (1990) 'The mechanism of internationalization', *International Marketing Review*, VII, 11–24.

Johanson, J. and Vahlne, J-E. (2003) 'Business relationship learning and commitment in the internationalization process', *Journal of International Entrepreneurship*, I, 83–101.

Lu, J.W. and Beamish, P.W. (2006) 'Partnering strategies and performance of SMEs' international joint ventures', *Journal of Business Venturing*, XXI, 461–86.

Marshall, A. (1927) *Industry and Trade* (London: Macmillan).

Oviatt, B.M. and McDougall, P.P. (1994) 'Toward a theory of international new ventures', *Journal of International Business Studies*, XXV, 45–64.

Owen, D. (1999) 'Economic geography rewritten', *The Business Economist*, XXX, 23–38.

Oxford Economic Forecasting (2005) *The Economic Contribution of the UK Film Post-Production and Visual Effects Industry* (report commissioned by UK Post) (Oxford: Oxford Economic Forecasting).

Pinch, S., Henry, N., Jenkins, M. and Tallman, S. (2003) 'From "industrial districts" to "knowledge clusters": A model of knowledge dissemination and competitive advantage in industrial agglomerations', *Journal of Economic Geography*, III, 373–88.

Piore, M. and Sabel, C. (1984) *The Second Industrial Divide: Possibilities for Prosperity* (New York: Basic Books).

Porter, M.E. (2000) 'Locations, clusters and company strategy', in G.L. Clark, M.P. Feldman and M.S. Gertler (eds) *The Oxford Handbook of Economic Geography* (Oxford: Oxford University Press).

Porter, M.E. (1990) *The Competitive Advantage of Nations* (London: Macmillan).

Requena-Silvente, F. (2005) 'The decision to enter and exit foreign markets: Evidence from U.K. SMEs', *Small Business Economics*, XXV, 237–53.

Rocha, H.O. and Sternberg, R. (2005) 'Entrepreneurship: The role of clusters, theoretical perspectives and empirical evidence from Germany', *Small Business Economics*, XXIV, 267–92.

Saxenian, A. (1994) *Regional Advantage: Culture and Competition in Silicon Valley and Route 128* (Cambridge, MA: Harvard University Press).

Scott, A.J. (2006) 'Entrepreneurship, innovation and industrial development: geography and the creative field revisited', *Small Business Economics*, 26, 1–24.

Scott, A.J. (ed.) (2001) *Global City-Region* (Oxford: Oxford University Press).

Scott, A.J. (2000) 'Economic geography: The great half century' in G.L. Clark, M.P. Feldman and M.S. Gertler (eds) *The Oxford Handbook of Economic Geography* (Oxford: Oxford University Press).

Scott, A.J. (1988) *New Industrial Spaces: Flexible Production, Organization and Regional Development in North America and Western Europe* (London: Pion).

Storper, M. (1997) *The Regional World: Territorial Development in A Global Economy* (New York: Guilford).

Tallman, S., Jenkins, M., Henry, N. and Pinch, S. (2004) 'Knowledge, clusters and competitive advantage', *Academy of Management Review*, XXIX, 258–71.

Television Research Partnership (2005) *Rights of Passage: British Television in a Global Market* (London: UK Trade & Investment).

Wernerfelt, B. (1984) 'A Resource-based view of the firm', *Strategic Management Journal*, V, 171–80.

Zacharakis, A.L. (1997) 'Entrepreneurial Entry into Foreign Markets: A Transaction Cost Perspective', *Entrepreneurship, Theory and Practice*, XXI, 23–39.

Part III
Emerging Market Challenges

11
Learning in International Joint Ventures in Central and Eastern European Countries: System of Innovation Approach

Irina Jormanainen

Introduction

The strategy of local firms in Central and Eastern European (CEE) transition economies to establish International Joint Ventures (IJVs) with western multi-national corporations (MNCs) has become increasingly popular during the past two decades, and it has been widely recognized that such IJVs provide an excellent opportunity for local partner firms' learning (Lyles and Salk, 1996; Sadowski, 2001). Previous research recognizes learning as a main source for developing and sustaining competitive advantage, and the burgeoning micro-level literature on learning in IJVs has investigated its antecedents and consequences focusing on the assessment of partners' characteristics, knowledge attributes and relationship factors (Cohen and Levinthal, 1990; Inkpen, 1998). The outcomes of learning have been measured in terms of IJVs' performance and innovativeness (Lane, Salk and Lyles, 2001).

However, although firm-level determinants are important for the understanding of learning in IJVs, this study argues that it is vital to account for macro-level factors originating from the external environment. Specifically, the innovation literature suggests that System of Innovation (SI) has a strong impact on the activities of local and foreign firms in host economy. Therefore, the main objective of the present paper is to develop a systemic theoretical approach for gaining a deeper understanding of the scope of learning in IJVs, by bridging several streams of macro- and micro-literature. The SI approach is employed in order to explain how the structural characteristics of the national economy such as its specific production structure, basic and knowledge infrastructure and institutional set-up influence the types of established IJVs in terms of foreign and local partners' strategic objectives, resource contributions and learning intents. Further, the study suggests that possibilities for and consequences of local partners' learning in IJVs vary across different types of IJVs, depending on quality and quantity of knowledge-based resources transferred to the IJV and the nature of co-operation between partners. The developed theoretical framework demonstrates causal links existing between different elements of SI and scope of learning in IJVs. This framework allows for a better understanding that due to the differences in SIs in different national contexts as well as sector-specific determinants, not all IJVs provide local firms with equal opportunities for the acquisition of the advanced knowledge. Theoretical discussion is supported by the analysis of manufacturing IJVs in Russia, Poland, the Czech Republic and Hungary established during the 1998–2006 period. The IJV database was created on the basis of several secondary sources, including databases reporting newspaper announcements on the IJVs, national statistics offices and foreign direct investment agencies.

The structure of the chapter will be as follows. Sections 'Firm-level perspective on learning in IJVs' and 'Macro-level perspective at learning' provide a discussion of theoretical approaches to learning, including micro- and macro-streams of research emphasizing their relevance for a better understanding of learning in IJVs. 'Impact of SI on learning in IJVs' presents the theoretical framework of the study, demonstrating the causal relationships between various elements of SI and learning in IJVs. 'Methodology' explains the empirical methodology of the research. 'The empirical evidence of System of Innovation impact on scope of learning in IJVs in CEE countries' describes the nature of SIs in CEE countries and their influence on the sectoral distribution of manufacturing IJVs and scope of learning in IJVs in Russia, the Czech Republic, Poland and Hungary. The last section provides the reader with conclusions of the study and suggests avenues for future research.

Firm-level perspective on learning in IJVs

The management literature recognizes IJVs as an opportunity for learning and knowledge acquisition where partners have close access to each other's knowledge (Hamel, 1991; Khanna, Gulati and Nohria, 1998), and thus, the number of IJVs has significantly grown over the last few decades in both developing and developed countries. Management scholars define learning as a process of improving actions through increased knowledge and understanding (Fiol and Lyles, 1985), and argue that learning takes place at the individual level and moves upward to firm level (Nonaka and Takeuchi, 1995). Hence, studies to date have investigated various firm-level factors influencing learning in IJVs including its antecedents and the process (Cohen and Levinthal, 1990; Inkpen, 2000). However, less attention in the management literature has been paid by scholars to the examination of measurements of learning and its outcomes for partner firms.

Although extensive, the firm-level literature has several limitations. Specifically, it overlooks the importance of the external environment influence, which, from our perspective, has a significant impact on the structural characteristics of IJVs and antecedents of learning. As Hennart (2006) suggests, the structure of an IJV to a large extent explains the outcomes of the processes taking place in IJVs. Hence, we assume that structural features of IJVs will significantly influence the scope and outcomes of learning. We will next discuss other streams of literature which take different approaches to learning, but are considered relevant to our deeper understanding of learning in IJVs.

Macro-level perspective at learning

The macro-level literature on development argues that learning and knowledge acquisition lie at the heart of the development of firm- and national-level technological capabilities (Lall, 1992). It is worth noting that these streams of the literature focus explicitly on the technological learning, suggesting that development of technological foundations in firms and industrial restructuring are the most important factors for economic development. Several features of technological learning and capabilities building have been distinguished in development literature, which are also applicable to learning in general.

First, technological learning requires firms to allocate significant investment and acquire knowledge and other resources from domestic and non-domestic sources (Wignaraja, 2002). Foreign sources of knowledge have long been recognized as essential elements in the technological development of local firms in less developed countries (Bell and Pavitt, 1993; Kim, 1998). Second, technological learning and capabilities development is an incremental and cumulative process (Wignaraja, 2002). Firms gradually develop their technological foundations over time, and this process is influenced by the factors of the external environment. The particular approach of technological capabilities development which domestic firms follow in each country has historical origins, and thus, these processes have specific features in each of the national contexts. Hence, it was recognized that firm-level technological capabilities development is embedded in the national SI.

The SI was defined as 'all parts and aspects of the economic structure and the institutional set-up affecting learning as well as searching and exploring – the production system and the system of finance present themselves as sub-systems in which learning takes place' (Lundvall, 1992, p. 12). In other words, the SI includes elements and relationships which interact in the production, diffusion and use of new knowledge. Edquist (1997) argues that this approach allows for including a broad spectrum of factors that influence knowledge development in firms such as economic, institutional, organizational, social and political factors. Three main groups of elements could be distinguished in SI (Lundvall, 1992; Edquist, 1997; Narula, 2003): (1) private organizations represented by domestic firms including networks between customers, suppliers and competitors; in-house R&D, professional and industrial organizations and foreign affiliates; (2) public organizations including governments, universities and R&D institutes; and (3) formal and informal institutions, such as intellectual property rights, technical standards, investment incentives, taxation, competition policy and so on. These elements are interconnected through numerous links which are evolving over time. Changes in one element of the system will lead to various adjustments in the others. Each element of SI has a significant impact on the process of capabilities development in firms, and there is interdependence between firm-, industry- and country-level technological accumulation. Thus, there are factors which are firm-specific and those that are common to given countries depending on their policy regimes, skills endowment and institutional structures (Lall, 1992).

To summarize, the important finding of the innovation and technological capabilities studies is that the process and outcomes of learning and capabilities building in firms are embedded in, and influenced, by the external environment, specifically the SI of the home country. Therefore, we find the SI approach highly applicable for understanding the nature of IJVs operations and scope of learning. The next section will elaborate on these aspects in greater detail.

Impact of SI on learning in IJVs

Recognizing the importance of the findings of previous macro-level studies, this chapter aims to improve understanding of the nature of learning in IJVs by incorporating insights from those studies with literature on learning in IJVs. The main objective of this research is to examine how SI affects the scope of learning in an IJV, and the framework developed in the chapter aims to demonstrate the causal links existing between SI and scope of learning in IJVs. Figure 11.1 provides an illustration of the framework.

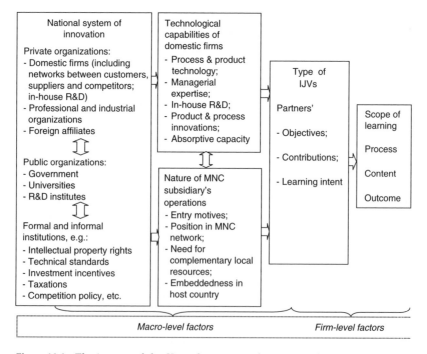

Figure 11.1 The impact of the SI on the scope and outcome of learning in IJVs

Impact of SI on local firms' activities

The innovation literature argues that the stock of knowledge of the firms in a given location is defined to a large extent by the external environment consisting of economic actors and institutions, which are closely interconnected (Edquist, 1997; Narula, 2003). Therefore, the SI approach allows for a deeper understanding of local companies' stock of knowledge in the areas of process and product technologies as well as managerial expertise. Also, the stock of knowledge available in local firms affects their ability to further develop their technological foundations and acquire knowledge-based resources from domestic and non-domestic sources (Cohen and Levinthal, 1990).

As was discussed in the previous section, SI consists of various interconnected elements (Figure 11.1). The first element of SI, which is private organizations, influences the capabilities development of local firms by being involved in interactive knowledge-sharing between customers and suppliers in the process of imitating competitors, as well as by joining forces in R&D activities. Moreover, industry associations and scientific and professional societies contribute to enhancing the knowledge-base of local firms by conducting research and allocating resources to innovative activities.

The second element of the SI is public organizations which are represented by the organizations formulating and implementing technology policy, regulatory agencies, organizations for higher education and research, technology support entities, standard setting organizations and patent offices (Edquist, 1997). Furthermore, they can be classified as organizations for knowledge production (for example, universities), knowledge distribution (for example, science parks) and knowledge regulation (for example, standard setting committees and patent offices). These organizations could be described as knowledge infrastructure due to their functions of defining the mechanisms and structure of knowledge production and distribution. It is worth noting that physical infrastructure such as roads, electricity production and distribution systems and telecommunication networks also play an important role in knowledge production and distribution. Furthermore, the strength of influence of each of the components varies amongst the countries where local firms succeed to different extents in capabilities generating activities.

The third element of SI is formal and informal institutions. The concept of institutions is very heterogeneous and broad, including the range of formal and informal institutions which are represented by normative structure, regimes and various kinds of organizations (Carlsson and Stankiewicz, 1995). North (1990, p. 3) suggests that 'institutions are the rules of the game in the society'. Edquist (1997) points to several important functions of institutions: (1) reduce uncertainty by providing information; (2) manage conflicts and co-operation; and (3) provide incentives. Thus, institutions allocate resources for the development of technological competences of indigenous companies in various ways, and they might create both obstacles or stimulate the processes of the technological change. Institutional set-up changes over time, and therefore, forces influencing the resources and capabilities of local firms also evolve.

The SI approach also emphasizes that it is important to account for industry differences when investigating the process of technical change and patterns of technological accumulation. The sectoral approach suggests that features of technological capabilities development are technology and industry specific and tend to vary among sectors in terms of technological opportunities, cumulativeness and other conditions.

Impact of SI on MNC subsidiaries' scope

The other important aspect having an impact on structural features of IJVs and scope of learning, which also depend on the functioning of national SI, is the nature of MNC subsidiaries' operations in host economies. Subsidiaries as units of a MNC adopt different roles as part of the wider strategic focus of the MNC in respect of innovation, internal differentiation and exchange of knowledge (Yamin, 2005). Hence, the subsidiary's role will determine the extent to which they receive knowledge from a parent organization (Gupta and Govindarajan, 2000), the degree of interdependence with other MNCs' units, the ability to innovate and the subsequent relationships and networks they create in the host economies. Therefore, this study emphasizes that the structure of the IJVs in terms of western partner contributions and objectives depends, to a large extent, on the scope of the MNC's subsidiary operations and the amount and quality of knowledge transferred by the MNC to the IJV (Figure 11.1). Thus, it is particularly important to investigate the rationale behind the MNC's decision to allocate resources for the operations in a given foreign country and incorporate this into the analysis of learning processes taking place in IJVs.

Previous literature suggests that the type of activities in the host country is defined by two main groups of factors (Narula, 2003): (1) internal, such as the MNC's global strategy, the role of the subsidiary in the MNC network and investment motives and (2) external, such as the host country's opportunities including the level of technological capabilities of local firms, knowledge and physical infrastructure, economic stability and so on. It is important to stress that external and internal factors are closely interconnected and evolve over time, influencing the decision of MNCs regarding the scope and competence of their subsidiaries. One of the most vital external factors having an impact on MNCs' decisions is availability of the educated work force in the host country, which defines the position of the MNC subsidiary's operations in the value chain, and the types of knowledge flows to domestic economy. Presence of local skills, educational resources and advanced knowledge infrastructure is critical for the attraction of direct investment of better quality, which in turn offers better opportunities for knowledge spillovers to domestic factors. Basic infrastructure also plays an important role in attracting foreign firms, since it affects the ease of entry and further operations in the host country.

Importantly, the strategies of MNCs also depend on the local firms' capabilities and competitiveness. Thus, Figure 11.1 shows a link between these two groups of factors. When deciding what type of operations to set up, MNCs seek complementary resources in host locations which will allow for the sustaining and development of the competitive advantage. Thus, the availability of various types of capabilities in local firms is an important factor which foreign MNCs consider before investing in the host country, and, as the literature suggests, they are more likely to set up production subsidiaries in locations which provide complementary knowledge and capabilities.

To conclude, SI greatly influences activities of local firms and their absorptive capacity, as discussed in 'Impact of SI on local firms' activities'. It also affects the scope of MNC subsidiaries in terms of the amount of knowledge they bring to the host country and the level of embeddedness as shown in 'Impact of SI on MNC subsidiaries' scope'. Further, as IJV has been defined as 'an alliance that combines resources from more than one organization to create a new organizational entity (the "child"), which is distinct from its parents' (Inkpen and Beamish, 1997, p. 178), the nature of operations of the local firms and MNC affiliates has an impact on the structural characteristics of established IJVs in terms of both partners' resource contributions, objectives and learning intent. Hence, it can be argued that the propensity of firms to establish certain types of IJVs is affected by the external environment, and thus, the framework of the study – (Figure 11.1) shows those relationships as 'macro-level factors'. Further, management studies suggest the scope and outcomes of learning depend on the structural characteristics of the IJV. Thus, the framework shows these relationships as taking place under the influence of micro-level factors. To summarize, the study argues that in order to get a systemic and holistic understanding of learning in IJVs, both macro- and micro-perspectives should be incorporated into the analysis.

Methodology

The empirical research is conducted in the context of CEE transition economies, namely Russia, the Czech Republic, Poland and Hungary, which offers a particularly appropriate ground for explaining the theoretical model developed in the previous section since these countries include features of both developed and developing economies. Specifically, the present chapter is based on the analysis of secondary data on manufacturing IJVs established in Russia, the Czech Republic, Poland and Hungary in the 1998–2006 period. For the purpose of this study, the choice of countries has been made based on data suggesting that Russia, the Czech Republic, Poland and Hungary have received the largest amount of FDI (UNCTAD, 2007). The full dataset, collected from several sources, consists of 239 IJVs. The databases reporting newspaper announcements on the IJVs were used as a main source of the empirical material for the paper. Also, the materials provided by national statistics offices and foreign direct investment agencies were carefully analysed. When collecting the data, several selection criteria were employed. Hence, we included in our dataset those IJVs which were established: (1) in manufacturing industries; (2) in the 1998–2006 period, and most importantly, (3) outside the operations of both partners. Thus, we aimed to exclude partial acquisitions from our study where nature, incentives and outcomes of learning differ from those in IJVs.

The empirical evidence of System of Innovation impact on scope of learning in IJVs in CEE countries

This section aims to provide empirical evidence of the influence of the external factors originating from SI on the structural characteristics of JVs and scope of learning in IJVs in the context of CEE countries.

The nature of the System of Innovations in CEE countries and
their impact on the local firms' technological capabilities

Governments of CEE countries have undertaken a serious effort to transform Science and Technology Systems functioning in centrally planned economies into conventional Systems of Innovation suitable for market-oriented economies. However, several features of the 'old' systems have been inherited by new SI. The first and very important feature is a relatively well-developed education sector (Radosevic, 1998) Hence, local firms have the availability of well-educated and highly skilled personnel. Table 11.1 illustrates that the number of students in tertiary education measured as a percentage of total population in CEE countries is at the same level as that in developed countries (UNCTAD, 2007). The previous literature argues that the presence of qualified employees has a highly positive impact on the firms' capabilities to absorb and develop new knowledge. This also implies that foreign firms can potentially find in host countries a high level of expertise allowing for co-operation with local firms in technologically advanced sectors.

However, the education system existing in centrally planned economies also had several serious drawbacks. One worth mentioning is that education was technically oriented and produced engineers and technical specialists in great numbers whereas insufficient attention has been paid to the educating of experts in

Table 11.1   Number of students in tertiary education (percentage of total population)

CEE countries	Students in tertiary education (as a % of total population)	Developed countries	Students in tertiary education (as a % of total population)
Russia	6.0	Australia	5.0
Czech Republic	3.1	Canada	4.0
Poland	5.3	Denmark	4.0
Hungary	4.2	Finland	5.7
Estonia	4.9	France	3.6
Kazakhstan	4.5	Germany	2.4
Latvia	5.5	Italy	3.4
Lithuania	5.3	Netherlands	3.4
Romania	3.2	Portugal	3.8
Slovakia	3.0	Spain	4.3
Slovenia	5.3	United Kingdom	3.8
Ukraine	5.3	United States	5.7

the economics and management fields. Thus, after the beginning of the reforms, local firms in CEE countries lacked the ability to function efficiently in new economic conditions (Moore, 1994). This fact had an impact by incentivizing local firms to enter IJVs with foreign firms possessing advanced managerial knowledge and skills (Lyles and Salk, 1996).

The second characteristic of SIs of CEE countries is that the structure of the non-firm R&D sector remains inappropriate for the efficient creation and development of innovations, as R&D activities are to a large extent concentrated outside industrial enterprises (Radosevic, 1998). Table 11.2 indicates the number of US patents produced in CEE countries in the 1969–1994 period, and clearly illustrates that the share of CEE enterprises was relatively small in US patenting (Radosevic and Kutlaca, 1999). This implies that due to inefficient organization of SI, local firms lack capabilities to develop innovative products internally and have to seek advanced technological knowledge from external sources, particularly from foreign partners in IJVs. Importantly, the institutional distribution of R&D activities (Table 11.2) partly explains the inadequately developed R&D capabilities and resulting technological 'gap' between CEE enterprises and their western rivals.

As Table 11.2 shows, there are some differences in the distribution of US patents by institutional sectors across the countries. The former Soviet Union had the lowest level of US patents produced by industry (13 per cent) whereas industrial enterprises in Hungary were involved in innovative activities to the largest extent (65 per cent). This different structure of the R&D activities in selected countries sheds light on differences in local firms' capabilities to produce innovative products that are competitive in the market-based economy, and arguably, on their motives in establishing IJVs.

The third feature of the SIs is that enterprises lack economic incentives to innovate and invest in their technological development (Radosevic, 1998). Criscuolo and Narula (2002) argue that the presence of relevant institutions and motives for investment is crucial for technological upgrading, and mere availability of a skilled and qualified labour force is not a sufficient condition for the development of technological capabilities. This feature has been preserved from the pre-transition time when state-owned enterprises were politically and

Table 11.2 Number of foreign US patents by institutional sectors, 1969–1994 (percentage)

	Former Soviet Union	Former Czechoslovakia	Poland	Hungary
Enterprises	13	47	35	65
Industrial institutes	53	32	36	15
Foreign organizations	17	8	9	10
Academy of Science	11	3	8	5
Universities	5	7	12	2
Government	0	0	0	0
Non-classified	1	3	0	3
Total	100	100	100	100

economically dependent upon higher authorities that were co-ordinating their activities through state plans of production, various supporting subsidies, and supply of critical resources (Child and Markoczy, 1993). Therefore, after rapid transition from central planning to market orientation, local managers lacked knowledge and skills regarding how to operate under conditions of market economy, and were forced to learn from scratch about how to run the business in a competitive way in domestic and foreign markets (Markoczy, 1993).

Moreover, prior to the transition, local companies were embedded in networks within traditional large state-owned enterprises which were disorganized after the break-up of most state-owned enterprises (Sadowski, 2001). Local enterprises faced the challenge of re-establishing production and technology networks by finding new partners among domestic and foreign firms. In addition to the organizational deficiencies mentioned above, underdeveloped financial markets and the absence of resources for development and restructuring constrained the opportunities for development of enterprises in CEE countries (Peng and Heath, 1996), and created an incentive to pursue the strategy of partnering with foreign MNCs through IJVs.

The processes of economic transformation have deepened the deficiencies inherited from the socialist SI discussed earlier. The mixture of changes in incentives has played a negative role in the capabilities of development and sustaining of competitive advantage in local firms in CEE countries. During the transition period, the governments of CEE countries failed to create an efficient SI for stimulating growth of domestic enterprises. One of the main problems of Russian SI is that although many new policies were introduced and oriented towards the development of new commercial culture in the science and technology area as well as support of innovative activities in the private sector, these have not yet been efficiently implemented. As a result, local enterprises still face numerous problems in organizing their operations to meet the requirements of a market-oriented economy and to manufacture competitive products.

The impact of the external environment in
CEE countries on the activities of MNCs subsidiaries

As we discussed in the theoretical section, the nature of MNCs affiliates' operations influences the amount of knowledge transferred to local economy, and specifically to IJVs established with local companies. In order to understand the nature of MNCs operations, we need to consider two major aspects of their entry strategy: (1) MNCs' motives to establish FDI operations in CEE countries and (2) MNCs' incentives to do so through IJVs. In respect to the first aspect of the entry strategy, which is the decision to invest in CEE, several motives can be pointed out: market size; the availability of a relatively inexpensive and well-educated labour force; and the availability of natural resources, particularly in Russia. Thus, market-seeking and resource-seeking FDI are the most popular types of investments in CEE countries. An underdeveloped system of intellectual property rights, the absence of the well-developed knowledge infrastructure and the lack of technological expertise in local firms prevent foreign companies from high quality investments in CEE countries such as R&D subsidiaries. After the transition period, some CEE countries have succeeded better than others in improving, for example, the level of protection of property rights and political and economic stability. The second part of the decision regarding the operations of MNC affiliates in host economies is whether to form an IJV with the local firm or set up a wholly-owned subsidiary. One of the main incentives for MNCs choosing the former option has been to assure operational support and access to the knowledge of local conditions necessary for survival in the turbulent environment of transition economies. However, as the economic and political environment becomes more stable, the need for local partners decreases and MNCs are more likely to establish wholly-owned subsidiaries. It has been documented in previous research (Sadowski, 2001) that the number of IJVs has decreased during the later phase of economic transformation.

*Empirical evidence on the patterns of IJVs in
CEE countries in manufacturing industries*

This section will provide an analysis of empirical data on manufacturing IJVs in Russia, Poland, the Czech Republic and Hungary. Table 11.3 shows how IJVs included in the dataset are distributed across industrial sectors in these CEE countries. It is important to emphasize that although patterns of the IJV distribution are different (Table 11.3), there are also noticeable similarities which are argued to exist due to their comparable models of SIs.

Inter-country similarities/differences in sectoral distribution of IJVs

Table 11.3 shows that the sectoral distributions of IJVs in four CEE countries have several features in common. Specifically, the highest percentage of IJVs is found in automotive and chemical industries. These results can be explained by the fact that technology-intensive industries traditionally represent an area of comparative advantage for CEE countries as reflected by Revealed Technology

Table 11.3 Sectoral distribution of IJVs in manufacturing industries in Russia, Czech Republic, Poland and Hungary (percentage)

Manufacturing Sectors	IJVs (%)			
	Russia	Czech Republic	Poland	Hungary
Automotive	21.5	21.4	7.2	18.2
Chemical	24.9	25.0	32.1	21.2
Machinery	26.0	17.9	7.1	6.1
Food/beverage/tobacco	9.9	3.6	14.3	9.0
Clothing/footwear	1.1	3.6	3.6	2.3
Electronics	6.6	7.1	14.3	19.0
Consumer products	3.9	10.7	10.7	15.1
Paper/packaging	3.3	0.0	0.0	0.0
Pharmaceutical	2.8	10.7	10.7	9.1

Advantage indices (see in Radosevic and Kutlaca, 1999). These industries are, therefore, particularly attractive to foreign investors seeking local technological expertise.

However, there are also some important differences. Table 11.3 demonstrates that the pattern of sectoral distribution in Russia differs from those in the Czech Republic, Poland and Hungary. Specifically, Russian firms are the most attractive for the foreign investors in the machinery sector where IJVs represent 26 per cent of the total number of IJVs, whereas in the Czech Republic, Poland and Hungary, this industry has a significantly smaller percentage of IJVs – 17.9 per cent, 7.1 per cent and 6.1 per cent respectively. Furthermore, Russian partner firms attract foreign investors in the paper/packaging industry, which is not the case in the other Central European countries due to their lack of natural resources. Finally, local firms in electronics and pharmaceutical industries in the Czech Republic (7.1 per cent and 10.7 per cent respectively); Poland (14.3 per cent and 10.7 per cent respectively); and Hungary (19.0 per cent and 9.1 per cent respectively) are significantly more attractive partners for western MNCs than those in Russia (6.6 per cent and 2.8 per cent respectively). These inter-country differences can be explained by the fact that CEE countries followed divergent patterns of emerging systems of innovations. As we discussed previously, SIs in Russia, the Czech Republic, Poland and Hungary differ in terms of the degree to which R&D was carried out in industry and non-firm R&D centres such as Universities, Academies of Sciences and Governments (Table 11.2). Further, the different paths of economic restructuring in CEE countries during the transition period resulted in recombination of existing competencies into new organizational forms, thus increasing the diversity of competences available to local firms in these countries (Radosevic and Sadowski, 2004). Table 11.4 indicates that, for example, GDP growth per capita in 2007 varies significantly between CEE countries from 10,449.0 dollars in Czech Republic to only 1426.9 dollars in Ukraine (UNCTAD, 2007). Also, as a result of reforms, CEE countries have achieved different degrees of economic and political stability, which is also affected by the propensity of foreign firms establishing IJVs in CEE countries, and specifically in such sectors as electronics or pharmaceuticals where well-developed property rights regulation is of particular importance.

Overall, the analysis of the empirical data seems to support the proposition that foreign firms are mostly interested in co-operating with CEE firms in those sectors with a small technology gap where technological knowledge contribution of the local partner has a value for western MNCs.

Influence of the sector-specific factors on
the scope of technological learning in IJVs

The other aspect stressed by the SI approach is that learning is an industry specific phenomenon. Specifically, the gaps between domestic companies and their western rivals in terms of technological development, availability of financial resources and managerial skills necessary for development differs across industrial sectors. Thus, this section will discuss the nature of learning in those

Table 11.4 Indicators of economic development in transition economies and developed countries

	Real GDP growth % (Average 1995–2005)	GDP per capita (Dollars)	R&D expenditures (% of GDP)
CEE countries			
Russia	4.4	4,141.0	1.2
Czech Republic	2.3	10,449.0	1.3
Poland	3.7	6,407.0	0.6
Hungary	4.3	9,652.0	0.9
Estonia	6.3	8,284.0	0.9
Kazakhstan	6.8	2,945.0	0.2
Latvia	6.8	5,735.9	0.4
Lithuania	5.6	6,376.8	0.7
Romania	2.1	3,573.1	0.4
Slovakia	3.9	7,416.0	0.6
Slovenia	3.9	15,975.0	1.6
Ukraine	3.8	1,426.9	1.2
Developed countries			
Australia	3.6	31,905.0	5.0
Canada	3.6	30,911.0	4.0
Denmark	1.9	44,178.6	4.0
Finland	3.4	34,471.6	5.7
France	2.3	33,136.9	3.6
Germany	1.4	32,218.9	2.4
Italy	1.4	28,687.6	3.4
Netherlands	2.3	36,334.8	3.4
Portugal	2.4	16,477.3	3.8
Spain	3.8	23,817.9	4.3
UK	2.8	34,392.3	3.8
US	3.2	39,832.8	5.7

manufacturing sectors where IJVs were the most frequent in four selected CEE countries.

The chemical industry, where present research has documented a high percentage of IJVs in all four countries included in the study, is a science-based sector. Technological development requires co-operation at the level of academic research and applied research and to a large extent product-innovation driven (Sadowski, 2001). Therefore, IJVs were established in this industry for the mutual development of new products where co-operation occurs at the higher levels of the industry's value-added chain. This type of co-operation is beneficial for local firms due to the acquisition of advanced technological knowledge allowing for the enhancement of their technological capabilities.

In the car industry, which accounts for 21.5 per cent of IJVs in Russia, 21.4 per cent in Czech Republic, 7.2 per cent in Poland and 18.2 per cent in Hungary (Table 11.3), local producers lack the knowledge to upgrade their products and process engineering as well as the financial resources for modernization (Radosevic and Sadowski, 2004). At the same time, the size of domestic markets (especially in case of Russia) and proximity to Europe have been the major strategic attraction for foreign investors. This is a production-intensive sector where production engineering is an important source of process innovation. The technological capabilities, which local firms need to become more competitive, are related to the improvement of operating skills, product quality and design. The co-operation in automotive IJVs has been mostly manufacturing related and the main objective of the local firms has been to gain complementary assets for process innovations from their western partners. These ventures are also beneficial for the local firms and provide them with the opportunity to acquire advanced technological knowledge necessary for manufacturing competitive products.

In other manufacturing sectors such as food/beverage, clothing, consumer products, paper/packaging, the integration took place at the lower stage of the added-value chain, and thus the IJVs have provided limited opportunity for local companies to acquire technological competencies (Sadowski, 2001). Thus, it can be argued that in CEE countries, only few sectors such as chemical, automotive, machinery and electronics opened up opportunities for the further development of technology-related capacities in local firms. This supports the conclusion that MNCs have primarily been following the strategy of partnering with local firms to establish manufacturing and supply base in these emerging markets and to leverage resources of local companies in IJVs according to their global manufacturing needs.

Conclusions and implications

The study examines the relationships between the factors of external environment rooted in the SI and scope of learning in IJVs in CEE countries. Hence, the macro-level SI approach has been employed to provide a complementary explanation of the scope of learning and its potential outcomes in IJVs. We illustrated that structural characteristics of SI influence the amount and quality of resources and capabilities of local firms as well as the nature of MNCs' subsidiaries operations, which in turn affects the types of IJVs established in host countries and scope of inter-partner learning in those IJVs. The important argument of the research is that differences in knowledge acquisition and learning opportunities in IJVs across countries and industries occurs, to a large extent, due to the differences in functioning of SIs. Therefore, the study brings a better understanding of how country- and sector-specific factors rooted in SI may affect the scope of learning in IJVs and its potential outcomes for local firms.

The empirical part of the study has been conducted in the context of CEE transition economies, namely Russia, Poland, Czech Republic and Hungary. The analysis of the empirical data supports our theoretical argument and shows that sectoral distribution of IJVs varies across these countries due to the differences in models of 'old' Science and Technology systems as well as divergent transition paths. Importantly, the majority of IJVs have been established in a few industries with a small technology gap where technological contribution of local companies has a value for MNCs. Arguably, partners co-operate in these ventures on a parity basis and learning occurs at the high stage of the value-added chain. Thus, local partners have the opportunity to benefit from the establishment of IJVs and acquire the advanced knowledge of foreign MNCs. However, in other industries co-operation between local firms and foreign investors occurs at the lower stages of the value-added chain and provide local partners with access to the knowledge-based resources of foreign MNCs, albeit to a significantly lower extent.

Overall, the chapter contributes to the existing firm-level research on learning in IJVs by developing a broader perspective for the understanding of how the external environment influences learning in IJVs in transition economies. The developed approach allows us to comprehend that due to the differences in SIs in different national contexts as well as sector-specific determinants, not all types of IJVs provide local firms with equal opportunities for learning, and for catch-up with firms from developed countries. It is also worth noting that, although CEE economies provide an excellent illustration of how differences in national SIs affect the learning in IJVs, the idea of the combination of macro- and micro-level factors for the investigation of learning in IJVs is, in our view, equally applicable to developed countries. This adds to the generalizability of the theoretical arguments suggested in this study.

This chapter also aims to remind international business scholars of the continuing importance of inter-disciplinary research, which bridges several literature streams and takes a holistic perspective, for gaining a better understanding of the global business environment and a deeper knowledge of the multifaceted phenomena of international business.

The important implication of the study for policy makers is that the presence and extent of knowledge spillovers to local firms depends on the extent of development of SI, and requires conscious efforts from the host government to provide incentives for MNCs to establish operations at the higher levels of the value-added chain. Moreover, the development of appropriate government policies to attract high quality foreign investment can promote growth in various sectors of the economy.

There is fruitful ground for future research in this area. Scholars should continue attempts to link various streams of literature, and in particular, for the better understanding of the nature of learning in IJVs. One avenue for the future work is to implement a qualitative study on learning in IJVs and acquire insights from IJVs' partners regarding their perception of each other's objectives for learning and its outcomes. The other suggestion is to conduct a comparative analysis using data from both developed countries and transition economies; this may enable a better understanding of how different types of SI affect learning in IJVs and allow broader implications to be drawn on the antecedents and outcomes of learning. Finally, there is a need for the development of more comprehensive measurements of learning outcomes for the partner firms in terms of their technological and innovative capabilities development.

References

Bell, M. and Pavitt, K. (1993) *Technological Accumulation and Industrial Growth: Contrast between Developed and Developing Countries* (Oxford: Oxford University Press).

Carlsson, B. and Stankiewicz, B. (1995) 'On the nature, function and composition of techno-logical systems', in Carlsson, B. (ed.), *Technological Systems and Economic Performance: The Case of Factory Automation*, 21–56 (Dordrecht, Kluwer Academic Publishers).

Child, J. and Markoczy, L. (1993) 'Host-country managerial behaviour and learning in Chinese and Hungarian joint ventures', *Journal of Management Studies*, 30(4), 611–31.

Cohen, W.M. and Levinthal, D.A. (1990) 'Absorptive capacity: A new perspective on learn-ing and innovation', *Administrative Science Quarterly*, 35(2), 128–52.

Criscuolo, P. and Narula, R. (2002) 'A novel approach to national technological accu-mulation and absorptive capacity: Aggregating Cohen and Levinthal', Working paper. MERITInfonomics Research Memorandum series.

Edquist, C. (1997) *Systems of Innovation: Technologies, Institutions, and Organizations* (London and Washington: Pinter).

Fiol, C.M. and Lyles, M.A. (1985) 'Organizational learning', *Academy of Management Review*, 10(4), 803–13.

Gupta, A.K. and Govindarajan, V. (2000) 'Knowledge flows within multinational corpor-ations', *Strategic Management Journal*, 21, 473–96.

Hamel, G. (1991) 'Competition for competence and inter-partner learning within interna-tional strategic alliances', *Strategic Management Journal*, 12(Summer Special Issue), 83–103.

Hennart, J-F. (2006) 'Alliance research: Less is more', *Journal of Management Studies*, 43(7), 1621–28.

Inkpen, A.C. (1998) 'Learning and knowledge acquisition through international strategic alliances', *Academy of Management Executive*, 12(4), 69–80.

Inkpen, A.C. (2000) 'Learning through joint ventures: A framework of knowledge acquisi-tion', *Journal of Management Studies*, 37(7), 1019–43.

Inkpen, A.C. and Beamish, P.W. (1997) 'Knowledge, bargaining power and international joint venture stability', *Academy of Management Review*, 22(1), 177–202.

Khanna, T., Gulati, R. and Nohria, N. (1998) 'The dynamics of learning alliances: competi-tion, cooperation, and relative scope', *Strategic Management Journal*, 19(3), 193–210.

Kim, L. (1998) 'Crisis construction and organizational learning: Capability building in catching-up Hyundai Motor', *Organization Science*, 9, 506–21.

Lall, S. (1992) 'Technological capabilities and industrialization', *World Development*, 2, 165–86.

Lane, P.J., Salk, J.E. and Lyles, M.A. (2001) 'Absorptive capacity, learning, and performance in international joint ventures', *Strategic Management Journal*, 22, 1139–61.

Lundvall, B. (1992) *National Systems of Innovation: Towards Theory of Innovation and Interactive Learning* (London and New York: Pinter).

Lyles, M.A. and Salk, J.E. (1996) 'Knowledge acquisition from foreign parents in inter-national joint-ventures', *Journal of International Business Studies*, 27, 905–27.

Markoczy, L. (1993) 'Managerial and organizational learning in Hungarian – Western mixed management organizations', *The International Journal of Human Resource Management*, 4(2), 277–304.

Moore, J. (1994) 'Science and technology in Central and Eastern Europe: After revolution', *European Business Journal*, 6(1), 8–20.

Narula, R. (2003) *Globalization and Technology. Interdependence, Innovation Systems and Industrial Policy* (Malden MA: Polity Press).

Nonaka, I. and Takeuchi, H. (1995) *The knowledge-creating company* (New York: Oxford University Press).

North, D. (1990) *Institutions, Institutional Change and Economic Performance* (New York: CUP).

Peng, M. and Heath, P.S. (1996) 'The growth of the firm in planned economies in transi-tion: institutions, organizations and strategic choice', *Academy of Management Review*, 21(2), 492–528.

Radosevic, S. (1998) 'National systems of innovation in economies in transition: Between restructuring and erosion', *Industrial and Corporate Change*, 1, 77–108.

Radosevic, S. and Kutlaca, D. (1999) 'Technological "catch-up" of Central and Eastern Europe: An analysis based on US foreign patenting data, Technology analysis and strategic management', 11(1), 95–111.

Radosevic, S. and Sadowski, B. (2004) *International Industrial Networks and Industrial Restructuring in Central and Eastern Europe* (Boston/Dordrecht/London: Kluwer).

Sadowski, B. (2001) 'Towards market repositioning in Central and Eastern Europe: International cooperative ventures in Hungary, Poland and Czech Republic', *Research Policy*, 30, 711–24.

UNCTAD (2007) *World Investment Report: Transnational Corporations, Extractive Industries and development* (Geneva: United Nation Publications).

Wignaraja, G. (2002) 'Firm size, technological capabilities and market-oriented policies in Mauritius', *Oxford Development Studies*, 30(1), 87–104.

Yamin, M. (2005) 'Subsidiary business networks and opportunity development in multinational enterprises: A comparison of the influence of internal and external business networks', in P.N. Ghauri and A. Hadjikhani (eds), *Business Opportunity Development in Business Networks* (London: Palgrave, Macmillan).

12
Returning Entrepreneurs vs Indigenous Entrepreneurs: An Investigation of High Technology SMEs in Emerging Markets

Ou Dai and Xiaohui Liu*

Introduction

International human mobility has recently increased significantly, and two-way flows of human capital between emerging economies and OECD countries have become a new phenomenon. For example, more than 275,000 overseas Chinese scientists and students had returned to China by 2006. Among these, 5000 returnees have set up 2000 new high-tech firms in Zhongguancun Science Park (ZSP), China's Silicon Valley[1]. Returnees are defined here as scientists and engineers, or students who were trained or studied/worked in the OECD countries, and returned to their native countries to start up a new business venture. Taiwan and South Korea have benefited enormously from this trend. Migrants returning from overseas have played an important role in the economic development of Taiwan and South Korea (Saxenian, 2001, 2005).

However, only a few comparative, descriptive studies have been carried out on the issue. Although Saxenian (2002) has examined the role of transnational entrepreneurs in transforming the global organization of semiconductor production in Silicon Valley, Hsinchu Science Park in Taiwan and Science Park in Shanghai, very little is known about how the backgrounds and characters of returning entrepreneurs affect the performance of their ventures. There is a lack of formal evidence showing to what extent returnee-owned firms confer a substantial competitive advantage compared with local-entrepreneur-owned firms. What are the differences in performance between returning entrepreneur and local-entrepreneur-owned firms?

We aim to fill these gaps by examining the performance of returning-entrepreneur-owned firms compared with local-entrepreneur-owned firms in Zhongguancun Science Park. Specifically, we identify how knowledge and social capital factors of returnee entrepreneurs influence firm performance.

China provides an excellent opportunity to examine these issues. The Chinese government has designed various preferential policies to attract Chinese overseas talent as developing an adequate scientific, technological and business environment will provide rewarding opportunities for the return of individuals who have upgraded their skills abroad (OECD Observer, 2002). Following the collapse of the dot-com boom in the late 1990s, the United States and other developed countries have become less attractive than some large emerging economies, such as China and India, where new entrepreneurial opportunities are associated with exploiting a relatively low-cost skill base and targeting the potentially vast domestic market. Therefore, it is not surprising that China has attracted a large number of talented returnees. This group of returnees is usually attracted to science parks where inducements to the establishment of high-tech firms including tax incentives, cheap office space, start-up loans, venture capital, advice centres and other incentives for new start-ups are available (Li, Zhang and Zhou, 2004).

In this chapter, we consider returning entrepreneurs in China as one particular group and compare them with home-grown entrepreneurs. Both groups studied are based in ZSP in the same business environment. Using an integrated framework which embraces a knowledge-based view (KBV) and social capital theory, we investigate the interaction of internal and external factors in terms of the combination of technological knowledge, commercial knowledge and networks, and their effects on entrepreneurial venture success. The results provide new insights into whether these intangible assets play an important role in high-tech industries. In particular, the findings advance our understanding of whether complementary resources can be a new source of sustained competitive advantage in high-tech industries.

The following section situates our analysis in the literature of the KBV and social capital theory before developing our hypotheses. This is followed by a description of our data and methodology, while the subsequent section presents and analyses the empirical results. We then discuss our findings and finally conclude with policy and managerial implications.

Theory and hypotheses

In this study, we employ a combined research framework, namely the KBV and social capital theory. The KBV proposes that knowledge is the firm's most valuable strategic resource and the principal basis for creating competitive advantage. Knowledge is created and stored within individuals. The primary role of the firm is to apply the knowledge to the production process of goods and services, and its source of unique advantage rests in its ability to integrate the knowledge of different individuals (Ghoshal and Moran, 1996; Grant, 1996). The possession of advanced technology and commercial knowledge is the essential tool for the successful development of technology-based firms in emerging economies. We expect that the business performance of entrepreneurial ventures will be driven and distinguished by the combined characteristics that they have developed in the past.

Entrepreneurs not only depend on internal knowledge sources for business success, but also need to be able to obtain knowledge and business information externally within the firm's networks and through human relations. Social capital theory places a greater emphasis on human relations and on the elicitation of tacit knowledge in the context of the global economy. Specifically, social relations underline the links between social capital and access to resources including both interpersonal relationships and the resources embedded in the relationships. It can be regarded as an intangible resource that is difficult to replicate, thus providing start-ups with a significant advantage (Burt, 1992; Peng and Luo, 2000; Lin, 2001). Such social capital is particularly important to many small firms as it provides access to information and resources not available internally, as found in some studies (Davidsson and Honig, 2003; Peng and Zhou, 2005).

Social capital in the form of networks is viewed as the relational and structural resources attained by individuals/firms through a network of social relationships (Adler and Kwon, 2002; Cooper and Yin, 2005). The commercial working experience of returning entrepreneurs may be associated with the development of international business networks. Returning entrepreneurs who have developed social capital in the form of international networks can act as a bridge between the Chinese context and international markets. Zweig et al. (2005) perceive returning entrepreneurs as 'transnational capital' that results from overseas links, foreign education or training, or transnational networks. This type of social capital may help returning entrepreneurs access valuable resources, thus enhancing their firm's business performance.

Building on these theoretical perspectives, we adopt an integrated theoretical framework to examine the relationship between the characteristics of entrepreneurs and firm performance. In particular, we are interested in how returning entrepreneurs' knowledge and social networks established abroad affect firm performance using local-grown entrepreneurs as a control group. We explore the issues defined above in two directions. First, international education and working experience not only reflect international entrepreneurial orientation, but also provide returning entrepreneurs with opportunities to access advanced technological knowledge and commercial knowledge abroad. Hence, their firms may exhibit better performance than local-entrepreneur-owned firms. Second, we argue that the competitive advantage derived from the integration of technological knowledge, commercial knowledge and social networks plays an important role in business growth. In particular, international networks may help returnee-entrepreneur-owned firms to grow rapidly. Based on the integrated framework discussed above, we develop a number of testable hypotheses as follows.

International entrepreneurial orientation and performance

An international entrepreneurial orientation is associated with innovation, managerial vision and a proactive competitive posture (Covin and Slevin, 1989; Lumpkin and Dess, 1996; Dess et al., 1997). Returnee entrepreneurs may have an international entrepreneurial orientation because of their educational background and experience of working abroad, which provide unique entrepreneurial competences and outlook (for example McDougall et al., 1994; Autio et al., 2000).

Having international entrepreneurial orientation signifies the transformation of scientific and technological knowledge into products and services. Combining international entrepreneurial orientation with other resources such as technological knowledge and commercial knowledge enables returning entrepreneurs to exploit opportunities in both domestic and foreign markets.

Existing studies show that firms that exhibit a global mindset have a competitive advantage (Levitt, 1983). Based on a five-year study of nine of the world's largest corporations at Harvard Business School in the 1970s, the transnational mindset was suggested as leading to superior long-term performance (Orly et al., 2007). More recent studies on the interrelationships between an entrepreneurial orientation, markets and business performance indicate that venture performance is positively related to the innovativeness component of an entrepreneurial orientation, a market orientation and learning orientation (Fredric et al., 2006). Therefore, we propose that:

> **Hypothesis H1:** *SMEs of returnee entrepreneurs with international entrepreneurial orientation will perform more strongly than local-entrepreneur-owned SMEs.*

Technological knowledge and performance

Entrepreneurship often involves the development and application of new technology in high-tech industries. Taking advantage of technological breakthroughs is a driving force in entrepreneurial activity (Schumpeter, 1950). Exploiting what returnee entrepreneurs have obtained abroad is a critical factor driving them to become reverse migrants. Most returning entrepreneurs have had the opportunity to acquire technological knowledge through general education, scientific and technical training and experience working abroad. The importance of technological knowledge in generating superior performance is widely recognized. In particular, the introduction of new or improved products and processes is widely believed to be a main determinant of competitive advantage, organizational performance and survival (Damanpour, 1991). Recent theoretical and empirical research suggests that it is not the total stock of knowledge, but specific characteristics of the knowledge stock that is important for sustained competitive advantage (Winter, 1987; Henderson and Clark, 1990; Prahalad and Hamel, 1990; March, 1991; Starbuck, 1992; Christensen, 1993; Helleloid and Simonin, 1994).

Patents are used as an indicator of the possession of technology knowledge. Patents are not only considered as a proxy of commercializing the outcome of formal research processes, but also constitute important intellectual property which permit companies to gain full economic value of their ideas and inventions. We expect that patents help returning entrepreneurs exploit niche business opportunities and gain first-mover advantages. As a result, patents may enhance firm performance. Hence, we propose:

> **Hypothesis H2a:** *SMEs of returnee entrepreneurs possessing more patents will perform more strongly than local-entrepreneur-owned firms.*

However, patents do not cover all the outcomes of innovative activity. In particular, patents relate to pre-commercial inventions rather than innovation that can readily be developed into new products. R&D investment consists of searching among various novel and uncertain pathways. R&D activity may develop new capabilities that a firm can use to develop new products. Through complementarities, R&D increases the likelihood that firms will engage in external knowledge sourcing, and hence the likelihood that they will be able to obtain successfully the knowledge necessary for technical innovation. Moreover, R&D contributes directly to enterprises' knowledge stock and increases innovation intensity. Some studies have found that innovation is a mechanism by which organizations can draw upon core competencies and transfer these into performance outcomes critical for success (Barney, 1991; Reed and DeFillippi, 1991). In particular, new business enterprises, or 'start ups', may still depend on in-house R&D labs to take the first innovative step and create sustainable competitive advantage. Thus, we propose

Hypothesis H2b: *SMEs of returning entrepreneurs with more R&D spending perform more strongly than local-entrepreneur-owned firms.*

Commercial knowledge and performance

Depth and breadth of technological knowledge may help nascent entrepreneurs identify opportunities. However, technological knowledge and R&D investment do not guarantee entrepreneurs' business success (Casson, 2003). A successful new venture requires not only the capabilities to exploit opportunities, but also the skills for managing the venture and commercializing the new ideas.

The commercialization of high-tech opportunities will require access to manufacturing and marketing techniques as well as distribution channels. Commercialization may also require access to other technological developments to create a product that fits customer needs. Hence, successful commercializing of ideas involves bringing knowledge from a variety of sources and effectively meeting performance criteria in terms of discovery, exploration and exploitation of business ideas and opportunities (Patel and Pavitt, 1998; Shane and Venkataraman, 2000).

Returning entrepreneurs may have obtained practical business knowledge from either working in a commercial environment or through having started a business abroad. For example, working in MNCs enables them to understand the complexities of global operations, the characteristics of foreign markets, the business climate and cultural patterns (Downes and Thomas, 1999). We argue that the prior commercial knowledge from working in developed commercial markets such as business knowledge, management skills and marketing techniques enables returning entrepreneurs to manage their ventures well in the global context.

In addition, returning entrepreneurs may also have the knowledge to seek out funding; for instance, to contact venture capital firms abroad which provide funds and professional guidance. Thus, they may have developed transferable expertise in accessing such funding in China as well (Saxenian, 2006). Hence, we propose:

Hypothesis 3a: SMEs of returning entrepreneurs who acquired commercial knowledge abroad will perform more strongly than local-entrepreneur-owned firms.

Besides advanced technological and commercial knowledge acquired abroad, these returning entrepreneurs also face new challenges in their home country as the overwhelming variety, complexity of business relationships and differences in market conditions require returning entrepreneurs to have local knowledge. This kind of knowledge is specific to each country with regard to language, culture, politics, society and economy (Makino and Delios, 1996; Inkpen and Beamish, 1997). For instance, when running a successful business in any country, entrepreneurs need to understand and have sufficient knowledge of local culture and the business environment. The cultural elements provide a sustainable system of values, beliefs, artifacts and art forms and help sustain social organizations and rationalize action (Norgaard, 1994).

Possessing local knowledge can, indeed, contribute to firm performance. Local commercial knowledge includes local competitors, local laws, the local business climate and the local customer base. Such commercial knowledge constitutes intangible assets and comprises information about how to access the labour force, distribution channels, infrastructure, raw materials and other factors required for conducting businesses (Makino and Delios, 1996). Local knowledge is deeply spatially embedded. It may take time for returning entrepreneurs to learn and/or update their local knowledge (Nonaka and Takeuchi, 1995). Hence, we propose:

Hypothesis 3b: The local commercial knowledge possessed by returning entrepreneurs may moderate their business performance compared with local-entrepreneur-owned firms.

International networks and performance

Social capital theory provides the theoretical foundations to understand the impact of the special character of entrepreneurs on firm performance. The theory stresses that social capital in the form of business networks is a powerful tool for entrepreneurs, enabling them to gain access to resources and improve their strategic position (Hitt and Ireland, 2000; Alvarez and Barney, 2001). Managers or founders with such social capital are well-positioned to identify and develop opportunities (Burt, 1997). Being embedded in social networks gives entrepreneurs the opportunity to acquire information and ideas, and helps entrepreneurs to establish credibility and access critical resources, including knowledge and technology (McDougall et al., 1994). For SMEs, knowledge and social capital are positively interrelated because social capital directly affects the combine-and-exchange process and provides relatively easy access to network resources (Nahapiet and Ghoshal, 1998). The interplay of this type of special social capital with knowledge enables firms to realize their new resource configurations, and hence create unique competitive advantage (Shane and Stuart, 2002).

We argue that returnee entrepreneurs' international networks may have an important impact on firm performance by reducing information asymmetries and providing the focal firm with important knowledge and resources. Such social capital-related factors may enable entrepreneurs to access valuable information and create global value chains to target international niche markets. These factors also provide the resources for returnee-owned firms (Coviello and Munro, 1997; Zahra et al., 2000). Davidsson and Honig (2003) find a significant positive association between social capital and performance. Therefore, SMEs whose owners are heavily involved in networking should outperform SMEs whose owners make limited (or no) use of networks (Havnes and Senneseth, 2001). Hence, we propose:

Hypothesis H4: *SMEs of returning entrepreneurs who have established international networks will perform more strongly than local-entrepreneur-owned firms.*

The sample and method

To test the hypotheses proposed above, we conducted a questionnaire survey. The sample firms were selected within the largest science park in China, ZSP in Beijing, which has attracted a large number of returning overseas Chinese entrepreneurs. All firms in our sample are from high-tech industries, following the definition of the Ministry of Finance and China National Bureau, comprising electronics and information technology, bio-engineering and new medical technology, new materials and applied techniques, advanced manufacturing technology, aviation and space technology, modern agricultural technology, new energy and high-power conservation technology, environmental protection technology, marine engineering technology and nuclear-applied technology. Since returnee-owned firms are a recent phenomenon in China, we limited the sample to SMEs, according to the official Chinese definition, where an SME has fewer than 300 employees, and a total value of sales below five million RMB.

The key informant at firm level is usually the founder/owner/entrepreneur. By applying the criterion of high-tech SMEs founded for around three to five years, populations of 1003 returnee-owned and 1138 local firms were identified from a list obtained from the management committee of ZSP. A willingness to participate in our survey was indicated by 857 returnee-owned firms and 976 local entrepreneurial firms, representing 85.4 per cent and 85.6 per cent of the population respectively. Postal questionnaires were distributed among these two groups of firms and followed up with random phone calls and visits to 84 sample firms. A total of 353 usable questionnaires from returning entrepreneurs (a 41.2 per cent response rate), and 358 questionnaires from local firms were returned (36.7 per cent).

The questionnaire had been developed through an interactive process of interviewing, drafting and pilot-testing. The questionnaire was translated from English into Mandarin Chinese. Then it was back-translated by two Chinese Professors in Beijing to ensure its validity. A pilot study was carried out in ZSP where two workshops were organized involving groups of six and eight returning and local entrepreneurs who completed the questionnaire and were asked to identify any unclear questions. We modified the questionnaire according to feedback received from the workshops.

Data was collected on board composition, and technological and financial performance, as well as controls such as firm size, industrial classification and the age of the firm. The possibility of non-response bias was checked by comparing the characteristics of the respondents with those of the original population sample. The calculated t-statistics for the number of employees and R&D expenditures of the firms are all statistically insignificant, indicating that there are no significant differences between the respondent and non-respondent firms. The variables used in the estimation are defined as follows:

Dependent variable

Business Performance (BP) is measured by the entrepreneurs' satisfaction with their business performance. The problems of measuring firm performance in transition economies are widely recognized, and quantitative and qualitative measures have their own relative merits (Hoskisson et al., 2000). Financial measures are unreliable in a transitional environment where asset values still rely on historic cost and crude depreciation charges, and the quality of local auditors is variable (Liu, 2005). Similarly, measuring the performance of newer, smaller firms even in developed economies can also be problematic due to the lack of published information. Satisfaction is a fundamental measure of performance for the individual entrepreneur and may bear on decisions about whether to continue or close a business (Cooper and Artz, 1995). Satisfaction-with-performance measures have been shown to possess strong internal consistency and reliability (Chandler and Hanks, 1993; Cooper and Artz, 1995).

Bearing this in mind, we used subjective performance measures together with *Exploratory Factor Analysis* to measure the extent to which returnees and local entrepreneurs were satisfied with firm performance in terms of market share, sales growth and the pre-tax profitability of their sales in both Chinese and international markets. The items were measured on a seven-Likert-point scale which measured the extent to which respondents were satisfied with the performance of their firms; point seven being the highest level of satisfaction. The results show that these four items – in terms of sales growth in local markets; sales growth in international markets; pre-tax profitability in local markets; and pre-tax profitability in international markets – loaded on a single factor with a reliability coefficient or *Cronbach's Alpha* of 0.847. Satisfaction-with-performance measures have been shown to possess strong internal consistency and reliability (Chandler and Hanks, 1993; Naman and Slevin, 1993; Cooper and Artz, 1995). The correlation between this subjective performance measure and employment growth was 0.56, indicating that entrepreneurs' perceptions of firm performance were in line with employment growth, and they constitute reasonable measures of firm performance in the context of high-tech SME start-ups in an emerging economy.

Independent variables

International entrepreneurial orientation (***IEO***) is used to measure entrepreneurs' international vision, management experience, marketing position and risk-taking attitude. This measure is adopted from Knight and Cavusgil (2004). IEO is calculated based on 5 items with a seven-Likert-point scale (see the Appendix). Its reliability coefficient or *Cronbach's Alpha* is 0.806. We use the number of patents possessed by the sample firms (***PAT***) to measure technological knowledge acquired, and R&D (***RD***) expenditure is used to represent internal technological capability. Commercial knowledge is measured by the following items: (1) new commercial technologies; (2) new business ideas and opportunities; (3) new marketing knowledge; and (4) new financial knowledge; obtained a) from abroad; or b) locally. Hence, the items above are used to construct two composites of commercial knowledge obtained abroad *(KI)* and locally (***KL***). The reliability coefficients or *Cronbach's Alpha* for these two constructs are 0.7373 and 0.712 respectively.

The variable of international networks (***IN***) was created using three questions in our questionnaire. These seven-Likert-point questions focused on the degree of importance of three types of networks: business networks established with firms in major markets; business contacts maintained with people in foreign markets; and membership of business and professional associations abroad. The reliability coefficient or *Cronbach's Alpha* for the variable *IN* is 0.843.

Control variables

Our sample firms mainly fall into ten sub-sectors in high-tech industries, including electronics and information technology (42.9 per cent of the sample firms), bio-engineering and new medical technology (12.1 per cent), new materials and applied techniques (7.8 per cent), new energy and high-power conservation technology (4.8 per cent) and others. Therefore, we included industry dummy variables in the estimation equation to capture the impact of industrial sectors on firm performance. In addition, we controlled for firm age (years since founding). The proposed hypotheses are tested based on the following equation:

$$BP_i = \alpha_0 + \alpha_1 IEO_i + \alpha_2 KI_i + \alpha_3 KL_i + \alpha_4 R\&D_i + \alpha_5 PAT_i + \alpha_6 IN_i + \alpha_7 Age_i + {}_i \qquad (1)$$

BP represents entrepreneurs' satisfaction regarding their firm performance. IEO, KI, KL, PAT, R&D and IN denote the explanatory variables as described above. Age and industry dummies are standard control variables which are used to differentiate their possible impact on business performance. The Equation is estimated by applying the *OLS*. In order to investigate in more detail whether the different characteristics of returnee firms and local firms are associated with firm performance, the overall sample is divided into two sub-samples, returnee-owned firms and local-entrepreneur-owned firms. We compare the results from the overall sample and two sub-samples. A *Chow test* is applied to test the equivalence of *regression estimates* for Equation (1) between sub-samples. If differences between estimations are statistically significant, then the division of the overall sample into two sub-samples is justified.

Empirical results

Table 12.1 reports the descriptive statistics for the variables used in the analysis and the matrix of correlation coefficients. As it is shown in Table 12.1, the average age and size of firms in our sample are 4.6 years and 50 employees, respectively. Returnee firms are more internationally orientated, and 37 per cent of returnee firms export their products, whereas only 18 per cent of non-returnee firms are engaged in exporting. The correlations between the variables show the predicted signs and most of the coefficients are statistically significant, providing preliminary support for the proposed hypotheses.

We estimated the overall sample first, and then divided it into two sub-samples, returning entrepreneurs and local-grown entrepreneurs. Two specifications for Equation 1 were estimated with and without industry dummy variables. However, the industry dummy variables are not statistically significant in the estimation for different specifications, indicating that firm performance is independent of industry and therefore internal factors are the main driving force for firm performance. The results summarized in Table 12.2 show that the six hypotheses specified above receive partial support for the overall sample and sub-samples.

The results from the overall sample in Model One indicate that firm performance is strongly related to in-house R&D (one per cent level), entrepreneurs' local knowledge (five per cent level) and international business networks (one per cent level). However, other factors such as international entreprencurial orientation, technological knowledge in the form of patents and commercial knowledge are not significantly associated with business performance. The firms' age is not statistically significant in the estimation, indicating that the performance of high-tech firms is not directly linked with firm age. In fact, all these sample high-tech firms are quite young.

The result of the *Chow test* is statistically significant at the one per cent level ($F = 2.83$ with $p = 0.01$), showing that there are distinctive differences in performance between returnee and local-entrepreneur-owned firms, and the regression estimates using a pooled sample may be biased. Therefore, it is appropriate to divide the overall sample into the two sub-samples. Based on the sub-sample of returnees in Model Two, the six hypotheses receive most support. The international entrepreneurial orientation variable is significant at the ten per cent level, thus H1 is weakly supported. Patents possessed and transferred by returnees from abroad are significant at the one per cent level as hypothesized in H2a. R&D expenditure is positively associated with the performance of returnee-owned firms, which is the same as the result obtained from the overall sample. Hence H2b is fully supported.

The variable, commercial knowledge obtained abroad by returning entrepreneurs, is statistically significant at the ten per cent level, which produces weak

Table 12.1 Correlation matrix and descriptive statistics

Variables	Mean	Std. Dev	1	2	3	4	5	6	7	8	9
1. Business performance	4.2324	1.311	1.000	–	–	–	–	–	–	–	–
2. Patents	3.91	11.95	0.227	1.000	–	–	–	–	–	–	–
3. R&D expenditure	340.5	11.84	0.252	0.758	1.000	–	–	–	–	–	–
4. International entrepreneurial orientation	3.671	0.611	0.126	0.090	0.024	1.000	–	–	–	–	–
5. Knowledge obtained abroad	5.000	1.257	0.245	0.035	0.000	0.329	1.000	–	–	–	–
6. Knowledge obtained locally	5.037	1.245	0.298	0.035	–0.008	0.101	0.551	1.000	–	–	–
7. International networks	4.486	1.401	0.508	0.190	0.065	0.469	0.262	0.178	1.000	–	–
8. Age	4.67	2.604	0.010	0.118	0.142	0.263	–0.004	–0.049	0.111	1.000	–
9. Size	50.21	1.066	0.53	0.427	–.230	0.338	0.299	0.148	0.267	0.487	1.000

Note: All correlation coefficients more than 0.13 or less than −0.13 are significant at 5% level or higher.

Table 12.2 The dependent variable: business performance (BP)

Independent variables	Model I OLS The overall sample	Model II OLS The sub-sample returnee-owned firms	Model III OLS The sub-sample local-entrepreneur-owned firms
(H1) IEO	.395	.934*	.803
(H2a) PAT (Patents)	.272	.009***	.343
(H2b) R&D	.003***	.056*	.040**
(H3a) KI	.798	.071*	.746
(H3b) KL	.011**	.106	.127
(H4) IN	0.000***	0.000***	0.000***
Control variables			
Firm age	.133	.202	.179
Industry dummy	0.550	0.313	0.904
Constant	1.109	2.067	1.097
Adjusted R^2	.406	.283	.515
Observations	711	353	358

Notes: ***, ** and * represent the 1%, 5% and 10% significance levels, respectively.

evidence for H3a, but there is no significant association between commercial knowledge obtained locally and firm performance, so H3b is not supported. The possession of international networks contributes to firm performance of returnee-owned firms at the one per cent significance level as predicted by H4.

The results from Model Three, based on the sub-sample of local-entrepreneur-owned firms, shows that there is no a significant association between international entrepreneur orientation and business performance. This finding supports H1 as local entrepreneurs may have weak international entrepreneurial orientation. Hence, the business performance of their firms is not as strong as those of returning entrepreneurs. The variable of patents is not statistically significant indicating that the SMEs of local entrepreneurs perform less strongly than returnee-owned firms due to fewer patents. The variable of R&D investment for both groups is positively associated with their venture performance.

There is not a positive association between the commercial knowledge obtained abroad and firm performance for local-entrepreneur-owned firms. However, international networks also positively affect the business performance of local-entrepreneur-owned firms.

Discussion and conclusions

This study is probably one of the first to compare the business performance of two groups of firms with different characters in an emerging economy. We have identified an important phenomenon, returning entrepreneurs. We have provided insightful evidence on how the characteristics of returning entrepreneurs affect firm performance compared with local-entrepreneur-owned firms, in relation to different types of accumulated technological and commercial knowledge, and the international networks they developed in the past.

Our finding shows that having international entrepreneurial orientation is important. Based on education and working experience abroad, returning entrepreneurs' international entrepreneurial orientation is (as hypothesized in H1) significantly and positively associated with firm performance. Nonaka (1991) states the essence of innovation is to *recreate the world according to a particular vision or ideal*. The international vision of returning entrepreneurs reflects an innovation-focused managerial mindset that levers the competitive advantage of their firms and maximizes business performance. The entrepreneurs who have international vision make the leap into international markets due to their unique entrepreneurial competence (McDougall et al., 1994; Autio et al., 2000). Their international orientation is reflected by the firm's overall innovativeness and proactiveness in the pursuit of both domestic and international markets (Knight and Cavusgil, 2004).

Knowledge is the most important resource, and the integration of individuals' specialized knowledge is essential to business success (Nelson and Winter, 1982; Conner and Prahalad, 1996). In particular, tacit knowledge is embedded in individuals and cannot be expressed explicitly or codified in written form (Nonaka, 1994). The availability of academic technological knowledge is found to be important in the growth of returnee ventures through knowledge transfer (patents) and R&D investment. The support for these two hypotheses H2a and H2b is consistent with the special features of returning entrepreneurs who are well-stocked with patents from abroad and subsequently are rewarded with a positive performance outcome.

We find that commercial knowledge accumulated from abroad positively affects the business performance of returnee-owned firms. This result suggests that returnee entrepreneurs have played an important role in transferring commercial skills as well as technological knowledge. It supports the view that returnee entrepreneurs have developed human capital related to how enterprises abroad work in the international context, which helps returnees develop their own businesses in China. The support for H3a reflects the special features of returnee entrepreneurs. The finding also supports the Chinese government's policy which aims to attract overseas Chinese back to the country. Returnees not only bring physical capital back to their home country, but also human and social capital which they accumulated abroad. This type of human and social capital positively affects their performance as shown in the results.

Our finding suggests that international networks are an important factor affecting the performance of both returning and local-entrepreneur-owned firms. One important aspect of Chinese returning entrepreneurs is that they have well-established networks in major global markets, such as the US and EU. This kind of international network enables them to access valuable information and create global value chains to target international niche markets. Hence, international networks have contributed to firm performance. The significant result for the sub-sample of local firms may reflect the fact that local-entrepreneur-owned firms not only produce and provide products and services to the home market, but also extend their business to international markets. Our finding indicates that engaging in international business may also help local firms generate high levels of sales and profits.

Our study makes a number of contributions to understanding the relationship between firm performance, knowledge and social capital in emerging markets. First, we develop a complementary approach which combines technological knowledge and commercial knowledge. This perspective may be extended usefully to other emerging economies where returning entrepreneurs have also increased substantially. Our findings suggest that intangible assets and knowledge play an important role in high-tech industries. Second, our investigation contributes to the KBV and network literature by linking knowledge and social capital together. These two types of complementary resources enable returning entrepreneurs to establish an effective mechanism to integrate knowledge into business activities and gain sustained competitive advantage in high-tech industries. Hence, the findings shed light on the relationship between performance, knowledge and social capital, and provide evidence that emphasizes the need to consider the impact of a wide range of factors such as social capital and networks on firm performance. Third, it seems likely that the findings from the study are generalizable, and advance our understanding of returning entrepreneurs. We believe that this start of a complementary line of research provides novel explanations for the new phenomenon of returning entrepreneurs worldwide.

We should acknowledge some empirical limitations of the study which suggest further research possibilities. With respect to performance, we were constrained by the lack of published information and sensitivity on the part of respondents to report details on levels of profitability. In addition, the study was also restricted to a single science park in the Chinese context. Further research might extend to returnee entrepreneurs in science parks within and outside China, such as India and Russia.

Notes

* Acknowledgements: Financial support from the British Academy, grant number LRG-39371 is gratefully acknowledged.
1. People Daily, Overseas Edition, 21 September 2007.

Appendix

International Entrepreneurial orientation:

- See the world instead of just China as its marketplace
- Top management is experiences in international business
- Market its products in foreign markets
- Market its products in HMT
- Management Communicates information throughout the company in relation to customer experience abroad

Knowledge obtained abroad

- New Technology
- New Business idea and opportunity
- Marketing Knowledge
- Finance knowledge

Knowledge obtained locally

- New Technology
- New Business idea and opportunity
- Marketing Knowledge
- Finance knowledge

International business networks

- Networks established in the major markets
- Contacts maintained with people in foreign countries
- Membership of different associations abroad

Business Satisfaction of firm performance

- Sales growth in local markets
- Sales growth in international markets
- Pre-tax profitability in local markets
- Pre-tax profitability in international market

Factor measures

Measure	Items	Reliability Coefficient Cronbach's Alpha
International entrepreneurial orientation	5 items	0.806
Knowledge obtained abroad	4 items	0.737
Knowledge obtained locally	4 items	0.712
International business networks	3 items	0.843
Business performance	4 items	0.847

References

Adler, P. and Kwon, S. (2002) 'Social capital: Prospects for a new concept', *Academy of Management Review*, 27, 17–40.

Alvarez, S. and Barney, J. (2001) 'How entrepreneurial firms can benefit from alliances with large partners', *Academy of Management Executive*, 15, 139–48.

Autio, E., Sapienza, H. and Almeida, J. (2000) 'Effects of age of entry, knowledge intensity, and imitability on international growth', *Academy of Management Journal*, 43, 909–24.

Barney, J.B. (1991) 'Firm resources and sustained competitive advantages', *Journal of Management*, 17(1), 99–120.

Burt, R. (1992) *Structural Holes: the Social Structure of Competition* (Cambridge, MA: HUP).

Burt, R. (1997) 'The contingent value of social capital', *Administrative Science Quarterly*, 42, 339–65.

Casson, M. (2003) *The Entrepreneur: an Economic Theory*, 2nd edn (Cheltenham: Edward Elgar).

Chandler, G. and Hanks, S.H. (1993) 'Measuring the performance of emerging businesses: A validation study', *Journal of Business Venturing*, 8, 391–408.

Christensen, C.M. (1993) 'The rigid disk drive industry: A history of commercial and technological turbulence', *Business History Review*, 67, 531–88.

Conner, K.R. and Prahalad, C.K. (1996) 'A resource-base theory of the firm: Knowledge versus opportunism', *Organization Science*, 477–501.

Cooper, A.C. and Artz, K.W. (1995) 'Determinants of satisfaction for entrepreneurs', *Journal of Business Venturing*, 10, 439–57.

Cooper, A.C. and Yin, X. (2005) 'Entrepreneurial networks', in M.A. Hitt and R.D. Ireland (eds), *The Blackwell Encyclopaedia of Management (second edition), Entrepreneurship*, 98–100 (Oxford: Blackwell Publishing).

Coviello, N. and Munro, H. (1997) 'Network relationships and the internationalization process of small software firms', *International Business Review*, 6(4), 361–86.

Covin, J.G. and Slevin, D.P. (1989) 'Strategic management of small firms in hostile and benign environments', *Strategic Management Journal*, 10(1), 75–87.

Damanpour, F. (1991) 'Organizational innovation: A Meta-analysis of effects of determinants and moderators', *Academy of Management Journal*, 34(3), 555–90.

Davidsson, P. and Honig, B. (2003) 'The role of social and human capital among nascent entrepreneurs', *Journal of Business Venturing*, 18(3), 301–31.

Dess, G.G., Lumpkin, G.T. and Covin, J.G. (1997) 'Entrepreneurial strategy making and firm performance: Tests of contingency and configurational models', *Strategic Management Journal*, 18, 677–95.

Downes, M. and Thomas, A. (1999) 'Managing overseas assignments to build organizational knowledge', *Human Resource Planning*, 22(4), 33–48.

Fredric, K., Noel, J.L. and Aviv, S. (2006) 'Entrepreneurial, market, and learning orientations and international entrepreneurial business venture performance in South African firms', *International Marketing Review*, 23(5), 504–23.

Ghoshal, S. and Moran, P. (1996) 'Bad for practice: a critique of the transaction cost theory', *Academy of Management Review*, 21, 13–47.

Grant, R.M. (1996) 'Towards a knowledge-based theory of the firm', *Strategic Management Journal*, 17. Special Issue entitled Knowledge and the Firm.

Havnes, P.A. and Senneseth, K. (2001) 'A panel study of firm growth among SMEs in networks', *Small Business Economics*, 16(4), 293–302.

Helleloid, D. and Simonin, B. (1994) 'Organizational learning and a firm's core knowledge', in G. Hamel and A. Heene (eds), *Knowledge-based Competition*, 213–39 (Chichester: John Wiley).

Henderson, R. and Clark, K. (1990) 'Architectural innovation: The reconfiguration of existing product technologies and the failure of established firms', *Administrative Science Quarterly*, 35, 9–30.

Hitt, M. and Ireland, D. (2000) 'The intersection of entrepreneurship and strategic management', in D. Sexton and H. Landstrom (eds), *Handbook of Entrepreneurship* (Oxford: Blackwell).

Hoskisson, R.E., Eden, L., Lau, C-M., and Wright, M. (2000) 'Strategy in emerging economies', *Academy of Management Journal*, 43(3), 249–67.

Inkpen, A.C. and Beamish, P. (1997) 'Knowledge, bargaining power, and the instability of international joint ventures', *Academy of Management Review*, 22(1), 177–202.

Knight, G. and Cavusgil, S. (2004) 'Innovation, organisational capabilities, and the born-global firms', *Journal of International Business Studies*, 35, 124–41.

Levitt, T. (1983) 'The globalization of markets', *Harvard Business Review*, 61, 92–102.

Li, H., Zhang, W. and Zhou, L.A. (2004) *'Ownership, efficiency and survival in economic transition: evidence from a Chinese science park'*, Chinese University of Hong Kong, Department of Economics Discussion Paper.

Lin, N. (2001) *Social capital* (Cambridge, MA: Cambridge University Press).

Liu, Q. (2005) *'Corporate governance in China: Current Practices, Economic Effects and Institutional Determinants'*, Hong Kong Institute of Economics and Business Strategy. Working Paper HIEBS/1125, Hong Kong University.

Lumpkin, G.T. and Dess, G.G. (1996) 'Clarifying the entrepreneurial orientation construct and linking it to performance', *The Academy of Management Review*, 21(1), 135–72.

Makino, S. and Delios, A. (1996) 'Local knowledge transfer and performance: implications for alliance formation in Asia', *Journal of International Business Studies*, 27(5), 905–27.

March, J.G. (1991) 'Exploration and exploitation in organizational learning', *Organization Science*, 2, 71–87.

McDougall, P., Shane, S. and Oviatt, B. (1994) 'Explaining the formation of international new ventures: The limits of theories from international business research', *Journal of Business Venturing*, 9, 469–87.

Nahapiet, J. and Ghoshal, S. (1998) 'Social capital, intellectual capital, and the organizational. Advantage', *Academy of Management Review*, 22(2), 242–66.

Naman, J.L. and Slevin, D.P. (1993) 'Entrepreneurship and the concept of fit: A Model and empirical Tests', *Strategic Management Journal*, 14, 137–53.

Nelson, R.R. and Winter, S. (1982) *An Evolutionary Theory of Economic Change* (London: The Belknap Press of Harvard University).

Nonaka, I. (1991) 'The knowledge-creating company', *Harvard Business Review*, November–December, 96–104.

Nonaka, I. (1994) 'A dynamic theory of organizational knowledge creation', *Organization Science*, 5(1), 14–37.

Nonaka, I. and Takeuchi, H. (1995) *The Knowledge Creating Company: How Japanese Companies Creates the Dynamics of Innovation* (New York: Oxford University Press).

Norgaard, R. (1994) *Development Betrayed* (London: Routledge).

OECD Observer (2002) International Mobility of the Highly Skilled, *Policy Brief*, July 2002.

Orly L., Schon, B., Sully, T. and Nakiye, B. (2007) 'What we talk about when we talk about "global mindset": Managerial cognition in multinational corporations', *Journal of International Business Studies*, 38(2), 231–58.

Patel, P. and Pavitt, K. (1998) 'National systems of innovation under strain: The internationalization of corporate R&D', *SPRU Electronic Working Papers Series*, 22, Science Policy Research Unit, University of Sussex.

Peng, M.W. and Luo, Y. (2000) 'Managerial ties and firm performance in a transition economy: The nature of a micro-macro link', *Academy of Management Journal*, 43(3), 485–501.

Peng, M.W. and Zhou, J.Q. (2005) 'How network strategies and institutional transitions evolve in Asia', *Asia Pacific Journal of Management*, 22(4), 321–36.

Prahalad, C.K. and Hamel, G. (1990) 'The core knowledge of the corporation', *Harvard Business Review*, 68, 79–91.

Reed, R. and DeFillippi, R.J. (1991) 'Causal ambiguity, barriers to imitation and sustainable competitive advantage', *Academy of Management Review*, 15, 80–102.

Saxenian, A. (2001) 'The role of immigrant entrepreneurs in new venture creation', in C.B. Schoonhoven and E. Romanelli (eds) *The Entrepreneurship Dynamic: Origins of Entrepreneurship and the Evolution of Industries* (Stanford, Calif.: Stanford University Press).

Saxenian, A. (2002) *Local and Global Networks of Immigrant Professionals in Silicon Valley'* San Francisco (CA: Public Policy Institute of California).

Saxenian, A. (2005) 'From brain drain to brain circulation: Transnational communities and regional upgrading in India and China', *Studies in Comparative International Development*, 40(2), 35–61.

Saxenian, A. (2006) *The New Argonauts: Regional Advantage in a Global Economy* (Cambridge, MA: Harvard University Press).

Schumpeter, J.A. (1950) *Capitalism, Socialism, and Democracy* (New York: Harper and Row).

Shane, S. and Stuart, T. (2002) 'Organizational endowments and the performance of university start-ups', *Management Science*, 48(1), 154–70.

Shane, S. and Venkataraman, S. (2000) 'The promise of entrepreneurship as a field of research', *Academy of Management Review*, 25, 217–26.

Starbuck, W.H. (1992) 'Learning by knowledge-intensive firms', *Journal of Management Studies*, 29, 713–40.

Winter, S.G. (1987) 'Knowledge and knowledge as strategic assets', in D.J. Teece (eds), *The Competitive Challenge*, 159–84 (Ballinger, Cambridge, MA).

Zahra, S.A., Ireland, R.D. and Hitt, A.H. (2000) 'International expansion by new venture firms: International diversity, mode of market entry, technological learning, and performance', *Academy of Management Journal*, 43(5), 925–50.

Zweig, D., Vanhonacker, W., Chung, S.F. and Rosen, S. (2005) *'Reverse and Migration and Regional Integration: Entrepreneurs and Scientists in the PRC'*, Centre on China's Transnational Relations, Working Paper No. 6, The Hong Kong University of Science and Technology.

13

The Emergence of Low-Cost Airlines in Africa: A Preliminary Analysis of Internal and External Drivers

Joseph Amankwah-Amoah and Yaw A. Debrah

Introduction

Recent progress in economic growth and policy environment in Africa has led to improving perception of the region as one of the largest and most exciting groups of frontier markets (Chung, 2007). According to the IMF, private capital flow to Sub-Saharan Africa has tripled since 2003. In 2006, total gross private capital flows amounted to about US$45 billion, almost six per cent of gross domestic product, compared to about US$9 billion in 2000 (Chung, 2007). Some private capital and foreign direct investments have been made in areas such as transport infrastructure development, which are essential to sustainable economic development in Africa (Africa Research Bulletin, 2006).

Against this backdrop, we are witnessing the emergence of fierce competition in the air transport sector in Africa. The collapse of some national carriers/ traditional airlines (also known as legacy airlines) such as Air Afrique, Ghana Airways, and Nigerian Airways, and the dire state of some national airlines such as Air Zimbabwe, have created opportunities for carriers from Europe and North America to increase their presence on the continent. At the same time, conditions created by globalization, in particular advances in electronic booking/ticketing, have also given birth to low-cost airlines (LCCs – also known as low-cost carriers, no-frills airlines and budget airlines) in Africa. These LCCs are exploiting the opportunities created by the inefficiencies of the traditional airlines. Many LCCs are doing brisk business while the national legacy carriers are struggling to survive. This, then, brings to the fore one of the challenging questions facing International Business (IB) research in a globalized era, that is, *what determines the international success and failure of firms?* (Peng, 2004, p. 106). This chapter seeks to contribute to this topic by exploring the factors that promote or hinder the emergence and internationalization of LCCs in Africa.

The rest of the chapter is organized as follows. The next section briefly reviews the emergence of LCCs and outlines the key questions guiding the study. This is followed by a discussion of the changing airline sector in Africa. The penultimate

218

section focuses on a framework for analysing the development of LCCs in Africa. The final section presents the conclusions and strategic implications of the emergence of the LCCs for traditional airlines in Africa.

The emergence of low-cost airlines

The emergence of LCCs in the global airline industry is a relatively new phenomenon. It started in the USA but has now spread to other parts of the world. Some studies have shed light on the regional expansion of LCCs and the intense competition it has generated in the airline industry (Franke, 2004; Tretheway, 2004; Evangelho et al., 2005). It is generally agreed that the emergence of LCCs can be attributed to liberalization/deregulation in the airline industry globally (Gilbert et al., 2001; Piga and Filippi, 2002; Evangelho et al., 2005; Lawton and Solomko, 2005; CAA, 2006; de Neufville, 2006; Doganis, 2006). The emergence of LCCs exemplifies the competitive forces unleashed by deregulation, globalization and regionalization (Levy, 1997; Rugman and Hodgetts, 2001; Rugman, 2003; Rugman and Verbeke, 2004; Collinson and Rugman, 2008).

Historically, the growth of the global airline industry has been affected by the decisions of politicians and governments. Until the mid-1980s, the majority of the world's airlines were state-owned (Shaw, 2004; Doganis, 2006). It was, therefore, understandable that decisions by state-owned airlines on route entry, capacity and frequency were more or less part of public policy, often not supported by commercial reasons, but by the wishes of politicians. Such policies on routes and market access effectively constrained the globalization of the airline industry for decades. This, nevertheless, gathered pace following the establishment of the European Common Aviation Market (ECAM) in 1997 and enactment of the Airline Deregulation Act of 1978 in the US (Button, 2002; Doganis, 2006). Restrictions on fares, market access and frequency were all eased, thus, removing a major impediment in the way of new entrants.

Arguably, the most significant outcomes of liberalization have been the unleashing of new competitive forces and the emergence of LCCs. Southwest Airlines in the US pioneered the low-cost model in the 1970s and since then, a number of European low-cost carriers such as easyJet and Ryanair have adopted the principles and applied them to the European (CAA, 2006; Doganis, 2006) and North African market (Roberts and Harrison, 2006). LCCs are able to connect travellers to new and unexploited routes.

LCCs were absent from the European market before the 1990s due to the restrictions in the operating environment (CAA, 2006). However, the establishment of the ECAM in 1997 eased some of the restrictions on European Union (EU) airlines, which allowed them to make their own decisions regarding market access, capacity and prices. This brought major structural changes, which led to the emergence of LCCs in the European aviation market. In fact, the low-cost sector has seen rapid growth since the emergence of Ryanair in 1991 and EasyJet in 1995, following the liberalization of the UK aviation market (The Economist, 2004; Mason and Alamdari, 2007).

A recent study by Mason and Alamdari (2007) found that in 2002 and 2004, the UK low-cost market competition intensified following the emergence of Buzz, Bmibaby, MyTravelLite and Jet2. They further noted that the acquisitions of BA's subsidiary Go by EasyJet and KLM's subsidiary Buzz by Ryanair also led to consolidation in the low-cost sector. The growth in the UK market has been replicated in continental Europe. The recent accession of new countries to the European Union has also increased activity in the low-cost airlines sector with new entrants such as Wizz Air in Poland, and SkyEurope in Slovakia and Hungary establishing a foothold in the EU market (Mason and Alamdari, 2007). Other studies such as Evangelho et al. (2005) have focused on the Brazilian market and noted deregulation in the early 1990s as the underlining factor that paved the way for LCCs such as Gol to emerge. It is generally acknowledged that liberalized air transport markets attract new entrants, which are generally expected to increase competition, producing benefits for air travellers in the form of lower fares, improved frequency and service levels (Doganis, 2006).

Much of the literature has focused on mainly the European Union and US with little emphasis on developing countries (with the exception of South-East Asia). However, interest is now emerging on the study of LCCs in Africa. For example, Fourie and Lubbe (2006) investigated factors that influence business travellers in their selection of traditional airlines or low-cost carriers in South Africa. Their findings show similarities with studies conducted by Mason (2001) and Evangelho et al. (2005) on the UK and Brazilian markets respectively. However, it is unclear whether liberalization in Africa is driven by similar factors as those in Europe and the United States.

What is, however, known is that African ministers responsible for civil aviation met in Yamoussoukro, Ivory Coast in 1988 to seek ways to liberalize air transport markets (Akpoghomeh, 1999). The Yamoussoukro Declaration (YD), which emerged seeks to remove all restrictions in intra-Africa routes by allowing free access of air traffic between member states in order to create a single African aviation market. To date, however, the YD has not been fully implemented, as more than 50 per cent of African airlines are state-owned carriers (Airline Business, 2006a). As a result, airlines cannot fly to new markets in Africa without an international agreement and cross-border mergers and consolidations are restricted. Progress in the industry has, thus, stalled and new entrants face high market entry barriers.

Despite the above factors, LCCs have emerged in South and North Africa raising a number of interesting questions about what factors have contributed towards this trend. In November 2006, a new LCC, Mango, was launched in South Africa to compete with established LCCs such as Kulula and 1Time. Other carriers such as Atlas Blue and Jet4you have emerged in North Africa. Furthermore, Europeans budget carriers such as EasyJet, Air Berlin and Ryanair have expanded their services to North Africa. Table 13.1 illustrates point-to-point flights connecting city-pairs served by some LCCs in South and North Africa. It suggests that the new carriers have managed to build domestic, regional and international connections to cities in Africa and Europe. For instance, some carriers in South Africa have

Table 13.1 Sample route networks of LCCs in Africa

Route/Airport	Carrier
Marrakech – Orly, Paris.	Jet4you
Fes – Orly, Paris.	Jet4you
Johannesburg – Harare, Zimbabwe	Kulula
Johannesburg – Durban	Kulula, 1Time, Mango
Johannesburg – Cape Town	Kulula, Mango, 1Time
Johannesburg – Ndola, Zambia	Kulula
Johannesburg – Lusaka, Zambia	Kulula
Johannesburg – Port Elizabeth	1Time
Johannesburg – Windhoek, Namibia	Kulula
Johannesburg – Plaine Magnien Mauritius	Kulula
Johannesburg – Bloemfontein	Mango

Sources: 1Time, 2007; Kulula.com, 2007; Mango; www.jet4you.com

been able to launch services on profitable routes to countries such as Namibia and Zimbabwe.

In the light of the foregoing developments, the following questions are raised:

(a) What are the main internal factors underpinning the emergence and regional expansion of LCCs in North and South Africa?
(b) What are the key external factors driving the emergence and regional expansion of LCCs in North and South Africa?

The chapter is guided by the above key questions. Many international managers and foreign investors are sceptical about the prospects for any profitable investment in Africa (Debrah and Toroitich, 2005). This is partly due to political interferences, obstacles and constraints in the operating environment. But, it appears that some sectors are bucking the trend and are benefiting from the injection of foreign private capital (*The Economist*, 2008a, b). This chapter provides an example of an emerging sector, which has overcome some of the scepticism and hindrances, and whose seeming prosperity should be of interest to foreign investors, aviation companies and IB scholars.

The changing airline industry in Africa

Arguably, the airline industry in Africa exhibits similar characteristics to its European and US counterparts, though the stages of development differ widely. Since the mid-1980s, widespread privatization of state-owned airlines (SOAs) has occurred in the global airline industry partly due to the pressures to liberalize and free state resources from the unsustainable burden of continuing public ownership, and the push on these traditional airlines to discard inefficient practices such as revenue-pooling agreements and to become competitive and customer oriented (Doganis, 2006). In spite of the privatization trend, many African airlines are still characterized by state-ownership and involvement and many, including

Air Namibia and Air Zimbabwe, still perform social roles. Some governments regard the existence of a state-owned carrier as a sign of national pride and the carriers are often asked to serve international destinations that purely commercial consideration would not support (Ramamurti and Sarathy, 1997; Gourdin, 1998; Doganis, 2006). Providing such public services not only diverts resources from essential investments in areas such as new aircrafts, but also increases their operating costs (Akpoghomeh, 1999). But changes in the airlines' external environment are forcing African governments to deregulate the industry.

The South African government deregulated its air services in 1991 and allowed entrants such as 1Time to enter the market. The state transport controlling body in South Africa, Transnet has 98.2 per cent stake in South African Airways (SAA) (Birn, 2006). This enables the airline to enjoy state support in the form of financial aid and subsidies. Such on-going support has imposed a burden on taxpayers of South Africa and has adversely affected the efficient running of the airline. Since 2002, SAA has made losses of R16 billion (US$2.2 billion) and is insolvent to the tune of nine billion rand (Airline Business, 2007). In addition, there is evidence to suggest that some of the SOAs in Africa have abused their dominant position. For instance, SAA signed an agreement that encourages travel agents to increase their sales of SAA tickets at the expense of other airlines. The agreement was subsequently ruled by the South Africa's Competition Tribunal in 2006 as anti-competitive (Airline Business, 2007). The case of SAA not only illustrates the prevailing conditions in South Africa, but is also a reflection of operating tactics of many African state-owned or traditional carriers. Recently, it has been suggested that the South African government should follow its global counterparts and privatize SAA (Airline Business, 2007).

The problems of under-capitalization and large accumulated debts have forced some governments to adopt privatization as a means of attracting foreign direct investment. Two recent cases are Ghana Airways and Nigeria Airways. Following years of under performance, the governments of Ghana and Nigeria respectively privatized the two carriers (Airline Business, 2006b). The two carriers were characterized by problems such as over-employment, political interference and the servicing of too many routes. These problems made them vulnerable to global competition and prone to what is described by Doganis (2006) as 'distressed state airline syndrome'. The drain on the government resources in terms of subsidies and tax relief was no longer sustainable. Their demise resulted in the formation of Ghana International Airline (GIA) and Virgin Nigeria with a mix of foreign and domestic capital to help fill the vacuum left. Private investment from Virgin Atlantic helped to establish Virgin Nigeria to compete with other carriers such as Bellview. Currently, Virgin Atlantic Airways have a 49 per cent stake in Virgin Nigeria.

A proposed framework for analysing the development of LCCs in Africa

The IB literature has identified several categories of drivers propelling exports, markets and industries (Yip, 1992, 2003; Ibeh and Wheeler, 2005; Wheeler et al.,

2008). Building on work of these researchers, we have proposed a modified framework for analysing the factors responsible for the emergence of LCCs in Africa.

As can be seen from Figure 13.1, the proposed framework identifies two broad categories of factors, internal and external, as underpinning the emergence of LCCs in Africa. The internal environmental drivers encompass decision-maker attributes and firm resources, capabilities and strategies. These, in a sense, represent their strengths and weaknesses. As widely noted in the literature, decision-maker characteristics such as prior business experience and international orientation have a positive influence on firm international expansion (Miesenbock, 1988). Such managerial attributes and other organizational resources and capabilities play pivotal roles in achieving competitive advantage (Wernerfelt, 1984; Barney, 1991, 2001; Barney et al., 2001; Spanos and Lioukas, 2001). While numerous internal resources may influence a firm's strategy and performance, the key resources that lead to competitive advantage must meet four conditions: valuable, rare, imperfectly imitable and imperfectly substitutable (Barney, 1991). This means that to outwit competitors, firms need to develop distinct and innovative strategies and processes. These strategies can be developed using the internal resources of the airline, including physical assets such as aircraft/fleet and machinery, and intangibles such as unique business processes, licences and patents, and reputation.

The external environment is viewed as encompassing the relevant industry and home and foreign market factors, including the opportunities and threats in the firm's operating environment. This aspect utilizes some of the factors identified by Yip (1992, 2003) as 'globalization drivers', which include cost, governments, markets and competitive drivers, to examine the factors accounting for the emergence of LCCs in Africa. As implied by the direction of the arrows in Figure 13.1,

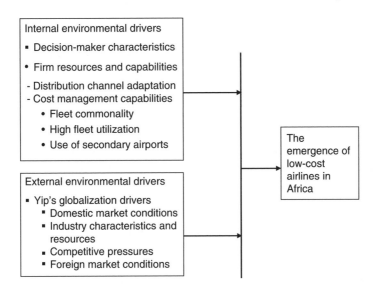

Figure 13.1 A proposed framework of the emergence of low-cost airlines in Africa

these external and internal drivers combine to influence the emergence of low-cost airlines in Africa.

We now examine the impact, if any, of these internal and external factors on the emergence and regional expansion of African LCCs.

Analysis and discussion

Internal drivers – Decision-maker characteristics

Evidence from the present study appears to reinforce the importance of decision-maker characteristics, as suggested in the literature. In the case of 1Time, the five entrepreneurs who started the company in 2004 have had several years of experience in the aviation industry and were determined to succeed (1Time, 2008). Indeed, three of the five entrepreneurs had over 20 years experience each in the industry ranging from starting up aircraft maintenance companies, that is, Bop Air and Sun Air, to working as a commercial pilot (*Financial Times*, 2008; *Newsweek*, 2008). Sobie (2006), for example, highlighted the importance of the previous competencies gained by some members of the management team of 1Time at South Africa's other regional and international carrier, Comair. One member of the management team had served as financial director with Comair and gained expertise in financial management, which proved crucial in enabling them to secure funding from local investors to buy and lease aircrafts at highly favourable rates (Sobie, 2006). This is because in 2003, in the aftermath of the 9/11 terror attacks, aircraft acquisition costs were still low, so 1Time was able to secure a lease agreement for two Boeing MD-83s for only R500,000 ($71,000) per month (1Time, 2008; Sobie, 2006). This was a crucial period because the South African Rand was also strong relative to the US dollar (Sobie, 2006). As Sobie (2006) noted, the management team managed to lock-in aircraft at a fraction of the cost so they were assured of a long-term cost advantage. The management took advantage of the exchange rate to secure competitive rates to establish low start-up cost, which provided the springboard for them to launch services on both domestic and international routes. It further helped that the other member of the management team had over ten years experience in information technology, which helped in designing and implementing the 1Time on-line booking reservation system (*Newsweek*, 2008; *Financial Times*, 2008). This combined set of skills put the company on a sound footing to overcome some of the inherent human resource constraints and the lack of managerial expertise that characterize small firms in Africa and act as major barriers to their internationalization.

In summary, the individual team members are part of networks of specialized expertise in areas such as business start-up, information technology, financial and international management, and technical acumen relating to aircraft maintenance and commercial piloting. These equipped the organization with expertise across all functional areas. As Ibeh (2004, p. 106) points out, 'given decision-makers with the appropriate mix of qualities, firms, whatever their nationality or the nature of their operating environment, would tend to exhibit favourable export behaviour'. This appears to be the case with the new LCCs in

Africa. The study data also reflects Loane et al. (2007) observation that firms formed by teams tend to demonstrate superior internationalization performance, influenced by the greater resource capabilities and skills vested in members of the teams. Therefore, it can be concluded that small firms in Africa aiming to achieve improved export performance or undertake international expansion could benefit from the introduction of top management teams with a 'mix of qualities' across functional areas. In this respect, future government policy direction in Africa should focus on capacity enhancement measures such as training and human resources development, which are consistent with the recommendations by Wheeler et al. (2008).

Internal Drivers – Distribution channel capabilities

Evidence also suggests that the distribution channel capabilities developed by African LCCs have been instrumental in their regional expansion. These firms have innovatively changed the ways of organizing their value-chain activities by mimicking strategies adopted by carriers in Europe, US and elsewhere. For instance, LCCs such as 1Time, Kulula and Mango operate 100 per cent e-ticketing, which differentiates their services from traditional airlines such as SAA. The adoption of innovative technologies and Internet-based platforms, therefore, seems to have assisted these African LCCs to overcome some size-related impediments and engage in international expansion (see Ibeh, 2000, 2003). By relying mainly on online booking, LCCs are not only able to eliminate commissions paid to travel agents by directly dealing with customers, but also provide up-to-date information to their customers. Online bookings offer the carriers the opportunity to manage their revenue management system by receiving direct revenue of all bookings. In addition, they help to ensure that the airlines capture key details regarding customers for their database, which can be used to provide services more closely attuned to customers' needs and to market directly to them. As observed by Wheeler et al. (2008), good distribution channels and customer relationships impact favourably on firms' international expansion.

Internal Drivers – Cost management capabilities

Evidence suggests that effective management of value-chain activities – through *fleet commonality, higher fleet utilization and use of secondary airports* – are enabling African LCCs to achieve cost advantages (Evangelho et al., 2005; Flouris and Walker, 2005; CAA, 2006; Doganis, 2006) and exploit these in regional markets. *Fleet commonality* means operating a single-class aircraft layout and using aircraft made by one manufacturer; this can reduce operational cost by two per cent (Doganis, 2006). For instance, since 2004, 1Time has moved three of the four DC-9s in its fleet to its charter unit and replaced them with mainly 157-seat MD-83s to enable it to achieve cost savings (Sobie, 2006). Another carrier, Kulula, operates a fleet consisting entirely of Boeing MD-82s (Birn, 2006). The underlining motive for this fleet commonality is to enable the carriers to reduce the cost of training pilots and maintenance personnel since additional training on other types of aircraft would not be required. This and other cost advantages have enabled LCCs to not only offer lower fares to travellers, but also encourage people to make journeys they would otherwise not have made. Higher fleet utilization involves scheduling flights to increase the number of take-offs and landings. This enables LCCs to spread cost over a greater quantity of output, and reduce cost per seat-km since fixed costs such as insurance, maintenance and depreciation are largely unaffected by the number of flights made by an aircraft. Furthermore, using mainly under-utilized airports enables LCCs to achieve direct cost savings through paying relatively cheaper landing fees, passenger-loading fees, aircraft parking fees and noise surcharges (Done, 2005). In addition, congestion at second-ary airports is rare, which provides opportunity for carriers to follow schedules on time and avoid costs of delays (Barbot, 2006). A case in point is Kulula, which uses Johannesburg's secondary airport, Lanseria International Airport, where landing fees are around a tenth of those of Johannesburg's Tambo International Airport (Flight International, 2003). Security and safety is not compromised at Lanseria Airport since it complies with the standards set by International Civil Aviation Organization. The partial implementation of the YD has enabled secondary air-port based airlines to operate a limited number of fights. For instance, Lanseria-based carriers have rights to fly to up to three destinations in Mozambique (Flight International, 2003). Arguably, this would help to facilitate the emergence of LCCs across Africa.

External drivers – Domestic market conditions

The emergence and regional expansion of Africa would seem to have been facili-tated by the policies of individual African governments to improve market access and the working of air travel markets. As mentioned earlier, the South African government deregulated its air services in 1991, which paved the way for entrants, meeting the necessary safety, insurance and financial requirements, to enter the market and compete against the state-owned flag carrier, SAA (Wastnage, 2003). There, thus, emerged LCCs such as Kulula (owned by Comair) in 2001, 1Time in 2004 and Mango in 2006. These South African LCCs have, since 2001, doubled their market share to about eleven million passengers (Birn, 2006), using their lower prices to gain market share from traditional carriers in Southern Africa such as SAA, Zambia Airways and Air Zimbabwe (Sobie, 2006). Recently, the LCCs have recognized that operating mainly in South Africa may not be sufficient to ensure their long-term survival. As a result, some started exploring means to expand in the Southern African region. In 2006, Zambian Airways signed a lease agreement with Kulula to fly the Johannesburg–Lusaka route; Zambian Airways had discon-tinued its services leaving SAA as the sole operator (Myburgh et al., 2006). This was a strategic opportunity for the low-cost carrier to extend its activities beyond its domestic market by adding extra routes. Similar arrangements enabled the car-rier to extend its services to other Southern African cities, including Harare.

The emergence of two Morocco-based LCCs, Atlas Blue in 2004 and Jet4you in 2006, also seems to have been encouraged by the liberalization of the air trans-port sector in Morocco during the 1997–2004 period (Buyck, 2006). Jet4you cur-rently has services to several Moroccan, French and Belgian airports, whilst Atlas

Blue, which is a subsidiary of Royal Air Maroc, operates charter and scheduled services to destinations in Europe. Air traffic between the EU and Morocco has been rising due to tourism and the fact that about 2.8 million Moroccans reside in Europe (Buyck, 2006).

External drivers – Industry characteristics

The reference, in the preceding sentence, to tourism brings us to another factor that has been suggested as influential in the emergence of LCCs in North Africa: rising tourism levels and the importance of the tourism industry to the national economies (Buyck, 2006). International tourist arrivals to Morocco increased 13 per cent in 2005 compared to 2004, with 1.3 million arriving from France, 368,000 from Spain, 194,000 from the UK and 144,000 from Germany (Buyck, 2006). An estimated 60 per cent of international tourists visit Africa for leisure, recreation and holiday purposes (WTO, 2003). As Gray (2000) observes, tourism is one of the priority sectors for North Africa, and governments in the region have taken several measures to help attract tourists. These include the EU–Morocco aviation agreement and the liberalization of the Moroccan air transport sector, which, as indicated earlier, facilitated the emergence of Atlas Blue and Jet4you. The prevalence of new holiday destinations has created further regular traffic streams for LCCs to exploit (Bieger and Wittmer, 2006).

The fact that South Africa and Morocco account for the LCCs discussed here appears to follow the European example. In their early development phase, European no-frills airlines focused mainly on the British Isles due to the liberal regulatory regime, which fostered a more conducive environment for airline start-ups (Flottau and Taverna, 2001; CAA, 2006). The four major European carriers, namely Ryanair, EasyJet, Go and Buzz were based in the UK or Ireland, which provided the platform for them to expand across Europe. African LCCs may follow a similar pattern and continue to extend their activities across Africa.

Conclusions and implications

This chapter has examined the internal and external factors that have contributed towards the emergence and regional expansion of LCCs in South and North Africa, and the challenges that LCCs pose to the traditional airlines. The conceptual framework employed represents an attempt to draw upon relevant models, notably Yip's (1992; 2003) globalization drivers framework and the resource-based view (Barney, 1991, 2001; Spanos and Lioukas, 2001; Wernerfelt, 1984) to explain the factors driving the emergence of LCCs in Africa. The framework suggests that considering both external and internal factors is likely to result in a better understanding of the environmental drivers of growth and development of firms in the airline industry and beyond. Such theoretical integration may lead to quality answers to the big question in IB research: *what determines the international success and failure of firms?* (Peng, 2004, p. 106). Building on the analytical framework developed in this chapter, several future research directions can be pursued to illuminate our understanding of regional expansion of airlines. First, since both the resource-based view and Yip's globalization drivers are integrated into the framework, researchers examining international expansion of firms can employ both approaches to provide a better understanding of a firm's regional expansion strategy. Second, future research can focus on using fieldwork/empirical evidence to assess the impact of the emergence of LCCs on the traditional airlines operating in Africa.

Managerial implications

The application of the framework also suggests several implications for traditional airlines, governments, low-cost airlines in Africa and other stakeholders. First, the low-cost phenomenon in Africa is in its infancy and therefore unless the YD is fully implemented, LCCs are unlikely to take off in a great wave across Africa. If the LCCs expand successfully from both South and North Africa to other parts of Africa, the phenomenon is likely to catch many traditional carriers in sub-Saharan Africa off guard as many rely on governments for protection against competition and have not developed strategies for competing with LCCs. Second, the failure of some African governments to pursue privatization of state-owned airlines has hindered the traditional carriers' ability to attract foreign investment and compete in the global era. Therefore, by removing political and financial support in terms of subsidies, traditional airlines would be more able to focus on reducing cost. This action will force many state-owned airlines to stop servicing too many routes and withdraw from unprofitable ones. In the long term, this is bound to benefit both companies and passengers.

Some of Africa's traditional airlines such as SAA and Royal Air Moroc have responded to the threats from LCCs by setting up subsidiaries based on the LCC model as a competitive response to the growth of new entrants. In 2006, SAA launched Mango as its low-cost subsidiary to compete with established carriers such as Kulula and 1Time, but more importantly, to stop losing market share to the new entrants. Royal Air Moroc has also launched its own low-cost subsidiary, Atlas Blue to provide charter and scheduled services on some routes and to compete with some African and European airlines. As Dennis (2007) pointed out, traditional airlines in North America and Europe adopted a similar approach in response to low-cost competition. In Europe, traditional airlines such as Alitalia and Olympic continue to incur huge losses whilst others such as BA, Lufthansa and KLM/Air France have to some extent weathered the initial threats posed by the emergence of low-cost airlines (Dennis, 2007). The differences in performance are partly due to the strategic responses adopted by these carriers to liberalization, which enabled the emergence of LCCs in their previously restricted markets.

The lesson here for Africa's traditional airlines is the need to develop a responsive and robust strategy to counter the threats posed by LCCs or risk losing further market share. Some of Africa's traditional airlines such as Kenya Airways, South African Airways, alongside new entrants such as Ghana International Airline and Virgin Nigeria have adopted the online booking technology in their attempt to reduce cost. For instance, they all have extensive online booking sites to support the use of travel agents. This suggests that the presence of technology savvy LCCs has a positive impact on traditional airlines not least on the adoption of online booking practices to reduce operating costs. Therefore, the introduction of the low-cost model to the African context has some potential benefits for traditional carriers.

References

1Time (2007) 'Bookings', available at https://www.1time.aero/aqueduct/1time/Booking (accessed 19 June 2007).

1Time (2008) 'All about us', available at https://www.1time.aero (accessed 19 June 2008).

Africa Research Bulletin (2007) 'Economic, financial and technical series', 43(11), 17171–17206.

Airline Business (2005) 'Africa's era of liberalization', available at http://www.flightglobal.com/articles/2005/08/22/201007/africas-era-of-liberalization.html (accessed 22 August 2006).

Airline Business (2006a) 'Africa: Consolidation is essential', available at http://www.flightglobal.com/articles/2006/04/26/206244/consolidation-is-essenti (accessed 11 November 2006).

Airline Business (2006b) 'Africa report: Survival test', available at http://www.flightglobal.com/articles/2006/11/21/210613/africa-report-survival-test.html (accessed 21 November 2006).

Airline Business (2007) 'Privatise South Africa', available at http://www.flightglobal.com/Articles/2007/03/19/212632/privatise-south-africa.html (accessed 23 March 2007).

Akpoghomeh, O.S. (1999) 'The development of air transportation in Nigeria', *Journal of Transport Geography*, 7, 135–46.

Barbot, C. (2006) 'Low-cost airlines, secondary airports, and state aid: An economic assessment of the Ryanair–Charleroi Airport agreement', *Journal of Air Transport Management*, 12, 197–203.

Barney, J. (1991) 'Firm resources and sustained competitive advantage', *Journal of Management*, 17(1), 99–120.

Barney, J. (2001) 'Is the resource-based "view" a useful perspective for strategic management research? Yes', *Academy of Management Review*, 26(1), 41–56.

Barney, J., Wright, M. and Ketchen, D. (2001) 'The resource-based view of the firm: Ten years after 1991', *Journal of Management*, 27, 625–41.

Bieger, T. and Wittmer, A. (2006) 'Air transport and tourism – Perspectives and challenges for destinations, airlines and governments', *Journal of Air Transport Management*, 12, 40–46.

Birn, H. (2006) 'South Africa: Mango in the mix', *Flight International*, 5060(170), 32–34.

Button, K.J. (2002) 'Toward truly open skies', *Regulation*, 25(3), 12–16.

Buyck, C. (2006) 'Air souk', *Air Transport World*, 43(10), 44–47.

Chung, J. (2007) 'Investors focus on Africa's potential', *Financial Times*, 18 November.

Civil Aviation Authority (CAA) (2006) *No-Frills Carriers: Revolution or Evolution? A Study by the Civil Aviation Authority*, CAP 770 (London: The Stationery Office).

Collinson, S. and Rugman, A.M. (2008) 'The regional nature of Japanese multinational business', *Journal of International Business Studies*, 39(2), 215–30.

De Neufville, R. (2006) 'Planning Airport Access in an era of low-cost airlines', *Journal of the American Planning Association*, 72(3), 347–57.

Debrah, Y.A. and Toroitich, O.K. (2005) 'The making of an African success story: The privatization of Kenya Airways', *Thunderbird International Business Review*, 47(2), 205–30.

Dennis, N. (2007) 'End of the free lunch? The responses of traditional European airlines to the low-cost carrier threat', *Journal of Air Transport Management*, 13, 311–21.

Doganis, R. (2006) *The Airline Business*, 2nd edn (London: Routledge).

Done, K. (2005) 'A new wave of privatization', *Financial Times Aerospace*, 1(13 June).

Evangelho, F., Huse, C. and Linhares, A. (2005) 'Market entry of a low cost airline and impacts on the Brazilian business travelers', *Journal of Air Transport Management*, 11, 99–105.

Financial Times (2008) Companies research: 1Time Holding Ltd, available at markets.ft.com (accessed 18 January 2008).

Flight International (2003) 'Kulula.com considers expansion', available at http://www.flightglobal.com/articles/2003/11/25/174202/kulula.com-considers-expansion.html (accessed 18 January 2007).

Flight International (2006a) 'Another bad year for Africa', 5018(169), 32.

Flouris, T. and Walker, T.J. (2005) 'The financial performance of low-cost and full-service airlines in times of crisis', *Canadian Journal of Administrative Sciences*, 22(1), 3–21.

Fourie, C. and Lubbe, B. (2006) 'Determinants of selection of full-service airlines and low-cost carriers – A note on business travellers in South Africa', *Journal of Air Transport Management*, 12, 98–102.

Franke, M. (2004) 'Competition between network carriers and low-cost carriers – Retreat battle or breakthrough to a new level of efficiency?' *Journal of Air Transport Management*, 10, 15–21.

Gilbert, D., Child, D. and Bennett, M. (2001) 'A qualitative study of the current practices of "no-frills" airlines operating in the UK', *Journal of Vacation Marketing*, 7(4), 302–15.

Gourdin, K.N. (1998) 'U.S. International aviation policy into the new millennium: Meeting the global challenge', *Transportation Journal*, 37(4), 13–21.

Gray, M. (2000) 'The political economy of tourism in North Africa: Comparative perspectives', *Thunderbird International Business Review*, 42(4), 393–408.

Ibeh, K.I.N (2000) 'Internationalization and the small firm', in S. Carter and D. Evans (eds), *Enterprise and Small Business: Principles, Practice and Policy* (London: Financial Time and Prentice Hall).

Ibeh, K.I.N. (2003) 'On the internal drivers of export performance among Nigerian firms: Empirical findings and implication', *Management Decision*, 41(3), 217–25.

Ibeh, K.I.N. (2004) 'Furthering export participation in less performing developing countries: The effects of entrepreneurial orientation and managerial capacity factors', *International Journal of Social Economics*, 31(1/2), 94–110.

Ibeh, K. and Wheeler, K. (2005) 'A resource centred interpretation of export performance', *International Entrepreneurship and Management Journal*, 1(4), 539–56.

International Air Transport Association (IATA) (2005) 'Four point agenda for Africa', available at http://www.iata.org/pressroom/pr/2005-10-05-03 (accessed 21 July 2006).

Kulula.com (2007) 'New flight booking', available at http://www.kulula.com/Default.aspx (accessed 19 June 2007).

Lawton, T.C. and Solomko, S. (2005) 'When being the lowest cost is not enough: Building a successful low-fare airline business model in Asia', *Journal of Air Transport Management*, 11, 355–62.

Levy, J.D. (1997) 'Globalization, liberalization, and national capitalisms', *Structural Change and Economic Dynamics*, 8, 87–98.

Loane, S., Bell, J.D. and McNaughton, R. (2007) 'A cross-national study on the impact of management teams on the rapid internationalization of small firms', *Journal of World Business*, 42, 489–95

Mason, K.J. (2001) 'Marketing low-cost airline services to business travelers', *Journal of Air Transport Management*, 7, 103–09.

Mason, K.J. and Alamdari, F. (2007) 'EU network carriers, low cost carriers and consumer behaviour: A Delphi study of future trends', *Journal of Air Transport Management*, 13, 299–310.

Miesenbock, K.J. (1988) 'Small business and exporting: A literature review', *International Small Business Journal*, 6(2), 42–61.

Myburgh, A., Sheik, F., Fiandeiro, F. and Hodge, J. (2006) *Clear Skies over Southern Africa* (Woodmead: The ComMark Trust).

Newsweek (2008) '1timeholdings', available at www.newsweek.com (accessed 19 June 2007).

Peng, M.W. (2004) 'Identifying the big question in International Business research', *Journal of International Business Studies*, 35 (2), 99–108.

Piga, C.A. and Fillipi, N. (2002) 'Booking and flying with low-cost airlines', *The International Journal of Tourism Research*, 4(3), 237–47.

Ramamurti, R. and Sarathy, R. (1997) 'Deregulation and globalization of airlines', *The International Trade Journal*, 11(3), 389–432.

Roberts, G. and Harrison, M. (2006) 'Budget airlines spread their wings to Africa', *The Independent*, 2 March, 3.

Rugman, A. (2003) 'Regional strategy and the demise of globalization', *Journal of International Management*, 9, 409–17.

Rugman, A. and Hodgetts, R. (2001) 'The end of global strategy', *European Management Journal,* 19(4), 333–43.

Rugman, A. and Verbeke, A. (2004) 'A perspective on regional and global strategies of multinational enterprises', *Journal of International Business Studies,* 35, 3–18.

Shaw, S. (2004) *Airline Marketing and Management*, 5th edn (Aldershot: Ashgate).

Sobie, B. (2006) 'Leading South Africa's other low-cost carrier', *Airline Business*, 22 December.

Spanos, Y.E. and Lioukas, S. (2001) 'An examination into the causal logic of rent generation: Contrasting Porter's competitive strategy framework and the resource-based perspective', *Strategic Management Journal*, 22, 907–34.

The Economist (2004) 'Low-cost airlines – turbulent skies', 372(8383), 67–9.

The Economist (2005) 'Lining up for profits', 377(8452), 95–9.

The Economist (2007) 'African and the Internet: The digital gap', 385(8551), 72.

The Economist (2008a) 'Africa calling', 387(8583), 82.

The Economist (2008b) 'An up-beat assessment of Africa', 387(8576), 87.

Tretheway, M.W. (2004) 'Distortions of airline revenues: Why the network airline business model is broken', *Journal of Air Transport Management*, 10, 3–14.

Wastnage, J. (2003) 'Open skies promise', *Flight International*, available at http://www.flight global.com/articles/2003/12/16/175324/open-skies-promise.html (accessed 16 December 2006).

Wernerfelt, B. (1984) 'A resource-based view of the firm', *Strategic Management Journal*, 5, 171–80.

Wheeler, C., Ibeh, K. and Dimitratos, P. (2008) 'UK Export Performance Research', *International Small Business Journal*, 26(2), 207–39.

World Tourism Organization (WTO) (2003) 'WTO in Africa 1996–2003', available at, http://www.world-tourism.org/newsroom/Releases (accessed 14 February 2007).

www.jet4you.com

Yip, G.S. (1992) *Total Global Strategy: Managing for Worldwide Competitive Advantage* (Englewood Cliffs, NJ: Prentice Hall).

Yip, G.S. (2003) *Total Global Strategy Ii: Updated for the Internet and Service Era* (New Jersey: Pearson Education Inc).

14

Re-examining Women's International Management Experiences: A Middle Eastern Perspective

Beverly Dawn Metcalfe, Kate Hutchings and Brian Cooper

Introduction

Globalization of business has reinforced the importance of international assignments for career advancement, both within and across organizations (Hartl, 2004). Yet, a key concern for Human Resource (HR) talent specialists is the under-representation of women amongst international and expatriate managers (Organization Resources Counsellors, 2002; Harris, 2004; Hearn, Jyrkinen, Piekkari and Oinonen, 2008). Though women in Western nations are increasingly represented in senior management positions, particularly in the public sector and government roles, they remain very under-represented in international management (IM) positions with recent research suggesting that women account for only 14 per cent of expatriate executives posted from the USA, and less than five per cent of those sent abroad from European companies (Van der Boon, 2003). Women from developing countries in Eastern Europe, Asia, South America, Africa and the Middle East (ME) are even less represented amongst international managers, even though their numbers are increasing at senior political and executive levels in their own countries (Walby, 2005).

Pioneering research undertaken by Adler (1984a, b, 1994) has suggested three primary reasons for women's under-representation, including company resistance, foreigner prejudice, and women's own lack of interest in undertaking international assignments. Subsequent scholars have highlighted a fourth barrier to women's international employment opportunities, namely, lack of family and network support systems (Harris, 2001, 2004; Linehan, Scullion and Walsh, 2001). What has not been explicitly explored within this literature, however, is the impact of home country cultural and institutional influences on international employment opportunities and perceptions of opportunities.

In this chapter, we advance current knowledge of women's work orientation towards international careers through detailing an exploratory scoping study, which was designed to test and question whether the barriers to women taking international assignments are similar to those highlighted by western-oriented

232

investigations. The study reports on survey responses from 97 women managers in selected Arab ME nations (Bahrain, Egypt, Jordan, the Kingdom of Saudi Arabia (KSA), Oman, Qatar and the United Arab Emirates (UAE)) and their attitudes towards undertaking international assignments and perceived barriers to doing so. This study complements earlier research, but also considers ME women's own perceptions about national, cultural and institutional barriers to their participating in international work. We argue that the social and political context, particularly in those regions that have very different governance and institutional structures, needs to be carefully unravelled in order to appreciate the complexity of HR and business systems and gender relations. Further, we highlight that international business (IB) scholars need to reassess current understanding of what constitutes international work, since the majority of our sample gain international work experience and challenges via international development and aid agencies and non-government organization (NGOs) agencies. Underpinning our arguments, we stress that gender dimensions of IM should continue to be investigated.

Gender and international human resource management (HRM)

Women and IM assignments

International business research has tended to ignore the gender and diversity aspects of HRM policy formation and development; Hearn et al. (2006) and Nishii and Ozbilgin (2007) are exceptions. The reasons for women's limited advancement in organizations and the public sphere is well documented, including the persistence of gender stereotypes; biases in recruitment and selection processes; few female role models; and limited training opportunities (Adler, 1997; Harris, 2004; Hearn et al., 2006). Many international and cross-cultural studies have shown that individualized management practices adopted as part of HRM strategies, such as training and development, are inherently gendered (Harris, 1995; Zanani and Janssens, 2003; Janssens, Cappellan and Zanoni, 2007). Recent research on expatriate management in international employment policies has found that strategic HRM codes of Western MNCs when implemented in developing regions have not promoted equality as an organizing principle. Rather, they have perpetuated inequalities between men and women (Hartl, 2004; Hearn et al., 2006).

As part of the now expansive gender and HRM literature, women's role in IM has emerged as a distinct field in it own right. Adler has provided the most comprehensive examination of the role of women in IM. She and her successors attribute the scarcity of female expatriates to three principal causes: foreigners' prejudice (Adler, 1994), corporate resistance (Adler, 1984b, b, 1987, 1994; Harris, 1995; Selmer and Leung, 2002; Hearn et al., 2006), and female managers' disinterest (Adler, 1984b; Stroh et al., 2000; Sinangil and Ones, 2001). Recent research has also suggested additional barriers to international employment opportunities for women, specifically limited social network support available to female expatriates and work–family conflict (Linehan, 2000; Linehan et al., 2001).

The barriers to women's international work noted above are primarily based on *Western, developed* and *secular* economies (Metcalfe, 2006). The plethora of studies of gender and management tell us little of the HRM dynamics in regions where religion, notably Islam, has a significant influence on economic and political organization and on gender and human relations (Tayeb, 1997; Walby, 2005). This is all the more important given *Islamic Revivalism*, the high profile of Islam in internationalization debates, and, as part of that debate, women's role in the economic and political sphere (UNIFEM, 2004).

Women, management and development in the ME

The increasing engagement of ME nations in the global economy and rising FDI flows into the region have provided opportunities for ME women in the political and business spheres (Moghadam, 2005). Measurements of women's economic and social development by international indicators show that progress has been mixed and uneven, with oil-rich economies providing greater opportunities especially in public employment (UNDP, 2005; Metcalfe, 2008). United Nations' Development reports indicate that ME nations compared to other developing regions have made significant strides in the empowerment of women, especially in education achievements, and have, to a limited extent, improved political participation (UNIFEM, 2004; UNDP, 2005, 2006). Women's employment, however, is still the lowest in the world. Tables 14.1 and 14.2 provide comparative data on human development (HDI) and gender development (GDI) indicators pertaining to ME and Western (UK, Australia and USA) countries.

Women's slow but steady entry into the economy, perhaps, explains why investigation of women in management in the ME is still an emerging field (Budhwar and Mellahi, 2006). Related, the paucity of scholarship on HRM in the ME can be attributed the fact that the phenomena is relatively recent within ME organizations' strategic planning units.

Current gender research in the ME (for example, El-Azhary, 2003; Barlow and Akbarzadeh, 2006) largely focuses on political participation, women's family roles and health issues rather than providing detailed critiques of corporate leadership and management. Metcalfe's (2006) research is one of the first studies to unravel the cultural and institutional practices that impact ME women's career advancement. She identified work–family conflict, lack of diversity or equality frameworks in both organizational and government machineries, together with limited training support as significant barriers against women's career mobility. These findings suggest that the experiences of women professionals in the ME are comparable to those of female managers in the West. Metcalfe's research (2006, 2007) highlights, however, the cultural dynamics of the 'Islamic Gender Order', which create social and work organization structures that are premised on Islamic principles. The *Islamic Gender Order* is based on sexual difference and recognizes that men and women have different economic and social roles. The importance of Islam as an organizing influence is highlighted in scholarship that shows how the *Qu'ran* and *Hadith* provide a moral framework that guides the behaviour of men and women in organizational and social relations. Significantly, readings of Sharia call for men and women to be treated *equally* but *differently*. As UNIFEM notes, this position may be a 'reflection of equity considerations rather than

Table 14.1   HDI, GDI and GEM rankings

Nation	HDI	GDI	GEM
Bahrain	39	38	–
Egypt	111	–	73
Jordan	86	69	–
KSA	76	72	74
Oman	56	57	–
UAE	49	49	70
Australia	3	3	8
UK	18	16	16
USA	8	8	12

Note: The Human Development Index (HDI) is a composite index that measures the average achievement in a country on three basic dimensions. The Gender Development Index (GDI) adjusts the HDI to penalize for disparities between women and men. The Gender Empowerment Measure (GEM) measures women's and men's abilities to participate actively in economic and political life and their command over economic resources.

Source: Adapted from UNDP 2006 Human Development Report.

Table 14.2   Gender and employment measures

Nation	Income in US Dollars		Economic Activity Rate % (15 and over)	Women in Government Ministerial Level %	Seats in Lower House %	Seats in Upper House %
	Male	Female				
Bahrain	29,107	9,654	29.2	8.7 9 (2005)	0 (2006)	15 (2006)
Egypt	6,817	1,588	20.1	5.9 (2005)	2.0 (2006)	6.8 (2006)
Jordan	7,038	2,143	27.0	10.7 (2005)	5.5 (2006)	12.7 (2006)
KSA	22,617	3,486	17.3 (2004)	0	0	0
Oman	23,223	4,273	21.9	10	2.4 (2006)	15.5 (2006)
UAE	31,788	7,630	37.4	5.6	0	0
Australia	35,832	24,277	56.1	20.0 (2005)	24.7 (2006)	35.5 (2006)
UK	37,506	24,448	55.0	28.6 (2006)	19.6 (2006)	17.5 (2006)
USA	4,075	30,581	59.6	14.3 (2005)	15.2 (2006)	14.0 (2006)

Notes: 1. No wage data is available. For the purposes of calculating the estimated female and male earned income, a ratio of 0.75:1 was used for female agricultural/rural wage and male agricultural/rural wage respectively.
2. Note that women are not allowed to vote in KSA or UAE. Also note that UAE has not signed the UN Convention on the Elimination of All Forms of Discrimination Against Women.
3. Women are appointed by the ruling government to ministerial seats in Bahrain and UAE.

Source: Adapted from UNDP 2006 Human Development Report.

biases against women' (UNIFEM, 2004, p. 26) – see also Rice (1999), Moghadam (2005), and Al-Hamadi et al. (2007).

Nonetheless, there are many institutional and cultural practices in the ME that disadvantage women. Sex segregation in work and public spaces is commonly observed in KSA, UAE, Kuwait and Bahrain, together with facilities for segregated education provision. New universities opening in recent years, for example, Zayed University in the UAE, and Women's Royal University in Bahrain, are solely for women. Women's educational opportunities reinforce traditional gender stereotypes with women barred from entry into engineering, medicine and technical professions. Finally, women's private role in the home as caretaker of the family is highlighted as her natural and important role for an Islamic society. These principles are acknowledged in the Islamic governance and political constitutions (for example, Bahrain Charter and Jordanian Constitution), which stress the family as central to the foundations of an Islamic state and of the role of women as caretakers of the family. Few organizations, therefore, have developed equality HR planning systems. Likewise, legislative frameworks provide minimal protection for any form of discrimination.

While the *Islamic gender order* provides career constraints, Metcalfe (2006) reports a positive outcome of gender segregation which encourages women's engagement in entrepreneurship development. In addition there has been an expansion in professional women's associations and NGOs in the ME which are dedicated to promoting women's rights in employment, providing employment development and training, as well as political advocacy. Metcalfe (2006) identifies these women's networks as significant sources of business connections within the ME for international corporations.

The forgoing discussion suggests that in order to develop an accurate picture of the ME HRM system for Western international corporate expansion into the region, it is imperative for research to see beyond the simplistic stereotypical vision of ME society as oppressive and limiting for women. The current social, political and economic human relations development efforts in the ME endeavour to attain a specific form of liberalization, based on a framework of equality and difference.

Method

Sample and procedure

This research is based on an analysis of a semi-structured survey conducted from August to December 2007 in Bahrain, Egypt, Jordan, KSA, Oman, Qatar and UAE. The selected seven Arab ME nations were chosen because they represent the diversity of economic and political development within the region and include oil and natural gas rich economies as well as those with less abundant natural resources. All countries adhere to Islamic Sharia. As well as being representative, the chosen nations were also those in which one of the authors had previously conducted research and consulting and, hence, had a large pool of contacts and business association networks through which the survey could be administered. The questionnaire was developed in English and was largely administered in English to 110 middle- and senior-level ME female managers and business owners, who are conversant in the language and many of whom also work in international organizations that have English as their working language. For some respondents (25 in total), the questionnaire was translated and back-translated into Arabic by a research assistant fluent in Arabic and English. Although 103 questionnaires were returned, seven were found to be incomplete, resulting in 97 usable responses.

The questionnaire was administered electronically by ME business contacts. Potential respondents were approached by the aforementioned contacts and asked to respond to the survey and to send their responses electronically to the first author. This snowballing/convenience sampling does suggest the potential for sampling bias. However, it is a strategy that has been successfully used in the international HRM field and in developing and beyond countries as a means of gaining access (Piekarri and Welch, 2004; Hutchings and Weir, 2006; Hearn et al., 2008). The survey was conducted in accordance with ethics clearance obtained through the participating universities.

Characteristics of the sample

Analysis of the background information on the 97 respondents shows that the women are employed across a range of industries and occupations, with the majority being employed in public or non-government organizations, as is consistent with general trends in women's work in the region (UNIFEM, 2004). Some of the women already had international work experience while others did not. Respondents with a mix of experience were important for the analysis as the research focuses not just on ME women's perceptions of barriers to international work, but also their disposition towards participating in international work.

Measures

The survey instrument was adapted from surveys which had been pre-validated in IM research by Stroh et al. (2000), who examined barriers and opportunities for women in international employment. Additional ME, culturally-specific, questions and subsets of questions were developed by the authors. The attitudinal items were rated on Liker-type rating scales. Further details on the wording of the survey items can be accessed via the lead author.

Results

Cultural and organizational barriers

Analysis results show that over half of the respondents (53.5 per cent) reported stereotypical perceptions of women managers as being a barrier to their international career opportunities. In addition, limited training and education opportunities, lack of female role models, the business culture of the home country, and family commitments related to child rearing were identified by approximately 40 per cent of the women.

Training and professional development and organization support

It also emerged that leadership and team building were the most commonly mentioned education and training needs (67 per cent) by the women. Other education and training needs mentioned by over half of the respondents were interpersonal skills (56.7 per cent) and human resource management (54.6 per cent). Some 51.5 per cent of respondents had attended business/industry seminars as part of their professional development. However, far fewer women had developed an individual career plan (28.9 per cent) or had been advised/supported by a mentor (34 per cent). About a half of the sample (49.5 per cent) had attended NGO training programs, and unlike western female executives, 20 per cent of our sample had participated in specialized women's development programmes organized by the United Nations. With regard to organizational support, over a third of the respondents reported a lack of opportunities for part-time and flexible working (36.1 per cent) and 32 per cent cited lack of child care facilities.

Prejudice and cultural adjustment

Data analysis shows that just over a third of respondents (36.2 per cent) either agreed or strongly agreed that host country cultures disadvantage ME women. A similar proportion either agreed or strongly agreed that 'host country nationals both inside and outside the company are prejudiced against female ME expatriates'. About half of the respondents (49.5 per cent) reported that female ME executives generally have more difficulty than do their male counterparts in coping with the aggressive atmosphere of business in an international context.

Corporate resistance

Analysis results show that 59 per cent of respondents either agreed or strongly agreed that ME companies are reluctant to send women on international assignments. The corresponding figure for international companies is 30.2 per cent. Just over half of the respondents (51.6 per cent) either agreed or strongly agreed that ME women who have children are offered fewer international assignments than ME women who do not have children. A slightly lower proportion of respondents (44.8 per cent) either agreed or strongly agreed that ME women who have a husband are offered fewer international assignments than ME women who do not have a husband; 38.5 per cent, however reported a neutral opinion on this matter. There were no statistically significant differences in attitudes to corporate resistance by size or organization or industry.

Women and international assignments

In general, the women had positive attitudes to international assignments. Analysis results show that the majority of respondents (66.0 per cent) either disagreed or strongly disagreed with the proposition that they are not personally interested in going on international assignments. Interestingly, nearly a quarter of respondents (23.4 per cent) stated they were not personally interested in going on international assignments, and just over a third (34.0 per cent) either agreed or strongly agreed with the proposition that ME women in general are not interested in going on international assignments.

Attitudes to international assignments varied by age, marital status and presence of children. All of those respondents who were aged 18–24 years expressed an interest in going on international assignments, compared with just over half

(55.6 per cent) of those aged 35 years and over, and 64.5 per cent of those aged 25–34. Those women who were single were more likely to express personal interest in going on international assignments (81 per cent), compared with those who were married (54.5 per cent). Similarly, those respondents with no dependent children were more likely to express personal interest in going on international assignments (78.6 per cent) compared with those with children (47.4 per cent).

Interestingly, there was little variation in attitudes to international assignments by perceptions of corporate resistance or host country prejudice. However, women who disagreed or strongly disagreed that female ME executives have more difficulty than do their male counterparts in coping with the aggressive atmosphere of business in an international context were more likely to express interest in going on international assignments (82.6 per cent) relative to those who indicated feeling such difficulties (54.1 per cent).

A large majority of respondents (71.9 per cent) either agreed or strongly agreed that ME women who have children accept fewer international assignments than women who do not have children. A much smaller majority (54.7 per cent) either agreed or strongly agreed that ME women in dual-career relationships accept fewer international assignments than women who are single or whose husbands do not work. While the majority of women (64.2 per cent) either disagreed or strongly disagreed that female ME executives generally are not as qualified for extended foreign work assignments as are male executives, about a quarter (24.2 per cent) either agreed or strongly agreed with this proposition.

In addition to the quantitative data presented above, we also asked survey participants to respond to several open-ended questions which asked them about instances in which they had been rated unfairly at work, instances where they believed they had been treated unfairly in respect to international experiences, and organizational, cultural or institutional issues which they believe affect international work opportunities for them or other ME women.

Networks, gender identity and motherhood

Several respondents argued that while qualifications and status are important aspects of ME society and business, personal connections override them in recruitment and selection choices as well as opportunities for promotion. The significance of *wasta* (interpersonal relations) and how to navigate personal networks is a key component governing business systems and personal relationships in the ME (Hutchings and Weir, 2006). One respondent argued that 'the recruitment procedure and ... job title ... doesn't give the true appreciation of the person, and it all depends on personal connections' (Jordan 35). Importantly, such connections are not necessarily gender-related, with women from prominent political and business families having better opportunities than men from poorer families. So, in some instances, class may be a more important consideration than gender in affecting opportunities, although it should be noted that many women will suffer double disadvantages on gender and class grounds. This highlights the ways in which the intersections of differences can result in marginalization in organizations (Metcalfe, 2007).

Cultural values and organization attitudes about women's social role and ability greatly impact women's opportunities and their own sense of self-identity. One respondent argued that there are 'general cultural perceptions of women's inadequacy for managerial roles' (Oman 13), while another suggested that it is 'women's own belief in themselves that impacts on empowerment and advance' (Bahrain 44). As she proffered, 'in the ME women mistakenly believe that they are weak, sensitive and not able to handle sophisticated tasks. This common misconception is negatively influencing women in the workplace and is creating fewer opportunities for them' (Jordan 18). This suggests that building women's confidence and awareness of international opportunities is important for HR specialists working in the ME.

There was also general concern that equal opportunity employment codes were disadvantageous to women. Concurrent with survey data, it was generally reported by respondents that there were limited HR initiatives that targeted women's management training and development. Similar to western counterparts, respondents suggested that they did not have the same opportunities as men who had equal or lesser qualifications and work experience. One respondent argued that 'women are passed over for promotion...they are not seen as being able to support departments' (Bahrain 44), while another argued that 'men are always seen as more superior and given more opportunities – as a woman I constantly feel the need to prove myself' (Jordan 68). One woman academic provides details of how her gender affected her opportunities to obtain support from her university to undertake PhD studies. As she stated

> ...men are preferred to women. My experience where I felt I was not fairly treated is that I wanted to continue my personal and professional development through pursuing my PhD degree. Another male colleague who is older than me...and less experienced in teaching and research applied at the same time to obtain his PhD. For him it took only two months to have the organisation's approval. For me it took more than three years to have the organization's approval. They [referring to the head office, who are men]...tried to [discourage me with various reasons]...My colleague finished his PhD and now he is looking for another promotion. Why they did that to me is because I am a woman and they do not want me to compete with them (men)...the good opportunities...only reserved for male. (KSA 6)

One variable that seems to shape women's opportunities is marital or motherhood status (or potential to marry and bear children). One woman from Jordan reported that 'I was supposed to be the second in charge in the bank two years ago, but when I gave birth to my baby someone else was promoted though he is less experienced and qualified' (Jordan 36). Another maintained that their organization 'fears training the female...after a couple of months/years she is well trained...she may get married and have babies...then she may quit' (Jordan 70). Interestingly, even though many professional women in the ME have full-time housekeepers and child carers, the importance of their standing as wife and mother, and the perception that this is their primary role in life, blurs the lines between public and private spheres and affects their employment opportunities. Women's development is thus both gendered and classed since few women of lower birth status will be afforded education and work opportunities.

It was also found that being a ME woman is a double burden reflecting stereotypical views about being a woman and a woman in Islamic societies (El-Azhary, 2003; Barlow and Akbarzadeh, 2006). This, to some extent, reflects the cultural values about men and women's different roles in society. The women surveyed reported that opportunities were affected by either perceptions that ME organizations had about ME women's abilities, or perceptions which they believed that organizations or individuals in foreign nations had about ME women. In respect to the former issue many respondents suggested that ME organizations or foreign organizations operating within the ME would not provide opportunities for ME women to work internationally because they believed that either they would not be accepted as international managers. The 'think international manager, think male' construct was strongly embedded in organization hiring practices (Harris, 2004). As one respondent argued, 'there is an Arabic mentality that only males can work internationally' (Jordan 70). Similarly, there was a perception that Western organizations are culturally prejudiced against ME women. One woman argued that 'foreign managers want foreigners, not ME women as managers' (UAE 17). Respondents also suggested they believed that the lack of opportunities provided to them by foreign organizations was because of a combination of cultural stereotyping as well as political tensions between the ME societies and the Western world. One respondent claimed that 'I am faced with mistreatment as a woman – people in the US/Europe have stereotypes of Arab women' (Jordan 72). These political tensions about Islamic identity in a globalized world are far different from the pressures that female expatriate managers normally experience and may suggest that understanding how to 'position' oneself and understand 'positioning' can aid women's expatriate assignment experiences (Janssens et al., 2007). It is, therefore, likely in the current international relations climate that the adjustment of both Muslim men and women on international assignments will be more challenging (Caligiuri and Cascio, 1998).

ME women in international development

While the forgoing suggests that women's advancement in international assignments is still limited, a key aspect emerging from our study is the vital contribution that women are making to social and economic regeneration. Indeed, many ME women felt that their role was in contributing to the social advance and political reform of societies. Several respondents identified the value of having opportunities to work in international organizations while in their home country and the enriched work experience that could be leveraged for future international employment opportunities. Where respondents believed that they had skills and knowledge that were highly valued by international organizations, they were largely referring to work that they had undertaken for the UN or ILO projects or for other non-government organizations. As one respondent noted, 'the biggest issue I saw in my working experience was that when our own organizations and companies bring in specialists from overseas who are women, they believe in their abilities and treat them professionally, and likewise they view our experience as invaluable' (Jordan 15). There was, therefore, a strong belief that women need targeted support strategies to enable them to participate in international work assignments. The most frequently cited issue for advancing women's opportunities was the general need for belief in, and support for, ME women in their roles in organizations – support which needs to come from family, organizations and government. One respondent suggested the 'need for a husband's understanding and support, and support by management' (Jordan 75) while another maintained that

> my family is supportive but not all families are supportive of women working generally or working internationally. The Sheikh needs to do more to encourage women's roles in families as more than just a mother...we are intelligent, have business skills and usually more qualifications than many men. Women can lead the international development process...if they receive support to do so. (Oman 16)

Discussion

The findings support earlier research, namely Adler's, which suggested that women's international opportunities were affected by foreigner prejudice and corporate resistance. While some of our survey respondents maintained that their organizations were opposed to women working internationally, most suggested that the problem was not actually about organizations directly preventing women from working internationally, but a lack of initiatives to assist their management development for international experience. Like Adler (1984a, b, 1994), our research also found females' own disinterest in international employment, with older married women with dependants being much more likely to report a lack of interest in undertaking international work. Few respondents believed that there was lack of support in expatriate communities, as had been previously suggested (Linehan, 2000; Hutchings et al., 2008), but this could be because respondents had limited international experience or because of the nature of their work in NGOs rather than MNCs. A further reason for women's disinterest could be the stronger emphasis that is placed on family relations and associated roles of men and women in Islamic societies. This *Islamic Gender Order*, which fosters an 'equal but different philosophy', provided both constraints and opportunities for women's development.

The findings further suggest that there is much to be gained by government interventions, which provide leadership and training programs for women as well as industry meetings and NGO training programs. Respondents also argued that organizations provide very little in the way of equal employment opportunity at the workplace, and called for the introduction of workplace crèches, and anti-sexual harassment and discrimination practices in a domestic context, which would then provide a foundation for women to leverage international opportunities. In addition to a lack of supportive practices, many women also commented that there are still organizational barriers to employment within ME nations (which then impacts on opportunities for international work), citing stereotypes of women managers, lack of a family-friendly work culture and lack of strong female role models. In respect to the latter issues, the evidence suggests that ME women are calling for the equal employment practices that were enacted in most Western nations throughout the 1980s and 1990s and view this as fundamental to achieving equal opportunities from which international employment opportunities may then grow.

While much of the findings are consistent with earlier research suggesting lack of corporate support and perceived (or real) foreigner prejudice, what is most interesting about our research is the impact of the local cultural environment in the ME on women's domestic and international work opportunities. Significantly, a number of respondents pointed to the role of *wasta* (interpersonal connections) in affecting women's opportunities and argued that such connections can override gender in the workplace, that is, if women are from well-connected, prominent, wealthy families, then they may have equal or better opportunities than their less well-connected male counterparts. And, while there may be more male recruitment, and training and promotion opportunities for males, women who come from wealthy families may actually be able to find international work assignments irrespective of women generally receiving less support in HR functional areas.

A key finding from our study is that international work experiences need to be more broadly defined to incorporate those activities outside of transnational corporations, namely all forms of international development and associated human rights and social justice roles. Importantly, while ME women may suffer from foreigner prejudice based on cultural and religious stereotypes and may not be considered by private and MNC organizations for international work, they do benefit from training and job opportunities being provided by women's NGOs, women's professional organizations and governmental agencies responsible for women's issues which, they argued, tend to be less gender factionalized than MNCs. It is certainly a weakness that the current IM literature is dominated by concerns about the HR practices and institutional structures of MNCs and has ignored managerial systems in international agencies such as NGOs, the ILO and UN subsidiaries. As our study exemplifies, international organizations play a vital role in economic and social development and contribute to learning and knowledge transfer, within/across organizations and cultures. International agencies and NGOs also play a pivotal development role in educating women about employment rights, opportunities and professional skills.

While respondents suggested that there is a need for government policies and organizational support for women's opportunities, this should be complemented with the provision of support from husbands and families to allow women to manage their work/family responsibilities and to provide them with the capacity to undertake international work. This aspect of our research extends prior international HRM literature on expatriate management, by underlining the need for changing thinking about the gendered nature of economic earning and dominant partners on international assignments. Our findings also add to extant research on barriers to women's international assignments by highlighting the need for national social change to support women's perceived value as potential international managers.

Conclusions

The foregoing analysis presents significant challenges for advancing understandings of gender and HRM policy development in ME Islamic states. The issue of women's liberation is one that has greatly influenced global work culture (Hearn et al., 2006, 2008). Women's rights, in terms of work, family and society are an accepted part of public discourse in Western societies. And yet, economic evidence suggests that reducing gender inequality can, for example, increase growth overall; improve investments in health and education for long term development; and raise productivity and household saving and investment. To some extent, organizations and the government are going to have to carefully manage this gender and work tension between espoused labour market goals to support gender and globalization on the one hand, and the prevailing social views about women and family responsibilities on the other.

While there is a concern to expand development opportunities for women in the work and political sphere, these are framed by recourse to the *Islamic Gender Order* (Metcalfe, 2007). Women are largely expected to leave the workforce when they marry, and what is often termed 'protective socialization' (Kingdom of Bahrain and ILO, 2000) are a set of gendered social and work relations that position men and women in different spheres. The separate public and private worlds of men and women, however, should not always be interpreted (from Western eyes) as oppressive and limiting for women, but as structures and relations that respect and value women and their family role. And, unlike dominant conceptualizations of equality and HR planning, which focus on diversity (incorporating ethnicity, age, sexual orientation), efforts in a ME societal context promote sexual difference and are clearly centred on *women's* empowerment and development. An Islamic lens would, thus, support the development of women and HRM policies that *value* sex differences, acknowledging that men and women may require different policy frameworks to enable equal participation in the public sphere (Tayeb, 1997). Managing difference and the legitimacy of women's needs is an important political tactic in fostering social and economic transformation (Hearn et al., 2006). That is, women's unity is not essentialized but constructed in relation to the organization of social and economic relations (Harris, 2004; Hearn et al., 2006).

It is important to recognize that this research questions the universalism of Western women's IM experience (Tayeb, 1997). This is borne out by the fact that economic growth and development is occurring in developing and transition economies and that the experience of internationalization in these regions is markedly different. In particular, the politicization of Islam and global debates about both the rights and status of Muslims and Muslim women create potential challenging organization dynamics.

Managerial/HRM implications

This research has identified the need for organizations and ME governments to provide initiatives to assist ME women's work and employment opportunities domestically and internationally within and outside the Middle East. Consistent within the Islamic framework discussed above, a women's HR development programme requires 'selective equality action', which values sex difference (Hakim, 1996) and encompasses work-life balance programs such as provision of child care or child care subsidies and flexible or teleworking work hours. Organizations also need to provide career development plans for women that recognize the importance placed on child rearing and family responsibilities within the Arab nations. Further, organizations need to provide mentors and role models for women and showcase the achievements of successful women within their organizations to provide impetus to other women to aim for senior positions, as well as communicating clearly all policies and training staff in equal employment opportunity practices.

To assist ME women to maximize their potential for international employment, organizations in the ME could provide secondments and short-term international assignment postings or cultural exchanges to other counties as well as ensuring that women have equal access to training and cross-cultural training. Moreover, as already practised in the Western world, there is need for cognizance of dual-career issues and assistance in providing jobs for male trailing spouses where women are posted internationally.

There is a also a necessity for overall value-change in ME nations; change which can be led by government plans to promote the empowerment for women through enactment of Anti-Sexual Harassment and Anti-Discrimination legislation, and to reform existing government machineries to fully acknowledge the active role of women in public policy and planning. While focus on the current UN's Millennium Development Goals (MDGs) have improved women's opportunities, there needs to be further stress on inequalities in the Middle East and North African (MENA) region in terms of access to work and training.

Limitations and issues for future research

There are a number of limitations of the present study, which highlight the need for further research. First, we surveyed women currently working within the selected seven ME nations, meaning that the reported perceptions refer only to the experience of working within other ME nations. Future research should aim to survey ME women who are currently on an international assignment, or have previously held an assignment, outside the ME. Second, the study's relatively small sample size and focus on seven ME Arab nations may limit its generalizability to other Islamic or developing nations. Future scholars are, therefore, encouraged to utilize larger study samples and broaden the geographical contexts of their research. It would also be beneficial for future work to survey men in the ME and compare their perceptions with the responses provided by women. Another interesting future research idea might be to explore women's positive experiences with work and employment internationally, by asking them to report situations and experiences in which their skills and knowledge are valued by organizations, government and society. Finally, we would strongly argue that IHRM literature needs to consider HR practices in international development agencies.

References

Adler, N. (1984a) 'Expecting international success: Female managers overseas', *Columbia Journal of World Business*, 19, 77–83.

Adler, N. (1984b) 'Women in IM: Where are they?' *California Management Review*, 6, 79–89.

Adler, N. (1994) 'Competitive frontiers: Women managing across borders', *Journal of Management Development*, 13(2), 24–41.

Adler, N. (1997) 'Global leadership: Women leaders', *Management International Review*, 371(1), 171–96.

Al-Hamadi, A.B., Budhwar, P.S. and Shipton, H. (2007) 'Management of human resources in Oman', *The International Journal of Human Resource Management*, 18(1), 100–113.

Barlow, R. and Akbarzadeh, S. (2006) 'Womens rights in the Muslim world? Reform or reconstruction', *Third World Quarterly*, 27(8), 1481–94.

Budhwar, P.S. and Mellahi, K. (2006) *Managing Human Resources in the Middle East* (Abingdon: Routledge).

Caligiuri, P. and Cascio, W. (1998) 'Can we send Her there? Maximising the success of Western women on global assignments', *Journal of World Business*, 33(4), 394–417.

El-Azhary, A. (2003) *Women of Jordan, Islam, Labor and the Law* (New York: Syracuse University Press).

Hakim, C. (1996) *Key Issues in Women's Work: Female Heterogeneity and the Polarization of Women's Employment* (London: Athlone Press).

Harris, H. (1995) 'Organizational influences on Women's career opportunities in IM', *Women in Management Review*, 10(3), 26–31.

Harris, H. (2001) 'Researching discrimination in selection for IM assignments: The role of repertory grid technique', *Women in Management Review*, 16(3), 118–25.

Harris, H. (2004) 'Global careers: Work-life issues and the adjustment of women international managers', *Journal of Management Development*, 23(9), 818–32.

Hartl, K. (2004) 'The expatriate career transition and Women managers' experience', *Women in Management Review*, 19(1), 40–51.

Hearn, J. Jyrkinen, H., Piekkari, R. and Oinonen, E. (2008) 'Women home and away: Transnational managerial work and gender relations', *Journal of Business Ethics*, Online First.

Hearn, J., Metcalfe, B.D. and Piekkari, R. (2006) 'Gender and international human resource management', in I. Bjorkman and G. Stahl (eds) *Handbook of International Human Resource Management*, 502–22 (London: Edward Elgar).

Hutchings, K., French, E. and Hatcher, T. (2008) 'Lament of the ignored expatriate: An examination of organisational and social network support for female expatriates in China', *Equal Opportunities International*, 27(4), 372–91.

Hutchings, K. and Weir, D. (2006) 'Understanding networking in China and the Arab World: Lessons for international managers', *Journal of European Industrial Training*, 30(4), 272–90.

Janssens, M., Cappellan, T. and Zanoni, P. (2007) 'Successful female attributes as agents: Positioning oneself through gender, hierarchy and culture', *Journal of World Business*, 41(2), 13–148.

Kingdom of Bahrain and ILO (2000) *Employment, Social Protection and Social Dialogue: An Integrated Policy Framework for Promoting Decent Work in Bahrain.* Geneva: ILO.

Linehan, M. (2000) *Senior Female International Managers: Why So Few?* (Vermont: Ashgate Publishing).

Linehan, M., Scullion, H. and Walsh, J. (2001) 'Barriers to Women's participation in IM', *European Business Review*, 13(1), 10–18.

Metcalfe, B.D. (2006) 'Exploring cultural dimensions of gender and management in the Middle East', *Thunderbird International Business Review*, 48(1), 93–107.

Metcalfe, B.D. (2007) 'Gender and human resource management in the Middle East', *The International Journal of Human Resource Management,* 18(1), 54–74.

Metcalfe, B.D. (2008) 'Gender, globalization and management in the Middle East', *Journal of Business Ethics*, Online First.

Moghadam, V. (2005) 'Women's economic participation in the Middle East', *Journal of ME Women's Studies*, 1(1), 110–46.

Nishii, L.H. and Ozbilgin, M. (2007) 'Global diversity management: A conceptual framework', *International Journal of HRM*, 18(11), 1993–94.

Organization Resources Counsellors Inc (ORC) (2002) *Worldwide Survey of International Assignment Policies and Practices* (London: ORC).

Piekarri, R. and Welch, C. (2004) *Handbook of Qualitative Research for International Business* (Cheltenham: Edward Elgar).

Rice, G. (1999) 'Islamic ethics and the implications for business', *Journal of Business Ethics*, 18(4), 345–58.

Selmer, J. and Leung, A. (2002) 'Career management issues of female business expatriates', *Career Development International*, 7(6), 348–58.

Sinangil, H. and Ones, D. (2001) 'Expatriate management', in N. Anderson, D. Ones, H. Sinangil and C. Viswesveran (eds) *Handbook of Industrial, Work and Organisational Psychology* (London: Sage).

Stroh, L., Varma, A. and Valy-Durbin, S. (2000) 'Why are Women left at home: Are they unwilling to go on international assignments?' *Journal of World Business*, 35(3), 241–55.

Tayeb, M. (1997) 'Islamic revival in Asia and human resource management', *Employee Relations*, 19(4), 352.

United Nations Development Programme (UNDP) (2005) *The Arab Human Development Report: Empowerment of Arab Women* (New York: UNDP).

United Nations Development Programme (UNDP) (2006) *Human Development Report: Beyond Scarcity: Power, Poverty and the Global Water Crisis* (New York: UNDP).

UNIFEM (2004) *Progress of Arab Women* (New York, UNIFEM).

Van der Boon, M. (2003) 'Women in IM: An international perspective on Women's ways of leadership', *Women in Management Review*, 18(3/4), 132–46.

Walby, S. (2005) *Measuring Women's Progress in a Global Era*, report for UNESCO (Oxford: Blackwell)

Zanani, P. and Janssens, M. (2003) 'Deconstructing difference: The rhetoric of HR managers diversity discourses', *Organization Studies*, 25, 55–74.

Part IV
Emergent Challenges

15
Trends in International Terrorism against Business Targets
Andrew Lee

Introduction

A key challenge to contemporary international business (IB) is the management of international terrorism risk, in which the consideration of politically motivated violence is introduced into risk assessment. International terrorism poses a particular threat to businesses with a presence in non-domestic markets, where overseas holdings are vulnerable to terrorist attacks whose motivations for attack are unknown. The uncertainty caused by the unpredictable nature of terrorist attacks highlights the complex issues faced when managing organizational risks, for example, where the business might be attacked for what it symbolizes in the mind of the attacker, rather than the nature of the business itself (Czinkota, Knight and Liesch, 2004).

Poole-Robb (2002) highlights the growth in international terrorism as a specific threat to global business, noting how global businesses have become targets where previously terrorist activities were focused on military, political and individual person targets. One source of evidence for this growth in attacks against business targets is indirectly shown in changes in business insurance policies, for example, the increase in the number of insurance claims by global businesses due to the kidnap of business executives in non-domestic markets. In addition to direct physical threats to assets and the financial impact of attacks, terrorist attacks on businesses affect global business issues such as a decline in consumer demand, interruptions to supply chain inputs, increased bureaucracy from additional security legislation and policy, negative macroeconomic effects and deteriorating business relationships between countries (Liesch, Steen, Knight et al., 2006).

The actual direct and indirect effects of international terrorism are recognized as a challenge to business operations, but an analysis of the specific threats to businesses is required to identify appropriate risk assessment and mitigation strategies to determine how these challenges can be overcome. This is necessary to ensure that perceptions of international terrorism are in line with reality since these perceptions can influence risk assessments in internationalization decisions. This paper aims to address these issues by identifying the trends in international terrorism attacks directed specifically against business targets, identifying which geographical regions are more at risk from attack, whether business targets or business infrastructure targets are more at risk, what type of tactics and what weapons are most frequently used to determine what physical countermeasures can be prepared. Through these trends, a clearer picture of the threats to global businesses due to international terrorism can be determined to aid in the management of international risks and international business decisions.

International terrorism

Definitions of international terrorism vary, and no universally accepted version exists. The range of definitions depend on the purpose of the organization forwarding their interpretation of international terrorism, for example, the definition of international terrorism according to US Code 18USC2331 (2000), used by the US Federal Bureau of Investigation, encompasses violent acts to intimidate or coerce the government or civilian population, and violate US criminal laws outside of the territorial jurisdiction of the United States. This definition preserves the interests of the US regardless of the location of the attack by specifying that US criminal laws can be applied to terrorism incidents outside the United States. However, the definition in US Code 22UC2656f(d) (2000), as used by the Department of Justice, defines international terrorism as 'terrorism involving citizens or the territory of more than one country', with terrorism defined separately as premeditated politically motivated violence intended to influence an audience. This definition specifies that international terrorism involves two different countries without restricting the location of the attack to a domestic or foreign location. The RAND Corporation, a non-profit research and analysis organization to aid policy making, defines international terrorism as 'incidents in which terrorists go abroad to strike their targets, select domestic targets associated with a foreign state, or create an international incident by attacking airline passengers, personnel or equipment', placing the emphasis on the nationality of the target and location of the target as core definition of international terrorism (Hoffman and Claridge, 1998, p. 139).

These three definitions demonstrate a spectrum of interpretations of international terrorism. At one end are international companies or industries operating in non-domestic markets being attacked by a terrorist group from that region, for example when the Greek 17 November Revolutionary Organization bombed the Apple Computer Dealership in Athens in March 1999 (Associated Press, 1999). This demonstrated a representative of an American corporation operating in a non-domestic market being attacked by a terrorist group local to the region. At the other end of the spectrum are international businesses or industries being attacked by an international terrorist group, either in the domestic or the overseas market. For instance, the bombing of two hotels in Istanbul on the 9 August 2004 by the Kurdistan Freedom Hawks and Al-Qa'ida was specifically targeted against foreign tourists (AFX News, 2004). Although the bombing damaged a local business, the incident represented an international terrorism attack on foreign tourism industry.

The debates over what constitutes international terrorism have led to databases such as the Global Terrorism Database avoiding a definition altogether and allowing the data to be filtered in a way that matches the interpretation being used by the database interrogator. Given the range of definitions for international terrorism, an alternative approach could be to consider all terrorist activity excluding domestic terrorism incidents. Domestic terrorism has a narrow definition, applying to terrorist acts by a group or individuals within a country without foreign direction or involvement.

The Perception of international terrorism in global businesses

The perception of international terrorism threats to business leaders shows high expectations of attacks to their organizations. This can be seen in the Overseas Security Advisory Council top-ten list of worldwide security trends in the US private business sector in 2007, in which terrorism and political conflict occur five times (OSAC, 2008).

More specifically, Lloyds (2007) surveyed 154 global board level business executives on their perception of risks to their businesses from political violence and terrorism over the next five years from 2007 onwards. Findings from the survey included the following:

- 59 per cent or respondents believe that risks to their companies from political violence and terrorist activity would increase over the next five years;
- 36 per cent expect the highest risk to their company's operations to stem from international terrorism attacks on their businesses;
- 25 per cent believe the biggest threat to their business is political violence aimed at capitalism or business;
- 45 per cent believe the media have painted a bleaker picture than their own experience suggests.

The Lloyds survey shows that respondents are pessimistic in their assessment of terrorism threats to their businesses, whilst acknowledging a difference between the perception created by news media and the actual experience of terrorism risks. The perception of terrorism threat could then exert an influence over rational risk evaluation and mitigation when compared to the actual impact of international terrorism on business targets and have implications on the management of associated risks.

The portrayal of terrorism events in news media has an indirect effect on businesses, where the psychological impact of news media influences the performance of organizations and employees. Howie (2005, 2007) discusses how the psychological impact of media coverage of terrorism influences employee behaviour and the effect on organizational performance, identifying a negative impact on workplace relations with changes to working habits and culture. The heightened risk awareness of employees affects the performance of the organization, even when the organization is unlikely to be under direct threat of a terrorist attack. The public perception of terrorism risk is found to have a strong correlation with public policies used to combat terrorism (Haider-Markel, 2006), suggesting a link between how public perception can influence social and political factors which subsequently affect business operations. Furthermore, public concerns are influenced by media reporting, as evidenced by a survey showing that the media are referred to first when seeking credible information about terrorism in preference over governmental sources of information (Lemrye et al., 2007).

If this is so, one immediate question that arises is, how much does the portrayal of terrorism incidents by the media actually influence public perception of terrorism? Taylor (2002) argues that the perception of terrorism risk is predominantly based on media interest and portrayal of events, where the reporting of events is used to persuade an audience to the benefit of the originator of the news item. In addition, Norris, Kern and Just (2003) investigate how the framing of media issues influences public opinion, concluding that the media coverage reinforces public opinion when making predictions on future international terrorist attacks. These studies suggest that the media are a trusted source for information on terrorism, but the opinion formed from this information is not necessarily unbiased, depending on how the news is presented and for whose benefit.

This issue is highlighted in the Lloyds survey, which compares the opinions of the surveyed executives to results of the 2007 Human Security Report (HSRP, 2007) which concludes that the trend in the number of international terrorism incidents is decreasing. However, the Human Security Report is based on an analysis of all types of targets of international terrorism attacks without distinguishing attacks specifically aimed at business targets. Similar studies on trends on international terrorism also do not distinguish between types of target, for instance, the Memorial Institute for the Prevention of Terrorism (MIPT, 2006) analyses the trends in tactics used in terrorism attacks, applying the analysis to all types of terrorism targets, combining domestic and international terrorism incidents, and merging all types of target including business, government, academic and individual targets. Consequently, the trends for international terrorism attacks on business and infrastructure targets is not clear from these existing analyses, for instance the overall number of global terrorism incidents may be decreasing, but the attacks directed specifically against business targets may be increasing. Without examining historical trends in attacks specifically aimed at business targets, the actual impact on business cannot be measured and this has consequences on risk mitigation strategies (Wernick, 2006); for instance, a stress testing exercise may be simulating a threat that is perceived to be imminent but is unlikely according to historical trends.

Targets of international terrorism

The problems in identifying international terrorism threats to businesses can be seen in reports of incidents, for example, the London bombings on 7 and 21 July 2005 were directed at the transport infrastructure but had a secondary effect of damaging business confidence and causing a negative economic impact on businesses in the region, particularly for retail and tourism sectors (LCC, 2005). Although the terrorist incident affected several different targets (transport, tourism, local economy) the impact of the attack on each type of target could not be separated and measured independently from the others from the report alone.

In response to this problem, databases of terrorism incidents classify terrorism incident reports under the types of target affected and allow the data to be filtered accordingly. These types of target include a category for business, as seen in the Memorial Institute for the Prevention of Terrorism (MIPT), Terrorism Knowledge Base (TKB) and the START Global Terrorism Database (GTD). The TKB defines 21 types of target, including business targets, governmental and diplomatic targets and specific industries such as abortion-related targets, educational institutions, military targets and journalists and media targets. The GTD uses a similar list with slight variations, for instance, a category for agricultural targets is added (normally considered as part of Food and Water targets in the TKB) and renaming the TKB's Government and Diplomatic categories as Government (General) and Government (Diplomatic) (CETIS, 2007).

However, analysis of terrorism threats to business targets alone is not sufficient for a full risk assessment for internationalization decisions. Attacks on other targets can have severe consequences for businesses, for instance the loss of power or communications can paralyse overseas operations which normally require frequent contact with headquarters. The types of targets listed in the TKB and GTD can be utilized here to identify these infrastructure targets for inclusion into risk assessments to businesses, for example the TKB categories of utilities, airports and airlines and telecommunications can be seen as business infrastructure targets (Table 15.1) and used in an analysis of where businesses may be vulnerable.

Analysing trends in international terrorism activity against business targets

To identify the historical trends in international terrorism against business targets, data from the Memorial Institute for the Prevention of Terrorism (MIPT) Terrorism Knowledge Base (TKB) will be used (TKB, 2008). This is the same dataset used in the Human Security Brief analysis of terrorism trends, as cited in the Lloyds survey but which applied the analysis to all types of target. The data used by the TKB includes the type of target that each terrorism incident was directed against, allowing the trends in international terrorism attacks specifically directed against business targets to be identified. The interface to the data also allows the dataset to be filtered by international or domestic terrorist activity, geographical region, type of target (including business as a category), tactic used

Table 15.1 Types of target

Category	MIPT TKB target types
Political	Diplomatic, government
Ideological	Abortion related, journalists and media, educational institutions, food and water supply, maritime, military, NGO, police, private citizens/property, religious figures and institutions, terrorists and former terrorists
Business	Airports and airlines, business, telecommunications, tourists, transportation, utilities
Other	Other, unknown

Source: Adapted from MIPT TKB terrorism target categories.

by the terrorist group and weapon used, allowing a range of analyses to be made on the nature of international terrorism attacks against businesses.

Other datasets of global terrorism and political violence exist, but none of these are directly comparable to the TKB, for instance the Global Terrorism Database (START, 2008) has a more limited date coverage for international incidents (covering the period from 1975 onwards, compared to the TKB which starts from 1968); datasets such as Correlates of War (COW, 2008) and the Uppsala Conflict Data Programme (UCDP, 2008) focus on political violence and conflict rather than on terrorism activity specifically. The TKB also has the advantage of being publicly accessible, compared to terrorism data services such as Jane's World Insurgency data service (Janes, 2008) and the Political Risk Group's Country Risk data (PRS, 2008).

However, two limitations of the TKB must be noted here. The first is that the TKB data is proprietary and uses an interface that limits the depth of the analyses. Data can be filtered by either type of target, tactic used or weapon used, but not a combination of these. As a result, queries such as what types of bombs were used when bombing tactics were used against business targets could not be made directly. The second and more serious limitation is that the TKB ceased operations on 31 March 2008 (Houghton, 2008), with the existing data merged into the Global Terrorism Database from the 31 March 2008 onwards. This will affect the replication of the analyses in this chapter.

Methodology

Analyses of the TKB data were performed for international terrorism incidents directed against business targets for geographical region, type of business target, type of tactic used and type of weapon used. Time series data for each analysis was extracted from the TKB by querying the database with the data range limited from 1 January to 31 December of each year from 1968 to 2008. The results were compiled on spreadsheets and the gradient and intercept for a best fit trend line calculated so that the trend could be expressed as a formula. Where the total number of attacks could be calculated, the number of terrorism incidents was expressed as a percentage of the total number of incidents to give an indication of the relative numbers of incidents. This occurred on the type of business target and the type of weapon used.

Incidents by region

Nine geographical regions are defined in the TKB: Africa; East and Central Asia; Eastern Europe; Latin America and Caribbean; Middle East and Persian Gulf; North America; South East Asia and Oceania; South Asia; and Western Europe.

Incidents by target

The TKB lists 21 types of terrorism targets. For the purposes of this analysis, these were classified into four groups: business targets; political targets; ideological targets; and unclassified targets (Table 15.1). Six of these targets were grouped into the business targets category: airports and airlines; business targets; telecommunications; tourism; transportation; and utilities. These were selected because they either affected general business targets directly, or they posed a risk to the physical infrastructure required for international businesses to operate.

The decision to include tourism in the business category rather than the ideological category was made from the international business perspective where the risk of damage to the country reputation and security may have an impact on international businesses. An example of this is the London bombings, mentioned earlier as an example of how the intended target affected businesses in general. The other types of terrorism target on the TKB list were not considered in this analysis since they affected a specific business sector or localized area only, for example, attacks on educational institutions where the effect on business targets is limited.

Incidents by tactic

The TKB lists nine types of tactic used by terrorist groups: armed attack; arson; assassination; barricade/hostage taking; bombing; hijacking; other; unconventional and unknown. For the purposes of this analysis, three of these (other, unconventional and unknown) have been grouped together since they all relate to types of tactics that cannot be identified until they occur. Furthermore, the combined number of these three types of tactic has not exceeded one incident per year in the entire period studied (1968–2008). Hijacking is not included in this analysis since no incidents were reported between 1968 and 2008.

Incidents by weapon

The TKB lists nine types of weapon: biological agent; chemical agent; explosives; fire and firebombing; firearms; knives and sharp objects; other; remote detonated explosives (RDEs); and unknown. Two of these weapons were not included in the analysis – no attacks against business targets using biological weapons were made between 1968 and 2008, and only one incident of chemical weapons being used against a business target was recorded throughout the same period. In addition, other and unknown weapons were grouped together since they both represented unidentified threats.

Results

Terrorism attacks against IB by region

Increasing trends

Three regions show a distinct increase in the number of terrorism attacks against business between 1968 and 2008: Eastern Europe; Middle East and Persian Gulf; and South Asia.

Eastern Europe had a very low frequency of international terrorism incidents against business up until 1990. This may be attributable to the collapse of communism where international businesses had a very limited presence in former communist countries. However, several years of high international terrorism activity coincide with the opening up of the region for international trade. The trends in the data suggest 0.78 incidents in 2008 increasing at a rate of 0.022 incidents per year.

The Middle East and Persian Gulf have historically had a high number of international terrorism incidents against business targets (the average number of incidents between 1968 and 2000 is approximately 50 per year, whereas the highest number of incidents in five other international regions combined has not reached 50 (North America; Africa; East and Central Asia; Eastern Europe; South Asia). Unusually high numbers of international terrorism incidents have occurred in the Middle East and Persian Gulf region since 2001, peaking at nearly 300 incidents in 2004. With the recent increase in activity, the trend suggests 15.38 attacks against business targets, increasing at a rate of 0.38 attacks per year.

South Asia shows a noticeable peak of incidents between 2002 and 2005, with a rise in terrorist activity from groups in Afghanistan, Pakistan, India and Bangladesh. Even without these peaks, the trend suggests 4.7 attacks against business per year, increasing at a rate of 0.14 incidents annually.

Declining trends

Three geographical regions showed a decline in international terrorism incidents against business between 1968 and 2008: Western Europe; North America; and Latin America and Caribbean.

International terrorism incidents against businesses in Western Europe peaked in the 1980s and 1990s (with peaks of 59 incidents in 1992, 54 in 1991 and 54 in 1994, compared to an average of less than 20 between 1968 and 2008). The trend in the number of attacks has fallen, giving a declining trend of 0.0785 incidents per year, with the number of incidents in 2008 extrapolated to 17.8 attacks.

North America demonstrated a notable decline in international terrorism incidents over time, with incidents against international business peaking with between two and twelve attacks per year between 1971 and 1982, then falling to below five incidents from 1983 onwards. The overall trend falls below zero between 2007 and 2008, leading to the suggestion that terrorism attacks against business in the US have been eliminated. However, this is misleading since the impact of the 9/11 attack, the only international terrorist attack against a business target in the 14 year period between 1994 and 2008, caused more deaths and negative psychological impact than the entire history of international terrorist attacks in the region.

Latin America and the Caribbean had two peaks of international terrorism incidents against businesses: one between 1971 and 1977 with between 11 and 52 attacks, the other between 1984 and 1997 with an average of 20 attacks per year. All other years average less than ten attacks annually. The number of incidents has fallen sharply with fewer than 11 incidents per year since 2000. The overall trend shows a decline of 0.38 incidents per year, with 7.19 incidents expected in 2008.

Inconclusive trends

Three regions show a slight increase in international terrorism incidents against business between 1968 and 2008, but the trends are small and skewed with isolated years with high frequencies of incidents.

Africa shows an overall increasing trend in incidents due to two periods of increased activity – 1994 when 16 attacks were recorded, and 2006 with 14 attacks.

In other years, the number of attacks per year has consistently been below seven. East and Central Asia have very low numbers of international terrorism attacks on businesses, with the overall trend indicating a very slight increase of 0.0038 incidents per year, with 0.25 attacks expected in 2008. South East Asia and Oceania show an increasing trend in terrorism incidents of 0.092 incidents per year, with 3.87 attacks against business projected in 2008.

Global trends

The global total of international terrorism incidents against business is increasing but at a very slight rate (0.1295 incidents per year, with 64.23 attacks against business in all regions expected for 2008.) However, when considered in context of the global total number of terrorism incidents against all targets, the proportion of attacks against business is declining, where attacks against global business targets are 18 per cent of all terrorism attacks or 55 incidents in 2007, declining at a rate of 0.62 per cent per year.

Observations

Although international terrorism incidents against business targets shows increasing trends in Eastern Europe, Middle East/Persian Gulf and South Asia, these increases are very slight (0.02, 0.38 and 0.14 incidents per year respectively). In addition, when placed in context of the actual numbers of attacks expected in 2008 (0.78, 15.38 and 4.66 respectively), the probability of an international terrorism attack on business targets is low compared to other types of targets (Figure 15.1).

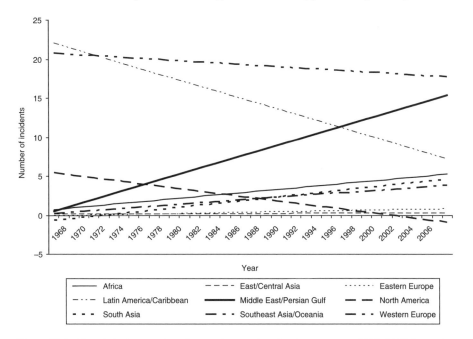

Figure 15.1   Trends in international terrorism against business targets 1968–2008 by region

The number of attacks against business targets in North America is remarkably low, considering the size of the region. In comparison, Western Europe has the highest number of international terrorism attacks against business targets. However, the data does not show which region the actual targets belong to, for instance how many of the attacks in South Asia are directed against businesses owned by North American organizations.

Terrorism attacks against business targets by type of target

Increasing trends

Three business targets showed increasing trends in the number of terrorist attacks between 1968 and 2008: telecommunications; tourist targets; and transportation.

Telecommunications show an increasing trend of 0.01 per cent in attacks per year, with 0.33 attacks expected in 2008. However, the actual number of attacks is historically low at less than one per cent of total attacks against all terrorism targets. One important consideration is that the TKB data only records physical terrorist attacks – the trend identified is likely to be much steeper if electronic attacks were also considered.

Tourist targets show an increase in the number of attacks at a rate of 0.08 per cent per year. However this trend is skewed by a high number of attacks between 1993 and 2000. Without this peak in activity, the number of attacks is historically less than three per cent of all attacks against all targets.

Transportation targets show an increase of 0.06 per cent attacks per year, with 3.78 attacks expected in 2008. The number of attacks shows a distinct increasing trend over time, with a peak of eight per cent of attacks in 2003.

Declining trends

Three types of terrorism target show a decline in the number of incidents between 1968 and 2008: Airports and airlines; business targets; and utilities.

Airports and airlines show a distinct decline of 3.755 incidents per year, with the trend showing 0.13 attacks expected for 2008. This suggests that no further attacks against airports and airlines should be expected after 2008. The decline could be attributable to increased security around international air transportation and the improved detection rate of threats before an attack can take place.

Business targets show a very slight decline in attacks over time. According to this trend, less than 20 attacks per year are directed towards business targets globally, with this trend declining at 0.06 attacks per year.

Utilities also show a decline in the number of attacks, although the number of incidents averages less than two per year globally. The historically low number of attacks against utilities could be attributed to awareness that disruption of utilities endangers unintended targets which terrorist groups may rely on for support, therefore doing more damage to the terrorist group in terms of support than to the target.

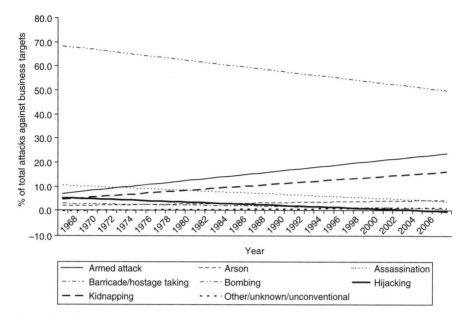

Figure 15.2 Trends in international terrorism against business targets 1968–2008 by type of target

Observations

Direct attacks on business infrastructure are relatively low, with the total number of attacks against tourism, transportation, utilities, telecommunications and airports/airlines being less than ten per cent of attacks on all types of target (Figure 15.2). This may be due to increased security around infrastructure facilities (for examples in airports and airlines), or that there is little motivation to attack these targets.

Terrorism attacks against business targets by tactic

Increasing trends

Four types of tactic used against business targets showed increasing trends over time between 1968 and 2008: armed attack; arson; kidnapping; and other/unconventional/unknown attacks.

Armed attack against business shows an increasing trend of 0.43 incidents per year, with 23.76 attacks expected in 2008. The trend was skewed by a high level of activity in 2005 (18 incidents, compared to less than four incidents from 1997 onwards). Although the peak in 2005 appears unusual, the value fits with the increasing trend seen between 1968 and 1994. Arson suggests an increasing trend of 0.06 incidents per year, but this is skewed by a high number of incidents in 1982 (13 incidents compared to less than seven throughout the remainder of the period between 1968 and 2008). The period from 1986 onwards suggests a flat trend with an average of three incidents per year, with very little activity before

1982. Kidnapping as a tactic against business targets shows an increasing trend of 0.124 incidents per year, with a peak in activity in 2005 of 23 attacks (compared to an average of 4.55 attacks between 1968 and 2008).

Other, unknown and unconventional attacks appear sporadically in the period between 1968 and 2008, occurring a maximum of once per year. However, the frequency of attacks has increased leading to a rising trend in the number of attacks, with one incident occurring between 1968 and 1995, and six incidents between 1995 and 2008.

Declining trends

Three types of terrorism tactic used against business targets in all regions between 1968 and 2008 showed a slight decline over time: assassination; barricade and hostage taking; and bombing.

Assassination against business targets in all regions peaked at nine incidents in 1976 but has subsequently declined at a rate of 0.032 per cent of all attacks against business per year. Four incidents occurred in 1989 and five in 1991, otherwise assassination is an uncommon tactic against business targets, with less than two incidents per year and no incidents reported since 2001. Barricade and hostage taking has only occurred against business targets nine times between 1968 and 2008. Six of these incidents occurred before 1986, with a resurgence of one incident approximately every five years since 1996. The over-all trend is a decline of 0.005 per cent of incidents per year. Bombing is the most frequently used terrorism tactic used against business targets, representing between 49 per cent and 100 per cent of tactics used between 1968 and 2008. However the trend is declining by 0.46 per cent incidents per year, with distinct falls in bombing activity as a percentage of all tactics against business targets in 1992 and 2004.

Observations

The trends in tactics used show a decline in bombing in favour of other attacks, particularly in armed attack and kidnapping (Figure 15.3). Reasons for this could include better bomb awareness and detection, and more control over access to bomb-making components. The instance of bombing being used in 100 per cent of attacks against business targets in 1968 highlights how the data at the start and end of the recorded time period cannot be relied upon. Incidents recorded at the start of the period will be sparse due to the reporting standards and convention still being established, whereas data at the end of the recording period will be incomplete since data collection is ongoing and incidents might not be added to the database for some time after the attack.

International terrorism attacks against business targets by weapon

Increasing trends

Five types of weapon show an increased use in attacks against business targets between 1968 and 2008: fire and firebombs; firearms; other; remote detonated explosives; and unknown weapons.

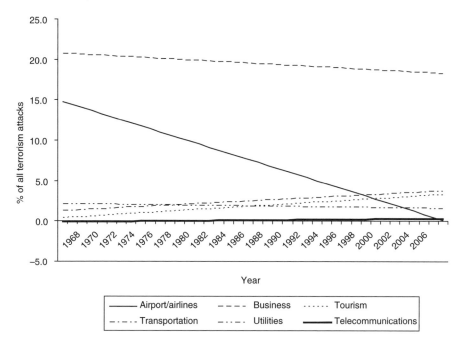

Figure 15.3   Trends in international terrorism against business targets 1968–2008 by tactic used

Fire and firebombs as weapons have increased in use slightly compared to other types of weapon, increasing at a rate of 0.14 per cent per year. Two noticeable peaks in activity occurred (with fire/firebombs accounting for 34.3 of attacks against business in 1971, and 61.3 per cent in 1995) but do not adversely skew the general trend. Firearms show a marked rise of 0.32 per cent of all weapons used in attacks on business targets per year. A noticeable peak in firearms use can be seen in 2005–06, without which the trend is more likely to be flat. Projecting the trend to 2008, firearms would account for 14.4 per cent of attacks against business targets globally. Other and unknown weapons (i.e., those not classified under other types of known conventional weapons) show an increase of 0.12 per cent of all types of weapon used against business targets per year. The increasing trend in other and unknown weapons highlights a move away from conventional weapons, with a projected 14.5 per cent of attacks in 2008 being unidentified. The use of Remote Detonated Explosives (RDEs) occurs at regular intervals from 1995 onwards, with an increasing trend of 0.24 per cent of all types of weapons per year, and 6.8 attacks projected for 2008. The lack of RDEs before 1995 may be explained by the technology or knowledge not being available to terrorist groups before that time, and subsequent data may significantly change the trend identified here.

Declining/flat trends

Declining trends were seen in the use of explosives, with a flat trend seen for knives and sharp objects.

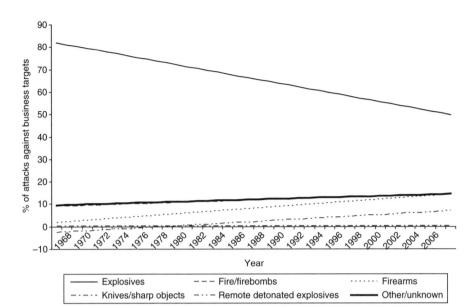

Figure 15.4 Trends in international terrorism against business targets 1968–2008 by weapon used

Explosives have declined significantly as a weapon against business targets between 1968 and 2008, at a rate of 0.826 per cent of incidents per year and a projected use in 49.8 per cent of attacks in 2008. Knives and sharp objects were reported in terrorism attacks against business in three incidents, occurring in 1979, 1992 and 1994, giving a flat and inconclusive trend. The use of knives/sharp objects as a weapon against business targets is not likely to be popular due to the limited range and damage that can be caused compared to other types of weapon.

Observations

The use of explosives as a weapon has declined significantly in favour of other types of weapon, although it is still the most frequently used type of weapon against business targets (Figure 15.4). However, the decline may not be due to a reduction in the use of explosives, rather it may be due to an increase in other types of weapon which have influenced the overall percentages of weapons used. Further investigation would be needed to confirm this. The remaining types of weapons show increasing usage, although outliers in the data have affected the trends slightly.

Analyses and conclusions

This paper has calculated trends in international terrorism attacks against business targets, showing which geographical regions are more prone to attack, the probability of attack to businesses and infrastructure, the types of tactic most frequently used in attacks and the weapons used. A brief comparison with the Lloyds survey of business leaders highlighted how the perception of terrorism threats by business leaders is very different from historical trends, demonstrating how the approach to managing risks from international terrorism may be based on the expectation of threat rather than actual data. These trends identify the actual risks to businesses and answer the following questions.

Where are risks to business from international terrorism more likely to occur?
Based on the TKB data, Western Europe and the Middle East/Persian Gulf have the highest numbers of terrorism attacks directed against businesses, with 17.75 and 15.38 attacks respectively expected for 2008 based on the trends and accounting for more than half of the total number of attacks worldwide. The trend for North America suggests that no international terrorism attacks against business are expected after 2008, a spurious result that requires only one incident to invalidate. Eastern Europe and East/Central Asia have the lowest numbers of international terrorism attacks against business, which may reflect the lack of businesses that are attractive as targets in these regions. The remaining regions of the world are projected to have fewer than ten attacks in 2008, with only slight changes to this trend over time. Compared to the perceptions of international terrorism threats to business in the Lloyds survey, the trends identified here show a large discrepancy (Table 15.2). Where the perception of the

Table 15.2   Regional trends in terrorism attacks against business targets compared to the Lloyds survey of perceived threat to businesses

Region	Projected number of incidents for 2012 based on historical trends	Projected % increase in incidents between 2007 and 2012 based on trends	Predicted % increase in risks from international terrorism between 2007 and 2012 (from Lloyds survey)
Global	54.87	+1.19	+59
Western Europe	17.35	−2.21	+39
Middle East/Persian Gulf	17.29	+12.39	+55
Latin America/Caribbean	5.29	−26.44	+23
Africa	5.84	+11.02	+32
South Asia	5.34	+14.63	−
South East Asia/Oceania	4.33	+11.89	−
Eastern Europe	0.89	+14.12	+25
East/Central Asia	0.27	+7.69	−
North America	−1.72	−90.02	+47
All Asia (South Asia, South East Asia/Oceania and East/Central Asia combined)	9.94	+13.22	+32

Note: The Lloyds survey groups all of Asia into a single region whereas the TKB divides Asia into three regions, making a direct comparison misleading.

respondents of threats in Western Europe is perceived to increase by 59 per cent over the next five years, the historical trend suggests a decrease of 2.21 per cent in the same period. Perceptions of terrorism attacks in the Middle East and Persian Gulf region predict an increase of 55 per cent in the number of attacks in five years, but the historical trends suggest an actual increase of 12.39 per cent over five years, showing that the perceptions of regional threats are widely out of step with historical trends.

What types of business are more at risk?
International terrorism attacks against business targets account for 18.28 per cent of all attacks; direct attacks on business infrastructure targets account for less than ten per cent of all international terrorism targets, suggesting that attacks on infrastructure are less likely to occur as an indirect attack on business targets. However, the data does not indicate which business sectors are attacked, or the sizes of organizations attacked. This analysis could be developed by identifying this information from qualitative descriptions of attacks.

What tactics are used in attacks?
What international terrorism threats should businesses be preparing for?
The most widely used tactic in international terrorism against business targets is bombing, currently averaging approximately 39 incidents per year globally. All other forms of attack average less than five incidents a year each. However, the use of bombing is declining in favour of other tactics, particularly armed attack.

What weapons are used in attacks?
What physical countermeasures should be prepared for?
Historically, approximately 50 per cent of terrorist attacks against business use explosives, with fire or firebombs, firearms, or other/unknown weapons occurring approximately 15 per cent each. The use of explosives is declining slowly in favour of other forms of attack, a trend that corresponds with the declining trend in bombing as a tactic against businesses. The other/unknown weapon category is difficult to protect against since the nature of the weapon used is not specified. Currently this is used in less than two per cent of all attacks against business but the trend is increasing over time, suggesting that weapons used in future attacks are becoming less predictable.

Recommendations for senior managers

The historical trends show a wide gap compared to the perception of terrorist risks to business targets between 2007 and 2012. Based on the trends identified in this paper, existing risk assessments with regards to international terrorism should be reviewed in the context of actual trends specific to business targets, since risk mitigation strategies based on perception may not be appropriate to the types of attack against business targets that occur in reality. With the increased expenditure on security and crisis planning in recent years, this may represent a substantial cost saving by targeting international terrorism risk mitigation strategies more effectively.

The historical trends highlighted the tactics and weapons used in international terrorism attacks against businesses. These results allow appropriate levels of physical countermeasures to be included in risk assessments, for example to evaluate whether insurance against biological attack is still reasonable when no attacks of this nature have been directed against businesses since the TKB started recording data in 1968. However, this needs to be balanced with the unpredictable nature of international terrorism where the absence of one type of attack does not discount future incidents from occurring.

Limitations and further work

An important limitation to note in this analysis is that the trends are based on historical data and do not necessarily represent an accurate prediction of the nature of future terrorist incidents, especially since short and medium term political, economic and social influences on political violence are not taken into account in the data. In addition, the trends apply to businesses as a primary target only and do not consider damage done to business as an innocent bystander in attacks on other targets.

The motivations behind international terrorism trends identified in this paper have not been explored. A fuller understanding of these would contribute to risk assessment and management decisions to protect international business, given the specific nature of the business, the local environment and profiles of potential attackers.

The impact of the perception gap between anticipated terrorism threats and the historical trends identified in this paper warrants further investigation, to evaluate how much risk assessment and management approaches have been influenced and whether risk management processes can be refined by putting international terrorism threats into context of historical trends. Finally, the trends identified in this paper are at a broad level, showing the tactics and weapons used against business targets worldwide. A more detailed study of the trends for specific regions would provide a clearer picture of threats from international terrorism when making internationalization decisions.

References

AFX News (2004) 'Bomb attacks in Istanbul leave one dead, seven injured', *AFX News*, August 10.

Associated Press (1999) 'Bomb blast damages Apple computer dealership', *Associated Press*, March 26.

CETIS (2007) *GTD2 (1998–2004) Codebook, draft version 1.0.* Center for Terrorism and Intelligence Studies. http://209.232.239.37/gtd2/gtd2_codebook.pdf

COW (2008) *Correlates of War. Datasets*, http://www.correlatesofwar.org/

Czinkota, M.R., Knight, G.A. and Liesch, P.W. (2004) Terrorism and international business: Conceptual foundations, in G.G.S. Suder (ed.) *Terrorism and the International Business Environment: the Security-Business Nexus* (Cheltenham: Edward Elgar).

Haider-Markel, D.P. (2006) *The Politics of Fear: Personal Concern and Perception of Public Concern about Terrorist Attacks.* Paper presented at the annual meeting of The Midwest Political Science Association, Chicago. http://www.allacademic.com/meta/p141154_index.html

Hoffman, B. and Claridge, D. (1998) 'The RAND-St Andrews chronology of international terrorism and noteworthy domestic incidents, 1996', *Terrorism and Political Violence,* 10(2), 135–80.

Houghton, B.K. (2008) 'Terrorism knowledge base: A eulogy (2004–2008)', *Perspectives on Terrorism,* II(7), 18–19.

Howie, L. (2005) *There is nothing to fear but fear itself (and terrorists): Public perception, terrorism and the workplace.* Paper presented to the Social Change in the 21st Century Conference, Centre for Social Change Research, Queensland University of Technology. http://eprints. qut.edu.au/archive/00003493/01/3493.pdf

Howie, L. (2007) 'The terrorism threat and managing workplaces', *Disaster Prevention and Management,* 16(1), 70–78.

HSRP (2008) *Human Security Brief 2007.* http://www.humansecuritybrief.info/HSRP_ Brief_2007.pdf

Janes (2008) *Jane's Terrorism and Insurgency Centre.* http://catalog.janes.com/catalog/public/ index.cfm?fuseaction=home.ProductInfoBrief&product_id=98796

LCC (2005) *The Economic Effects of Terrorism on London: Experiences of Firms in London's Business Community* (London Chamber of Commerce, August).

Lemrye, L., Turner, M.D., Lee, J.E.F. and Krewski, D. (2006) 'Public perception of terrorism risks and related information sources in Canada: Implications for the management of terrorism risks', *Journal of Risk Research,* 9(7), 755–74.

Liesch, P., Steen, J., Knight, G. and Czinkota, M.R. (2006) 'Problematizing the internationalization decision: Terrorism-induced risk', *Management Decision,* 44(6), 809–23.

Lloyds (2007) *Under Attack? Global Business and the Threat of Political Violence.* www.lloyds. com/NR/rdonlyres/0926E705-A16C-4432-B607-A4925A9EFEAB/0/360terrorismreport.pdf

MIPT (2006) *The MIPT Terrorism Annual 2006.* National Memorial Institute for the Prevention of Terrorism.

Norris, P., Kern, M. and Just, M. (2003) 'Framing terrorism', in P. Norris, M.R. Just and M. Kern (eds) *Framing Terrorism: The News Media, the Government and the Public* (London: Routledge).

OSAC (2008) *Top 10 Overseas Security Trends for the US Private Sector.* Overseas Security Advisory Council. http://www.osac.gov/Reports/report.cfm?contentID=77971

Poole-Robb, S. (2002). *Risky Business: Corruption, Fraud, Terrorism & Other Threats to Global Business* (London: Kogan Page).

PRS (2008) *Political Risk Services Group: Political Risk Services.* http://www.prsgroup.com/PRS. aspx

START (2008) *National Consortium for the Study of Terrorism and Responses to Terrorism Global Terrorism Database.* http://www.start.umd.edu/data/gtd/

Taylor, P.M. (2002) 'Perception management and the "war" against international terrorism', *Journal of Information Warfare,* 1(3), 16–29.

TKB (2008) *The National Memorial Institute for the Prevention of Terrorism Terrorism Knowledge Base.* http://www.mipt.org/

UCDP (2008) *Uppsala Conflict Data Programme.* http://www.ucdp.uu.se/

US Code 2000 Supplement 5 (18USC2331).

US Code 2000 Supplement 5 (22UC2656f(d)).

Wernick, D.A. (2006) 'Terror incognito: International business in an era of heightened geopolitical risk', in Gabriele G.S. Suder (ed.) *Corporate Strategies under International Terrorism and Adversity* (Cheltenham: Edward Elgar).

16

The Automotive Industry and Environmental Regulations: Challenges to Corporate Political Activities of Multinational Enterprises in the European Union

Sigrun M. Wagner

Introduction and literature background

This chapter deals with corporate political activities (CPA) of multinational companies in the European Union regarding environmental regulations for the automotive industry. The research covers an important aspect of the AIB 2008 theme on *Challenges to International Business*, that is, the impact of MNCs on the physical environment and attempts to mitigate this impact.

Three areas of literature provide the background for this study. The first is the *International Business* (IB) literature on MNE–Host-government relations. According to Boddewyn and Brewer (1994), political behaviour is intrinsic to IB as crossing borders means introducing companies into other sovereignties. Boddewyn (1988) criticizes previous work for having an economic bias and for viewing government policies as fixed dicta that are not amenable to the influence of MNEs. He emphasizes that even though MNEs' goals might be economic, they can still use political means to achieve economic ends. Blumentritt and Nigh point out that 'business–government interactions are a complex function for multinational corporations' (2002, p. 57). They strongly argue for a better integration of the IB and CPA literatures (ibid.). The second background source is *Strategic Management*, specifically its perspectives on CPA (US-American focus), which focuses on how corporations manage the political environment. The third stream of literature drawn upon is *Political Science,* more precisely, previous work on lobbying and interest group representation; this literature has EU emphasis, which partly mitigates the dominant US flavour of prior CPA research (Boddewyn and Brewer, 1994). Moreover, the Political Science literature provides important insights into the European Union (EU) as a political entity, which is distinct from any single country.[1]

The focus in the IB literature on business–government relations tends to be on business–host-government relations. In practice, however, MNEs face home governments as well as host governments. The EU as a political entity with state-like features (Grant, 1993) blurs the traditional borders between domestic and international business, as it is home and host country for European multinationals at one and the same time. In addition, for American and Japanese MNEs, the EU institutions are host governments although subsidiaries portray themselves as distinct European or national firms (for example, Opel in Germany, subsidiary of US-based General Motors, interview October 2006).

Regarding the terminology of this area, 'corporate political activities' will be the main term used, but 'government relations' or 'interest representation' will also be used. Corporate political activities are defined by Getz as 'any deliberate firm action intended to influence governmental policy or process' (Getz, 1997, p. 32). Here, the term will also include activities that keep relations with governments on an ongoing basis as a pre-condition for influence.

As the communication of information and positions to policy-makers by representatives of societal or corporate interests, interest representation involves three basic citizen rights in democracies and is thus a legitimate activity: the freedom of expression and information; the freedom of assembly and association; as well as the right to petition (Rieksmaier, 2007).

Within the context of the three literature streams described above, the main assumption of this chapter follows from the resource-based theory (RBT) which states that companies differ in their competitive strategies due to heterogeneous distributions of resources across firms and the immobile nature of resources (that is, they cannot be transferred between firms without costs) (Peteraf, 1993). The chapter transfers this hypothesis into the field of political strategies: firms differ in their political strategies and activities due to different competitive strategies and resource endowments. As the RBT is a theoretical framework that is used to explain differences between companies in a competitive environment (Hoopes, Madsen and Walker, 2003), it will be used as a framework to investigate firm differences in a political environment. The study aims to answer the following central research questions:

- How do firms of different national origins (the traditional Triad regions) differ in terms of their corporate political activities on particular environmental regulations? and
- Which resources and competencies do firms deploy in order to facilitate their corporate political activities?

These questions have been studied within the specific context of environmental regulations for the reasons outlined in the following paragraph.

The general increase in environmental regulations has been attributed to society's concern over negative environmental impacts of business activities (Rugman and Verbeke, 1998). The choice of the EU as context for studying firms' attempts to influence environmental policy may be regarded as fitting, because the EU is often seen as the most progressive region when it comes to environmental issues. Environmental regulations in the EU have grown immensely in number over the past two decades and pose new challenges for policy-makers and industry. Areas generally covered under environmental legislation include waste, noise, air, soil, nature, water and chemicals (Krämer, 1997; DG Environment, 2007). The general principles of environmental regulations comprise the precautionary principle, the prevention principle, rectification of damage at source and the polluter-pays principle (Krämer, 2000).

In the EU, automobile companies are subject to a whole range of regulations, not only environmental. Consequently, there is a tradition of interest representation of the automobile industry in the EU (Mazey and Richardson, 1993; McLaughlin and Jordan, 1993; Spell, 2000), and currently, all mass car producers have representative offices in Brussels. As all major car companies operate in the EU, that is, not only sell but also produce, it is possible to compare MNCs from the traditional Triad regions of Europe, North America and Japan in one single location, Brussels, the so-called capital of the EU. Also, the fact that the industry – the world's largest manufacturing industry (Nieuwenhuis and Wells, 2003) – faces significant market and technological challenges on account of climate change (Levy and Egan, 2003) and other environmental regulations, both in voluntary and legally binding form, makes it a suitable context for investigating MNCs' corporate political activities in relation to EU environmental regulations.

The issues chosen as environmental regulatory cases for the automotive industry are recycling (end-of-life vehicles – ELVs), global warming (carbon dioxide – CO_2 emissions) and pollutant emissions (Euro norms). These will be presented further in the section on methods and material. The rest of the chapter is structured as follows: conceptual framework; methods and material; presentation and discussion of preliminary results; and conclusion with an outlook.

Conceptual framework

In her comprehensive review, Getz (1997) assesses nine basic social science theories used to explain CPA: interest group theory (from political science); collective action, public choice and transaction cost theories (from economics and political economy); and resource dependency, exchange, institutions, behavioural theory of the firm and agency (from management). Theories that are related to the micro behaviour of firms are, for example, resource dependence, transaction cost and agency theories (Boddewyn and Brewer 1994). What is significant about Getz's (1997) review is that the resource-based view (RBV) is missing, although this has been applied to the study of CPA by other authors (for example, Hillman and Hitt, 1999; Moon and Lado, 2000; McWilliams, Van Fleet and Cory, 2002; Frynas, Mellahi and Pigman, 2006). The point must be made that these previous applications of the RBV in CPA analysis have mostly focused on the United States, suggesting that there is still room for extension to the EU setting, which is arguably very distinct from the US. This section gives an overview of the RBV and envisages transferring the RBV from the corporate competitive market context into a political context; that is, taking it from a competitive strategies setting to one of political strategies.

The emergence of the resource-based theory of the firm has been one of the main developments in recent international business and strategic management research, with Wernerfelt (1984) and Barney (1991) at the forefront (Peng, 2001). In the strategy literature, it has served as the dominant explanation for firm differences (Hoopes, Madsen and Walker, 2003). The main focus of the theory is how firm resources contribute to sustainable competitive advantage. In order to be a basis for sustainable competitive advantage, resources need the following characteristics: valuable, rare, imperfectly imitable and non-substitutable (Barney, 1991; Moon and Lado, 2000).

Furthermore, an elemental assumption of the theory is that resources need to meet the conditions of heterogeneity and immobility to exhibit aforementioned characteristics. Penrose (1959, p. 75) – an important precursor of the theory – points out that '[I]t is the heterogeneity, and not the homogeneity, of the productive services available or potentially available from its resources that gives each firm its unique character.' Among the required resource characteristics leading to uniqueness and competitive advantage, inimitability is a crucial factor as it inhibits other firms from obtaining valuable and rare resources. Imitation of innovations, for example, threatens the sustainability of competitive advantage (Rumelt, 1984, 1987). Barriers to imitation such as causal ambiguity, social complexity and unique historical conditions make resources imperfectly imitable. They exist when rivals cannot understand the competencies and capabilities on which competitive advantage is based (Fiol, 1991).

Boddewyn and Brewer (1994) criticize the resource-based theory for only looking at economic and organizational competences of firms, not at political capabilities. Moon and Lado (2000) point out that research of the MNE–Host-government relationship has not used insights from the RBT. The research presented here will use the theory to scrutinize political resources in the context of MNE government relations, specifically in the EU arena. Furthermore, resource-based-view-oriented strategists take the non-market environment as exogenous and neutral (Boddewyn, 2003), whereas this research views the non-market environment as endogenous to corporate strategy. This could therefore lead to an extension of the theory to include non-market factors in corporate strategy.

The RBT is, thus, tested and explored in a new context, and it is expected that it would explain differences in CPA due to its emphasis on internal firm-specific resources. Resources can be categorized as follows: financial resources; physical resources; human resources; technological resources; and organizational resources (Grant, 1991). Dahan's (2005) typology of firm political resources consist of expertise, financial resource, relational resource, organizational resource, reputation with other non-market actors, public image, support of stakeholders and recreational skills. As discussed in the next section, this typology forms part of the basis for the interview guide.

Figure 16.1 illustrates the focus of the research, which is how firm-specific political resources are directed into corporate political activities. Other moderating

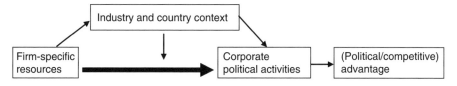

Figure 16.1   Resource-based determinants of MNE political activities
Source: Author, adapted from Moon and Lado (2000, p. 101).

influences on political activities are the context of the industry and the context of country or region. In the RBT, the main objective of companies is to attain (sustainable) competitive advantage. As political activities might not necessarily lead to competitive (market) benefits, but to legislative advantages, the chapter also uses the term political (non-market) advantage, thus illustrating the RBT's application in a different context. One example of political advantage is the reputation a firm has or enjoys among policy-makers, which makes it more likely for decision-makers to trust the firm's expertise and information provided through its interest representation.

Methodology and material

The research employs a case study approach to explore the corporate political activities of the major automobile manufacturers which are active in the European Union. The case study methodology is most appropriate as the relations among the actors and their context is complex. Case studies can offer the breadth and depth of information for descriptive, causal and inductive analysis to be performed (Miles and Hubermann, 1984; Eisenhardt, 1989; Yin, 1994; Levy and Rothenberg, 1999). Shaffer (1995) highlights the qualitative and longitudinal aspects of case studies as strengths that make the approach better suited to the investigation of CPA. He, nevertheless, acknowledges the classic limiting problem of generalizability.

The case study as applied here is of longitudinal nature as the regulatory areas investigated unfolded over time. As the policy process in the EU can take years from proposal to adoption of legislation,[2] the longitudinal element is deemed important. Corporate political activities are a contemporary phenomenon in a real-life context, where a case study's ability to handle a variety of evidence can offer benefits (Yin, 1994): as corporate political activities are often seen in a critical light because of 'lobbying scandals', it is important to not only collect data from companies, but also from other stakeholders (the 'lobbied' European institutions and other stakeholders and observers like non-governmental organizations and supplying industries). This is only possible with a case study, which allows for a multi-method approach that uses triangulation (Bryman and Bell, 2003).

Figure 16.2, based on Van Tulder and Van der Zwart (2006), demonstrates how triangulation of sources comes into play in the context of this paper. Investigating CPA from different sides will give a more holistic representation of the complex

Figure 16.2   The societal triangle – triangulating corporate political activities

reality involved in how firms respond politically to environmental policy-making. As well as sources, methods will also be triangulated by using documentation in addition to interviews.

The semi-structured interview is both flexible and standardized at the same time (Gillham, 2000). The standardized or structured element is important in case study research involving multiple cases in order to ensure cross-case comparability (Bryman and Bell, 2003).

The chosen organizations and interview partners were selected according to their role as stakeholders in the policy-making process of EU environmental regulations for the automobile industry. They were identified as stakeholders by investigating the contributions to the consultation process of EU legislation and following up references in organizational documents, and academic and professional publications related to the cases. Furthermore, the author was given recommendations by interviewees and contacted interview partners who were not available for interviews. The organizations chosen also provided the main source for documentation.

Three cases were chosen as a basis for comparison. Eisenhardt (1989) advocates choosing cases such as extreme situations or polar types. The cases chosen for this research would not normally be called extreme or polar. However, as they represent significant trade-offs for the industry's operations, they are to a certain degree polar: Reductions in CO_2 and pollutant emissions are in principle not compatible as equipment required for reductions in pollutant emissions can lead to heavier vehicles and consequently to increased fuel consumption and thus CO_2 (Keay-Bright, 2000). Similarly, reductions in CO_2 require lighter vehicles, whereas increased recycling rates for end-of-life vehicles (ELVs) requires higher proportionate contents of steel – easier to recycle than plastics – thus resulting in heavier cars and higher CO_2 emissions. A 'strategy of diverse sampling' (Eisenhardt 1989, p. 537) was, thus, followed to cover a broad range of environmental regulations for the automotive industry.

Interviews were conducted in two main stages with research excursions to Brussels, home to the EU institutions. Between the two main stages, the experience of the first stage was taken into account in modifying the approach. This included, for example, a change of terminology when contacting potential interviewees from 'corporate political activities of multinational enterprises' to 'government relations of multinational enterprises', as it had become apparent that the term CPA was used

Table 16.1 Interview guide

General questions on government relations	Association v firm level	European v national level	Environmental regulations	Assessment
Motivational factors	Coordination	Experiences	Interests and	Strengths
	Cooperation	Relations	Positions	Weaknesses
Approach	Competition	Headquarters v	Euro norms	Overall
Strategy	Preference for	Brussels	CO_2	
Tactics and	policy-makers	Producer	End-of-life	
instruments	Resources and	Regions	vehicles	
	competences	Europe, North		
	(Personnel,	America,		
	Expertise,	Japan		
	Organization,			
	Learning processes)			

more in academic than practitioner circles. Furthermore CPA seemed to be seen by interviewees as carrying potentially negative or contentious connotations ('political') in contrast to the more neutral term 'government relations'.

Interviews lasted between 15 minutes (telephone interviews) and two hours, with the majority ranging between 30 and 60 minutes. Interviews were mainly conducted in English; those with German targets were conducted in German and subsequently translated into English. The interview excerpts used have been left unedited in order to preserve the interviewees' intended meaning. Interview guides were discussed with several academics and they received minor modifications after the first stage of data collection. The following table shows the general guide, which was adapted according to interviewees' organizational backgrounds.

Miles and Hubermann (1994) define data analysis as three linked sub-processes: data reduction, data display and conclusion drawing and verification. A systematic, but not over prescriptive, approach (Coffey and Atkinson, 1996) has been adopted in analysing qualitative data for this study. The techniques suggested by Miles and Hubermann (1994) have been followed. These include a range of devices such as graphs and tabular displays to manage and present qualitative data 'without destroying the meaning of data through intensive coding' (Eisenhardt, 1989, p. 534). The process involved the coding of data, within-case and cross-case analysis. As the analysis process is still in progress, the following section can only present preliminary findings in form of interview extracts.

Results and discussion

In total, 73 interviews were conducted for this study, which is part of a larger research project. 140 potential interviewees were contacted and thus a response rate of about 52 per cent was achieved. Considering the contentious nature of the subject, this is considered a very high response rate. Table 16.2 displays the distribution of interviewees among the stakeholder organizations.

Table 16.2   Overview of distribution of interview partners

Organization/interview partner	Number of interviews	Total
Market side		
Corporate public affairs offices (automotive industry – other stakeholder industry)	(14 + 5)	36
Business associations (automotive industry – other stakeholder industry)	(7 + 10)	
State side		
EU Institutions	13	27
European Parliament	12	
Commission	2	
Council		
Civil society side		
Environmental NGOs	7	8
Consumer organizations	1	
Others and informal meetings	2	2
Total	–	73

It was ensured that within all sides of the societal triangle (state, market, civil society), interviewees were found for all three cases. Furthermore, with members of the European Parliament (MEPs), effort was made to talk to members of the four biggest groups, representing four-fifths of the whole assembly. The companies that were contacted included BMW, DaimlerChrysler, Fiat, Ford, General Motors (mainly Opel in Europe), PSA (Peugeot-Citroën), Renault and Volkswagen (all *Association des Constructeurs Européen d'Automobiles* [ACEA] or European Automobile Manufacturers' Association members); Honda, Nissan and Toyota (Japanese Automobile Manufacturers' Association [JAMA] members); and Hyundai (Korean Automobile Manufacturers' Association [KAMA] member). Nissan and Hyundai have not been available for any discussions, but as their market share in Europe averages only approximately two per cent each (ACEA, 2007), these omissions are not considered to be significant. More significantly, however, the two French companies PSA and Renault, whose combined market share is above 20 per cent, have not been willing to discuss their government relations. Thus France, as a significant manufacturing country in the automobile industry, is not represented in the sample.[3] Various attempts and requests for interviews have either been turned down or ignored. A general suspicion towards outside requests from researchers might be the reason for this. One interviewee described the climate pertaining to public affairs/government relations within the industry in Brussels as follows:

The people who are in it, they are wound up in these things. It's a climate where they think of plotting against us, it's an exaggeration, it's not plotting but inside the industry the people get paranoid and see threats and monsters everywhere. (Automotive industry representative)[4]

The next two sub-sections will present the preliminary findings in relation to the two research questions.

Differences in corporate political activities

According to a number of interviewees, national sensitivities play a significant role in this area. National peculiarities and backgrounds also proved to be a source of differences in companies' corporate political activities. These differences were manifest mainly between European producers. The European subsidiaries of the American firms, Ford and General Motors, were very much regarded as European firms in this context. This is in contrast to the subsidiaries of Japanese enterprises which are still distinctly Japanese, also in their approach to interest representation. The following paragraphs will discuss how the differences in interest representation manifested themselves across the three investigated cases of environmental regulations.

The Air Quality Agenda and the 'Euro Norms' on Pollutant Emissions[5]: As these norms have been successively tightened, starting with the introduction of the catalytic converter in the 1980s and the Euro norms in the 1990s (Euro 1 and 2 in 1991 and 1994, then Euro 3 and 4 in 1998, with the latest norms Euro 5 and 6 adopted in December 2006[6]), there has been a history of tensions. These are along two lines. First, French producers (and French governments) were trying to politically push the lean-burn engine, while German producers were arguing for the catalytic converter (three-way). The latest tension in this area has been the debate about the diesel particulate filter. Secondly, economically strong versus economically weak producers: for economically viable companies the fitting of an additional piece of equipment such as a catalytic converter or a particulate filter does not pose as great a problem as for financially struggling firms. Similarly, for producers of small cars, the costs of fitting an extra piece of kit to a car are proportionally higher than for producers of bigger cars. This distinction also plays a considerable role for the second case.

Voluntary Emission Reductions: The Climate Change Agenda and CO_2 from Passenger Cars: Similar to pollutant emissions, there was, and still is, a division between German and French and Italian producers. When the voluntary agreement was discussed in the 1990s, the French producers argued for a target expressed in grams per kilometre (140 g/km), whereas the German producers argued for a target expressed in relative terms (25 per cent reduction). A relative target would have put the German producers of rather large, heavy and luxury cars at an advantage (These have higher CO_2 emissions which are directly related to higher fuel consumption caused by heavier vehicle weight). Similarly, an absolute target would have, and has, benefited French and Italian producers of rather small cars, who will be able to meet the 130g/km target for 2012 proposed by the European Commission (EC) in February 2007.

End-of-life Vehicles: The Waste Reduction Agenda and Scrap Cars: The main differences in terms of interest representation here were not on national lines, but more in terms of mass producers (Volkswagen, Ford, General Motors, French and Italian producers). These would be hit by free take-back policies for scrap cars compared to producers of luxury cars, whose cars do not end up as waste in the EU as they are exported from the EU to non-EU countries or become vintage cars and collectors' items. As a consequence, this was rather an intra-national issue within Germany: between Volkswagen as the biggest producer and with the largest vehicle stock on the roads in the EU and companies like BMW, Daimler-Benz and Porsche whose high-end range vehicles rarely end up as waste.

All these differences were recalled by several interviewees in Brussels as reflected in the following quotes:

> We feel that the automobile industry has no unanimity inside, for example 120g CO_2 per km. The French say yes, the Germans say no. (Brussels expert)

> So there's a national European tension inside ACEA, a constant struggle between French and Germans, the Italians are too weak, they fall behind the French. (Brussels expert)

> And still you see quite a nationalistic flavour to that so you will see each member state tending to reflect the interests of the OEMs based in their territory. (Civil servant in European Commission)

Overall, it seemed that the French producers especially and, to some extent, the Italian producers were very much using their own governments to pursue their own strategies. These governments were perceived to be protecting their 'national champions'. For the German producers such industrial policies were weaker, although the closeness of a former Chancellor to the car industry did play a great role in delaying the end-of-life vehicles directive. On the other hand, the erstwhile Swedish producers[7] and government showed a more distant and objective approach: during negotiations for a particular piece of legislation, the Swedish government was accused by another government of protecting the interests of its automobile industry, when the Swedish side had reportedly not even spoken to its indigenous producers about this (interview with Brussels expert of automotive industry, March 2007). With regards to the Japanese producers in the EU, it has to be mentioned that, although the Japanese Association, JAMA, does have an office in Brussels, it is not very vocal – it acts rather carefully and tends to follow the line of ACEA, the European Association. Two of JAMA's member companies show rather different approaches: Honda takes a very factual approach and only becomes active when there are objective technical concerns with proposed legislation. Toyota, on the other hand, was pointed out as a positive example by numerous interviewees for taking a proactive and positive stance, especially with regards to environmental regulations in its interactions with policy-makers.

Table 16.3 Matrix of corporate political activities across cases and countries (less/medium/high and yes/no, blank)

	In general	CO_2	ELV	Euro norms
European firms				
German firms		Yes	Yes	Medium
BMW	Less		Yes	
DaimlerChrysler	High		Less	
Volkswagen	High		High	
French firms		Yes	Less	
PSA	Medium			High
Renault	Medium			Less
Italian firm			–	
Fiat	Less	Medium		Yes
American firms			–	
Ford	High	High		Yes
General Motors	Less	Less		
Japanese firms		Less		Less
Honda	Less		Medium	
Nissan	Less			
Toyota	High			

The observed differences in CPA, thus, have their basis in the different countries of origins on the one hand and in different product portfolios on the other. The results could tentatively be schematized in Table 16.3.

Resources and competencies used in corporate political activities

Under this sub-heading, preliminary findings on resources and competences deployed in MNCs' CPA (regardless of the particular environmental regulation involved) are presented and discussed. Interview questions are based on Dahan's (2005) typology and include human resources and expertise, financial resources, relational resources, organizational resources, reputation with other non-market actors, public image, support of stakeholders as well as recreational skills. The interview extracts have partly been condensed as similar responses were given by several interviewees. The analysis is still tentative; hence the sample quotes presented below represent initial insights.

Human resources, that is, personnel and their expertise, seem to be of paramount importance in CPA within the EU automotive industry. An interviewed representative of a Japanese automotive company highlighted as much, whilst also emphasizing the need for expert knowledge on the part of those undertaking this role: '... People ... doing it need to be an expert in their activity ...' This point is further developed by an EC staff, thus: 'with studies [relevant expertise] you can steer the kind of debate, you establish a nomenclature, ideas that can't be debated away, ideas that can't be taken out again'. Effectiveness in communicating this expert knowledge appears to be equally crucial, as interview data suggests:

It is very important that the person who deals with the topic knows what he's talking about, and can communicate complex, technical interrelations and where I have the feeling he is telling the truth. (Current Member of the European Parliament)

The aspect of expertise and communicating this expertise is significant as policy-makers depend on outside information to make informed policy decisions. Expertise, however, is not easily acquired – several interviewees pointed out a 'learning by doing' process through which relevant skills are acquired:

> It's learning by experience, within two years you're not efficient, there is no school to address regulatory business, with technical studies very little is said about regulation. (Industry Association representative)

The reputational and relational resources of the people engaged in the actual interest representation also emerged as important. As one interviewee, a company representative, remarked 'reputation plays a big role, credibility is the strongest capital'. This is understandable since reputation is related to credibility, which is a crucial asset when representing corporate interests. An interesting additional insight is the observed tendency among government stakeholders to distinguish between corporate and individual reputation. As one source in the EU Parliament puts it '... reputation of the company doesn't matter. Reputation of the individual who is doing the lobbying does, because lobbying is a social activity as well as a political activity'. This may explain the observed value placed by these policy makers (Commission officials and politicians in the European Parliament) on continuity of contacts: 'Continuity is a keystone in order to create mutual trust and that's where companies have made mistakes in their strategies in the past' (former Member of the European Parliament). This illustrates that the reputation of individuals may matter more than the reputation of the employer, that is the (parent) company, and the image of its respective brands.

Relational resources such as contacts and relations within a network are also inextricably linked to individual representatives and may represent the most important pre-conditions for influencing policy-makers favourably. An interviewed company representative emphasized thus: 'That is the basis, without relations and contacts to relevant decision-makers you will not be heard, not be noticed' – a view echoed by a current member of the European Parliament: 'Relationships are crucial.' Other aspects of companies' relational resources highlighted as important by the interviewees include skills and capabilities in organizing recreational and networking events, arranging targeted visits to plants and working with environmental organizations.

Financial resources appear to play only a limited role in CPA within the EU automotive industry, mainly in setting up and maintaining lobbying operations. One company source reported that 'there was one big budget increase when the department was set up, but since then, it has been stable'. This is in stark contrast to the United States where financial contributions from firms through Political Action Committees (PACs) are very common.

It would seem from the foregoing that, more than anything else, human resources provide the crucial resource for companies when interacting with political institutions. Unlike in day-to-day production operations, there are no technologies or patents to be protected, but the contributions of individuals, through their expertise, their networks, their built-up credibility and their provision of continuity.

Conclusions and outlook

The first conclusion that can be reached from the present study data pertains to the continued importance of national culture and nationality on how corporate political activities are exercised among automotive multinational enterprises in the EU. This might mean that these dimensions, the industry and the country or regional contexts, are stronger than shown earlier in Figure 16.1. In this respect, it would be beneficial in the future to draw upon the business-systems literature in order to understand how different cultures and business climates play a role in CPA. Future investigations could draw upon Morgan, Kristensen and Whitley (2001), Morgan, Whitley and Moen (2005) and Whitley (1991, 1992).

Secondly, in terms of resources and competences used and how firm-specific political resources are directed into corporate political activities, the findings strongly suggest the crucial importance of human resources and their assets regarding expertise, network, provision of continuity, reputation and credibility. Even though possibilities for CPA might be the same for every company, the way a firm carefully builds up its political resources may ensure that the work leads to sustainable advantage in terms of contacts, reputation and credibility. The process, above all, takes time and is, thus, not easily imitated.[8] This is where firms can gain advantage in their government relations, by providing valuable expertise through credible and trustworthy human resources.

The differences in the actual daily work of interest representation are rather subtle. They do vary in emphasis and in style, as pointed out above, among firms of different origins or nationalities. The main reason for firms' divergence lies in their respective positions in the market place: Different competitive positions (for example, regarding end-of-life vehicles over pollutant emissions to CO_2 emissions) lead to different political strategies. This is an important conclusion, which may explain the increased significance of lobbying activities for individual car manufacturing firms. It may also explain why an industry that used to rely mainly on industry associations for representation has more recently witnessed the opening of individual firms' representative offices in Brussels. Future research could look into this interesting dichotomy between particularized CPA and collective interest representation.[9]

In concluding this chapter, the author would like to recommend that firms (not only those in the automotive industry) should view environmental regulations as challenges, and not threats, and improve their relations and interest representation with political institutions. They should also contribute positively to the protection of the natural environment and, hence, sustainable development. To take on this challenge in a convincing and effective manner, companies need to ensure that the human resources they employ – the most significant resource identified above – are appropriately equipped to rise to the challenge.

Acknowledgements

The author would like to thank all interviewees for their valuable contribution to this research.

Notes

1. For overviews of these two streams of literature, see Hillman, Keim and Schuler (2004) and Pedler (2002).
2. In the case of the end-of-life vehicles directive it took more than three years between the publication of the EC proposal and the final adoption of the directive by the European Parliament and the Council of Ministers.
3. It has to be noted that at a later stage of this research project, after the submission of this contribution, the two companies agreed to be interviewed.
4. As interviews were conducted confidentially, only the side of the triangle will be indicated in quotes and in some cases interviewees only wanted to be identified as a 'Brussels expert'.
5. Regulating tail-pipe emissions like carbon monoxide (CO), Hydrocarbons (HC), Nitrous Oxide (NOx) and particulate matter (PM).
6. The standards came/come into force in the following years: Euro 1 – 1993, Euro 2 – 1996, Euro 3 – 2000, Euro 4 – 2005, Euro 5 – 2009, Euro 6 – 2014 (Dieselnet, 2007).
7. Saab and Volvo have been under the ownership of General Motors and Ford respectively since the late 1990s.
8. In the resource-based theory, Dierckx and Cool (1989) speak of *asset stock accumulation* and *time compression diseconomies*.
9. At the annual conference of the European Centre for Public Affairs, March 2007, there was little support for industry federations and overwhelming support for individual company interest representation.

References

ACEA (2007) *New passenger car registrations*. Retrieved 12 July 2007, from http://www.acea.be

Barney, J.B. (1991) 'Firm resources and sustained competitive advantage', *Journal of Management*, 17, 99–120.

Blumentritt, T.P. and Nigh, D. (2002) 'The integration of subsidiary political activities in multinational corporations', *Journal of International Business Studies*, 33(1), 57–77.

Boddewyn, J.J. (1988) 'Political aspects of MNE theory', *Journal of International Business Studies*, Fall, 341–63.

Boddewyn, J.J. (2003) 'Understanding and advancing the concept of "nonmarket"', *Business and Society*, 42(3), 297–327.

Boddewyn, J.J. and Brewer, T.L. (1994) 'International-business political behavior: New theoretical directions', *Academy of Management Review*, 19(1), 119–43.

Bryman, A. and Bell, E. (2003) *Business Research Methods* (Oxford: Oxford University Press).

Coffey, A. and Atkinson, P. (1996) *Making Sense of Qualitative Data: Complementary Research Strategies* (Thousand Oaks, CA: Sage).

Dahan, N. (2005) 'A contribution to the conceptualization of political resources utilized in corporate political action', *Journal of Public Affairs*, 5(1), 43–54.

DG Environment (2007) Directorate General Environment of European Commission, Website. Retrieved July 12, 2007, from http://ec.europa.eu/dgs/environment/index_en.htm

Dierckx, I. and Cool, K. (1989) Asset Stock Accumulation and Sustainability of Competitive Advantage, *Management Science*, 35(12), 1504–11.

Dieselnet (2007) *Emissions Standards Europe: Cars and Light Trucks*. Retrieved 11 October 2007, from http://www.dieselnet.com/standards/eu/ld.php

Eisenhardt, K.M. (1989) 'Building theories from case study research', *Academy of Management Review*, 1989, 14(4), 532–50.

Fiol, C.M. (1991) 'Managing culture as a competitive resource: An identity-based view of sustainable competitive advantage', *Journal of Management*, 17(1), 191–211.

Frynas, J.G., Mellahi, Kamel and Pigman, G.A. (2006) 'First mover advantages in international business and firm-specific political resources', *Strategic Management Journal*, 27(4), 321–45.

Getz, K.A. (1997) 'Research in corporate political action: Integration and assessment', *Business and Society*, 36(1), 32–72.

Gillham, B. (2000) *Case Study Research Methods* (London: Continuum).

Grant, R.M. (1991) The resource-based theory of competitive advantage: Implications for strategy formulation, *California Management Review*, 33(3), 114–35.

Grant, W. (1993) 'Pressure Groups and the European Community', in S. Mazey and J.J. Richardson (eds) *Lobbying in the European Community*, 27–46 (Oxford: Oxford University Press).

Hillman, A.J. and Hitt, M.A. (1999) 'Corporate political strategy formulation: A model of approach, participation, and strategy decisions', *Academy of Management Review*, 24(4), 825–42.

Hillman, A.J., Keim, G.D. and Schuler, D. (2004) 'Corporate political activity: A review and research agenda', *Journal of Management*, 30(6), 837–57.

Hoopes, D.G., Madsen, G.L. and Walker, G. (2003) 'Guest editors' introduction to the special issue: Why is there a resource-based view? Toward a theory of competitive heterogeneity', *Strategic Management Journal* (Special issue), 24(10), 889–902.

Keay-Bright, S. (2000) *A critical analysis of the voluntary fuel economy agreement, established between the European automobile manufacturers and the European Commission, with regard for its capacity to protect the environment*, European Environmental Bureau, available at http://www.eeb.org/publication/2000/ACEA-10-final-complete.pdf (accessed 17 February 2006).

Krämer, L. (1997) *Focus on European Environmental Law*, 2nd edn (London: Sweet & Maxwell).

Krämer, L. (2000) *E.C. Environmental Law*, 4th edn (London: Sweet & Maxwell).

Levy, D.L. and Egan, D. (2003) A neo-Gramscian approach to corporate political strategy: Conflict and accommodation in the climate change negotiations, *Journal of Management Studies*, 40(4), 803–29.

Levy, D.L. and Rothenberg, S. (1999) *Corporate Strategy and Climate Change: Heterogeneity and Change in the Global Automobile Industry*. ENRP Discussion Paper E-99-13, Kennedy School of Government, Harvard University.

Mazey, S. and Richardson, J.J. (eds) (1993) *Lobbying in the European Community* (Oxford: Oxford University Press).

McLaughlin, A. and Jordan, G. (1993) 'The Rationality of Lobbying in Europe: Why are Euro-Groups so Numerous and so Weak? Some Evidence from the Car Industry', in S. Mazey and J.J. Richardson (eds), *Lobbying in the European Community*, 122–61 (Oxford: Oxford University Press).

McWilliams, A., Van Fleet, D.D. and Cory, K.D. (2002) 'Raising rivals' costs through political strategy: An extension of resource-based theory', *Journal of Management Studies*, 39(5), 707–23.

Miles, M.B. and Hubermann, A.M. (1984) *Qualitative Data Analysis: a Sourcebook of New Methods* (Newbury Park, CA: Sage).

Miles, M.B. and Hubermann, A.M. (1994) *Qualitative Data Analysis: an Expanded Sourcebook*, 2nd edn (Thousand Oaks, CA: Sage).

Moon, C.W. and Lado, A.A. (2000) MNC-host government bargaining power relationship: A critique and extension within the resource-based view, *Journal of Management*, 26(1), 85–117.

Morgan, G., Kristensen, Peer Hull and Whitley, R. (2001) *The Multinational Firm: Organizing Across Institutional and National Divides* (Oxford: Oxford University Press).

Morgan, G., Whitley, R. and Moen, E. (eds) (2005) *Changing Capitalisms? Internationalization, Institutional Change, and Systems of Economic Organization* (Oxford: Oxford University Press).

Nieuwenhuis, P. and Wells, P. (2003) *The Automotive Industry and the Environment* (Cambridge: Woodhead Publishing).

Pedler, R.H. (ed.) (2002) *European Union Lobbying: Changes in the Arena* (Basingstoke: Palgrave).

Peng, M.W. (2001) 'The Resource-Based View and International Business', *Journal of Management*, 27, 803–29.

Penrose, E.T. (1959) *The Theory of the Growth of the Firm* (Oxford: Blackwell).

Peteraf, M.A. (1993) 'The cornerstones of competitive advantage: A resource-based view', *Strategic Management Journal*, 14(3), 179–91.

Rieksmaier, J. (ed.) (2007) *Praxisbuch: Politische Interessenvermittlung: Instrumente – Kampagnen – Lobbying (Manual: Political interest representation: Instruments – Campaigns – Lobbying).* Wiesbaden: VS Verlag für Sozialwissenschaften.

Rugman, A.M. and Verbeke, A. (1998) 'Corporate strategies and environmental regulations: An organizing framework', *Strategic Management Journal*, 19, 363–75.

Rumelt, R.P. (1984) 'Towards a strategic theory of the firm', in R.B. Lamb (ed.), *Competitive Strategic Management*, 556–70 (Englewood Cliffs, NJ: Prentice Hall).

Rumelt, R.P. (1987) 'Theory, strategy, and entrepreneurship', in D.J. Teece (ed.), *The Competitive Challenge*, 137–158 (Cambridge, MA: Ballinger Publishing Company).

Shaffer, B. (1995) 'Firm-level responses to government regulation: Theoretical and research approaches', *Journal of Management*, 21(3), 495–514.

Spell, S. (2000) *Japanese Automobile Lobbying in Brussels: the Role of the Japanese Motor Car Industry in EU Policy Networks*. PhD Thesis, Stirling, University of Stirling, Scottish Centre for Japanese Studies, United Kingdom.

Van Tulder, R. and Van der Zwart, A. (2006) *International Business-Society Management: Linking Corporate Responsibility and Globalization* (London: Routledge).

Wernerfelt, B. (1984) 'The resource-based view of the firm', *Strategic Management Journal*, 5, 171–80.

Whitley, R. (1991) 'The social construction of business systems in East Asia', *Organization Studies*, 12, 1–28.

Whitley, R. (1992) *European Business Systems: Firms and Markets in Their National Contexts* (London: Sage).

Yin, R.K. (1994) *Case Study Research: Design and Methods*, 2nd edn (Thousand Oaks: Sage Publications).

17
Intra-Community Fraud among UK and German Expatriate Entrepreneurs in Spain: A Trust and Social Networks-Based Explanation

Andreas Hoecht*

Introduction: Background and research aims

In a recent comparative study undertaken in 2006, the present author investigated the business strategies of German and UK emigrant entrepreneurs based in Spain, with particular attention to their risk mitigation strategies and the role of trust and social networks in mitigating risks among these expatriate groups (see Wilson-Edwardes and Hoecht, 2008). While undertaking our empirical research, the author was alerted by interviewees and desk research to the substantial amount of intra-community fraud that takes place among UK and German emigrant entrepreneurs in Spain. This observation had not been anticipated when the initial research commenced, but it was later found that intra-community fraud within the German and UK expatriate communities in Spain is now such a widespread phenomenon that it has been featured in German media (for example, 3 SAT, 14 July 2006), and to a lesser extent in UK media. During the empirical research, it was found that almost all of the interviewees reported such intra-community fraud and all the key informants (solicitors, accountants and business advisors) reported such incidences.

This chapter attempts to provide an explanation for the significant amount of fraud that occurs within both nationality groups of entrepreneurs in their host country, and a trust and social networks analytical framework derived from relevant literature is used for this purpose. The key research aims for this paper are twofold:

(a) To identify whether there is a link between the risk mitigation strategies of different types of expatriate entrepreneurs that were identified in the original research and their likelihood of falling victim to intra-community fraud; and
(b) To identify under which conditions and to what extent the effective use of social networks can make expatriate entrepreneurs less vulnerable to this type of fraud.

It is argued, in this chapter, that trust and networks can play a very positive role in facilitating new ventures in an unfamiliar environment, but, under certain conditions, can also give rise to broken trust and fraud. In the following section, a review is conducted of the literature on the role of social networks in the creation of enforceable trust among group members and hence the prevention of fraud. From this literature, the conditions that have to be met for social networks to be able to prevent and sanction malfeasance of individual members will be identified, and the literature on ethnic entrepreneurial communities will be briefly scanned to see which type of these communities meet the required conditions and which do not. The latter point is very important for this chapter's argument as the empirical research suggests that the majority of both UK and German expatriate entrepreneurs are strongly oriented towards and perceive themselves as being part of their own expatriate communities and some of them tend to have a marked lack of trust towards the institutions and the people of their host society. It will be shown, however, that these expatriate communities are far different from immigrant ethnic entrepreneurs that support enforceable trust among their members and that this misperception of the nature of their own communities goes a very long way in explaining why intra-community fraud occurs and who is particularly vulnerable to it.

Literature review: The role of dense social networks in fostering trust and preventing fraud

Since the work of Granovetter (1985) on the role of embeddedness of economic decisions in social relations, economic sociologists have mainly focused on the protective and beneficial role of social networks. A wealth of studies undertaken by economic sociologists in the tradition of Granovetter have strongly put forward a case for the protective and beneficial role of social networks, in particular in cases of risk and uncertainty. Social networks can provide resources such as valuable information to their members and can be an effective means for identifying transaction partners who can be trusted not to default on their obligations towards other members of their group. The most widely cited example in this context is the case of rotating credit associations that have very low default rates due to their capacity for monitoring and social sanctioning (Biggart, 2001). More generally, in any transaction context, social ties are believed to offer ex-ante and ex-post advantages in economic exchanges: ex-ante, social ties reduce the information asymmetry between buyers and sellers and ex-post, social ties reduce opportunism by imposing social obligations and effective sanctions on the transaction partners not to cheat on the buyer (Baker and Faulkner, 2004). In particular, in situations where exchanges are risky and the environment is uncertain, economic agents prefer to transact with individuals who they already know and to use their social networks to identify honest transaction partners. They use what DiMaggio and Louch (1998, p. 620) call strategies of 'within-network exchange' – choosing persons with whom they have pre-existing non-commercial ties as transaction partners; and strategies of 'search embeddedness' – using social relationships to identify and assess the reliability of potential transaction partners with whom they have no direct or close indirect social ties in order to reduce their transaction risks.

Both strategies reduce the information asymmetry between exchange partners (buyers and sellers) before the decision to transact is made. 'Within-network exchange' also provides an ex-post beneficial effect of reducing the likelihood of opportunistic behaviour on the part of the seller, 'by introducing obligations and sanctions external to the transaction' (DiMaggio and Louch, 1998, p. 625). Portes (1994, p. 430) expresses the same powerful concept: 'Trust in informal exchanges is generated by both shared identities and feelings and by the expectation that fraudulent actions will be penalized by the exclusion of the violator from key social networks.'

Portes and Sensenbrenner (1993) identify four different sources of social capital that can be beneficial to distinct social groups such as immigrant communities.[1] The most relevant source of social capital they identify in the context of our discussion is 'enforceable trust'. If outside social and economic opportunities are very limited or blocked, if the group has sufficient in-group economic resources that can be made available for economic ventures and if the community has strong internal monitoring and sanctioning abilities, then trust can be enforced in the sense that trust default is not a feasible option for any community member. The intra-community sanctioning capacity is the crucial factor for enforceable trust and the blockage of outside social and economic opportunities to group members a pre-condition for the sanctioning capacity of the group. Enforceable trust leads to privileged access to the economic resources of the group for group members wishing to draw upon them, a reduced need for formal contracts and law enforcement (as its transactions are based on trust) and reliable expectations that group members will not default.

At this point it may be useful to briefly explain the different types and sources of trust. For our purposes here, a useful pragmatic definition of trust is that 'an agent exhibits trust when he/she exposes herself/himself to the risk of opportunistic behaviour by others and when he/she has no reason to believe that the trusted other will exploit this opportunity' (Humphrey and Schmitz, 1996, p. 4). A key point on which the literature on trust agrees is that trust makes the trustor vulnerable to the behaviour of the trustee, but the trustor ignores this possibility. This chosen ignorance makes social interaction possible.[2] According to Zucker (1986), trust can be based on ascription (such as membership of same group), can be process-based (tied to past or expected exchange such as previous interaction experience and reputation) and can be institutional-based (where trust is tied to formal structures, depending on individual or organization-specific attributes, for example membership in professional associations). Sako (1992) distinguishes between competence trust (confidence in the other's ability to perform properly), contractual trust (honouring the accepted rules of exchange) and goodwill trust (mutual expectations of open commitment to each other beyond contractual obligations).

Characteristic-based trust (Zucker, 1986) is a common phenomenon among ethnic entrepreneurial groups and, as we will see below, has advantages for setting up businesses, in particular for first generation immigrants: it provides access to crucial resources that are not available or difficult to obtain in the host society such as capital, labour and information. Trusting fellow group members is also rational in the sense that enforcement and monitoring costs are reduced within close-knit communities and the ultimate sanction for betrayal of community members – the expulsion from the community and hence the loss of the economic livelihood where no alternative employment in the host society is available to members – works as a very powerful incentive against intra-group fraud and betrayal. The preconditions for the sanctioning mechanisms to work are, however, very specific (Portes and Sensenbrenner, 1993): dense networks with good information flow; willingness of network members to monitor and sanction malfeasants; lack of economic opportunities outside the network; and lack of members' ability to leave the network without being easily traced and found. For our purpose, a key question is whether these conditions hold for UK and German entrepreneurs migrating to Spain: do expatriate communities exist among these groups that fulfil the necessary network conditions for enforceable trust and hence for preventing fraud?

We can draw some initial insights from a brief look at the general literature on ethnic minority entrepreneurship. The ethnic entrepreneurship literature (for example, Waldinger, 1995) has identified a number of 'social capital' and trust-related factors that are directly linked to ethnic group membership and provide resources such as pooled finance, access to information and cheap family labour. Differences among ethnic entrepreneurship groups in terms of start-up rates and business success can, according to this literature, be explained by the different degrees in social capital and trust that arise from the quality and density of these social networks (Ram and Jones, 1998). However, the density and quality of these networks does not only differ between different groups of ethnic entrepreneurs, but also changes over time within these groups. Peters (2002), for example, has identified marked differences between different generations of Dutch, Italian, Greek and Vietnamese entrepreneurs in Western Australia.

Such inter-generational studies on ethnic entrepreneurs appear to be still relatively sparse, but the existing studies point towards second generation ethnic entrepreneurs being generally better educated than their parents, having wider career options and often seeking employment in professions or starting businesses in more innovative sectors in preference to the ethnic community-niche based enterprises of their parents, that was often necessity rather than opportunity entrepreneurship (Metcalf, Modood and Virdee, 1996; Chan, 1997; Janjuha-Jivraj and Woods, 2002). Similarly, Ram and Smallbone (2002) found second generation ethnic entrepreneurs not only to be more innovative but also more open to external sources of business support, and Peters (2002) found that while ethnicity was largely a source of ethnic group social cohesion for first generation ethnic entrepreneurs, for the second generation, it was a resource that could be either deliberately suppressed or invoked by choice. Peters (2002) also found that second generation ethnic entrepreneurs could exploit both their own ethnic as well as the 'mainstream' cultural milieu for information, finance, labour and customers.

The key point here is that according to this literature, second and third generation ethnic entrepreneurs are much less dependent on their ethnic networks for their economic livelihood and are, therefore, no longer controlled by the economic sanctioning mechanisms of their ethnic group. As will be discussed later in the findings section, this situation is similar for UK and German expatriate entrepreneurial groups in Spain whose members are very mobile and principally not economically dependent on their peers but where, as was found in the interviews, some members tend to rather naively believe that they are operating within a dense network of communality that satisfies the conditions of mutual trust akin to the situation that prevails in first generation immigrant groups.

Approach

In order to examine the incidence of and reasons for fraudulent practices within the focal expatriate communities in Spain, pertinent data was drawn from a 2006 comparative study into the business and risk mitigation strategies of these German and UK emigrant groups. That original data-gathering effort involved semi-structured in-depth interviews with two matched sub-samples of roughly equal number of respondents from both nationality groups in Spain, and covered general business and personal background questions as well as specific questions addressing risk and risk mitigation in the emigrant entrepreneurs' new business environment. Sampling was purposive rather than strictly systematic, and the sample size was comparatively small (less than 30). Hence, the results should be treated as indicative and do not allow for generalization in a strict scientific sense. However, the representation of characteristics such as professional background and length of stay was reasonably well matched between the sub-samples and a sizeable number of key informants (solicitors, accountants and business advisors) were interviewed in addition to undertaking a substantial amount of desk research. In the light of this, the author is confident that these results will be confirmed by more extensive future research in this area.

The specific questions that guided the analysis for this chapter are: how prevalent is intra-community fraud among the German and British entrepreneur groups in Spain? Is there a link between the risk mitigation strategies of the different expatriate groups and their likelihood of falling victim to intra-community fraud? To what extent does effective use of social networks make expatriate entrepreneurs less vulnerable to this type of fraud? and under what conditions?

Analysis and findings

Incidence of intra-community fraud among UK and German entrepreneur groups in Spain

The study evidence points to the existence of a highly problematic sub-group, including fraudsters and small-time crooks that prey on fellow expatriates, among the investigated expatriate German and British entrepreneurs. Every interviewee knew of cases or had experienced another national defrauding a fellow expatriate.

It became apparent that the fraudsters managed surprisingly easily to gain the trust of their fellow countrymen and defrauded them with 'business opportunities' in financial services or offering themselves as mediators and facilitators in property purchase or contract negotiation. Almost all of the interviewees reported of such intra-community fraud and all the key informants (solicitors, accountants and business advisors) reported such incidents. Typically, a newly arrived expatriate would turn to a fellow expatriate that he or she had been befriended by for advice and help in finding a home or setting up their business in Spain. According to the key informants, the newly arrived individuals would entrust large amounts of money without careful checks or security 'on trust' to their new 'friend', only to find that this person would disappear with their assets very quickly. 'It is as if they had left their brains at the departure airport' and 'they act as they would never do at home' were typical comments made by the interviewed accountants and solicitors.

Interestingly, the most likely victims of such intra-community fraud were found to be individuals with the lowest levels of trust in the host society's people and institutions; such individuals tend to address their lack of (institutions-based) trust in the host society not necessarily by using a professional advisor from their own country group, but by misplacing such trust in recently befriended 'informal advisors' from their expatriate nationality group.

Risk mitigation strategies, social networks and intra-community fraud

It was found that the German migrant entrepreneurs, relative to their British counterparts, manifested certain patterns of behaviour that can be interpreted as risk reduction strategies and general risk averseness. These include a strong preference for working in their previous profession or line of work; a preference for employing business support services when starting their business; a greater likelihood to invest time in learning Spanish and informing themselves in some depth about the institutional business environment, culture and society of their destination country; and more extensive and exclusive use of social networks in their business operations.

These characteristics reflect attempts to reduce and manage risks arising from entrepreneurship in an unfamiliar and new environment. For example, working in the same profession and employing business support services when setting up a new business abroad appear to reduce the range of unfamiliar challenges and raise the general competence level of migrant entrepreneurs. Such decisions also provide some degree of insurance against liability risks during these expatriate entrepreneurs' familiarization period with the host country culture. Furthermore, acquiring some degree of linguistic competence helps to reduce the likelihood of severe expectation–reality gaps and generally assists in the process of settling into the new society. In a similar vein, the use of social networks for business purposes can be instrumental in reducing risks in uncertain environments, provided that the network is able to sanction misconduct among its members effectively (Portes and Sensenbrenner, 1993).

The research also revealed significant differences in the quality of risk mitigation strategies among different types of emigrant entrepreneurs. The following categories can be identified based on preparation strategies and use of social networks and business advice resources:

(a) The Professional Prepared: This group consisted of very well educated and well prepared, self-employed entrepreneurs with extensive professional experience at home prior to relocation. Most entrepreneurs in this group had a good level of knowledge about their destination country, including appropriate language skills, and most were equipped with sufficient capital resources. Many had developed extensive business and networking contacts in Spain before migrating, see their relocation as long term and continue to develop their business network in their host country. Their networks can be very exclusive and only open to new entrants if they are recommended by existing members. This group was the economically most successful group that we were able to identify.

(b) The Artisans: This group consisted of entrepreneurs operating on a smaller scale typically in professions such as in the building trade and some specialized service sectors (for example IT, media, telecommunication) with prior qualifications and business experience 'at home'. 'Artisans' do their 'homework' before moving and have sufficient capital resources to overcome the initial settling-in period, which can last up to three years. They draw their customers predominantly from fellow expatriates of their own nationality group and engage in some level of business networking (making referrals within their group).

(c) Tradespeople: These were small-scale entrepreneurs in lines of business such as building-related work (plumbers, decorators) and some services. Tradespeople are generally less well prepared than the group above, but they tend to be successful if they are able to establish a reputation for the quality of their work among fellow expatriates (intermediated trust).

(d) The Accidental Tourists: This group comprised entrepreneurs with some or little previous experience and professional qualifications in their new roles, who vacationed extensively in Spain prior to relocation and sought the 'living in the sun' experience. They can be ill-prepared to tackle bureaucracy and sometimes lacked sufficient capital and language skills. Typically, this group were the owners of small bars, restaurants, small shops and boutiques – a wide range of retail, service and manufacturing enterprises. Business networking took place, if at all, at a low level in this group.

(e) The Drifters: This group appeared to be made of individuals who have 'escaped' from their home country, believing it easier or preferring to establish themselves in Spain rather than at home. Usually they had little or no experience in their adopted line of work, were often exploited by other expatriates and were to be found in the restaurant trade and working for builders as paid labour on an ad hoc basis. Some offered gardening, other domestic and pool cleaning services and some were loosely involved with craft and design. Drifters often had no social security or other means of supporting themselves when work dried up.

Overall, extensive differences were found in the risk mitigation strategies pursued by the two nationality groups and between the different types of entrepreneurs that were identified above. It also emerged that it is largely the 'professional pre-pared' and the 'artisans', comprising more German than British entrepreneurs, that appear to more clearly understand the risks associated with their decisions whilst also making more astute and comprehensive effort to reduce their exposure to risk. The sample of UK entrepreneurs, on the other hand, comprised more indi-viduals from the entrepreneurial groups that tended to use business networks less extensively and effectively and are more prone to preferring the 'help' of compat-riot 'informal advisors' rather than qualified professional advice. UK expatriate entrepreneurs, thus, appeared more vulnerable to intra-community fraud than their German counterparts.

Synthesis: Towards a trust-based explanation of fraud among German and UK expatriates

As discussed above, characteristic-based trust (Zucker, 1986) is a common phe-nomenon among ethnic entrepreneurial groups and, as the brief review of litera-ture has shown, has advantages for setting up businesses, in particular for first generation immigrants. Trusting fellow group members is also rational in the sense that enforcement and monitoring costs are reduced within close-knit com-munities and the ultimate sanction for betrayal of community members – the expulsion from the community and probable loss of economic livelihood – works as a very powerful incentive against intra-group fraud and betrayal. The precondi-tions for the sanctioning mechanisms to work are, however, as has been seen, very specific (Portes and Sensenbrenner, 1993). It was also found that second gener-ation ethnic entrepreneurs are much more likely to have economic opportunities outside their ethnic group context due to better education and better socializa-tion into their host societies, and are, therefore, socially less dependent on their ethnic group than first generation immigrant groups. According to Peters (2002), they can choose to use the resources from both groups as they require. They are, therefore, in the unique position of being able to utilize their trustworthiness as social capital within their ethnic group, but without having to rely on it for their economic survival.

   This position opens the door for fraud and betrayal, in particular where the ethnic networks do not function very well (any longer) in their monitoring and sanctioning function, and where there is a strong perceived need for intra-community support by some members but not others. If this interpretation of the literature on ethnic entrepreneurs and on networks is correct, then it can also serve to explain the level and ease of fraud among UK and German expatriates in Spain. Compared with the post-war first generation immigrant ethnic entrepre-neurs who migrated to Northern Europe, the USA and other OECD countries, the German and UK expatriate communities in Spain appear to be rather loose-knit, with a constant stream of new arrivals and easy opportunities to disappear and move elsewhere within the EU to escape network sanctions (where they exist at all) and legal prosecution. There is, thus, a strong need for characteristic-based trust among new arrivals who do not have a good understanding upon arrival of the loose networks.[3] they move into. In cases where more direct sources of trust (including intermediated trust, recommendation, knowledge-based trust and direct interaction experience – see Sako, 1986) are uncertain, other trust sources such as institutions-based trust and characteristic-based trust can be expected to be of high importance. In the present study's case, institutions-based trust appears to be rather low and, therefore, characteristic-based trust becomes very predominant for those immigrants who have no recommendations to go by.

The foregoing does not, however, explain why so many new immigrants do not seek professional advice – from business advisors of their own nationality group – which would be the rational approach as far as this analysis is concerned. One possible explanation could be that they have very low competence or contractual trust (Sako, 1992) in professional advisors from their own nationality group; this, however, seems very unlikely given their generally high (sometimes unjustifiably high) level of characteristic-based trust towards members of their own expatriate group and the very low level of characteristic-based trust and institutional-based trust in the host society.[4] Also no confirmation was found of any pronounced lack of competence and contractual trust in expatriate group professional advisors in the interviews. This means that it is possible to explain reasonably well why betrayal happens within the two groups of immigrant entrepreneurs, but it appears more difficult to explain why many expatriates do not mitigate against this risk of betrayal by the 'rational' use of intra-group professional advisors.

Conclusions

This chapter has explored the incidence of, and reasons for, the intra-community fraud among German and UK expatriate entrepreneurs in Spain. Among the main findings are that the 'professional prepared' and the 'artisans' subgroups make best use of their network contacts and of professional advice available, making them less vulnerable for being defrauded; and that the lower the level of trust in the people and institutions of the host society, the more likely it is for expatriates to fall into the trap of bestowing exaggerated characteristic-based trust upon fraudsters within their own community. It was also found, rather surprisingly, that the 'rational' solution for the problem of working in an unfamiliar and uncertain environment – using the services of professional advisors – is often not chosen. No evidence was found to indicate that this is due to a general lack of competence and contractual trust in such advisors, and believe that it is linked with the varying levels of professionalism found among the different groups of expatriate entrepreneurs identified by the study.

This chapter has also provided a trust and network-based explanation for fraud within the investigated groups of expatriate entrepreneurs. It can be concluded from the research that adequate risk awareness, careful preparation and business networking on the basis of trust-based business relationships can greatly facilitate entrepreneurial venturing and that emigrant entrepreneurs should make good use of networks, but should be careful not to bestow blind characteristic-based trust on fellow expatriates. Finally, it can be concluded that the expatriate groups themselves should strive to improve the quality of the business networks they work with, using the effective, exclusive and selective way in which many of the 'professional prepared' and the 'artisans' employ their business and social networks as a model.

Notes

* The author wishes to acknowledge the outstanding contribution that Laura Wilson-Edwardes has made to the original research project on entrepreneurs and risk that was funded by the Anglo-German Foundation for the Study of Industrial Society. This chapter draws on some of the results from this joint work (see references) and hence the author is indebted to both the Anglo-German Foundation and to Laura Wilson-Edwardes.

1. For a recent discussion of the concepts of social capital, entrepreneurial relationships, networks and their inter-relationships, see Bowey and Easton (2007).
2. The essence of most definitions of trust is the suspension of doubt about the possible harmful behaviour of others. Moellering (2006, p. 111) defines trust as 'an ongoing process of building on reason, routine and reflexivity, suspending irreducible social vulnerability and uncertainty as if they were favourably resolved, and maintaining thereby a state of favourable expectation toward the actions and intentions of more or less specific others.' Goel and Karri (2006) put forward the argument that entrepreneurs as such have a tendency to 'over-trust', mainly based on recourse to effectuation theory. They have, however, not yet tested the prepositions on which their argument is based and it is unlikely to hold equally for all (personality) types of entrepreneurs.
3. One could argue that the expatriate communities at large are too loose to function properly as networks and that only the more organized professional groups (in particular the 'professional prepared', but also 'artisans' and 'tradespeople') operate in proper networks within their expatriate communities. However, the key point in the network and trust-based explanation for fraud advanced in this paper is that individuals, and in particular new arrivals, perceive their nationality groups as communities or networks of individuals that share a common ground in terms of their nationality background and are, therefore, trustworthy. Furthermore, in particular where expatriate communities are geographically concentrated as, for example, in the Balearic Islands, expatriates do not necessarily all know each other directly, but they tend to know of each other.
4. There is some indication that the UK expatriate group generally has a lower level of contractual and competence trust than the German expatriates. This could be a reflection of the different legal and institutional systems of the two 'home' countries, but it could also reflect the lower proportion of 'professional prepared' in our UK sub-sample.

References

3 SAT (14 July 2006, 20.15) 'Mallorca: Paradies der Gesetzlosen?' Documentary produced by E. Meinert and G. Enwaldt for NDR television in association with Arte television, broadcast by 3 SAT on 16 July at 20.15.

Bagwell, S. (2006) 'UK Vietnamese businesses: Cultural influences and intercultural differences', *Environment and Planning C: Government and Policy*, 24, 51–69.

Baker, W.E. and Faulkner, R.R. (2004) 'Social networks and loss of capital', *Social Networks*, 26, 91–111.

Biggart, N.W. (2001) 'Banking on each other: The situational logic of rotating savings and credit associations', *Advances in Qualitative Organization Research*, 3, 129–53.

Bowey, J.L. and Easton, G. (2007) 'Entrepreneurial social capital unplugged: An activity based analysis', *International Small Business Journal*, 25(3), 273–306.

Chan, S. (1997) 'Migration, cultural identity and assimilation effects on entrepreneurship for the overseas Chinese in Britain', *Asia Pacific Business Review*, 3, 211–22.

DiMaggio, P. and Louch, H. (1998) 'Socially embedded consumer transactions: For what kinds of purposes do people most often use networks?' *American Sociological Review*, 63, 619–37.

Goel, S. and Karri, R. (2006) 'Entrepreneurs, effectual logic and over-trust', *Entrepreneurship Theory and Practice*, July, 477–93.

Granovetter, M.S. (1985) 'Economic action and social structure: The problem of embeddedness', *American Journal of Sociology*, 91, 481–510.

Humphrey, J. and Schmitz, H. (1996) 'Trust and economic development', Discussion Paper No. 355, Institute of Development Studies, University of Sussex, Brighton.

Janjuha-Jivraj, S. and Woods, A. (2002) 'Successional issues within Asian family firms: Learning from the Kenyan experience', *International Small Business Journal*, 20(1), 77–94.

Metcalf, H., Modood, T. and Virdee, S. (1996) 'Asian self-employment: The interaction of Culture and Economics in England', Policy Studies Institute, London.

Moellering, G. (2006) *Trust: Reason, Routine, Reflexivity* (Oxford: Elsevier).

Peters, N. (2002) 'Mixed embeddedness: Does it really explain immigrant enterprise in Western Australia?' *International Journal of Entrepreneurship Behaviour and Research*, 8(1/2), 32–53.

Portes, A. (1994) 'The informal economy and its paradoxes', in N.J. Smesler and R. Swedberg (eds), *The Handbook of Economic Sociology*, 98, 426–49 (New Jersey: Princeton University Press).

Portes, A. and Sensenbrenner, J. (1993) 'Embeddedness and Immigration: Notes on the Social Determinants of Economic action', *American Journal of Sociology*, 98(6), 1320–50.

Ram, M. and Jones, T. (1998) 'Ethnic Minorities in Business', *Small Business Research Trust Report*, Milton Keynes.

Ram, M. and Smallbone, D. (2002) 'Ethnic minority business policy in the area of small business service', *Environment and Planning C: Government and Policy*, 20, 235–49.

Sako, M. (1992) *Prices, Quality and Trust: Inter-firm Relations in Britain and Japan* (Cambridge: Cambridge University Press).

Waldinger, R. (1995) 'The other side of embeddedness: A case study of the interplay of economy and ethnicity', *Ethnic and Racial Studies*, 18, 555–580.

Wilson-Edwardes, L. and Hoecht, A. (2008) 'Entrepreneurs and risk: A study of German and UK entrepreneurs in Spain', Research Report to the Anglo-German Foundation, Project grant no 1507, available online, http://www.agf.org.uk/cms/upload/pdfs/R/2008_R1507_e_entrepreneurs_and_risk.pdf.

Zucker, L. (1986) 'Production of trust: Institutional sources of economic structure, 1840–1920', *Research in Organizational Behaviour*, 8, 53–111.

Index